Wetlands

CHARACTERISTICS AND BOUNDARIES

Committee on Characterization of Wetlands

Water Science and Technology Board
Board on Environmental Studies and Toxicology

Commission on Geosciences, Environment, and Resources

National Research Council

NATIONAL ACADEMY PRESS
Washington, D.C.   1995

NATIONAL ACADEMY PRESS • 2101 Constitution Avenue, N.W. • Washington, DC 20418

NOTICE: The project that is the subject of this report was approved by the Governing Board of the National Research Council, whose members are drawn from the councils of the National Academy of Sciences, the National Academy of Engineering, and the Institute of Medicine. The members of the committee responsible for the report were chosen for their special competencies and with regard for appropriate balance.

This report has been reviewed by a group other than the authors according to procedures approved by a Report Review Committee consisting of members of the National Academy of Sciences, the National Academy of Engineering, and the Institute of Medicine.

Support for this project was provided by the U.S. Environmental Protection Agency under Agreement No. CX-821125-01-0 and the U. S. Department of Agriculture Natural Resources Conservation Service under Agreement No. SCD-68-3475-3-161.

The Director, Grants Administration Division, has approved a deviation from 40 CFR 30.518 of EPA's Assistance Regulations. This approval permits a waiver of EPA's peer review process and submission of the draft final report. The recipient agrees that the following disclaimer will be added to all documents published under this project.

"Although the results described in this document have been funded wholly or in part by the United States Environmental Protection Agency under Assistance Agreement X821125010 to the National Academy of Sciences, it has not been subjected to the Agency's peer and administrative review and therefore may not necessarily reflect the views of the Agency and no official endorsement should be inferred."

Cover art by Raphael Lopez, San Diego, California

Library of Congress Cataloging-in-Publication Data

Wetlands : characteristics and boundaries.
    p. cm
  William M. Lewis, Jr., chair.
  Includes bibliographical references and index.
  ISBN 0-309-05134-7 (cloth)
  1. Wetlands. 2. Wetland ecology. 3. Wetland conservation—
Government policy—United States. I. Lewis, William M., 1945-.
II. National Research Council (U.S.). Committee on Characterization
of Wetlands.
QH87.3W475   1995
333.91′8′0973—dc 20   95-440

Staff

SHEILA D. DAVID, Study Director, WSTB
DAVID POLICANSKY, Study Director, BEST
TANIA L. WILLIAMS, Research Associate, BEST
GREGORY K. NYCE, Senior Project Assistant, WSTB

The National Academy of Sciences is a private, nonprofit, self-perpetuating society of distinguished scholars engaged in scientific and engineering research, dedicated to the furtherance of science and technology and to their use for the general welfare. Upon the authority of the charter granted to it by the Congress in 1863, the Academy has a mandate that requires it to advise the federal government on scientific and technical matters. Dr. Bruce Alberts is president of the National Academy of Sciences.

The National Academy of Engineering was established in 1964, under the charter of the National Academy of Sciences, as a parallel organization of outstanding engineers. It is autonomous in its administration and in the selection of its members, sharing with the National Academy of Sciences the responsibility for advising the federal government. The National Academy of Engineering also sponsors engineering programs aimed at meeting national needs, encourages education and research, and recognizes the superior achievements of engineers. Dr. Harold Liebowitz is president of the National Academy of Engineering.

The Institute of Medicine was established in 1970 by the National Academy of Sciences to secure the services of eminent members of appropriate professions in the examination of policy matters pertaining to the health of the public. The Institute acts under the responsibility given to the National Academy of Sciences by its congressional charter to be an adviser to the federal government and, upon its own initiative, to identify issues of medical care, research, and education. Dr. Kenneth I. Shine is president of the Institute of Medicine.

The National Research Council was organized by the National Academy of Sciences in 1916 to associate the broad community of science and technology with the Academy's purposes of furthering knowledge and advising the federal government. Functioning in accordance with general policies determined by the Academy, the Council has become the principal operating agency of both the National Academy of Sciences and the National Academy of Engineering in providing services to the government, the public, and the scientific and engineering communities. The Council is administered jointly by both Academies and the Institute of Medicine. Dr. Bruce Alberts and Dr. Harold Liebowitz are chairman and vice chairman, respectively, of the National Research Council.

Acknowledgments

Many individuals assisted the committee in its task by participating in committee meetings, helping to plan field trips, and providing background information. The committee is especially thankful for the generous assistance provided by Mike Fritz, EPA; Mike Long, FWS; Billy Teels, NRCS; and Russell Theriot and Karen Kochenbach of USACE. The committee received valuable advice and assistance from Greg Peck, EPA; Marge Kohlar, FWS; and Mike Davis, USACE.

Field trips held in conjunction with committee meetings helped the committee better understand the problems of wetlands delineation. We would like to express our appreciation to the following people who assisted the committee and NRC staff during these field trips.

Kent Island, Maryland
Leander Brown, USACE
Woody Francis, USACE
Alex Dolgos, USACE
Tom Filip, USACE
Charlie Rhodes, Jr., EPA
Norman Melvin, NRCS

Vicksburg, Mississippi
James Gosselink, Louisiana State University
Randy Pearson, Space Remote Sensing Center, Stennis Space Center, MS
Larry Harper, USACE

David Lofton, USACE
Harvey Huffstatler, USACE
Tom Welborn, EPA
David Jones, NRCS
Raymond Callahan, NRCS
David Pettry, Mississippi State University

Sedona, Arizona
Kevin Martin, Soil and Environmental Consultants, Inc., Raleigh, NC
Robert Pierce, Wetlands Science Applications, Inc., Poolesville, MD
Duncan Patten, University of Arizona
Tom Yocum, EPA
Wendy Melgin, EPA
Kathy Kunz, USACE
Fred Weinman, EPA
Mary Butterwick, EPA
David Cooper, Colorado State University
Marie Sullivan, FWS

Ft. Myers, Florida
Maurice Mausbach, NRCS
Kevin Reush, consultant, Lakeland, FL
Kevin Erwin, consultant, Ft. Myers, FL
Robin Lewis, Lewis Environmental Services, Tampa, FL

Public Session in Ft Myers:
Jim Shepard, National Council of the Paper Industry for Air and
    Stream Improvement
Susan Asmus, National Association of Home Builders

Jamestown, North Dakota
Ned Euliss, FWS
Porter Reed, FWS
Arnold van der Valk, Iowa State University
Dan Smith, USACE
Lewis Cowardin, FWS
Jimmie Richardson, North Dakota State University
Harold Kantrud, FWS

Public session in Jamestown:
Don Parrish, American Farm Bureau
Don Etler, Iowa Drainage District Association
Vic Legler, Landowners Association of North Dakota

Gerald Eid, North Dakota Home Builders Association
Kenneth Dierks, Lanley and McDonald Consultants, Virginia Beach, VA
Greg Larson, Minnesota Board of Water and Soil Resources
Jay Leitch, North Dakota State University

Others
Gary Jellick, Greenhorne & O'Mara, Inc.
Ralph Tiner, FWS
Kim Santos, FWS
Dennis Tressel, NRCS

Preface

Principles for federal regulation of wetlands have been fundamentally challenged several times over the past 20 years. One legacy of these challenges has been a reduction in the credibility of all regulatory practice related to wetlands. For this reason, the U.S. Congress requested that the Environmental Protection Agency ask the National Research Council (NRC) to create a committee that would study the scientific basis for characterization of wetlands. This committee was formed in 1993 through the NRC's Water Science and Technology Board and its Board on Environmental Studies and Toxicology. The committee was asked to review and evaluate the consequences of alternative methods for wetland delineation and to summarize the scientific understanding of wetland functions. Specifically mentioned in the committee's charge are the issues of wetland definition, the structure and functioning of wetlands, and regional differences among wetlands. Members of the committee were drawn from a broad range of expertise, regional perspectives, and professional experience.

After its first meeting in Washington, D.C., the committee met in eastern Maryland, the lower Mississippi River valley, Arizona, southwest Florida, and the prairie pothole region of North Dakota. At each of these locations, the committee spent some of its time on field investigations organized under the direction of federal agency personnel and private consultants familiar with regional problems of delineation. This field experience assisted the committee members in their discussion of regional issues. The meetings also included two special sessions for public commentary (in Florida and in North Dakota) and presentations by nongovernment specialists in delineation.

The NRC committee has reached broad consensus on the issues related to its charge. In this report, the committee presents a reference definition of wetlands that sets the stage for a fresh look at existing regulatory definitions and for reconsideration of the confusion surrounding parameters, criteria, and indicators. In addition, the committee offers an overview of wetland functions as they relate to the protection of wetlands. Finally, the committee provides many recommendations and conclusions related to criteria and indicators. Although these recommendations and conclusions do not in themselves constitute a new delineation manual, they specify the essential framework and principles around which a new universal federal manual can be prepared by federal agency personnel. Many of the conclusions and recommendations underscore the committee's confidence in the fundamental soundness of current regulatory practice for characterizing and delineating wetlands. Changes that have been suggested by the committee typically involve refinements of practice rather than drastic change.

The committee's report will be scrutinized carefully for bias favoring or opposing the protection of wetlands. The committee members hold a range of personal viewpoints on the degree of rigor with which wetlands should be protected and on the uniformity with which protection should extend across wetlands, but the committee leaves these matters for resolution through law and administrative policy. The committee's task has been to analyze present regulatory practice in relation to wetland delineation and to recommend changes that might bolster the objectivity and scientific validity of wetland delineation and identification. In general, the committee has been impressed with the professionalism and scientific credibility that make up the foundation of federal expertise in characterization and delineation of wetlands. This foundation, when combined with a federal commitment to the use of scientific principles applied with regional realism, should steadily improve public confidence in the national system for characterization of wetlands.

The Committee on Wetlands Characterization has placed extraordinary demands on members of the NRC staff. The rapid pace of work, extensive logistical arrangements, and coordination of two NRC boards required experience and great dedication from the staff. The committee is indebted particularly to Sheila David, David Policansky, Tania Williams, and Greg Nyce of the National Research Council, and to David Greene of the University of Colorado's Center for Limnology, for extensive staff work on this project. In addition, the committee greatly appreciates the many briefings and assistance with field trips provided by the staff of the U.S. Environmental Protection Agency, the U.S. Army Corps of Engineers, the U.S. Natural Resources Conservation Service, the U.S. Fish and Wildlife Service, and others.

William M. Lewis, Jr., *Chairman*

Contents

Wetlands

Executive Summary

Until very recently, policies of the United States federal government were intended to encourage or subsidize the conversion of wetlands to filled or drained lands that could be used for agriculture or other purposes not compatible with the existence of wetlands. These federal policies, in addition to extensive private efforts of a similar nature, reduced the total wetland acreage in the contiguous United States by approximately 117 million acres, or half of the original total, by the mid-1980s. While this conversion of wetland produced extensive amounts of new cropland that bolstered the agricultural potential of the United States, and eliminated some of the socioeconomic nuisances associated with wetlands, it also reduced many of the valuable attributes of wetlands, including support of water-fowl and maintenance of water quality. An increasingly broad concern for these losses created political support for comprehensive protection of wetlands. Federal regulation of wetlands began to take effect on a broad scale in the 1970s, and now encompasses virtually all wetlands. Wetlands are the only ecosystem type to be comprehensively regulated across all public and private lands within the United States.

The 1972 amendments to the Federal Water Pollution Control Act gave the U.S. Army Corps of Engineers (USACE) and the Environmental Protection Agency (EPA) authority to regulate pollution of waters in the United States. The coverage of the 1972 act extended to wetlands, but was narrowly construed at first and extended to only approximately 15% of the total wetland acreage in the United States. Between 1972 and 1977, judicial decisions greatly broadened the coverage of the statute and created for the first time a need for a regulatory definition of wetlands and for federal conventions by which a definition could be

1

applied. The USACE finalized a regulatory definition in 1977, but delegated to its district offices the development of procedures for identifying and delineating wetlands. Section 404 of the 1977 Federal Water Pollution Control Act amendments (Clean Water Act) confirmed the national commitment to regulation of wetlands, and broad federal application of the 1977 act to wetlands was upheld judicially in 1985. In the same year, the Food Security Act established a separate regulatory definition of wetlands for application to agricultural lands.

Foreseeing the need for greater national uniformity in the identification and delineation of wetlands, the USACE issued in 1987 a national delineation manual ("1987 Corps manual"). Subsequently, USACE collaborated with the U.S. Fish and Wildlife Service (FWS), EPA, and the U.S. Department of Agriculture (USDA) in the preparation of a revised manual, which was released in 1989 ("1989 interagency manual"). The 1989 interagency manual was strongly criticized, however, by individuals and groups who perceived it as being excessively inclined toward the regulation of lands that might not be properly classified as wetlands. A second attempt at the creation of a revised manual was initiated by the Bush administration in 1991 ("1991 proposed revisions"). The 1991 proposed revisions were criticized for excluding many wetlands from regulatory coverage, and were not implemented. Thus USACE and EPA have continued to use the 1987 Corps manual. In the meantime, the Soil Conservation Service (now the National Resources Conservation Service [NRCS]) had implemented the 1985 Food Security Act through the preparation of a separate delineation manual ("1985 Food Security Act manual") for use on agricultural lands.

The preparation and withdrawal of the 1989 interagency manual and the 1991 proposed revisions, and the adoption of a separate manual designated specifically for agricultural lands, created confusion and uncertainty about the scientific and technical validity of federal regulatory practice in the identification and delineation of wetlands. As a result, Congress requested in 1993 that the Environmental Protection Agency ask the National Research Council to create a committee to assess the adequacy and validity of wetland definitions, the basis for applying definitions through delineation manuals, present knowledge of the structure and function of wetlands, and regional variation among wetlands.

The regulatory definition of wetlands and the procedures by which wetlands are identified and delineated are of great practical concern because of the nationwide regulation of wetlands. If flawed definitions or flawed procedures lead to the identification of wetlands where wetlands do not exist, landowners will unjustifiably lose the flexibility to develop land for agriculture or other purposes. On the other hand, definitional or procedural flaws that lead to the exclusion of true wetlands will not reflect the intent of legislation and judicial decisions that have established federal regulatory authority over wetlands. The work of the NRC committee has been to analyze the scientific and technical basis for identification and delineation of wetlands, but not to analyze economic or social issues connected with wetlands.

In comparing the 1987 Corps manual with the 1989 interagency manual and the 1991 proposed revisions, the NRC committee concludes that the 1989 interagency manual would typically provide the most expansive interpretation of wetland boundaries. The 1987 Corps manual would produce delineations essentially the same as the 1989 interagency manual in some instances, but would be somewhat more restrictive than the 1989 interagency manual in most instances. Delineation by use of the 1991 proposed revisions would be considerably more restrictive than by use of either the 1987 or 1989 manuals, and would lead to outright exclusion of numerous true wetlands through impractical documentation requirements.

Improvements in the scientific understanding of wetlands since 1987 and refinement of regulatory practice through experience over almost a decade of intensive wetland regulation suggest that a new federal delineation manual should be prepared for common use by all federal agencies involved in the regulation of wetlands. This new manual should draw freely from the strengths of each of the existing manuals, but would not be identical to any of the present manuals. The new manual should incorporate some changes in present practice and some solutions to past problems of regulatory practice, as well as an increased emphasis on regionalization within a framework of national standards. In some instances, the unavailability of critical information also demonstrates an urgent need for study of selected wetland characteristics for which lack of information hampers the identification and delineation of wetlands.

DEFINITIONS, FACTORS, CRITERIA, AND INDICATORS

It is useful to maintain a reference definition of wetland that stands outside the context of any particular agency, policy, or regulation. This places a broad framework around regulatory practice and puts into perspective regulatory definitions and the selection of criteria and indicators for regulatory purposes. A regulatory definition, in contrast, might reflect in varying degrees regulatory policy or legislation that restricts or extends regulatory jurisdiction in ways that differ from the reference definition.

A reference definition of wetlands is as follows: *A wetland is an ecosystem that depends on constant or recurrent, shallow inundation or saturation at or near the surface of the substrate. The minimum essential characteristics of a wetland are recurrent, sustained inundation or saturation at or near the surface and the presence of physical, chemical, and biological features reflective of recurrent, sustained inundation or saturation. Common diagnostic features of wetlands are hydric soils and hydrophytic vegetation. These features will be present except where specific physicochemical, biotic, or anthropogenic factors have removed them or prevented their development.*

As shown by the reference definition, three major factors characterize a wetland: water, substrate (physicochemical features), and biota. Customary reference to these as "parameters" is not correct and should be avoided. Although wetlands depend for their existence on all three factors, it is often scientifically defensible, in the absence of alterations or ambivalent indications, to infer information about one factor from another. The states of the three factors that characterize wetlands are the criteria for identification of wetlands: recurrent, sustained saturation (the hydrologic criterion), physical and chemical conditions in the substrate that reflect recurrent, sustained saturation (the substrate criterion), and the presence of organisms that are specifically adapted to recurrent and sustained saturation of the substrate (the biological criterion).

Of the three factors that characterize wetlands, water has special status because neither the characteristic substrates nor the characteristic biota of wetlands can develop in the absence of specific hydrologic conditions. Disturbance of the biota or substrate can produce a wetland in which the characteristic substrates or organisms are absent, at least temporarily. In contrast, elimination of the characteristic hydrology of a wetland eliminates the wetland, even though the characteristic substrate and organisms can persist for some time after the hydrologic change. Thus, when hydrology has been altered, the presence of organisms and substrates that are characteristic of wetlands is not necessarily indicative of a wetland.

Although hydrologic conditions are paramount to the maintenance of a wetland, it is often more difficult to evaluate hydrology than it is to assess substrate or biota. Therefore, even though water is in a sense more important than any other factor, substrate and biota will typically provide the most easily obtained and reliable evidence for the presence of wetlands, except where hydrology has been altered.

A criterion is a standard of judgment or principle for testing. As shown by the reference definition, wetlands are associated with specific conditions of water, substrate, and biota. These specific conditions correspond to thresholds or criteria that are used to judge whether a particular ecosystem is a wetland.

Each of the three criteria (hydrology, substrate, and biota) must be interpreted in terms of indicators that can be documented under field conditions. Each criterion can be interpreted with reference to multiple indicators. Some indicators are general; others are more specific and can be used only as secondary evidence or to support a more general indicator. The two most broadly significant indicators of wetlands are hydrophytic vegetation and hydric soils. Because these indicators are so often associated with wetlands, they are sometimes mistaken for criteria. This is incorrect, however. Some wetlands develop where hydric soils are absent or where vascular plants cannot grow, and the wetland supports instead other kinds of organisms that are reflective of recurrent, sustained saturation. Wetlands that lack hydric soils or hydrophytic vascular plants, although unusual, should not be excluded from regulation simply because they lack the most common indicators.

WATER

Although specific hydrologic conditions are an absolute requirement for the formation and maintenance of wetlands, the direct assessment of these conditions in the field by use of information on water table depth or inundation is often infeasible and should not be held as a strict requirement for the identification and delineation of all wetlands. In some cases, however, a direct evaluation of hydrology is essential or extremely useful in supporting the reliability of delineation. In particular, hydrologic alterations could invalidate most or all indicators except direct indicators of hydrologic conditions, and in this case direct hydrologic evaluation is mandatory. In addition, neutral or mixed indications from substrate and biotic factors should be taken as a requirement for hydrologic analysis.

Direct hydrologic analysis requires, at a minimum, information on three related elements: the duration of saturation and its relation to the growing season, the critical depth for saturation, and the frequency of saturation. In the absence of specific regional information to the contrary, the threshold for duration of saturation can be approximated as 14 days during the growing season in most years (long-term mean exceeding 50% of years). The depth over which saturation should be evaluated is the upper plant rooting zone, which can be estimated as 1 ft (30 cm). The depth of the water table should be taken as a direct indicator of the depth of the saturated zone below the surface, except where the capillary fringe makes a significant extension of the saturated zone above the water table.

The 14-day duration threshold should be viewed as provisional because it does not account for factors that can cause variation in the threshold. Because of the strong influence of temperature on the rate at which anaerobic conditions develop in saturated soils, a more sophisticated approach should be developed from a concept, such as degree-days, that accounts simultaneously for time and temperature. The current growing-season concept cannot be applied reliably to subarctic, arctic, and alpine regions, or to the southwestern and tropical parts of the United States. These regions should be evaluated separately while a more credible system for defining saturation thresholds is developed for the nation as a whole. In particular, perennially cold soils can develop the anaerobic conditions necessary for the formation of hydric soils and for the establishment of wetland vegetation even when soil temperatures seldom or never exceed the temperature that is presently used in defining the growing season (41°F, or 5°C).

Visual indicators of hydrologic events such as drift lines or blackened leaves are not reliable without support from other hydrologic data. In some instances, small amounts of direct hydrologic information on water-table level or depth of inundation can be expanded through the use of modeling.

SUBSTRATE

Most wetlands are characterized by hydric soils, which carry physical and chemical indications of repeated and prolonged saturation at or near the surface. These indications derive from blockage of oxygen transport by water in the substrate. Steady depletion of oxygen in saturated soils is caused by roots as well as microbes and other soil organisms. Often this leads to complete loss of oxygen and in some cases to substantial accumulation of reduced substances. Manifestations of hydric soils include lack of oxygen or low redox (reduction-oxidation) potential during the period of saturation, characteristic irregularities in the color of the soil, and other so-called redoximorphic features. These features are directly significant as indicators of hydric soils; they are also significant in showing the recurrent development of conditions that exclude many upland plant species, which are intolerant of conditions that accompany the loss of oxygen.

The national Hydric Soils List (Hydric Soils of the United States) has been developed under the sponsorship of the NRCS through the National Technical Committee for Hydric Soils (NTCHS). This list represents sound application of the principles of soil science to the identification of hydric soils, and it should be maintained, revised, and reviewed under federal sponsorship. The primary data, however, as well as procedures for identification of hydric soils and changes in the designation of hydric soils, should be more thoroughly documented and reviewed and should be made more widely available than in the past. In addition, a wetlands fidelity system should be considered for use with hydric soils as it is for hydrophytic vegetation, and more studies should be done of soils that are difficult to classify in the field, and particularly those that require the use of water table data, which typically are not available from field surveys. More emphasis should be placed on the development of field indicators for hydric soils.

In some instances, substrates other than hydric soils (such as unconsolidated floodplain substrates) and biotic communities other than hydrophytic vascular plants (such as algae) are associated with wetlands. There is no scientific basis for excluding these environments from designation as wetlands, and delineation manuals should acknowledge the admissibility of their indicators, unless laws or regulations dictate explicitly that they be excluded. Identification of these wetlands can be facilitated by the broadening of biotic indicators to include aquatic invertebrates, algae, and mosses.

VEGETATION

Hydrophytic vegetation is assessed through use of the National List of Plant Species that Occur in Wetlands (Hydrophyte List). This list is a valid tool for identifying hydrophytic vegetation. It is important that refinement of the list continue under federal support. The fidelity rating (obligate, facultative, etc.) assigned to plants through the Hydrophyte List is a useful foundation for the evaluation of predominance of hydrophytic vegetation and is scientifically credible. For some species, however, the existence of genetically distinctive populations that have differing affinities for wetland conditions complicates the use of the list. More extensive study of these species, and appropriate identification of the regions in which the differing genetic types are present, will enhance the usefulness of the list.

Either a dominance measure (the 50% rule) or a prevalence index can be used in quantifying the predominance of hydrophytic vegetation. The dominance measure classifies plant communities as indicative of wetland if more than 50% of the dominant taxa are hydrophytic. The prevalence index is calculated from wetland fidelity indicator values for each species, weighted by abundance, and is indicative of wetland above a threshold value indicating predominance of hydrophytes. Correct application of either method requires extensive botanical background as well as field experience. All strata of vegetation should be considered for either method. The prevalence index has withstood extensive scientific scrutiny.

A prevalence index value that is near neutrality (3.0) or a dominance estimate near 50% is not a reliable indicator for assessment of vegetation in the absence of independent information on soils, hydrology, or both. Very high or very low values for dominance or for the prevalence index reliably distinguish wetland from upland, if hydrology has not been altered, but should be supplemented with information on soils. An array of simple but definitive indicators based on vegetation can and should be constructed for use in the field as a means of conserving time, effort, and expense in vegetation analysis.

Vegetation indexes are sometimes computed without the inclusion of facultative species ("FAC-neutral" tests). Present evidence indicates, however, that such procedures do not resolve the ambiguities of communities that cannot be easily classified. A better alternative under such circumstances is to place heavier weight on other indicators. Information on soils is critical in marginal cases or where transition from wetland to upland is gradual, particularly because soil is less responsive than is vegetation to short-term change.

COMBINATIONS OF INDICATORS FOR WATER, SOIL, AND VEGETATION

Federal support is needed for more extensive, regionalized studies of the relationships between hydric soils, hydrophytic vegetation, and specific hydrologic thresholds associated with the development of wetlands. In the past, field studies have tended to focus separately on soils, vegetation, or hydrology, rather than on the coincidence of the three, which is a critical matter for identification and delineation of wetlands. The research should have a long-term component that is based in part on the establishment of regionally dispersed reference wetlands from which information can be collected routinely.

Evaluation of the three factors that define wetlands should account for the causal relationships among water, substrate, and biota. Although wetlands are defined by all three factors, it is often scientifically defensible to infer information about one factor from another in the absence of alterations or mixed evidence. This is especially true for hydrology, which is adequately characterized by hydric soils or hydrophytic vegetation if there is no evidence for alteration of hydrologic conditions. If hydrologic information is unavailable, wetlands should be identified by rigorous joint consideration of substrate (typically soil), and biota (typically vegetation).

A modified approach to the assessment of wetlands could reduce the collection of unnecessary information and thus save considerable public and private money without sacrificing the accuracy of delineation, and should be considered for use by regulatory agencies. The approach would involve either the use of primary indicators or the use of a hierarchical method for the evaluation of evidence. Either method would reduce the collection of unneeded evidence for sites that are easily classified as upland or as wetland, thus allowing more resources to be used for cases with mixed evidence, uncertain indications, or complications that result from alteration.

ESPECIALLY CONTROVERSIAL WETLANDS

Classification of some kinds of wetlands has been particularly controversial, typically because of special legislative or regulatory treatment or because of special difficulties associated with identification or delineation. These especially controversial areas include permafrost wetlands, riparian zones, isolated and shallow wetlands, agricultural wetlands, altered wetlands, transitional or marginal wetlands, and especially shallow or intermittently flooded wetlands.

Many proposals have been made to regulate permafrost wetlands separately from nonpermafrost wetlands. Extensive permafrost wetlands are now excluded from the regulatory definition of wetlands by the Food Security Act. The regulatory treatment of permafrost wetlands is significant because of their abundance in Alaska, which has a high proportion of the nation's remaining wetlands. Although regulatory exclusions of wetlands can occur for political or administrative reasons without a scientific basis, it should be clearly recognized that permafrost wetlands of Alaska or at any other location fall well within the NRC committee's reference definition of wetlands, and would be regulated as wetlands by any system that purports to protect or regulate all wetlands.

Riparian zones, which are the lands immediately adjacent to rivers and streams, also have posed some difficult problems, particularly in the western United States. Riparian zones share some of the characteristics of wetlands and often include wetlands but cannot be defined wholly as wetlands by any widely used definition because they are often saturated at much lower frequencies than wetlands. Riparian zones suppress the undesirable effects of flooding, maintain water quality, and serve as centers of biological diversity, especially in the western United States, and in this way share some of the functions and values of wetlands. If national policy calls for protection of riparian zones pursuant to the goals of the Clean Water Act, regulation must be achieved through legislation that recognizes the special attributes of riparian zones, and not by attempts to define them as wetlands.

Isolated wetlands and headwater wetlands also have been a subject of controversy because of their differential protection under Section 404 of the Clean Water Act. Wetlands that are isolated from other surface waters or that occupy headwaters are not necessarily less valuable or less functional than other wetlands are, and they may even perform some unique or particularly valuable functions, including maintenance of water quality and the support of waterfowl. Even though such wetlands qualify for protection under Section 404, Nationwide Permit 26 allows them to be filled in amounts up to 1 acre (0.4 ha) with no review and 10 acres (4 ha) with minimal review, except where Nationwide Permit 26 is overridden by the USACE district engineer or state regulations. Nationwide Permit 26 has been controversial because of the cumulative wetland losses that can result through its application and is the cause of more litigation than any other nationwide permit. The rationale for extensive use of Nationwide Permit 26 for isolated and headwater wetlands should be reviewed.

Especially shallow wetlands that might be dry much of the year, but that are maintained by repeated seasonal saturation or inundation, require protection even at times when they are completely dry if they are to retain their functions.

Agricultural wetlands, which for present purposes include both farmed wetlands and nonfarmed wetlands within farmed areas, are extensive within the United States. They often perform functions that are similar in nature to those of nonagricultural wetlands. Use of special definitions or criteria for the identification of agricultural wetlands is not justified because it leads to differential delineation of wetlands on agricultural and nonagricultural lands.

Wetlands that have been altered through activities other than agriculture present special problems in delineation. Any federal manual applicable to such lands should instruct delineators on the valid use of inference for the purpose of assessing altered lands. Natural transitional zones, especially if they are very broad, also present special problems in delineation. Transition zones should be the subject of more extensive study for the purpose of strengthening the efficiency and accuracy of delineation.

REGIONALIZATION

Regionalization, which is the adaptation of wetland indicators to regional variation in wetland characteristics, is the best approach for establishing the relationship between growing season, duration of saturation, and the development of substrate and biota. The current federal regulatory system is regionalized to some extent through the delegated authority of the regional offices of federal agencies and through the use of the Hydrophyte List and Hydric Soils List. The administrative system for regionalization of wetland assessment is haphazard, however. Regions for wetland regulation need to be redefined around environmental factors such as physiography and climate and should be used in common by all agencies. More extensive development of regional analysis and regional protocols should be encouraged administratively and through research, provided that the outcome of federal regulatory practice is reasonably uniform across the nation. A uniform process should be used to develop regional standards, and the four federal agencies that assess wetlands (USACE, EPA, NRCS, FWS) should cooperate in the development of regional protocols.

MAPS, IMAGES, AND MODELING

Use of aerial photography and satellite images for identifying and delineating wetlands can be acceptable, but it requires extensive field validation and should be designed and timed for assessment of wetlands rather than assessment of crops. Conventions for interpretation should be standardized across agencies that are involved in the delineation of wetlands. The National Wetlands Inventory provides an important overview of wetlands for the United States, and should be completed. Mathematical and computer models, if verified in the field, are useful and reliable methods for evaluating the hydrology of certain types of wetlands and the effects of alterations on wetland hydrology and will in some cases make the delineation of wetlands more effective and expeditious.

REGULATORY PRACTICE

Training and certification of delineators should be facilitated by federal agencies involved in the regulation of wetlands. The expertise necessary for delineation of wetlands should be clarified by the federal agencies that establish delineation protocols. Because identifying and delineating wetlands is a complex task a delineator would be required to have a scientific education at the college level combined with specialized training in delineation methods and practices. All wetland assessment programs of regulatory significance should incorporate procedures for quality control and quality assurance.

A federal system should be created for maintaining computerized records of regulatory wetland assessments, and this information should be made available to federal agencies, states, and private parties. It should form the basis for periodic nationwide synthesis and reporting of information on the numbers, kinds, and outcomes of regulatory actions related to wetlands.

Consolidation of all wetland regulatory functions into a single federal agency would improve the consistency of wetland delineations. Even if several agencies continue to share responsibility for wetland delineation, they should use a single definition and one delineation manual for all regulatory purposes.

FUNCTIONAL ASSESSMENT

Many wetland functions are considered useful or important by society. For example, inundation of wetlands can prevent flood damage elsewhere, denitrification can improve water quality, wetland habitat can help maintain waterfowl populations, and anoxic conditions in the substrate can influence the development of unique plant communities that contribute to the conservation of biodiversity.

The value of a wetland is a measure of its importance to society. Wetland functions are valued to various degrees by society, but there is no precise, general relationship between wetland functions and the value of wetlands to society, and values can be difficult to determine objectively. A wetland's value can be weighed directly or relative to other uses that could be made of the site. For this reason, the location of a wetland may affect its value to society. For example, wetlands in urban settings might have higher value for recreation and education or for alternative uses than wetlands in undeveloped lands or far from population centers. Assessing the value of wetlands requires the use of methods from economics and other related fields, and is not yet well developed.

The societal priorities for protection of wetlands and for investment in wetland protection are matters of policy that must reflect in part the value that society places on wetlands. Assessment of value requires comprehensive scientific knowledge of wetland functions. Indeed, some groups have suggested the creation of a national scheme that would designate wetlands of high, medium, and low value based on some general guidelines involving size, location, or some other factor that does not require field evaluation. It is not possible, however, to relate such categories in a reliable way to objective measures of wetland functions, in part because the relationships between categories and functions are variable and in part because we still have insufficient knowledge of wetland functions. In general, the identification and delineation of wetlands must be kept separate from the functional analysis of wetlands.

Functional analysis of wetlands should be extended and refined; it should take into account the interactions between wetlands and their surroundings. The regulation of wetlands is an integral part of watershed management, which in turn is central to the objectives of the Clean Water Act.

GENERAL CONCLUSIONS

Federal laws, such as the Commerce Clause, or policies, such as those developed by federal agencies implementing the Clean Water Act, could intentionally exclude some wetlands from regulation. Therefore, it is important to maintain the distinction between a reference definition, which ignores the matter of jurisdiction, and a regulatory one, which takes into account the intent of laws or policies that do not necessarily encompass all wetlands.

The federal regulatory system for protection of wetlands is scientifically sound and effective in most respects, but it can be more efficient, more uniform, more credible with regulated entities, and more accurate in a technical or scientific sense through constructive reforms of the type suggested in this report.

Detailed recommendations can be found at the end of Chapters 2, 3, 5, 6, 7, 8, 9, and 10.

1

Introduction and Background

The wealth of the United States was drawn initially from the development and exploitation of its virgin lands. Until this century, use of land for agriculture and commerce must have seemed unlikely to exhaust the country's vast reserves. Population growth and an increasingly potent agro-industrial capacity have, however, brought most of the conterminous United States under some form of management. As a result, the form and function of the original landscape have changed, and continue to change.

The ecosystems that compose the landscape provide distributed benefits that extend well beyond the boundaries of any individual property. Consequently, society is a stakeholder in environmental change. It is widely accepted that a healthy environment is necessary for a healthy economy over the long term, but the appropriate balance of voluntary action and regulation for protection of the environment is often a matter of contention. Regulation of wetlands has raised this issue more forcefully than any other federal action related to the environment.

The United States first became broadly committed, beyond its stewardship of public lands, to protection of public interest in the environment through laws intended to preserve or enhance the quality of air and water. Because air and water seldom can be construed as amenities of a single property, protection of the common interest can occur through regulations that are universally applicable to private and public lands. Federal regulation of wetlands was the first major step toward broad protection of landscape features, rather than protection of environmental media. Whereas regulation of air and water applies primarily to public or corporate entities, regulation of wetlands extends to individual property owners.

A direct connection to human health also has motivated protection of air and water, but is not a major element in the debate over wetlands. The context for regulation of wetlands thus differs from that of air and water, even though wetlands are largely regulated through the Clean Water Act.

Protection of wetlands is based on the premise that preservation of a specific ecosystem type can be of sufficient common interest that its conversion or development should be prevented or restrained by law, even though much of its area might be found on private property. To some, the universal protection of wetlands seems an infringement of property rights. To others, it is a reasonable extension of the need to protect the public interest in environmental components that have exceptional value to society. Science cannot resolve the propriety or legality of regulating wetlands on private lands. Science can, however, support the development of objective and consistent means for identifying wetlands and their boundaries.

Scientists have not agreed on a single commonly used definition of wetland in the past because they have had no scientific motivation to do so. Now, however, they are being asked to help interpret regulatory definitions of wetlands. The application of scientific principles to the definition of wetlands and to the determination of wetland boundaries could help stabilize and rationalize the application of regulations, but it does not ensure that any resultant definition will be precise in its ability to distinguish wetlands from all other kinds of ecosystems, or in its ability to specify the exact boundary of a wetland. Judgment and convention will continue play a role, even following full application of scientific principles. In addition, the concept of wetland has a long history in Anglo-American law and carries with it important legal connotations that need to be considered in the application of any wetland definition.

PURPOSES OF THE NRC REPORT

Identification and Characterization

One purpose of this report is to review the scientific basis for identification and delineation of wetlands as currently reflected in federal manuals and regulatory conventions. The report is intended to identify both the strengths and weaknesses of current regulatory practice. The committee's charge also asks that we deal with the basis for translation of definitions into "practical, scientifically valid methods to efficiently and consistently identify wetlands." The committee decided that the translation of a definition or of particular standards or criteria into practical methods is also dependent on certain principles of regulatory practice and thus Chapter 9 titled Regulation of Wetlands and other discussion pertaining to regulation of wetlands (e.g., review of Nationwide Permit 26 and functional assessment) is included in this report.

Although the identification and delineation of wetlands can and should have a scientific basis, scientific principles will not always dictate the appropriate choice among several possible regulatory conventions. For example, the boundary between wetland and upland can be identified scientifically as a transition zone that incorporates a hydrologic gradient as well as gradients in soil type and in community composition of plants. If the regulatory objective is to protect the wetland absolutely, without regard to other considerations, the obvious choice would be to place a regulatory boundary at the outermost limit of the transition zone. Alternatively, regulatory practice that attempts to minimize economic dislocation while still protecting the core wetland area might set the boundary at the innermost part of the transition zone.

The scientific and technical aspects of wetland identification and determination of wetland boundaries should not be confused with the matter of federal jurisdiction over wetlands. As explained further in Chapter 3, jurisdiction is to some extent severable from the delineation of wetlands insofar as laws and their regulatory interpretations may exclude, for sociopolitical reasons, certain classes of ecosystems that might be identified on scientific or technical grounds as wetlands. While any practical evaluation of the wetland regulatory system must acknowledge the importance of both scientific and jurisdictional principles, the relationship between the two can be understood only in light of their separate origins and motivations.

Identification of Functions and Values

Legislation dealing with wetlands, wetland regulations, and public comment on wetlands contain references to the societal values that motivate protection of wetlands. Some functions of wetlands are directly associated with specific societal values. For example, suppression of floods is a value of wetlands, and the underlying function is seasonal water storage by wetlands. Associations between functions and values may also can be indirect. For example, the waterfowl of wetlands have value. Wetlands support waterfowl, but only as a result of hydrologic functions that maintain specific wetland vegetation, wetland food chains, and other habitat features that are necessary for the reproduction or maintenance of waterfowl.

The association between the value of wetlands to society and the functions that are characteristic of wetlands is important in the design of wetland protection systems. If one objective is preservation of wetland attributes that have societal value, the association between selected wetland values and their supporting wetland functions will dictate the kinds of protection mechanisms that will be most effective.

Variations

A third factor to be considered in this report is variation among wetlands.

ᵉ diverse physiographic regions of the United States support many kinds of wetlands (Mitsch and Gosselink, 1993), which vary functionally and in their value to society. For example, cypress swamps and mangrove swamps differ greatly from northern peatlands, and tidal salt marshes function differently from inland freshwater marshes. Different kinds of wetlands also present varying kinds of technical challenges for identification and boundary setting. Physiographic regions vary not only in their assortment of wetland types, but also in the abundance of wetlands and in the degree to which the wetlands are altered or eliminated.

Both within and among regions, points of particular interest for this report include the degree of variation, the practical difficulties that variation poses for centrally designed delineation systems, and the feasibility of regionalizing technical procedures to be used in the identification and delineation of wetlands.

Relationships of the Three Themes

The three themes for this report—wetland identification and delineation, functions and values of wetlands, and variation among wetlands—are interdependent. The identification of wetlands, the determination of boundaries for wetlands, and the characterization of wetland functions and values must be set within a framework that is broad enough to encompass the great physical and biotic variety of wetlands, while at the same time maintaining as clearly as possible the distinction between wetlands and other kinds of ecosystems.

PATH TO REGULATION

At the time of European colonization, the area that is now the conterminous United States contained about 220 million acres (90 million ha) of wetland, comprising about 9% of the landscape (Dahl, 1990). Colonists were sometimes attracted to wetlands because of the high agricultural potential of their rich hydric soils. For example, the wealthiest colonists of tidewater Virginia chose the lowlands for their large estates; the unproductive uplands were left to less prosperous landholders (Fischer, 1989). As the saturated wetland soils were drained and diked for agriculture, wetlands often extracted a heavy price in the form of vivax and falciparum malaria, as well as such waterborne diseases as typhoid and dysentery (Fischer, 1989). Wetlands as viewed through the agrarian eyes of early America are well portrayed by the Federal Swamp Land Act of 1850, which deeded extensive wetlands to the states for conversion to agriculture.

Between the first phases of European colonization and the 1980s, about one-half of the wetland area in the conterminous states was converted to other land forms, primarily by drainage, for promotion of agriculture (Table 1.1). Federal intervention through various swampland acts and through ambitious drainage projects of the U.S. Army Corps of Engineers (USACE) promoted wetland con-

TABLE 1.1 Estimates of Wetland Losses in the Conterminous United States (Modified from Mitsch and Gosselink, 1993)

Period	Hectares (millions)	Acres (millions)	Percentage	Annual Percentage	Reference
Presettlement to 1950s	18	45	35	0.14[a]	Shaw and Fredine (1956)
Presettlement to 1980s	47	117	53	0.19[a]	Dahl (1990)
1922-1954	4.5	11[a]	6.4[a]	0.20	Zinn and Copeland (1982)
1954-1970s	6.5	16[a]	11[a]	0.55	Zinn and Copeland (1982)
1950s-1970s	3.6	9	8.5	0.42	Frayer et al. (1983)
1970s-1980s	1.1	2.6	2.5	0.25	Dahl and Johnson (1991)

[a]Computed from the primary estimates.

version, but much wetland conversion was privately motivated and resulted in the creation of productive croplands that today form an important part of the agricultural resource base of the United States (Mitsch and Gosselink, 1993). Conversion was distributed very unevenly. The conversion, which had exceeded 80% in a number of states by the end of the 1980s, was highest where conversion was both feasible and profitable (for example, in Illinois and Ohio), or where wetlands were of limited extent but coincided with the most favorable areas for agriculture and population growth (as in California).

The national attitude and federal policy toward wetlands became ambivalent as early as the 1930s. The first point of national concern was a decline in waterfowl populations, which in part reflected loss of wetlands along flyways and in breeding grounds. Concern for waterfowl led to the introduction of the Federal Duck Stamp Program in 1934, which provided money for the purchase or protection of wetlands. At the same time, both the Department of Agriculture and the USACE continued to encourage, subsidize, and finance the conversion of wetlands.

By the early 1970s, interest in the protection of wetlands had extended well beyond the desire to maintain waterfowl populations. Three factors contributed to a shift in national attitude. First was the environmental movement, which opened to question many established policies of land use. A second factor was the increasing evidence that wetlands were being lost and converted at a rate that projected their virtual disappearance in many parts of the country. Third was a realization that wetlands have particular value to society, not only through the maintenance of waterfowl populations, but also in support of water quality, hydrologic buffering, and provision of refugia for many kinds of organisms that cannot be found elsewhere.

In the 1970s, the federal government began incrementally to protect wetlands through executive orders and legislation. Individual states also had begun their efforts as early as the 1960s. The keystone of the federal protection system was set in the early 1970s by court decisions interpreting the Clean Water Act as protective of wetlands. This was followed by a critical shift in federal policy for the agricultural sector through the Food Security Act of 1985, which contained the so-called "swampbuster" provisions denying some agricultural subsidies to property owners who converted wetlands after 1985.

CURRENT CONTEXT FOR REGULATION

Laws and regulations notwithstanding, the United States lacked until very recently a consistent national policy for regulation of activities in wetlands. Permitting of dredge-and-fill activities by the USACE under authority of the Clean Water Act, for example, could be administered with varying degrees of stringency ranging from virtual prohibition of wetlands conversion to accommodation of all but their most egregious destruction. Thus, the existence of laws and regulations is not a substitute for national policy. Because regulations affecting wetlands can be administered with broad discretion, the underlying national policy has often been unclear.

Perceiving the need for a guiding hand to direct regulators and to inform the public, the Environmental Protection Agency called for a National Wetlands Policy Forum in 1987 (The Conservation Foundation, 1988). Participants in the forum, which was charged with making recommendations for national policy on the protection of wetlands, represented a range of political and technical perspectives. The forum's central recommendation was that a national wetland protection policy should be established around the principle of no net loss of wetlands. The recommendation was actually more elaborate, but the core concept was no net loss (Clark, 1993). For the long term, the forum recommended restoration and creation of wetlands, where feasible, leading to an increase in the quality and quantity of the nation's wetlands.

The forum's central recommendation (The Conservation Foundation, 1988) was adopted by the Bush Administration and since has been endorsed by the Clinton Administration as well. At least in the executive branch, and presumably throughout the regulatory and management agencies that are directed by the executive branch, the cornerstone of national policy has been set. Both the interpretation and the application of the policy are, however, still to be worked out. The policy in its barest form seems unambiguous, but is not immune to variable interpretation. Clark (1993) points out that each of the three words that summarize the policy ("no net loss") was viewed in a variety of ways by members of the National Wetlands Policy Forum. For example, the word "no" may be taken as either categorical or suggestive, and "net" can be interpreted as allowing unlimited replacement of existing wetlands by hypothetical ones to be created at a time and date not specified. The word "loss" also may be variously interpreted to mean loss of selected functions, or complete loss of identity. Consequently, the availability of a national wetlands policy statement does not chart an entirely clear course for the regulators or the regulated.

Also at issue is whether the national policy of no net loss is a statement of intent to be realized quickly, or at some indefinite time in the future, or perhaps only to be approached incrementally but never actually reached. An aggressive interpretation of the policy would dictate that federal agencies charged with wetland protection use the full force of wetlands regulation to achieve the national goal as quickly as possible. This would require tightening of the permitting system, much greater investments in restoration through programs such as the Natural Resources Conservation Service (NRCS) Wetlands Reserve, further development of mitigation banking, and accurate national inventory of wetlands to establish the degree of deviation from the national goal. A more casual interpretation might emphasize flexibility and slow incremental progress. The policy statement itself does not distinguish between these two possible applications of the principle of no net loss.

Regulatory practice will set the boundaries of wetlands under any wetland protection system. Protection of wetlands in the U.S. must be guided from a technical base that is consistent, reflective of legislative intent, and capable of continually assimilating new knowledge about wetlands. The following chapters deal with this issue first by considering the fundamental nature of wetlands and the essential factors that define them, followed by an assessment and critical analysis of current and past practice for identification and delineation, and finally by a treatment of regionalization, especially controversial wetlands, administrative issues, and functional assessment of wetlands.

2

Ecology of Wetland Ecosystems

INTRODUCTION

Many kinds of wetland ecosystems are found within the United States (Table 2.1). These range from small, discrete sites, such as Thoreau's Bog in Massachusetts or Four Holes Swamp in South Carolina, to large, spatially complex ones, such as the Great Dismal Swamp in Virginia and North Carolina or the peatlands of northern Minnesota. The characteristics and functions of any given wetland are determined by climate, hydrology, and substrate, as well as by position and dominance in the landscape. In many cases, wetlands occupy a small portion of the total landscape (usually less than 10%), but have extensive boundaries with both terrestrial and aquatic ecosystems. In some cases, they occupy virtually the entire landscape. Despite their great range in size and other features, wetlands share specific characteristics, some of which are structural (water, substrate, biota), while others are functional (nutrient cycling, water balance, organic production). Analysis of these characteristics shows how wetlands are distinct from other kinds of ecosystems, and illustrates the reasons for variation among wetlands.

In very large wetlands, such as extensive peatlands, marshlands, bottomlands, and river floodplains, internal spatial variation can be great. Examples include the Great Dismal Swamp, which consists of at least four major wetland plant communities integrated with lakes and streams (Kirk, 1979); the Everglades, which includes sloughs, sawgrass prairies, and wet shrub islands (Kushlan, 1990; Davis and Ogden, 1994); the Mississippi delta, which has swamps, marshes, lakes, and rivers (Day et al., 1977); and peatlands of northern Minnesota

TABLE 2.1 Major Classes of Wetlands in the United States and Some of Their Characteristics

Common Term	Distribution and Hydrology	Biota
Freshwater marsh	Widespread; seasonal to permanent flooding	Grasses, sedges, frogs
Tidal salt and brackish marsh	Intertidal zones; semidiurnal to fortnightly flooding	Salt-tolerant grasses and rushes, killifish, crabs, clams, snails
Prairie pothole	Northern plains states; temporary to permanent flooding; fluctuating water levels	Grasses, sedges, herbs
Fen	Associated with mineral-rich water; permanently saturated by flowing water	Sedges, grasses, shrubs, trees
Bog	Abundant in recently glaciated regions; precipitation principal source of water	Sphagnum moss, shrubs, trees, desmids
Swamp	Prolonged saturation and flooding	Cypress, gum, red maple
Bottomland	Seasonal flooding; annual dry periods	Oaks, sweetgum, other hardwoods
Mangrove	Subtropical, tropical regions; intermittent flooding by seawater through tidal action	Red, black, white mangroves

(Heinselman, 1970; Glaser et al., 1981). For such large areas, the gain, loss, and transformation of elements takes on continental or biospheric proportions (Elder, 1985; Gorham, 1991). For large river and floodplain systems, wetland complexes become landscape entities that rival major biomes in the context of global change (Lewis et al., 1990).

This chapter provides an overview of wetlands. It does not address specific questions about delineation. Instead, it serves as background for the analysis of the delineation issues that are discussed in other chapters. It begins with an overview of the nature of wetland ecosystems and the response of wetlands to various alterations, progresses to a summary of the functions of wetlands, and it closes with a consideration of boundaries between wetlands and terrestrial ecosystems.

THE NATURE OF WETLANDS

Because wetlands are neither aquatic nor terrestrial, they have not been easily assimilated by the well-established scientific disciplines of terrestrial and aquatic ecology. Wetlands have some of the same features as deepwater systems, including frequently anoxic substrate and some species of algae, vertebrates, and

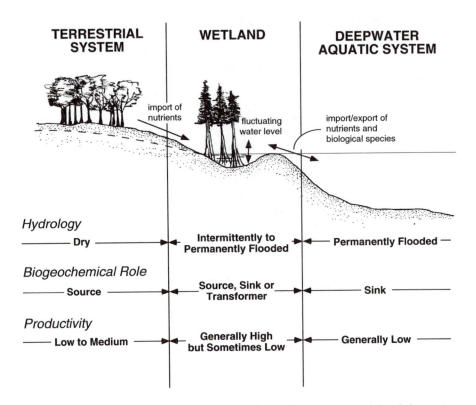

FIGURE 2.1A Wetlands can be part of a continuum between terrestrial and deepwater aquatic systems. Source: Mitsch and Gosselink, 1993.

invertebrates. Most wetlands share with terrestrial ecosystems a flora dominated by vascular plants, although the species composition of wetlands generally differs from that of uplands. Wetlands often are found at the interface of terrestrial ecosystems (such as upland forests and grasslands) and aquatic systems (such as lakes, rivers, and estuaries, Figure 2.1A,B). Some are isolated from deepwater habitats, and are maintained entirely by ground water and precipitation. Even though they show structural and functional overlap and physical interface with terrestrial and aquatic systems, wetlands are different from these other ecosystems in so many respects that they must be considered a distinctive class.

Hydrology as a Driving Force

Hydrology controls the abiotic and biotic characteristics of wetlands (Figure 2.2). Abiotic characteristics such as soil color, soil texture, and water quality depend on the distribution and movement of water, as do the abundance, diver-

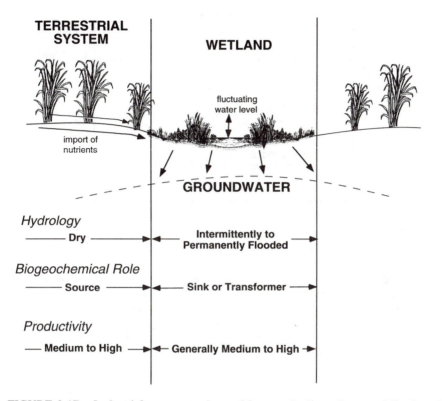

FIGURE 2.1B   Isolated from connections with water bodies. Source: Mitsch and Gosselink, 1993. Copyright Van Nostrand Reinhold, with permission.

sity, and productivity of plants, vertebrates, invertebrates, and microbes. Control is not unidirectional, however. For example, the biotic component of a wetland also can affect hydrology by increasing or decreasing water level or flow. Low rates of decomposition in some types of wetlands can cause basins to fill with undecomposed plant material, thus altering hydrologic conditions. Also, the water tables of some forested wetlands are held down in part by evapotranspiration; if trees are removed, standing water and marsh vegetation can develop. Muskrats, beavers, and alligators also can change hydrologic conditions in wetlands (Johnston, 1994a). Thus, wetland ecosystems are more than simple mixtures of water, soil, and organisms.

Water flows and levels in most wetlands are dynamic (Kusler et al., 1994). The temporal pattern of water level, or hydroperiod, for an individual wetland is part of its ecological signature (Mitsch and Gosselink, 1993). Water level fluctuates daily in coastal marshes and seasonally in almost all wetlands, as shown in Figure 2.3 on arbitrary scales referenced to the surface of the substrate. It also

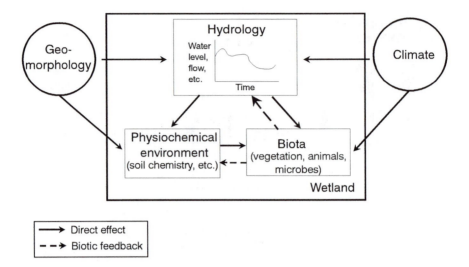

FIGURE 2.2 The relationships among hydrology, physicochemical environment, and bio-ta in wetlands. Vegetation provides important feedback to hydrology through evapotrans-piration and increase in flow resistance and to the physicochemical environment by af-fecting soil properties (organic content, dissolved oxygen) and elevation (accumulating organic matter, trapping sediment). Animals such as beaver, muskrat, and alligators can also significantly affect hydrology, soils, and other biota.

varies significantly from year to year in some wetlands, such as prairie potholes. For these reasons, Fredrickson and Reid (1990) criticize the practice of stabiliz-ing water level in managed wetlands. They point out that resource managers can be misled by the notion that most wetland wildlife species require year-round standing water for their life cycles. In fact, dry periods are often important for reasons that are less obvious but no less important.

Moisture gradients vary temporally and spatially at the margin of a wetland, and plants, animals, and microbes often orient in predictable ways to the gradient. Figure 2.4 illustrates the zonation of vegetation that develops in four wetland types. It is this gradient, and particularly the junction between upland and wet-land, that is central to the wetland characterization issue in the United States. The junction between wetlands and deepwater systems, while also incorporating a gradient, raises fewer regulatory issues.

Causes of Variation

Three factors explain many of the differences among wetlands (Figure 2.5): geomorphic setting (for example, floodplain, estuary fringe), water source, and hydrodynamics (such as unidirectional flow, reversing flow); these have been called hydrogeomorphic characteristics (Brinson, 1993a). Hydrogeomorphic characteristics are interdependent. For example, geomorphic setting is in part a product of water source and hydrodynamics, but it also places constraints on water source and hydrodynamics. Hydrogeomorphic classes are distinctive combinations of the three factors (Figure 2.5). Depressional wetlands are maintained by overland flow, ground water, and precipitation rather than channelized flow. Riparian wetlands show seasonal or periodic pulses of water level (Figure 2.3) that are delivered from overbank flows carrying nutrients and organic matter. Estuarine fringe wetlands are pulsed hydrologically by daily tides. Slope wetlands, such as the seeps that occur where ground water reaches the surface, are maintained by relatively constant sources of water. Peatlands occur in many settings, but can be maintained entirely by precipitation.

Organic Matter

The saturation of soils with water generally slows decomposition, which often causes wetlands to accumulate organic matter in the substrate. The organic-rich soil of wetlands, including peat in some wetlands (Glaser et al., 1981), is evidence of this accumulation. Even so, not all organic matter that enters or is formed by photosynthesis in wetlands remains within the wetland boundary. Many wetlands export organic carbon to streams and estuaries at a rate substantially higher than that of terrestrial ecosystems (Mulholland and Kuenzler, 1979). In this way, wetlands can make large contributions to the support of organisms that consume non-living organic matter. For example, in Arctic tundra, where most of the landscape is wetland underlain by peat, aquatic food webs are supported to a significant extent by fossil peat (Schell, 1983).

Natural Disturbance

Many wetlands are maintained in part by natural disturbances such as flood, fire, or herbivory. Ewel and Mitsch (1978), for example, found that fire prevents pines and hardwoods from invading cypress (*Taxodium*) swamps in Florida (Appendix B, Florida pine flatwoods). By occurring alternately, fire and inundation together maintain the characteristic plant communities of these wetlands (Figure 2.6). Riverine and riparian wetlands commonly change as meanders undercut banks to form point bars that can be colonized by hydrophytes. Muskrats (Errington, 1963) and Canada geese (Jefferies et al., 1979) can clear vegetation from large portions of freshwater marshes. Beavers can flood stands of upland vegetation, thus causing the development of wetland vegetation (Johnston, 1994a).

Nutrient Transformation

Nutrients such as nitrogen and phosphorus are carried into wetlands by precipitation, overbank flow from streams, lunar tides, movement of surface and

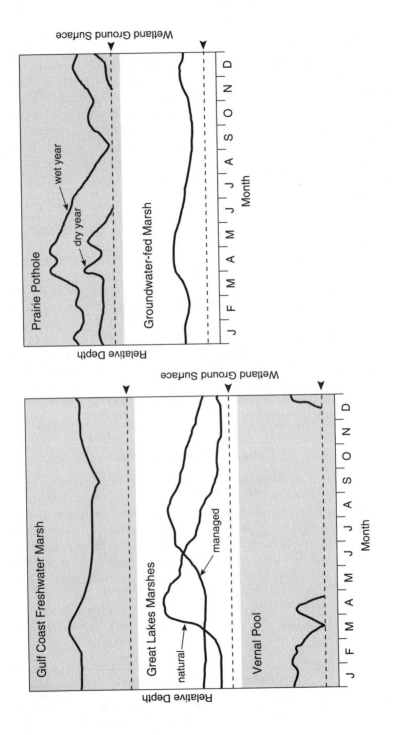

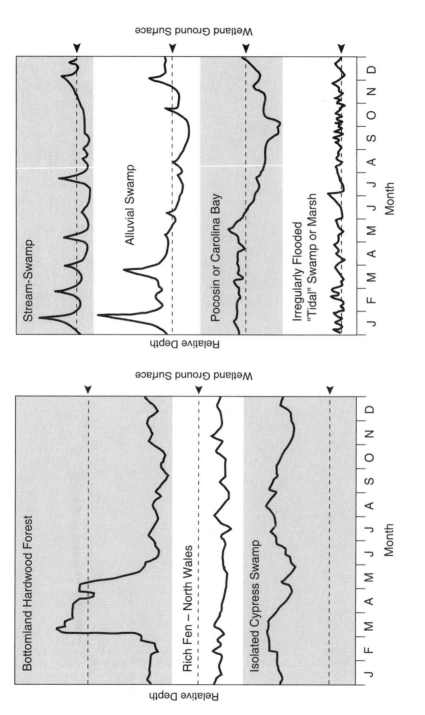

FIGURE 2.3 Hydroperiods for wetlands of several classes and physiographic regions. Source: Mitsch and Gosselink (1993); Brinson (1993a).

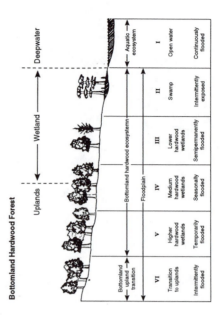

Bottomland Hardwood Forest

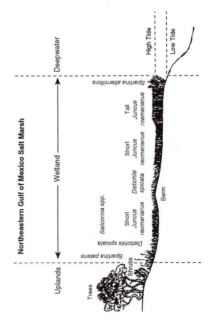

Northeastern Gulf of Mexico Salt Marsh

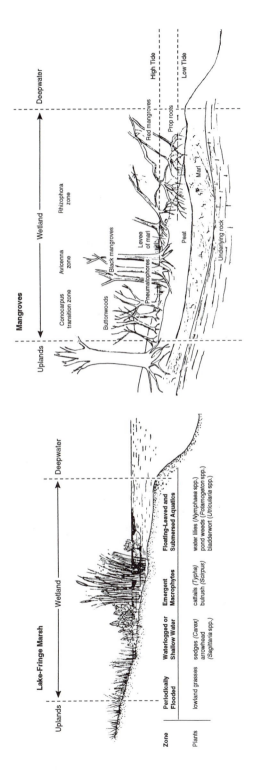

FIGURE 2.4 Zonation of vegetation in four kinds of wetlands. Source: Mitsch and Gosselink, 1993.

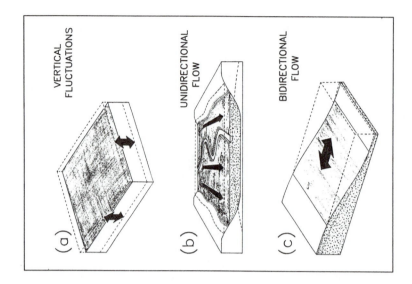

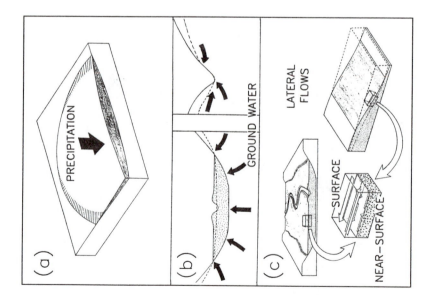

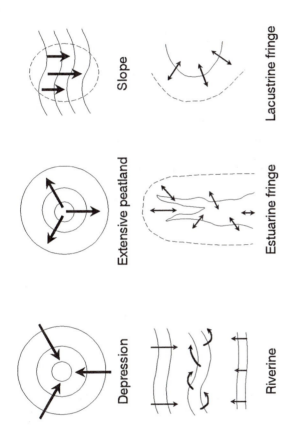

FIGURE 2.5 (A) Water source and hydrodynamics as they vary among hydrogeomorphic classes of wetlands. From Brinson (1993a). (B) Flow paths (arrows) and topographic contours for six hydrogeomorphic classes of wetlands (from Holland and Magee, in preparation).

B

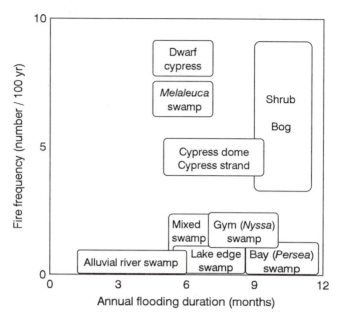

FIGURE 2.6   Interaction of hydroperiod and fire frequency for wetlands in Florida. Adapted from Ewel (1990); copyright University of Central Florida Press, Orlando.

ground water and, in the case of nitrogen, biological fixation from the atmosphere. Nutrients are exported by channelized and surface flows, seepage, and gas transfer via denitrification. Intrasystem nutrient cycling is to a large extent embedded in the pathways of primary production, food chain transfer, and decomposition. When production and decomposition rates are high, as is especially likely in flowing water or in wetlands that have pulsed hydroperiods, nutrient cycling is rapid. When rates of production and decomposition are low, as is most likely in nutrient-poor wetlands such as ombrotrophic bogs, nutrient cycling can be slow.

All wetlands, including those with high flows of water, tend to recycle nutrients repeatedly (Faulkner and Richardson, 1989). Wetlands can be sources, sinks, or transformers of nutrients (Figure 2.7). A wetland is a sink for a specific substance if it shows net retention of the substance, and it is a source if it shows net loss of the substance. If a wetland changes a substance from one oxidation state to another or from dissolved to particulate form, it is acting as a transformer. A given wetland can perform different functions for different substances. For example, a wetland could be a sink for phosphorus, at steady state for nitrogen, and an exporter of organic carbon (Figure 2.7).

Primary production can be limited by the availability of nutrients. Both low-nutrient (some bogs, cypress domes) and high-nutrient wetlands (floodplain wet-a.

b.

c.

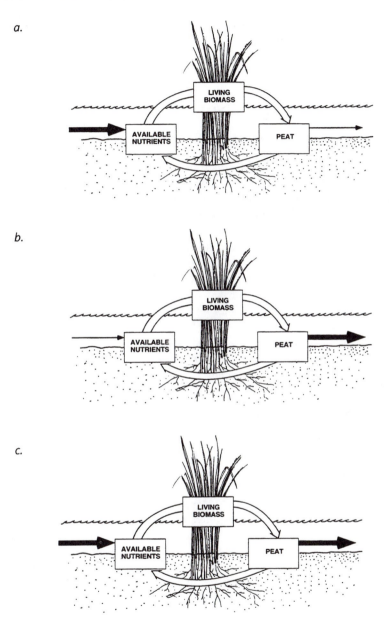

FIGURE 2.7 Wetlands alter the flow of nutrients, the magnitude of which is depicted by the width of the dark arrows. Wetlands can be: (A) net sink, (B) net source, or (C) in steady state with respect to a given nutrient. Reproduced with permission from Mitsch and Gosselink (1993), Van Nostrand Reinhold.

lands, tidal marshes) occur in nature, and each has special characteristics. Low-nutrient wetlands often support plant species that cannot compete with plants in high-nutrient wetlands. Consequently, low-nutrient wetlands support some of the rarest and most diverse plant communities (Keddy, 1990).

WETLAND FUNCTIONS

Functions of wetlands can be defined broadly as all processes and manifestations of processes that occur in wetlands. For example, denitrification is a function of wetlands that arises from a microbial process; maintenance of waterfowl populations, which results from production of food and cover by wetlands, is also a function of wetlands. Most functions fall into three broad categories: hydrologic, biogeochemical, and maintenance of habitat and food webs. Examples of each are listed in Table 2.2, although the table does not include all wetland functions, nor are all the functions shown in the table characteristic of every wetland. Functions of wetlands often have effects beyond the wetland boundary. For example, wetlands store surface water, and the effect of this function downstream is a reduction in flood peak. Indicators often correspond to specific functions (Table 2.2), which can vary with wetland class, physiographic region, and degree of disturbance.

Information on functions of wetlands has numerous uses, as explained in Chapter 10, but functional analysis is not necessary for the delineation of wetlands, as shown by Chapters 3 through 5.

Relationship to Value

Society does not necessarily attach value to all functions. Value is usually associated with goods and services that society recognizes. Thus, a connection can be made between the functions of wetlands, which are value-neutral, and to goods and services, which have value to society. Because value is a societal perception, it often changes over time, even if wetland functions are constant. It also can change over time, for example, as economic development changes a region. The value of a wetland in maintaining water quality near a drinking-water source can be great even if the wetland is small (Kusler et al., 1994). Some values can be mutually incompatible if they involve direct or indirect manipulation, exploitation, or management of a wetland. For example, production of fish for human consumption could conflict with the use of a wetland for improving the quality of water that contains toxins, if the toxins reduce fish production or contaminate fish flesh.

The alteration of wetland functions can impair the capacity of a wetland to supply goods and services. Alternatively, if the functions of the wetland are protected, many goods and services will be sustainable for the life of the wetland. The cost of functional protection of wetlands can be large, however, because it

TABLE 2.2 Functions, Related Effects of Functions, Corresponding Socie.
Values, and Relevant Indicators of Functions for Wetlands

Function	Effects	Societal Value	Indicator
Hydrologic			
Short-term surface water storage	Reduced downstream flood peaks	Reduced damage from floodwaters	Presence of floodplain along river corridor
Long-term surface water storage	Maintenance of base flows, seasonal flow distribution	Maintenance of fish habitat during dry periods	Topographic relief on floodplain
Maintenance of high water table	Maintenance of hydrophytic community	Maintenance of biodiversity	Presence of hydrophytes
Biogeochemical			
Transformation, cycling of elements	Maintenance of nutrient stocks within wetland	Wood production	Tree growth
Retention, removal of dissolved substances	Reduced transport of nutrients downstream	Maintenance of water quality	Nutrient outflow lower than inflow
Accumulation of peat	Retention of nutrients, metals, other substances	Maintenance of water quality	Increase in depth of peat
Accumulation of inorganic sediments	Retention of sediments, some nutrients	Maintenance of water quality	Increase in depth of sediment
Habitat and Food Web Support			
Maintenance of characteristic plant communities	Food, nesting, cover for animals	Support for furbearers, waterfowl	Mature wetland vegetation
Maintenance of characteristic energy flow	Support for populations of vertebrates	Maintenance of biodiversity	High diversity of vertebrates

includes not just the expense of regulatory programs, but also "opportunity costs" and "replacement costs" associated with a reduced range of economic choices. Costs of this type can be estimated (Farber and Costanza, 1987; Costanza et al., 1989; Gren, 1995), but they are beyond the scope of this report.

Unique Functions

Some of the functions of wetland ecosystems are shared by uplands. Even so, wetlands perform some functions, such as maintenance of breeding habitat for some bird species (Brinson et al., 1981), that are either unique or particularly efficient in proportion to their size. Also, wetlands are often the last portions of a landscape converted to alternative uses (Brinson, 1988, 1993b). Because many wetlands are adjacent to surface waters, they often represent the best opportunity for natural improvement of water quality because of their filtering and transformation capacity. Uplands also can provide retention and transformation, but they are often preferentially allocated to other land uses—such as agriculture and urban development—that generate nutrients and sediments, and are more remote from surface waters.

When wetlands are seasonally dry, they can be temporarily cease some functions, such as support of aquatic habitat, but retain others, such as the capacity to store surface water. Because the return of functions associated with saturation can be contingent on maintenance of the physical and hydrologic conditions under which the wetland developed, alteration of wetlands during dry phases is likely to be detrimental to their functional integrity.

Landscape Perspective

Individual wetlands function in part through interaction with the adjacent portions of the landscape and with other wetlands. For example, flyway support for waterfowl is a collective function of many wetlands. Likewise, no single wetland or aquatic site could support anadromous fish. The connections between individual wetlands, aquatic systems, and terrestrial systems are critical to the support of many organisms. Furthermore, flood control and pollution control are determined by the number, position, and extent of wetlands within watersheds. Thus, the landscape gives proper context for the evaluation of some wetland functions.

Maintenance of biodiversity, water quality, and natural hydrologic flow regimes in part depends on the total wetland area and on the types of wetlands within regions (Preston and Bedford, 1988). As wetland acreage declines within a watershed, some functional capacities, such as maintenance of water quality or waterfowl populations, also decline. In this way, cumulative loss of wetland gradually impairs some landscape-level functions (Gosselink and Lee, 1989; Gosselink et al., 1990; Preston and Bedford, 1988). This occurs not only through loss of surface area, but also through reduction in average size, total number, linkage, and density of wetlands (Johnston, 1994b). Many wetland functions and their associated value to society depend on the connections among wetlands and between wetlands and adjacent aquatic and terrestrial systems. For example, river floodplain wetlands form natural corridors for the migration of fish, birds, mammals, and reptiles (Brinson et al., 1981). Uses of uplands can affect the physical, chemical, and biotic characteristics of wetlands. Paving or agricultural uses, for example, affect the amount and quality of water that reaches adjacent wetlands. Where the use of uplands is intensive, as in urban areas, wetlands often show signs of stress (Ehrenfeld and Schneider, 1993).

Scarcity may magnify the value of wetlands. For example, in an urban environment, the remaining wetlands may provide the only refuge for many kinds of wildlife, protect large amounts of valued property against flooding, serve as the main remaining mechanism for natural improvement of water quality, and recharge groundwater (Tiner, 1984). In this way, the significance of wetland functions derives partly from the surrounding landscape (Chapter 10).

Relationship to Biodiversity

Reduction of the area of wetland in a landscape often reduces biodiversity because many organisms depend on the wetlands and riparian zones with which they are frequently associated. For example, Hudson (1991) concluded that about 220 animal and 600 plant species are threatened with serious reduction in California, and the state's high rate of wetland loss (91% since the 1780s) is in part responsible. Blem and Blem (1975) showed the importance of river bottom-lands to wildlife relative to adjacent uplands in Illinois. Ohmart and Anderson (1986) have shown that availability of large riparian areas, which include wet-lands, is the primary factor that explains the number of birds that breed at high elevations in central Arizona. Weller (1988) views wetlands as islands in a terrestrial sea, and suggests that bird diversity follows the rules of island biogeog-raphy (more species with larger island area), as shown for prairie potholes. Simi-larly, Leibowitz et al. (1992) conclude that many waterfowl species are sensitive to reductions in area, patch size, wetland density, and proximity to other wet-lands. They cite work that supports the need for many small wetlands as well as for large ones. Harris (1988) also points out that data on waterfowl, which provide some of the best long-term records of species that depend on wetlands, show steady declines (mallard down 35% from 1955 to 1985, pintail down 50%). Fish, which are good surrogates for aquatic biodiversity (Moyle and Yoshiyama, 1994), are sensitive to alteration of habitat, including wetlands. In the United States, 41 fish species have become extinct in the past century (Minckley and Douglas, 1991), and an estimated 28% of freshwater fish species in North America are seriously reduced in abundance or distribution. In addition, studies (Hickman, 1994; Weller, 1995) are beginning to document the extensive increase in biodiversity that occurs when wetlands are created or restored in a disturbed landscape. Factors other than reduction of area can cause a decline in biodiversity. For example, Moyle and Sato (1991) found that habitat heterogeneity is closely related to species diversity of fish communities, presumably because a more variable habitat provides a wider range of biological niches.

A large number of both invertebrates and vertebrates show some association with wetlands, but species vary widely in the nature of this association. Some taxa, including certain species of aquatic invertebrates and amphibians, may be confined to wetlands or dependent upon them for specific stages of the life cycle. Waterfowl and mammals also have a range of dependencies on wetlands for food and habitat. For individual species, the suitability of a particular wetland for habitat or for food may be critically dependent on the duration and time of year at which the wetland is inundated or saturated with water. In particular, species that require the presence of water for extended intervals will obviously not be able to live in a wetland that is inundated or saturated for a couple of weeks per year, but might be well suited to wetlands that show constant inundation.

Table 2.3 gives some information on the great range of temporal dependencies for species that might be associated with wetlands. For example, some invertebrates, such as fairy shrimp, are adapted to spring inundation, as is typical of vernal pools, and require only two weeks of standing water for the completion of the life cycle. In contrast, maturation of amphibians in some cases may extend over more than a year. Even among organisms of a particular group, there is considerable variation. For example, Wright (1907) found that the shortest period from hatching to metamorphosis of amphibian species in the Okefenokee Swamp was 15 days, the next shortest was 24 days, and the other 19 taxa required more than 30 days. Thus in evaluating the role of wetlands in maintenance of biodiversity, the duration of inundation is a significant consideration. Longer inundation does not necessarily increase biodiversity, however, because wetlands that are characteristically inundated for only brief intervals offer support organisms that are unable to withstand the competitive and predatory forces of environments that are inundated for longer intervals.

Removal of Nutrients and Sediments

The geology of most wetlands is depositional. In general, uplands lose mass that accumulates in wetlands. In many watersheds, wetlands process dissolved and suspended materials from an area much greater than their own, which explains their disproportionately strong influence on water quality. In watersheds subject to human activities, the importance of wetlands on water quality is exaggerated by two factors: disturbances to uplands that increase erosion and augment the fertility of the landscape, and reduction of wetland area through filling, diking, and draining.

Research has demonstrated repeatedly that natural wetlands enhance water quality by accumulating nutrients, trapping sediments, and transforming a variety of substances (Mitsch et al., 1979; Lowrance et al., 1984a,b; Whigham et al., 1988; Kuenzler, 1989; Faulkner and Richardson, 1989; Johnston, 1991). Whigham et al. (1988) observe that wetlands in different parts of a watershed improve water quality in different ways. For example, nitrogen processing and retention of large sediment particles might be more important functions of wetlands that border uplands where large particles are abundant, whereas phosphorus retention and trapping of fine particles might be more important in floodplain wetlands farther downstream (Mitsch et al., 1979; Cooper and Gilliam, 1987; Cooper et al., 1987). Stromberg et al. (1993) documented sediment accretion averaging 5-15 cm within a floodplain 150-200 m wide along the Hassayampa

TABLE 2.3 Name and Length of Limiting Portion of the Life Cycle for Invertebrates Commonly Associated with Wetlands (after Niering, 1985)

Species	Inundation Requirements
Corixa spp.	Eggs hatch 7-15 days; adults feed on water
Lethocerus americanus	Adult and nymph stage
Notonecta undulata	Entire life cycle
Notonecta kirbyi	Entire life cycle
Hydrophilus spp.	All but a few weeks
Dineutus spp.	All but pupal and part of adult stages
Thermonectes marmoratus	All but pupal stage
Chrysomela lapponica	None
Labidomera clivicollis	None
Xylotrechus insgnis	None
Brachinus spp.	None
Chlaenius seiceus	None
Donacia spp.	10 months
Gerris remigis	All but winter
Ranatra brevicollis	Entire life cycle
Chauliodes spp.	Larval stage
Corydalus cornutus	Two or three years
Acroneuria californica	One year or more
Grammotaulius bettenii	All but short adult stage
Nannothemis bella	Nymphs develop slowly
Libellula luctuosa	Egg to nymph
Boyeria vinosa	Egg to nymph
Anax junius	Overwinter
Argia spp.	Egg through naiad
Pachydiplax longipennis	Egg through nymph
Libellula pulchella	Egg through nymph
Celithemis elisa	Nymphs overwinter
Sympetrum illotum	Nymphs overwinter
Lestes congener	Eggs and nymphs overwinter until July
Tipula spp.	None
Agathos comstocki	All but adult
Baetis spp.	Eggs hatch 2-5 weeks; nymphs
Culex pipiens	Eggs hatch 1-5 days; larvae pupate 1-2 weeks
Chlorion cyaneum	none
Tabanus americanus	Two years
Simulium spp.	Egg and pupal stage
Drosophila melanogaster	None
Dolomedes triton	Most of life
Nephila clavipes	None
Limnochares americana	Much of life cycle

River in Arizona during a flood of 10-year recurrence in 1991. Unlike previous, smaller floods in which accretion was greatest adjacent to the main channel, the 1991 maxima were at elevations 1-2 m above the water table, indicating the functional importance of the broad floodplain for sediment retention during the larger, less frequent streamflow events.

As uplands become more intensively managed and as the area of wetlands is reduced, nutrient processing and retention become impaired. Cumulative effects are discussed by Gosselink and Lee (1989), who point out that concentrations of nitrogen and phosphorus increase as watersheds are cleared and that clearing bottomlands changes them from sediment sinks to sediment sources. They also note that there can be a long lag between clearing and sedimentation downstream. Similarly, Jones et al. (1976) report that in Iowa, nitrate concentrations in streams are inversely related to the percentage of total watershed area in wetlands.

Greatly increased sediment and nutrient transport from watersheds that experience urbanization or conversion of forest to agriculture can alter plant and animal species composition and even destroy wetlands. This is particularly true for isolated (depressional) and lakeshore (fringe) wetlands that have not historically received large amounts of sediment or nutrients. Many of the pothole wetlands in the glaciated regions of northern states are at particular risk from excessive sedimentation and nutrients because they lack flushing mechanisms. The original, heavily vegetated natural landscapes contributed small amounts of sediment and nutrients to these wetlands. Nutrient-poor wetlands, such as bogs, are also particularly vulnerable to watershed changes (Guntenspergen and Stearns, 1985). Other systems, such as riverine marshes, can better tolerate additional nutrients (Mitsch, 1992).

Too little sediment also can also be damaging. Decreased sediment transport downstream of reservoirs along rivers and streams can threaten delta and estuarine wetlands. This is particularly true for the wetlands of the Mississippi delta, where sediment deprivation caused by reservoirs throughout the Mississippi system and levees along the lower end of the river have changed natural sediment transport to the point that accretion no longer maintains coastal and estuarine marshes. An estimated area of 25,000 acres (10,000 ha) of marsh in the delta disappears annually because of land subsidence, sediment starvation, and saltwater intrusion (Kusler et al., 1994). Changes in land use and water diversions that decrease freshwater flows in rivers and streams similarly threaten many estuarine wetlands by reducing the quantity of fresh water.

Wetlands as Hydrologic Features of Watersheds

The hydrology of a regional landscape is often affected by the area and position of the wetlands within it. For example, peak flow in a stream leaving a watershed is directly related to the total amount of wetland in the watershed or to the amount of wetland in headwater reaches. The relationship of peak flow and wetland area may be nonlinear, however, in the sense that progressive loss of wetland may have an escalating influence on flood peaks (Novitzki, 1979; Gosselink and Lee, 1989; Johnston, 1994b). For example, in the Minneapolis metropolitan area, runoff per unit area of watershed increased rapidly when wetland area decreased to less than 10 percent of total watershed area (Johnson et al., 1990).

NATURE OF BOUNDARIES WITH UPLANDS

Wetlands frequently are bounded by uplands, but the boundary often lies within a broad transition zone. For gentle gradients, or where microtopography causes wetlands to be interspersed with uplands on very fine scales, the boundary of a wetland can be especially difficult to determine (Appendix B, hydric pine flatwoods of southwest Florida, and Chapter 8). Because vegetation analysis often is used in locating boundaries, the response of plant communities to environmental gradients is fundamentally important to the characterization of wetlands. Curtis (1959) and Whittaker (1967) introduced the continuum concept, which holds that vegetation changes gradually in response to environmental gradients because of the differing environmental optima among species. The continuum concept is now widely applied in vegetation analysis (Cox and Moore, 1993), and it is a useful basis for analyzing wetland boundaries.

Change in the plant community at the boundary of a wetland is determined not only by differing adaptations of plant species to abiotic conditions, but also by competition among species. The importance of competition has been demonstrated by Pennings and Callaway (1992) and by Bertness (1991), but there is little information on interactions among species along the wetland-upland transition, where boundary determinations of wetlands are of great practical importance. Beals (1969) suggests that competition between species can be a cause of more discrete boundaries on steeper environmental gradients than on gentle ones. He reasons that the individuals of any two species are closest together on steep slopes, where they will compete most strongly. It follows that the steepest environmental gradients at the margins of wetlands will show the most distinct vegetation boundaries.

The wetland boundary as judged by vegetation is not always stable. Natural hydrologic changes from year to year or from one decade to the next may cause the vegetation to shift. Changes in boundaries of wetland vegetation have been documented for prairie potholes (van der Valk and Davis, 1976; Weller, 1981; Kantrud et al., 1989a; Appendix B), for the riparian ecosystems of arid zones (Stromberg et al., 1991), for salt marshes (Morris et al., 1990; Zedler et al., 1992), and for vernal pools (Zedler, 1987). Although wetland plants respond to changing environmental conditions, they might not do so immediately. For example, forested wetlands respond more slowly than do marshes because of the long lives of trees. Soil morphology is less responsive than is vegetation and thus tends to integrate conditions over decades.

CONCLUSIONS

Wetlands have strong connections to adjacent uplands and deepwater environments. The interdependence between wetlands and associated aquatic ecosystems provides strong scientific justification for policies that make a connection between clean water and the protection of wetland ecosystems. Wetlands and associated terrestrial ecosystems are also interdependent, but alterations in terrestrial ecosystems usually affect wetlands more than the reverse. Watersheds and water bodies associated with wetlands control the quantity and quality of water reaching wetlands, and thus affect wetland functions. For this reason, regulation of activities within a wetland boundary is not always sufficient to maintain all wetland functions. Not all functions occur in all wetlands, nor are wetlands structurally uniform, but classification of wetlands into groups that share hydrogeomorphic and other properties clarifies similarities and differences in function. Wetlands often occupy only a small proportion of the watershed in which they lie, yet they often maintain exceptional biodiversity and process a large proportion of the dissolved and suspended materials leaving uplands, which typically occupy greater areas. When wetlands are removed, their collective functions are likely to decrease faster than the rate of reduction in surface area.

RECOMMENDATION

More intensive and regionally diverse studies of the following basic wetland phenomena should be undertaken in support of a stronger foundation for identification, delineation, and functional protection of wetlands:

- maintenance of biodiversity by wetlands,
- improvement of water quality by wetlands,
- flood abatement by wetlands,
- contributions of wetlands to functions occurring at the landscape scale, and
- effects of various kinds of land use of adjacent wetlands.

3

Wetland Definitions:
History and Scientific Basis

HISTORY OF TERMINOLOGY

The term "wetland" was not commonly used in the American vernacular until quite recently. It appears to have been adopted as a euphemistic substitute for the term "swamp" (Wright, 1907). Nineteenth-century scientists used terms such as mire, bog, and fen to describe the lands that are now called wetlands, and these terms are still used by scientists to describe specific kinds of wetland (Mitsch and Gosselink, 1986; Dennison and Berry, 1993). The term wetland has come gradually into common scientific usage only in the second half of the twentieth century.

Scientists have not agreed on a single commonly used definition of wetland in the past because they have had no scientific motivation to do so. Now, however, they are being asked to help interpret regulatory definitions of wetlands. The application of scientific principles to the definition of wetlands and to the determination of wetland boundaries could help stabilize and rationalize the application of regulations, but it does not ensure that any resultant definition will be precise in its ability to distinguish wetlands from all other kinds of ecosystems, or in its ability to specify the exact boundary of a wetland. Judgment and convention will continue play a role, even following full application of scientific principles. In addition, the concept of wetland has a long history in Anglo-American law and carries with it important legal implications that need to be considered in the application of any wetland definition.

Nineteenth-Century American Legislation

From the middle of the nineteenth century to recent times, Congress has passed legislation dealing with the lands now called wetlands, and in doing so has described these lands in a variety of ways.

Swamp and Overflowed Lands Acts

The U.S. Congress granted to Louisiana in 1849 certain wetlands, which were described as "those swamp and overflowed lands, which may be or are found unfit for cultivation. . . ." (Chapter 87, An Act to aid the State of Louisiana in draining the Swamp Lands therein, 9 Stat. 352, 1849). The purpose of the statute was to "aid the State of Louisiana in constructing the necessary levees and drains to reclaim the swamp and overflowed land therein. . . ." This statute was the prototype of a series of swampland acts by which Congress granted wetlands to the states, usually by means of a definition no more precise than the one quoted above. The statutes are codified in 43 U.S.C. §§ 981 et seq. (1988).

States with large amounts of wetland, such as Illinois, Michigan, and Florida, where only half the land was considered suitable for farming, joined a general move to have federal swamplands ceded to them (Gates, 1968). This led Congress to pass the Swamp Land Act of 1850, the intent of which was to enable Arkansas, Alabama, California, Florida, Illinois, Indiana, Iowa, Michigan, Mississippi, Missouri, Ohio, and Wisconsin to reclaim the swamplands within their boundaries (9 Stat. 519, 1850).

Before enacting the Swamp Land Act of 1850, Congress discussed the procedure for selection of swamplands. Advocates of the grants tried to assure opponents that descriptions on surveyors' plats could be the basis for selection, and that the states could finance drainage and development of the lands (Gates, 1968). The 1850 act stated that land should be transferred only when the greater part of a legal subdivision was wet and unfit for cultivation. The Land Office found many such lands, as evidenced by the ultimate transfer of 64 million acres under the act. The act's vague definition—"wet and unfit for cultivation"—led to substantial litigation. Almost 200 swampland cases reached the Supreme Court by 1888 (Gates, 1968). The confused state of the law led to a remedial act in 1855 (Hibbard, 1965).

The swampland acts largely failed to achieve their intended purpose. "In few instances in land history have the results deviated so widely from the plans. . . . The Swamp Act provided a means of getting rid of land but to a trifling extent of effecting drainage. The amount of money realized by the state out of the swamp land was small" (Hibbard, 1965).

Wildlife Refuge System

Beginning late in the nineteenth century, federal and state governments and private organizations started to acquire wetlands as waterfowl sanctuaries, including The National Wildlife Refuge System, which contains extensive wetlands acquired as waterfowl habitat through legislation to protect migratory birds (Bean, 1977; Fink, 1994). The federal acquisition of wetlands was important in stemming losses of waterfowl in the 1930s (Greenwalt, 1978), but acquisition did not follow any consistent policy, nor have any definitional criteria been used regularly in determining which wetlands should be purchased. Because much of the money for purchase of wetlands was derived from the sale of duck stamps to hunters, the protection of wetlands especially important to migratory waterfowl has received priority (Bean, 1977).

Rivers and Harbors Act

From the early days of the country's history, Congress gave the U.S. Army Corps of Engineers (USACE) the task of maintaining navigation throughout the United States. This authority was codified under the Rivers and Harbors Act of 1899, which gave USACE the responsibility to regulate dredging and filling of "navigable waters." This phrase, which was at one time interpreted narrowly (Silverberg and Dennison, 1993), was subsequently expanded by the courts to give USACE power to deny permits for the filling of submerged land on the basis of potential ecological damage (Want, 1989). This judicial interpretation was then extended to the water pollution legislation adopted by Congress in the 1970s, and it formed the foundation for a new legal status for wetlands.

New Legal Status

Federal authority for the general protection of wetlands developed only as recently as 1975. The source of this authority was somewhat convoluted, as described below.

Water Pollution Control Act Amendments of 1972

Even as late as 1972, Congress passed major water pollution control legislation without ever using the term "wetland." In the 1972 amendments to the Federal Water Pollution Control Act (FWPCA, later retitled the Clean Water Act), Congress gave USACE and the Environmental Protection Agency (EPA) authority to regulate water pollution in the "waters of the United States," but Congress failed to consider the application of that phrase to wetlands. The term "wetlands" was not used in the act, nor did the legislation use synonymous terms.

The legislative history did not discuss the concept of wetlands, but Congress did indicate that it would interpret the term "navigable waters" broadly.

The Senate's version of the 1972 FWPCA amendments was given by S. 2770. The Senate Committee on Public Works discussed the background of dredge-and-fill activity (FWPCA, Legislative History, Vol. 2: p. 1488). Historically, USACE had authority to regulate the discharge of "refuse" by issuance of permits under Section 13 of the Refuse Act of 1899 (33 U.S.C. § 407). This authority was largely ignored, however, until Executive Order 11574 of President Nixon directed the institution of a permit program under the terms of Section 13 of the Refuse Act "to regulate the discharge of pollutants and other refuse matter into the navigable waters of the United States or their tributaries and the placing of such matter upon the banks" (35 Fed. Reg. 19,627; 1970), which was then implemented by USACE regulation (35 Fed. Reg. 20,005; 1970).

The Senate Committee on Public Works considered integrating the permit program under Section 13 of the Refuse Act of 1899 with Section 402 of the FWPCA amendments of 1972 (FWPCA, Legislative History,Vol. 2: p. 1488). Section 402(m) of the Senate bill, S. 2770, would have transferred the 1899 Refuse Act permit program from USACE to EPA and would have treated the disposal of dredged soil like the disposal of any other pollutant. Sen. Allan Ellender's (D-Louisiana) proposed amendment, which would have retained the USACE's sole authority to issue dredge and fill permits, was successfully opposed by Sen. Edmund Muskie (D-Maine), who stated that the amendment would shift the environmental evaluation authority from EPA to USACE and that "the mission of [USACE] is to protect navigation. Its mission is not to protect the environment" (FWPCA, Legislative History, Vol. 2: p. 1389).

During the debate on S. 2770, the concept of wetlands was not mentioned explicitly, but "restoring the integrity of the nation's waters" was addressed in broad terms (FWPCA, Legislative History, Vol. 2: p. 1254). Sen. Muskie stated that "water moves in hydrologic cycles and it is essential that discharge of pollutants be controlled at the source" (FWPCA, Legislative History, Vol. 2: p. 1495).

The House amendment, H.R. 11896, established a separate USACE-administered permit program in Section 404 for the discharge of dredged or fill material into navigable waters (FWPCA, Legislative History, Vol. 1: p. 816). The House amendment said that "a determination is required that the discharge would not unreasonably degrade or endanger human health, welfare, or amenities of the marine environment, ecological systems, or economic potentialities" (FWPCA Legislative History, Vol. 1: p. 1063).

In the conference committee, the House prevailed in establishing a separate dredge-and-fill program under Section 404, but the disposal site had to be specified through the application of guidelines developed by EPA in conjunction with USACE (FWPCA, Legislative History, Vol. 1: pp. 324-25). Section 404(c) provided that EPA could prohibit disposal at a site if the discharge "will have an unacceptable adverse effect on municipal water supplies, shellfish beds, and fisheries areas (including spawning and breeding areas), wildlife, or recreational areas" (FWPCA, Legislative History, Vol. 1: pp. 324-25). In support of the compromise, it was argued that USACE and EPA had a responsibility to "identify land-based sites for the disposal of dredged spoil and where land-based disposal was not feasible, to establish diked areas for disposal" (FWPCA, Legislative History, Vol. 2: pp. 177-78).

The conference bill amended the term "navigable waters" to "waters of the United States, including the territorial seas" (FWPCA, Legislative History, Vol. 2: p. 327). During the House debate on the conference report in October, 1972, the House stated that the new and broader definition was in line with more recent judicial opinions, which substantially expanded the concept of navigability (FWPCA, Legislative History, Vol. 1: p. 250). The conference report states that "the conferees fully intend that the term navigable water be given the broadest possible constitutional interpretation unencumbered by agency determinations which have been made or may be made for administrative purposes" (FWPCA, Legislative History, Vol. 1: pp. 250-51).

Judicial Interpretation of the 1972 Statute

In commenting on judicial expansion of the concept of navigability, Congress was well aware that the trend of U.S. Supreme Court decisions had, in the words of one authority, reduced the idea that navigability was a limitation on federal jurisdiction to "a near fiction" (Tarlock, 1988). For example, cases such as *United States* v. *Grand River Dam Authority*, 363 U.S. 508 (1960) had extended federal jurisdiction to nonnavigable tributaries of navigable rivers.

In 1975, the Federal District Court in the District of Columbia ruled that the definition of navigable waters in Section 404 of FWPCA had the same meaning as did the broad definition used elsewhere in the statute, thus extending coverage of the act to wetlands regardless of actual navigability. *Natural Resources Defense Council* v. *Callaway*, 392 F. Supp. 685 (1975) held invalid USACE's earlier interpretation of the act, which had excluded some 85% of the nation's wetlands, and opened a new chapter in the history of wetland regulation (Tarlock, 1988). When the government accepted the new judicial interpretation of the act, USACE and EPA needed for the first time to adopt a regulatory definition of wetland.

EVOLUTION OF THE REGULATORY DEFINITIONS

Only in the 1950s were scientists beginning to use the term "wetland" as a category that would encompass terms such as bog, swamp, and marsh. Attempts of government agencies to define wetlands began at that time but developed momentum only in the 1970s.

1956 Fish and Wildlife Service Definition

The first official use of the term wetland in a government report was in 1956, when the U.S. Fish and Wildlife Service (FWS) issued Circular 39, a landmark report about the wetlands of the United States (Shaw and Fredine, 1956). Because the work was financed largely by the sale of federal duck stamps, the report focused on wetlands valuable to waterfowl, as was reflected in the definition from Circular 39:

> The term "wetlands," as used in this report and in the wildlife field generally, refers to lowlands covered with shallow and sometimes temporary or intermittent waters. They are referred to by such names as marshes, swamps, bogs, wet meadows, potholes, sloughs, and river-overflow lands. Shallow lakes and ponds, usually with emergent vegetation as a conspicuous feature, are included in the definition, but the permanent waters of streams, reservoirs, and deep lakes are not included. Neither are water areas that are so temporary as to have little or no effect on the development of moist-soil vegetation. Usually these very temporary areas are of no appreciable value to the species of wildlife considered in this report.

Circular 39 described 20 types of inland fresh, inland saline, coastal fresh, and coastal saline wetlands. Several of their names were or became standard terminology among wetland scientists and are still in common use. Even though Circular 39 was officially replaced in 1979, several states continue to use modifications of the original classification system in wetland regulations because of its simplicity.

1974 Wetland Inventory Project

In 1974, FWS directed its Office of Biological Services to design and conduct a new national inventory of wetlands. To prepare for this project, a dozen wetland scientists met in Bay St. Louis, Mississippi, in January 1975 to prepare the first draft of a new classification system for the new inventory (Cowardin and Carter, 1975). Six months later, FWS convened a workshop to review the draft (Sather, 1975). Several federal agencies with wetland-related missions gave presentations at the workshop: USACE, EPA, the U.S. Geological Survey, the U.S. Forest Service, the Soil Conservation Service (SCS), the Bureau of Reclamation, the Bureau of Land Management, the National Marine Fisheries Service, the Office of Coastal Zone Management, and the Tennessee Valley Authority, as did the Canadian Wildlife Service, the Nature Conservancy, the Wildlife Management Institute, the Institute of Ecology, the Sport Fishing Institute, the Conservation Foundation, and representatives of state wetland programs (Kusler and Bedford, 1975). Thus, the new classification system was subject to diverse influences, both organizationally and geographically.

1975 USACE Proposed Definition

Meanwhile, after the 1975 *Callaway* decision invalidating the initial USACE regulations that had excluded most wetlands from the jurisdiction of USACE, USACE quickly issued new proposed regulations that included the first regulatory attempt to define wetlands (40 Fed. Reg. 31, 328; July 25, 1975). USACE proposed a new definition that classified wetlands by function and treated as important only those lands that performed specific wetland functions. The 1975 definition is as follows:

(i) Wetlands are those land and water areas subject to regular inundation by tidal, riverine, or lacustrine flowage. Generally included are inland and coastal shallows, marshes, mudflats, estuaries, swamps, and similar areas in coastal and inland navigable waters. Many such areas serve important purposes relating to fish and wildlife, recreation, and other elements of the general public interest. As environmentally vital areas, they constitute a productive and valuable public resource, the unnecessary alteration or destruction of which should be discouraged as contrary to the public interest.

(ii) Wetlands considered to perform functions important to the public interest include:

(a) Wetlands which serve important natural biological functions, including food chain production, general habitat, and nesting, spawning, rearing and resting sites for aquatic or land species;

(b) Wetlands set aside for study of the aquatic environment or as sanctuaries or refuges;

(c) Wetlands contiguous to areas listed in paragraph (g)(3)(ii) (a) and (b) of this section, the destruction or alteration of which would affect detrimentally the natural drainage characteristics, sedimentation patterns, salinity distribution, flushing characteristics, current patterns, or other environmental characteristics of the above areas;

(d) Wetlands which are significant in shielding other areas from wave action, erosion, or storm damage. Such wetlands often include barrier beaches, islands, reefs and bars;

(e) Wetlands which serve as valuable storage areas for storm and flood waters; and

(f) Wetlands which are prime natural recharge areas. Prime recharge areas are locations where surface and ground water are directly interconnected.

As required by the Administrative Procedure Act, USACE published the proposed definition in the Federal Register and asked for comments.

1976 FWS Interim Classification

Concurrently with the work of USACE, the outcome of the 1975 FWS workshop was published in 1976 as the "Interim Classification of Wetlands and Aquatic Habitats of the United States" (Cowardin et al., 1976), which served as a precursor to the current FWS wetlands classification system (Cowardin et al., 1979). The four authors were wetland scientists from FWS, the U.S. Geological Survey, the University of Rhode Island, and the National Oceanic and Atmospheric Administration. The introduction to the document explained their concept of wetland (Cowardin et al., 1976):

> For centuries we have spoken of marshes, swamps and bogs, but only relatively recently have we attempted to group these landscape units under a single term, wetland. The need to do this has grown out of our desire: (1) to understand and describe the characteristics and values of all types of land, and (2) to wisely and effectively manage wetland ecosystems. Effective management requires legislation; out of such legislation, legal definitions are born. Unfortunately, legal definitions are usually based as much on facility and pragmatism as they are upon accuracy of meaning. Hence, legal definitions of wetland may bear little resemblance to the ecological concepts embodied in the term. There is no single, correct, indisputable, ecologically sound definition for wetland because the gradation between totally dry and totally wet environments is continuous. Moreover, no two people view the identity of any object in the same fashion. For these reasons, and because the reasons for defining wetland vary, a great proliferation of definitions has arisen. Our primary task here is to impose arbitrary boundaries on natural ecosystems for the purposes of inventory, evaluation and management. We are obliged to use sound reasoning as we attempt to describe the concepts of wetland and aquatic habitats in terms that past, present and projected future users will accept.
>
> The concept of wetland embraces a number of characteristics, including the elevation of the water table with respect to the ground surface, the duration of surface water, soil types that form under permanently or temporarily saturated conditions, and various types of plants and animals that have become adapted to life in a "wet" environment. The single feature that all wetlands share is the presence of more soil moisture than is necessary to support the growth of most plants. This excess of water creates severe physiological problems for all plants except hydrophytes, which are adapted for life in water or in saturated soil. Rather than attempt to place arbitrary limits on the fluctuation of the water table for the purpose of defining wetland, a task of great complexity at best, it seems more reasonable to define wetland broadly and simply, and then to place limits on the concept. The definition of wetland contained in the Interim Classification is as follows:
>
> Wetland is land where an excess of water is the dominant factor determining the nature of soil development and the types of plant and animal communities living at the soil surface. It spans a continuum of environments where terrestrial and aquatic systems intergrade. For the purpose of this classification system, wetland is defined more specifically as land where the water table is at, near or above the land surface long enough each year to promote the formation of hydric soils and to support the growth of hydrophytes, as long as other environmental conditions are favorable. Permanently flooded lands lying beyond the

deep-water boundary of wetland are referred to as aquatic habitats. In certain wetland types, vegetation is absent and soils are poorly developed or absent as a result of frequent and drastic fluctuations of surface-water levels, wave action, water flow, turbidity or extremely high concentrations of salts or other substances in the water or substrate. Wetlands lacking vegetation and hydric soils can be recognized by the presence of surface water at some time during the year and their location within, or adjacent to, vegetated wetlands or aquatic habitats.

There is great similarity between portions of this definition and the one that was adopted a year later by USACE.

1977 USACE Definition

USACE was inundated with comments on the definition of wetlands that it had proposed in 1975. As a result, its final definition of wetlands, which was issued in 1977 (42 Fed. Reg. 37, 125-26, 37128-29; July 19, 1977), was substantially revised:

Those areas that are inundated or saturated by surface or ground water at a frequency and duration sufficient to support, and that under normal circumstances do support, a prevalence of vegetation typically adapted for life in saturated soil conditions. Wetlands generally include swamps, marshes, bogs, and similar areas.

In explaining the new definition, USACE emphasized four important definitional issues. First, it noted that it was making no reference to traditional high-water-line boundaries or to distinctions between fresh and salt water. "Water moves in hydrologic cycles," it said, and the pollution of any part of the aquatic system will affect the water quality of the system as a whole. "For this reason, the landward limit of Federal jurisdiction under Section 404 must include any adjacent wetlands that form the border of or are in reasonable proximity to other waters of the United States, as these wetlands are part of this aquatic system."

Second, the USACE described the frequency with which a wetland is inundated:

The reference to "periodic inundation" has been eliminated. Many interpreted that term as requiring inundation over a record period of years. Our intent under Section 404 is to regulate discharges of dredged or fill material into the aquatic system as it exists, and not as it may have existed over a record period of time. The new definition is designed to achieve this intent. It pertains to an existing wetland and requires that the area be inundated or saturated by water at a frequency and duration sufficient to support aquatic vegetation.

Third, USACE dealt with the issue of normality:

The term ["normally"] was included in the definitions to respond to those situations in which an individual would attempt to eliminate the permit review requirements of Section 404 by destroying the aquatic vegetation, and to those areas that are not aquatic but experience an abnormal presence of aquatic vegetation. Several such instances of destruction of aquatic vegetation in order to eliminate Section 404 jurisdiction actually have occurred. However, even if this destruction occurs, the area still remains as part of the overall aquatic system intended to be protected by the Section 404 program. Conversely, the abnormal presence of aquatic vegetation in a non-aquatic area would not be sufficient to include that area within the Section 404 program.

But USACE said that it "did not intend, by this clarification, to assert jurisdiction over those areas that once were wetlands and part of an aquatic system, but which, in the past, have been transformed into dry land for various purposes."

Finally, USACE commented on the methods of identifying wetland vegetation. It noted that it was continuing to use the term "prevalence" so that it could eliminate reference to "those areas that have only occasional aquatic vegetation interspersed with upland or dry land vegetation." But it added language referring to vegetation "typically adapted for life in saturated soil conditions" because the old definition, by describing the vegetation as that which required saturated soil conditions for growth and reproduction, excluded "many forms of truly aquatic vegetation that are prevalent in an inundated or saturated area, but that do not require saturated soil from a biological standpoint for their growth and reproduction."

The 1977 definition is the one currently used by USACE and EPA.

Clean Water Act of 1977

In 1977, while USACE was revising its definition, Congress was adopting major amendments to FWPCA (and renaming it the Clean Water Act [CWA]). Congress expanded Section 404 by the addition of general permit provisions, exceptions, and provisions for the delegation to the states of Section 404 permitting responsibility. Although the legislative history provides little assistance in determining what Congress meant by the new reference to wetlands, that history does illustrate the extent to which Congress understood wetland issues.

The Senate Committee on Environment and Public Works, in its report, noted that "the 1972 Federal Water Pollution Control Act exercised comprehensive jurisdiction over the Nation's waters to control pollution to the fullest constitutional extent." Quoting a 1972 Senate report, the new report stated (FWPCA, Legislative History, Vol. 4: p. 708):

> that "waters move in hydrologic cycles and it is essential that discharge of pollutants be controlled at the source," and that the objective of the 1972 act is to protect the physical, chemical, and biological integrity of the Nation's waters. Restriction of jurisdiction to those relatively few waterways that are used or are susceptible to use for navigation would render this purpose impossible to achieve. The committee amendment does not redefine navigable waters. In-

stead, the committee amendment intends to assure continued protection of the Nation's waters, but allows States to assume the primary responsibility for protecting those lakes, rivers, streams, swamps, marshes, and other so-called phase I waters.

During the Senate debate, Sen. Lloyd Bentsen (D-Texas) introduced an amendment to Section 404 that would have redefined and narrowed the term "navigable waters" and would have defined the term "adjacent wetlands." Under Sen. Bentsen's amendment the discharge of dredged or fill material into waters other than "navigable waters" and in wetlands other that "adjacent wetlands" would not have been prohibited unless USACE and the governor of a state entered into a joint agreement that the waters should be regulated. In support of his amendment, Sen. Bentsen stated that Section 404 had "assumed an importance that extends far beyond dredge and fill activities; it has become synonymous with Federal overregulation; overcontrol, cumbersome bureaucratic procedures, and a general lack of realism" (FWPCA, Legislative History, Vol. 4: p. 901). The amendment drew some substantial support because of the court decision in *N.R.D.C. v. Callaway*, which had provoked opposition from agricultural and forestry interests (FWPCA, Legislative History, Vol. 4: pp. 931-936). Ultimately, the Senate rejected Sen. Bentsen's amendment, 51-45. Sen. Muskie stated that the Bentsen amendment, if adopted, would have left 85% of the wetlands of the United States unprotected (FWPCA, Legislative History, Vol. 4: p. 948).

The House committee proposed an amendment that was similar to the Bentsen amendment in that it would have limited the requirement for a permit to "navigable waters and adjacent wetlands," and would have defined "navigable waters" to mean those used or usable with reasonable improvement to transport interstate or foreign commerce (FWPCA, Legislative History, Vol. 4: p. 1195). In the debate, Rep. Smith (D-Iowa) supported the amendment that was designed to reverse the "March 25, 1975, District of Columbia District Court decision" (FWPCA, Legislative History, Vol. 4: pp. 1346-47).

The conference substitute left intact the prior definition of navigable waters (FWPCA, Legislative History, Vol. 3: p. 284), but also added subsection (g), which allowed a state to assume the authority to issue dredge-and-fill permits if EPA approved. The only place in the bill in which the term "wetland" appeared was in Section 404(g)(1), which dealt with the potential delegation to the states of administration of the Section 404 program. It provided that the governor of a state could administer a dredge-and-fill permit program for navigable waters "other than those waters which are presently used, or are susceptible for use in their natural condition or by reasonable improvement as a means to transport interstate or foreign commerce shoreward to their ordinary high water mark, including all waters which are subject to the ebb and flow of the tide shoreward to their mean high water mark, or mean higher high water mark on the west coast, including wetlands adjacent thereto." This language meant that if EPA approved delegation of permitting authority to a state, USACE would retain permitting authority over tidal waters and adjacent wetlands, and perhaps over large, inland navigable bodies of water such as the Great Lakes, while the state would have permitting authority over all other types of navigable waters, including nontidal wetlands.

The House debate on the conference report reflected the dissatisfaction of some members with the greatly expanded authority given to USACE by the courts, and the language relating to state delegation in Section 404(g) caused the members of the House to exhibit some jurisdictional confusion. On the other hand, some legislators expressed concern over the possibility of giving the states increased jurisdiction over wetlands. Rep. John Dingell (D-Michigan) said: "I personally do not think that transferring permit authority to the states in this regard is sound. . . . This is the dumping of dredge material and fill in our Nation's waterways and most importantly in our estuaries and wetlands which are important to our fish and wildlife resources, and yes, to pollution control. The states have shown a remarkable penchant toward development of those valuable and irreplaceable wildlife resources" (FWPCA, Legislative History, Vol. 3: p. 417). The result of this legislative process was to leave the Section 404 program substantially intact and to give the administering agencies little new guidance for the definition or delineation of wetlands.

1979 Cowardin Report

During this same period, FWS continued to work on its new definition and classification system to replace Circular 39. In 1979, the final report of the study that began in 1974 was issued under the title "Classification of Wetlands and Deepwater Habitats of the United States" (Cowardin et al., 1979).

The definition of wetlands contained in the final version of the new classification was substantially edited from the interim version, but contained the same basic concepts:

> Wetlands are lands transitional between terrestrial and aquatic systems where the water table is usually at or near the surface or the land is covered by shallow water. For purposes of this classification wetlands must have one or more of the following three attributes: (1) at least periodically, the land supports predominantly hydrophytes; (2) the substrate is predominantly undrained hydric soil; and (3) the substrate is nonsoil and is saturated with water or covered by shallow water at some time during the growing season of each year.

The limit between wetland and upland was further defined as:

> the boundary between land with predominantly hydrophytic cover and land with predominantly mesophytic or xerophytic cover; (2) the boundary between soil that is predominantly hydric and soil that is predominantly nonhydric; or

(3) in the case of wetlands without vegetation or soil, the boundary between land that is flooded or saturated at some time each year and land that is not.

Limits between wetland and deepwater systems also were distinguished, as they had been in the Circular 39 definition. Although the boundary between wetland and deepwater systems is important for inventory purposes, it is rarely at issue in regulatory disputes, and is not referred to at all in the regulatory definitions of wetland.

The 1979 report is significant for several reasons. First, it introduced the concepts of hydrophytes and hydric soils, and it was the impetus for the development of official lists of these (Chapter 5). Second, it embraced the concept of predominance (hydrophytes or undrained hydric soils had to be "predominant" in wetlands). Third, it introduced the use of three factors for wetland identification: soils, vegetation, and hydrology. Finally, it included some areas that lack vascular plants or soils. Each of these concepts was later developed in one or more of the wetland delineation manuals.

The hydrologic portion of the FWS definition is invoked only when the substrate is nonsoil, in which case the wetland must be "flooded or saturated at some time during the growing season of each year." This is the first appearance in a wetland definition of the concept of inundation or saturation during the growing season. Duration of flooding or saturation is not specified, although the classification system contains "water regime modifiers" that describe the duration of flooding in general terms.

Riverside Bayview Decision

Ten years after USACE began to regulate wetlands intensively, the Supreme Court, in *United States* v. *Riverside Bayview Homes*, 474 U.S. 121, 138 (1985), held that USACE had jurisdiction over discharges into wetlands adjacent to navigable waters, but it expressly left open the question of jurisdiction over wetlands that were not adjacent.

The Court looked at the legislative history of FWPCA and concluded that Congress's broad concern for protection of water quality and aquatic ecosystems made it reasonable for USACE to interpret the term "waters" to encompass wetlands adjacent to navigable waters. The Court also looked at the language in Section 404(g) concerning "adjacent wetlands" and construed the language to indicate that Congress intended "waters" to include "adjacent wetlands." However, the Court stated that "section 404(g)(1) does not conclusively determine the construction to be placed on the use of the term 'waters' elsewhere in the Act (particularly in section 502(7)), which contains the relevant definition of 'navigable waters'."

FOOD SECURITY ACT

In 1985, in response to the concern of agricultural interests about wetland issues, Congress enacted specific definitions of wetlands, hydric soils, and hydrophytic vegetation for Department of Agriculture programs. The "swampbuster" provisions of the Food Security Act (FSA) (P.L. 99-198, 99 Stat. 1504) were enacted on Dec. 23, 1985, with the premise that persons converting wetlands to agriculture would be denied agricultural loans, payments, and benefits. Further amendments were made by the Food, Agricultural, Conservation, and Trade Act of 1990 (P.L. 101-624, 104 Stat. 3587). The legislation now includes the following definition (16 U.S.C. § 801(a)(16)):

> The term "wetland," except when such term is part of the term "converted wetland," means land that—
>
> (A) has a predominance of hydric soils;
>
> (B) is inundated or saturated by surface or ground water at a frequency and duration sufficient to support a prevalence of hydrophytic vegetation typically adapted for life in saturated soil conditions; and
>
> (C) under normal circumstances does support a prevalence of such vegetation.
>
> For purposes of this Act and any other Act, this term shall not include lands in Alaska identified as having high potential for agricultural development which have a predominance of permafrost soils.

FSA directs the U.S. Department of Agriculture to develop criteria and lists of hydric soils and hydrophytic vegetation, and defines those terms as follows:

> "Hydric soil" means soil that, in its undrained condition, is saturated, flooded, or ponded long enough during a growing season to develop an anaerobic condition that supports the growth and regeneration of hydrophytic vegetation.
>
> "Hydrophytic vegetation" is a plant growing in
>
> (A) water; or
>
> (B) a substrate that is at least periodically deficient in oxygen during a growing season as a result of excessive water content.

The 1987 rule implementing FSA (7 C.F.R. § 12) further defines hydric soils as those that meet the criteria set forth in "Hydric Soils of the United States 1985" (National Technical Committee for Hydric Soils). It also states that a plant is considered to be a hydrophytic plant species if it is listed in "National List of Plant Species that Occur in Wetlands" (P.B. Reed, 1988), and it includes the formula for calculating the prevalence index that is used in determining whether hydrophytic plants predominate.

STATUS OF DEFINITIONS

Three definitions of wetlands are currently used in the United States: the 1977 USACE definition, the Natural Resources Conservation Service definition (1985 FSA definition), and the 1979 FWS definition, as derived from Cowardin et al. (1979). The USACE and FSA definitions have direct regulatory significance through implementation of the CWA and FSA. The 1979 FWS definition, although not directly regulatory, is also significant because it captures the perspective of a federal agency that interacts constantly with the regulatory agencies, comments on permits, and is charged with reporting to Congress on the status of the nation's wetlands.

1977 USACE Definition

The 1977 USACE definition references the importance of inundation and saturation—hydrologic conditions—as the prime determinant of wetland status. This definition also cites vegetation as a critical indicator of the hydrologic conditions that lead to the formation of wetlands. Although it refers to soil, it does not indicate that the physical and chemical condition of soil (or, more properly, substrate) is a critical criterion for distinguishing wetlands from other environments.

In referring specifically to soil, the 1977 USACE definition implies that wetlands cannot be supported on nonsoil substrates. Although most wetlands do form on soils and are specifically associated with hydric soils, a few types occupy substrates that are nonsoil or nonhydric soil (Chapter 5). Another difficulty is the specific reference to vegetation, which is commonly interpreted to mean vascular plants. For most regions of the United States, this is a reasonable approach, but some regional wetland types lack vascular plants entirely and instead show their wetland status through the presence of algae, mosses, and even invertebrates that require the basic hydrologic conditions associated with saturation or inundation of the substrate (Chapter 5). Finally, the 1977 USACE definition does not make sufficiently clear that wetlands are ecosystems, i.e., functionally integrated systems that reflect the hydrologic conditions leading to their formation.

1985 FSA Definition

The FSA definition emphasizes the importance of hydric soil as a critical indicator of wetland status. It implies that wetlands cannot exist without hydric soils. The vast majority of wetlands do in fact have hydric soils, and they can be identified by the presence of hydric soils in the absence of hydrologic alterations. Some wetlands do, however, develop on substrates that are not now classified as hydric soil (Chapter 5). Given that the FSA definition of wetlands was intended for application to agricultural areas, the emphasis on hydric soil is understandable. At the same time, it is clear that omission of wetlands lacking hydric soil renders the FSA definition inadequate for full coverage of wetlands (Chapter 6). In addition, the reference to vegetation, which is commonly presumed to be a reference to vascular plants, shows the same weakness as the 1977 USACE definition through its omission of wetlands that show a dominance of other indicator organisms that can be shown by field studies to be clearly indicative of wetland conditions. The FSA definition also does not underscore the importance of hydrologic factors in producing and maintaining wetlands.

The FSA definition of wetlands explicitly excludes Alaskan wetlands that have high potential for agriculture (Chapter 6). The connection of the FSA definition, and potentially any regulatory definition, to policy is evident from this example. Policy can legitimately dictate exclusion of any class of wetlands, but it should be clear that such exclusions are not based on scientific distinctions related to the characteristic properties of wetlands.

1979 FWS Definition

The FWS definition from the 1979 report of Cowardin et al. refers to wetlands as "transitional between terrestrial and aquatic systems," and in doing so introduces a potential complication that is not found in the 1977 USACE or the 1985 FSA definition. Wetlands are not always transitional either geographically or functionally. They are often found between deepwater and upland features of the landscape, but not necessarily. For example, wetlands sustained by ground water often are not bounded by deepwater habitats, and some wetlands that are bounded on all sides by water do not adjoin uplands. Furthermore, it is not always justifiable to invoke the concept of transition for the functional characteristics of wetlands. Functions and processes overlap across wetland boundaries, but they are not necessarily transitional. For example, the accumulation of organic matter under anaerobic conditions occurs not only in wetlands but also at the bottoms of lakes, and the retention of nutrients that occurs in wetlands can also occur in uplands and deepwater systems.

The special strengths of the 1979 FWS definition include its specific reference to nonsoil environments that can support wetlands and its reference to "systems," a critical concept that should always be coupled to wetland definitions.

FRAME OF REFERENCE FOR REGULATORY DEFINITIONS

The refinement and analysis of definitions is useful insofar as it focuses attention on the key characteristics of wetlands and on the factors that unify wetlands and separate them from other kinds of ecosystems. Of the three broadly recognized definitions of wetland, two are regulatory (USACE and FSA) and one serves as the basis for national assessment and mapping of wetlands (FWS).

These definitions reflect, in varying degrees, the intent of legislators, the missions of government agencies, and the influences of politics and administration on the evaluation of a technical issue. For these reasons, a separately derived reference definition is useful as a basis for the evaluation of regulatory definitions. A reference definition also highlights the substantive issues that need to be considered in the development of delineation manuals or in the design of research programs that are intended to make delineation more efficient and reliable.

Reference Definition

The Committee on Wetlands Characterization has developed a broad reference definition of wetland:

A wetland is an ecosystem that depends on constant or recurrent, shallow inundation or saturation at or near the surface of the substrate. The minimum essential characteristics of a wetland are recurrent, sustained inundation or saturation at or near the surface and the presence of physical, chemical, and biological features reflective of recurrent, sustained inundation or saturation. Common diagnostic features of wetlands are hydric soils and hydrophytic vegetation. These features will be present except where specific physicochemical, biotic, or anthropogenic factors have removed them or prevented their development.

All definitions, including this reference definition, are too broad to be applied directly to regulatory practice without substantial accompanying interpretation (Figure 3.1). Much of the following text of this report is devoted to a consideration of the evidence that supports the prevailing and alternative interpretations of regulatory definitions. The reference definition will provide a framework, outside of regulatory practice, against which current definitions and their interpretations can be compared.

The reference definition refers explicitly to the ecosystem concept of wetlands. The ecosystem concept, which is now being invoked widely in the management and regulation of environmental resources, acknowledges the integration of physical, chemical, and biological phenomena in the environment. Attempts to regulate, manage, protect, restore, or even identify wetlands without recognition of this underlying principle are likely to be ineffective. Consequently, the ecosystem concept is of definitional importance for wetlands.

The reference definition also recognizes the centrality of water in creating and sustaining wetland ecosystems. At the same time, the definition requires that wetlands show physical, chemical, and biological features that are manifestations of the hydrologic driving force.

The reference definition describes the biotic and physicochemical conditions of wetlands with sufficient breadth to encompass all wetlands. According to the definition, the physicochemical conditions of a wetland, which are properties of its substrate, must reflect recurrent, sustained saturation with water, but these

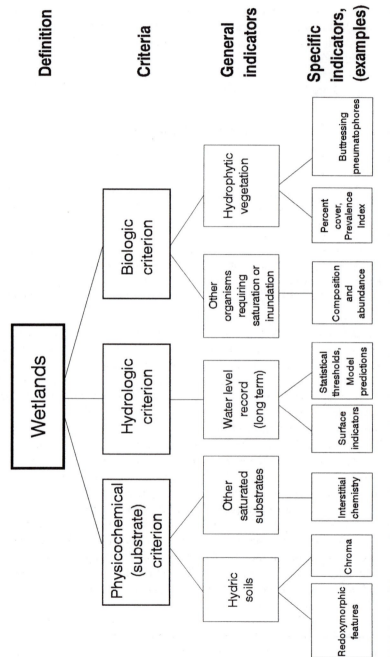

FIGURE 3.1 Diagram of relationships between the reference definition, criteria, general indicators, and specific indicators for wetlands.

substrate characteristics can take a range of forms, as described in Chapter 5. The redoximorphic features of hydric soils, which develop under low redox potentials that are produced by the repeated exclusion of oxygen from the soil, are the most common and easily recognizable examples of physicochemical conditions produced by saturation. The definition leaves open the possibility that other conditions, some of which might be more subtle, typify some wetlands. For example, soils and nonsoil substrates with especially small amounts of labile organic matter might show oxygen depletion in the pore waters without developing sufficient chemical reduction to create visible redoximorphic features. Similarly, the definition specifies that wetlands will have biotic features that reflect recurrent, sustained saturation, but these features can vary broadly among wetlands. The definition thus encompasses wetlands that do not support hydrophytes, but do support unicellular algae or invertebrates that have a scientifically demonstrated requirement for recurrent, sustained saturation. Inclusive phrasing of the physicochemical and biological portions of the definition is explicitly constrained by connection with the hydrologic driving factor of the definition: Physicochemical and biotic evidence of wetlands must be demonstrably maintained by recurrent, sustained saturation of the substrate at or near the surface to fall within the definition.

The last portion of the definition makes specific reference to the two most pervasive and reliable indicators of wetlands: hydric soils and hydrophytic vegetation. The definition acknowledges that these two indicators are so likely to accompany the presence of a wetland that their absence must be specifically explained in a wetland that lacks them. The most pertinent cases will be of a regional nature, as explained in Chapters 5 and 7.

The reference definition could be reworded several ways, but in any form would need to incorporate the concept of a wetland as an integrated ecological system (an ecosystem) that is distinguished from upland and deepwater systems by recurrent, sustained shallow inundation or saturation at or near the surface, and by a substrate and biota that show evidence of this distinctive hydrologic condition.

Terminology: Parameters, Criteria, Indicators

Application of regulatory definitions of wetlands is accompanied by confusion caused by three terms: parameter, criterion, and indicator. The term "parameter" is troublesome to the discussion of wetlands. This term is derived from mathematics and statistics, for which it refers to a component of a mathematical function or statistical distribution that determines the expression of the function or distribution. Transfer of this concept to a definition of wetlands is difficult at best. Except in relation to some specialized types of wetland research, wetlands are not defined by mathematical functions, nor do properties of wetlands show good analogs to mathematical or statistical parameters.

The 1977 USACE definition of wetlands and its accompanying regulatory guidance documents are often referred to as a "three-parameter approach" to the definition of wetlands because they mention three related factors: water, soil, and vegetation. These can be referred to more clearly and correctly as *factors* or *variables* than as parameters. The reference definition endorses the use of three factors, but designates the factors more generically than does the USACE definition.

It is important that both scientific inquiry and regulatory practice related to wetlands recognize the special status of hydrologic conditions in creating and maintaining wetlands. Recurrent saturation of the substrate at or near the surface is the one condition that sustains all other characteristics of wetlands. Water at or near the surface supports the development of characteristic organisms (hydrophytic vegetation) and substrate (hydric soils), rather than the reverse. Although there is some feedback between organisms and water (Chapter 2, Figure 2.2), the primary control is of water on substrates and organisms, rather than the reverse. Removal of water destroys the wetland, regardless of substrate or organisms. Thus, in the hierarchy of control or causation, the hydrologic factor has special status.

Criteria and Indicators

A criterion is a standard of judgment or principle for testing; it must relate directly to a definition (Figure 3.1). Wetlands are associated with specific conditions (variable states) for the master variable (water) and the two primary dependent variables (substrate, biota). These specific conditions are criteria in that they correspond to boundaries or thresholds that can be used to determine whether a particular ecosystem is a wetland.

The primacy of the hydrologic criterion must be recognized explicitly when wetlands have been altered or newly created by natural or anthropogenic processes. Removal of the hydrologic basis for the wetland eliminates its potential to remain a wetland, even if hydric soils and long-lived wetland vegetation persist. Also, if the hydrologic basis for a wetland exists and can be expected to persist, but the characteristic substrate or biota have been removed or have not had time to develop, their potential future development can be presumed. When hydrology has not been altered, it is sometimes possible to infer information about hydrology from the substrate of biota. This matter is discussed more fully in Chapter 5.

Any kind of evidence that bears on the evaluation of a criterion is an indicator. Indicators vary in specificity and are sometimes hierarchical: A specific indicator can support a more general one. For example, hydric soil is a general indicator that supports the substrate criterion, and characteristic chroma, or brightness of soil color, is a specific indicator that supports the identification of hydric soil.

The most general indicators often are confused with criteria. For example, because the substrate criterion is typically satisfied by the presence of hydric soils, except where hydrology has been altered, it is tempting simply to refer to hydric soil as a criterion. The reference definition of wetlands specifies, however, that hydric soil is an indicator, albeit a powerful one, whereas the criterion is somewhat broader because it extends to substrates other than hydric soils. Similarly, hydrophytic vegetation often is called a criterion. Hydrophytic vegetation, which customarily includes only vascular plants, is the most general biological indicator for wetland status, but it is not a criterion because other biological indicators, such as algae, mosses, or invertebrates, extend beyond hydrophytic vegetation. The distinction between indicators and criteria is valuable in maintaining a connection between a definition of wetland and the use of field evidence to support identification of wetlands.

APPLICATION OF DEFINITIONS

Any regulatory definition of wetlands has full practical significance only through interpretation at three levels: criteria, indicators, and recognition of regional variation. Criteria follow directly from the definition, and each must be dealt with explicitly by any regulatory system. Indicators then develop around the criteria. At this level, the interpretation of a definition becomes multifaceted and technically complex. Each of the criteria must be expressed in terms of empirical measurements or objective observations that can be used in establishing thresholds. This raises many questions. For example, what biotic indexes will best capture the presence of a substantial abundance of wetland organisms? How should the best possible biotic indicators be balanced against indicators that are slightly less accurate but more practical to use in the field? How should wetland substrates be identified in the field? What durations and recurrences of inundation or saturation are associated with the formation of physical, chemical, and biological features of wetlands?

The development of indicators is an endless process of refinement that is facilitated by research on wetlands. Research offers the possibility of improvement in indicators, with the beneficial consequence of greater reliability and repeatability in identifying and finding the boundaries of wetlands. Indicators are subject to strong regional variation that complicates the evaluation of criteria; this complexity can be revealed only through regional studies of wetlands (Chapter 7).

A reference definition of wetland that is derived from scientific principles may include some wetlands that the nation does not wish to regulate. Federal laws could for this reason exclude some wetlands from regulation. In such a case, a regulatory definition of wetlands might by intent fail to cover all wetlands. For this reason, it is important to maintain the distinction between a reference definition, which ignores the matter of jurisdiction, and a regulatory one, which reflects the intent of laws that do not necessarily encompass all wetlands.

The application of any definition to regulatory practice can be rational and defensible even when it is not very precise. Where the hydrologic conditions are marginally sufficient to maintain ecosystem characteristics that distinctively reflect recurrent inundation or saturation, the indicators of wetland often will be mixed, and regulatory practice must find a means of weighing indicators so that a final determination of wetland status can be made (Chapter 5). The same applies to the identification of wetland margins where the transition from wetland to upland is gradual. Although the weighing of mixed indicators is a form of judgment, and thus can be subject to multiple interpretations, the adoption of a fixed system for weighing indicators against one another can and should produce an outcome that is repeatable and in this sense reliable, even though it could be changed later as the understanding of indicators evolves.

RECOMMENDATIONS

1. A reference definition of wetlands is independent of legal jurisdiction and of administrative objectives and thus is distinct from a regulatory definition, which takes into account laws or policies that do not necessarily encompass all wetlands. A reference definition of wetlands should be used as a basis for evaluating regulatory definitions.

2. A reference definition of wetlands is as follows: *A wetland is an ecosystem that depends on constant or recurrent, shallow inundation or saturation at or near the surface of the substrate. The minimum essential characteristics of a wetland are recurrent, sustained inundation or saturation at or near the surface and the presence of physical, chemical, and biological features reflective of recurrent, sustained inundation or saturation. Common diagnostic features of wetlands are hydric soils and hydrophytic vegetation. These features will be present except where specific physicochemical, biotic, or anthropogenic factors have removed them or prevented their development.*

3. Three factors must be assessed in the identification or delineation of wetlands: water, substrate, and biota. It is not useful or correct to refer to these factors as parameters.

4. The states or conditions of the three factors (water, substrate, biota) that define wetlands are the criteria for identification and delineation of wetlands.

5. Indicators, which are the measurements or observations by which criteria are evaluated, should accommodate regional variation.

4

Wetland Delineation:
Past and Current Practice

INTRODUCTION

Technical manuals that provide agencywide guidance on wetland delineation are a relatively recent arrival in federal wetlands programs. Before 1986, none of the federal agencies with regulatory responsibilities—the U.S. Army Corps of Engineers (USACE), the Environmental Protection Agency (EPA), the Natural Resources Conservation Service (NRCS) (formerly the Soil Conservation Service [SCS])—had adopted a uniform technical manual or formal rules for delineation. Instead, the agencies used local and national aids, including draft and proposed manuals and district guidance documents, to assist individuals charged with delineating wetlands. In the late 1980s, each agency adopted its own delineation manual and then worked on the 1989 interagency manual. The manuals were intended to ensure consistent regulation of wetlands.

A delineation manual is not meant to define a wetland, but rather to aid a delineator in applying a definition of wetland; the manual gives details about what constitutes a wetland that must be confirmed during delineation. The complementarity of a regulatory definition and a delineation manual can be shown by juxtaposing the key words of the USACE regulatory definition with the implicit issues that each word raises (in bold):

Those areas (**distinguish wetland from upland**)
that are inundated (**specify depth**)
or saturated (**interpret proximity to surface, water table**)
by surface or ground water (**assess water source**)

at a frequency (**apply recurrence threshold**)
and duration (**apply duration threshold**)
sufficient to support (**identify requirements of vegetation**)
and that under normal circumstances (**adjust for altered conditions**)
do support a prevalence (**assess prevalence**)
of vegetation (**consider entire community**)
typically adapted (**categorize species**)
for life (**distinguish long term persistence from short term presence**)
in saturated (**relate vegetation and saturation**)
soil conditions (**characterize soils**).

This chapter summarizes the ways regulatory agencies have developed, interpreted, and applied such definitions.

WETLAND DELINEATION: MOTIVATION AND PROCEDURE

Wetlands are delineated primarily because property owners need to know which parts of their land could be within the regulatory jurisdiction of one or more federal statutes. As explained in Chapter 3, the primary regulatory programs arise under the Clean Water Act (CWA), which is administered by USACE and EPA, and the Food Security Act (FSA), which is administered by the NRCS. Some states also have wetland protection programs that require landowners to know the boundaries of wetlands on their properties. Although the U.S. Fish and Wildlife Service (FWS) is responsible for developing maps for the National Wetland Inventory (NWI), the inventory does not have regulatory effect, and it was not intended or designed for use in delineation. Other state and federal programs require wetland delineations as well; these include rules that tax undeveloped and developed property at different rates.

Clean Water Act

Wetlands are protected by the CWA (P.L. 95-217) and are subject to the act's prohibition against filling without a permit. The act's physical jurisdiction is defined in the statute and in its regulations. The act applies to "navigable waters," which the statute defines as "waters of the United States" (33 U.S.C. § 1362(7)). As explained in Chapter 3, USACE and EPA, acting in response to the *Calloway* decision as reflected in the 1977 CWA amendments, now regard waters of the United States to include wetlands and other bodies of water (33 C.F.R. §§ 328.3(a), (b); 40 C.F.R. §§ 230.3(s), 230.41). The CWA wetland protection feature is the statutory prohibition against discharging materials into U.S. waters without a permit (33 U.S.C. § 1311(a)). The permit program for discharges of fill material is established in Section 404 (33 U.S.C. § 1344) and administered by USACE.

Although USACE has administrative responsibility for Section 404, ultimate authority for determining the act's reach rests with EPA. In 1979, the U.S. Attorney General decided that, in light of the more extensive responsibility that EPA has under the CWA, it, and not USACE, should have final authority in deciding for the areal extent of the law's jurisdiction (43 Op. Att'y Gen. 15, 1979). USACE and EPA (1979) have entered into a memorandum of agreement (MOA) on delineation authority, which specifies that USACE will make most jurisdictional determinations in administering Section 404. EPA reserves the authority to determine jurisdiction in special cases, which it may designate either in generic or in project-specific instances. Jurisdictional determinations—or wetland delineations—made by either agency are binding on the other. Final jurisdictional determinations must be written and must be signed either by an EPA regional administrator or by a USACE district engineer. In the event of a disagreement, final authority rests with EPA.

Either USACE or EPA can make wetland delineations, but the responsibility for determining and knowing the boundaries of wetlands rests on the regulated entities (Want, 1989). A private party may request that USACE conduct a jurisdictional delineation (33 C.F.R. § 325.9), but USACE does so at its own discretion. Because many USACE offices lack the resources to provide timely responses to delineation requests, most entities pay private consultants to do them. A USACE delineation is valid for 3 years, although a period of up to 5 years may be justified by appropriate information (Regulatory Guidance Letter 90-06, 57 Fed. Reg. 6591; 1992).

The CWA and federal regulations establish a process for evaluating whether a person should be authorized to fill wetlands. In Section 404(f), the statute exempts certain filling activities, such as normal agriculture and silviculture, and minor filling associated with some construction activities such as temporary roads. In addition, some filling is authorized by general permits that are applicable nationwide. These general permits establish criteria for amount of filling and other management practices. As long as a person complies with the general permit criteria, no other authorization is required. If an individual permit is necessary, the permit application is evaluated under standards set out in EPA and USACE regulations. EPA's regulations, which are the 404 (b)(1) guidelines, establish environmental standards for issuance or permits. USACE regulations, which are known as the public interest standards, require evaluation of a broad range of environmental and legal criteria. USACE regulations also establish the procedures for consideration of permits, including public notice of permits and application of the National Environmental Policy Act.

A wetland delineation is often requested or contracted by a property owner who needs to know restrictions on the development or use of the land. In particular, a property owner might need a delineation when seeking an individual or nationwide permit. Nationwide permits, or "permits by rule," authorize filling of relatively small areas if the permitted activity is consistent with CWA regulations. For example, some nationwide permits cover modest bank stabilization or utility line backfill and bedding, or filling of wetlands in hydrologically isolated areas or headwaters (Chapter 6). A nationwide permit does not require an application if the activity is consistent with the scope of the permit, and if the activity can be expected to have minimal effect individually or in combination with other related activities. Some nationwide permits require landowners to file a predischarge notification, which includes a wetland delineation for review by USACE. USACE regulations encourage all permit applicants to consult with a USACE district office before making an application so that jurisdictional limits can be clarified (33 C.F.R. § 325.1(b)), and federal or state agencies can comment. Permits are generally valid from 3 to 5 years after issuance, and a wetland delineation that is made in connection with a permit is valid for the term of the permit.

The EPA may conduct a wetland delineation when it designates an area as a special case under the 1989 MOA. The EPA also has discretionary authority to identify wetlands in advance of any permit application through its program for advanced identification of wetlands (40 C.F.R. § 230.80; see Chapter 10). The program does not substitute for individual permit review, however. Instead, it categorizes wetlands either as suitable or as generally unsuitable for filling. The designations developed through the program are not binding in the review of a permit application.

Not all activities under Section 404 are regulatory. Inventory and nonregulatory protection of wetlands are examples of Section 404 activities that extend beyond permitting.

The Food Security Act

The Food Security Act of 1985 and its 1990 amendments established two conservation programs for the protection of wetlands: the "swampbuster" program and the wetland reserve program (16 U.S.C. §§ 3801-3862). Rather than prohibiting filling activities as the CWA does, the FSA specifies incentives and penalties to protect wetlands, and its programs require wetland delineations. The methods for delineation under FSA have been different from those of the CWA, although efforts are under way to create some concordance between the two.

NRCS, which is part of the U.S. Department of Agriculture, has primary responsibility for the FSA conservation provisions. The Agricultural Stabilization and Conservation Service (ASCS) also has FSA duties, however. NRCS does the wetland delineations; ASCS decides on the eligibility of farmers for exemptions. Each agency operates through local and county offices.

Both the CWA and FSA regulate agricultural activities. The CWA, however, exempts most routine agricultural practices from the Section 404 permit requirement. Exemptions include plowing; seeding; cultivating; and minor drainage associated with production of food, fiber, or forest products; construction or maintenance of farm or stock ponds or ditches; maintenance of drainage ditches;

and farm road construction or maintenance (33 U.S.C. § 1344(f)). The scope of these CWA Section 404 exemptions has been litigated frequently, and the courts have generally construed the exemptions narrowly: *United States* v. *Huebner*, 752 F.2d 1235 (7th Cir., 1985); *United States* v. *Akers*, 785 F.2d 814 (9th Cir., 1986). Converting wetlands to new uses as farmland is not within the scope of the Section 404 exemptions: *United States* v. *Cumberland Farms of Connecticut, Inc.*, 826 F.2d 1151, 1st Cir., 1987 (conversion to cranberry bogs is an illegal change of uses); *Hobbs* v. *United States*, 947 F.2d 941, 4th Cir., 1991 (conversion of wetland to hayfield is illegal).

The FSA wetland reserve program authorizes the federal government to purchase 10-year easements on wetlands, and it stipulates that the wetlands must be maintained in their natural state. The swampbuster provision of the law, in contrast, makes farmers who convert wetland acreage to cropland after Dec. 23, 1985, ineligible for agricultural subsidies—price supports, loans, or crop insurance, for example—for any agricultural commodity crop planted in the former wetland (16 U.S.C. § 1311, Supp. 1992). Agricultural commodity crops are specifically listed as sugarcane and crops that require annual tilling of the soil (16 U.S.C. § 3801(a)(1), Supp. 1992); 7 C.F.R. § 12.2(a)(1).

Some lands are exempted by definition (Chapter 3). Wetlands converted to farmable land before December 1985, or "prior converted cropland," are exempt (16 U.S.C. § 3801(A)(4)(a), Supp. 1992). Also exempt are artificial ponds that hold agricultural water; wetlands made farmable by natural conditions, such as drought; wetlands for which it is determined that the cropping would have only a "minimal effect"; wetlands for which the farmer demonstrates "undue economic hardship" based on conversion expenditures made before Dec. 23, 1985 (7 C.F.R. § 12.5(b)). Eligibility determinations, including decisions about exemptions under the swampbuster provision, are made by ASCS. NRCS applies the minimal-effect exemption.

Under the FSA, NRCS makes wetland delineations at the request of farmers and based on its own regulations and the National Food Security Act Manual (NFSAM). NRCS is authorized to make wetland delineations by use of soil maps and aerial photography, without field visits (Chapter 8).

The differences in objectives and statutory exemptions of the FSA and the CWA have caused some confusion over the regulatory status of wetlands on agricultural lands; the federal government has tried to resolve these. The Clinton administration issued a wetlands policy on Aug. 23, 1993, which notes that NRCS, USACE, EPA, and FWS signed an interagency agreement to develop consistent administration of their wetland programs (White House Office on Environmental Policy, 1993). USACE and EPA amended their regulations so that land qualifying as prior converted cropland under the FSA would not be treated as wetland under CWA (58 Fed. Reg. 45, 007, 1993; 33 C.F.R. § 328.3(a)(8); 40 C.F.R. §§ 110.1, 112.2, 116.3, 117.1, 122.2, 230.3). As a result, property designated by NRCS as prior converted cropland does not require a Section 404 permit regardless of the characteristics of the land.

In January 1994, USACE, EPA, and NRCS entered into an MOA regarding wetland jurisdictional delineations on agricultural lands (Memorandum of Agreement, 1994). The agreement states that NRCS is responsible for making wetland delineations on all agricultural lands and that the delineations are to be used for the swampbuster provisions and for CWA. NRCS is to use NFSAM for swampbuster delineations, and it uses the USACE 1987 manual for CWA delineations. The three agencies agreed to seek consistency in wetland delineations. Because NRCS relies heavily on maps and aerial photographs, the memorandum provides that the agencies are to agree on mapping conventions as well.

The FSA, like Section 404 of the CWA, motivates non-regulatory activities that supplement regulatory programs. Examples include inventory and conservation initiatives.

FEDERAL AGENCY MANUALS BEFORE 1989

As explained in Chapter 3, the federal wetland definitions embrace three factors: water, substrate, and biota. The characteristic state of each is a criterion for the identification of wetlands. All of the manuals prepared by the federal agencies provide guidance on the use of indicators for testing each of the criteria at specific sites. This kind of technical guidance is essential because the definitions themselves are too general to be used directly.

USACE Manual

Until 1987, USACE administered the CWA Section 404 program, including jurisdictional determinations and permit decisions on wetlands, without the benefit of a technical manual. In 1978, shortly after the 1977 CWA amendments and the consequential amendments to the USACE regulations that define wetlands, USACE assigned the Environmental Laboratory at the Waterways Experiment Station (WES) the task of developing a delineation manual. WES originally conceived of a two-volume manual: Volume I would specify criteria for hydrology, vegetation, and soils; Volume II would describe methods and procedures for delineation. The first draft of Volume I was circulated for review within USACE in 1982. Because of internal disagreements over this draft, it was held in draft form while WES continued to work on Volume II. During the early 1980s, WES worked with USACE districts to test the proposed methods and procedures in the field. Ultimately, the two-volume draft manual was combined into a single volume that was reviewed within USACE in 1985 and 1986. The final product was published in January 1987 as the U.S. Army Corps of Engineers Wetlands Delineation Manual (1987 Corps manual) (Environmental Lab, 1987). The 1987 Corps manual gave detailed guidance so that USACE personnel could perform wetland delineations simply and quickly. It also gave instructions on the exercise of professional judgment for atypical situations.

After the 1987 Corps manual was published, USACE evaluated its application by the districts. In early 1988, USACE (WES, headquarters, and district representatives) began to assess the need to modify the manual. In spring 1988, however, USACE joined EPA, NRCS, and FWS in developing a joint manual for wetland delineations. The result was the 1989 interagency manual (Federal Interagency Committee for Wetland Delineation, 1989), which was subsequently withdrawn from use. The federal government then proposed revisions to the manual in 1991.

When the 1989 interagency manual was withdrawn, and while proposed revisions were pending, USACE continued to use its 1987 Corps manual. In fact, Congress directed that USACE follow the 1987 Corps manual and that landowners who had delineations made under the 1989 interagency manual be given the opportunity to revise them according to the 1987 Corps manual (Energy and Water Development Appropriation Act of 1993, P.L. 102-377, 106 Stat. 1315, 1992).

EPA Manual

In April 1988, EPA (1988a) published its two-volume Wetland Identification and Delineation Manual. EPA began developing its manual with the issuance in 1980 of interim guidance for the identification of wetlands. In 1983, the rationale and guidance were revised and expanded, and a draft manual was prepared. A revised draft was prepared and circulated again in 1985 for agency and external review. After field testing and modification in response to review, the 1988 manual was published.

EPA stated, as had USACE, that it was following the "three-parameter" definition of wetlands found in USACE and EPA regulations and based on hydrology, soils, and vegetation. The 1988 EPA manual, however, allows delineators to rely on vegetation alone for routine delineations and when obligate wetland or upland species are dominant. According to the manual, soils and hydrology must be evaluated if the vegetation is not dominated by obligate wetland or upland species. The manual describes the difficulties of using hydrologic indicators for delineating wetland boundaries, and it justifies the heavier reliance on soils and vegetation in terms of these difficulties.

The field methodology in Volume II of EPA's 1988 manual, which was to be used by EPA personnel, includes a "simple approach" for "routine" jurisdictional determinations and a "detailed approach" for "large and/or controversial sites or projects." The simple approach uses vegetation to define the wetland unless there are reasons to look at other indicators. These approaches are analogous to the 1987 Corps manual's "routine approach" and "comprehensive approach." For vegetation units dominated by facultative species (not dominated by obligate wetland plants), the manual requires that soils and hydrology be checked; indirect indicators of hydrology are sufficient for this purpose. The detailed approach requires greater quantification of the composition of vegetation and an examination of soils and hydrology. Similarly, the manual requires a more detailed examination for atypical or disturbed areas.

Shortly after EPA published its 1988 manual, it collaborated in publishing the 1989 interagency manual. After the 1989 interagency manual was withdrawn and its proposed revisions were developed, EPA announced that it would follow the 1987 Corps manual (58 Fed. Reg. 4,995, 1993).

NFSAM

NRCS uses a wetland delineation manual that was developed in response to FSA. In March 1994, NRCS released the third edition of NFSAM, thus replacing the 1988 second edition and its amendments. The third edition incorporates changes that implement the 1994 MOA, although some important components were still under development when it was released. As these are finished, they will be published as amendments to NFSAM. In addition to wetland delineation, NFSAM discusses other NRCS programs, such as determination of highly erodible land, exemptions, and procedures for NRCS and ASCS.

Part 513 of the NFSAM describes the preparation for wetland determinations; part 514 describes the procedures for wetland determinations. Indicators for field delineation are given in part 527. The FSA requires NRCS to consult with FWS on wetland delineation matters; the 1994 MOA also requires coordination with USACE, EPA, and FWS. The NFSAM identifies the NRCS wetland decisions that require consultation or coordination with other agencies.

The 1994 MOA authorizes NRCS to make wetland delineations on agricultural lands and associated nonagricultural lands. The NFSAM makes it clear that NRCS will apply the FSA for agricultural lands and CWA for nonagricultural lands. Thus, for nonagricultural lands, NRCS will use the 1987 Corps manual. The NFSAM requires that, for agricultural lands, three factors—hydric soils, hydrology, and hydrophytic vegetation—be assessed independently. Appendixes to the NFSAM list indicators for soils, vegetation, and hydrology.

Under the terms of the FSA, farmers must obtain a wetland delineation before NRCS determines whether their lands qualify for statutory exemptions or exclusions. NRCS will perform wetland delineations at the request of a farmer. Some areas that would otherwise qualify as wetlands are exempt from NRCS-administered programs. These include artificial wetlands on farmland that was cropped before Dec. 23, 1985 (7 C.F.R. §§ 12.31-12.33), prior converted cropland, irrigation-induced wetlands, farmed wetlands on which farming is compatible with wetland status, wetlands created by mitigation, and wetlands or portions of wetlands covered by the minimal-effect exclusion. NRCS determines whether an exclusion applies and, if so, marks the excluded areas. Under the NFSAM, an

NRCS wetland delineation is valid for 5 years unless new information warrants a revision. The NFSAM also provides that an NRCS wetland determination stays with the land "until officially changed."

The NFSAM directs NRCS to make as many office determinations as possible. Office determinations are based on review of at least three aerial photographs, soil surveys, and other determinations previously made for the property (Chapter 8). NRCS, USACE, EPA, and FWS are continuing to work on protocols for mapping and photography that will be acceptable to all four agencies for wetland delineations. NFSAM provides that NRCS do a field wetland determination if the information is insufficient for an office determination. In practice, field determinations are done only when a farmer appeals an office determination.

NFSAM sets standards for classes of wetlands defined by FSA. These classes relate to the kinds of farming activities that are allowed or prohibited on farmed wetland—areas that were drained or otherwise manipulated before Dec. 23, 1985, and planted at least once with an agricultural commodity crop. A farmed wetland that is a playa, pothole, or pocosin must be inundated for at least 7 consecutive days or saturated for at least 14 consecutive days during the growing season. Farmed wetlands that are not potholes, playas, or pocosins must have a 50% chance of being seasonally flooded or ponded for at least 15 consecutive days during the growing season or for 10% of the growing season, whichever is less. NFSAM specifically acknowledges that these especially restrictive guidelines are intended to protect the unique wetland functions of potholes, playas, and pocosins. Wetland used for pasture or forage production, but not permanently drained or altered, qualifies as farmed wetland. The hydrologic thresholds for farmed wetland pasture require inundation for at least 7 consecutive days or saturation for at least 14 consecutive days during the growing season.

FSA requires coordination between NRCS and FWS on all wetland identification, exemption, and mitigation and restoration projects. NRCS participated with USACE, EPA, and FWS in the interagency efforts that resulted in the 1989 interagency manual. NRCS did not, however, formally adopt the 1989 interagency manual because it has its own regulations. Unlike USACE and EPA, NRCS does not apply the 1987 Corps manual to its wetland delineations on agricultural lands.

Attempts to Revise the Federal Manuals

As mentioned in Chapter 3, after the 1989 interagency manual was criticized, the Bush administration proposed a revised delineation manual (1991 proposed revisions, 56 Fed. Reg. 40,446; 1991). It initially announced that the 1989 interagency manual would remain in effect pending adoption of revisions. After Congress directed that USACE follow the 1987 Corps manual, however, EPA agreed to do the same (58 Fed. Reg. 4,995; 1993). NRCS has continued to use

NFSAM and its own regulations. The 1991 proposed revisions, which followed the 1989 interagency manual, also generated considerable public and serious scientific criticism. The controversy resulted in continued use of the 1987 Corps manual, and a congressional mandate that the National Academy of Sciences conduct a study, as described in Chapter 1.

COMPARING THE FEDERAL MANUALS

Table 4.1 lists some features of the 1987 Corps manual, the 1989 interagency manual, the 1991 proposed revisions, and NFSAM. Each manual applies a three-factor definition of wetland, yet each does so differently. Many of the differences among the manuals seem minor, but they can be significant in the field.

The 1987 Corps manual gives criteria and lists indicators for hydrology, hydric soils, and hydrophytic vegetation. Delineators must test hydrology, vegetation, and soils, but indirect indicators may be used to show that criteria are satisfied. Only for routine determinations affecting an area of less than 5 acres (about 2 ha) and in special cases, such as disturbed wetlands where vegetation has been removed, can evidence on specific criteria be omitted, however. The 1987 Corps manual is supplemented with USACE guidance letters and memoranda addressing specific issues pertinent to wetland delineation.

The 1989 interagency manual allows somewhat greater latitude in the use of indicators. For example, if hydric soils and wetland hydrology are present, a delineator can assume that the vegetation is hydrophytic. Similarly, if the hydrology is unaltered, wetland hydrology can be inferred from hydric soils or from characteristics of vegetation (plant adaptation to recurrent inundation or saturation) for routine and intermediate level determinations but not for comprehensive determinations. The 1991 proposed revisions require strict proof of hydrology, vegetation, and soils with separate field evidence. For example, hydrophytic vegetation or hydric soils cannot be used as indicators of hydrology.

TABLE 4.1 Comparison of Manuals

Characteristic	1987 Corps Manual	1989 Interagency Manual	1991 Proposed Manual	1993 NFSAM Manual
Factors	3	3	3	3
Allowable combinations	Show each separately; use fewer than three only for special cases (disturbed sites) or very strong evidence of two	Strong evidence of two sufficient to support the third	Show each separately	Show each separately

NFSAM requires independent assessment of hydric soil, hydrology, and hydrophytic vegetation. Because few NFSAM delineations are done in the field, however, it can be misleading to compare NFSAM's field requirements with those of the other manuals that require field delineations. NFSAM also incorporates by reference the field office technical guides, which provide specific information. For example, field indicators of hydric soils appear not in NFSAM, but in the technical guides maintained in NRCS field offices.

Hydrology

The manuals differ in their treatment of hydrology, as shown in Tables 4.2 and 4.3.

Hydrologic Evidence

The 1987 Corps manual establishes saturation thresholds as a percentage of growing season, which is defined by frost-free days. The manual also lists classes of hydrologic regimes that range from permanently inundated to intermittently or never saturated. The 1987 manual requires that saturation be to the surface. The surface can be dry, however, even though an area is considered saturated to the surface, because the critical water table depth is 12 in. (30 cm). The rationale is that capillary action saturates the upper surface of the soil above

TABLE 4.2 Comparison of Manuals: Hydrology

Characteristic	1987	1989	1991	NFSAM
Hydrologic threshold	Inundation or saturation at surface for >12.5% or 5-12.5% of growing season with other evidence	Inundation or saturation at surface for at least 7 days of growing season	Inundation at surface (15 days; saturation at surface (21 days during growing season	Inundation at surface for 15 days for most areas; 7 days for potholes, playas, or pocosins
Critical depth	Root zone (12 in.; 30 cm)	0.5 to 1.5 ft (15-46 cm); depending on soil	Surface	Surface
Growing season	Frost-free days, based on air temperature	Biological zero (41°F; 5°C) 20 in. (50 cm) below soil surface; soil temperature zones estimated	Three weeks before to 3 weeks after last killing frost	Biological zero, estimated from frost-free days

TABLE 4.3 Comparison of Manuals: Hydrology

Characteristic	1987	1989	1991	NFSAM
Periodically inundated, saturated to surface	Y	Y	Y	Y
Consider other factors (precipitation, stratigraphy, topography, soil permeability, plant cover)	Y	Y	Y	Y
Classification of hydrologic regime	Y	N	N	N
Minimum saturation, inundation 5% of growing season	Y	N	N	N
Indirect indicators of wetland hydrology allowed	Y	Y	Y	Y
Minimum saturation, inundation 7 days during growing season	N	Y	N	Y
Depth of water table differs by soil type, permeability, and drainage class	N	Y	N	N
Hydric soils, hydrophytic vegetation indicate wetland hydrology	N	Y	N	N
Minimum 15 days of inundation, 21 days of saturation to surface during growing season	N	N	Y	
Primary, secondary indicators indicated	N	N	Y	N

the water table (Letter to Honorable Owen Picketts from Lt. Col. R.O. Buck, Assistant Director of Civil Works, Atlantic Region, Feb. 2, 1994) (Chapter 5).

The 1989 interagency manual requires soil saturation or inundation to the surface for a fixed number of days rather than for a percentage of the growing season; critical depth is allowed to differ with soil type. The 1989 interagency manual notes that water is the overriding influence on vegetation and soils because of anaerobic conditions that occur when soil is saturated with water. Unlike the other manuals, NFSAM applies hydrologic thresholds separately to each of its wetland classes; thresholds can differ among classes.

All of the manuals allow the wetland hydrology criterion to be satisfied by specific indicators, some of which do not involve data on water (Table 4.4). Each manual, however, treats hydrology and its indicators differently. Only the 1991 proposed revisions divide the indicators into primary indicators, which are sufficient to determine wetland hydrology, and secondary indicators, which require some type of corroborative evidence. The 1989 interagency manual is unique in allowing hydrophytic vegetation and hydric soils as indicators of wetland hydrology. However, areas where the vegetation criterion is not met but wetland hydrology and hydric soils are present are termed "problem areas" and caution is advised. The 1989 interagency manual and the 1991 proposed revisions also allow plant adaptations to indicate hydrology as well as hydrophytic vegetation, as in the 1987 Corps manual. The 1989 interagency manual allows hydric soils to be used as an indicator of hydrology, but does not allow wetland delineation to be

TABLE 4.4 Comparison of Manuals: Hydrologic Indicators (P, Primary; S, Secondary)

Characteristic	1987	1989	1991	NFSAM
Recorded data on water depth	Y	Y	Y[a] P	Y
Visual observation of inundation	Y	Y[b]	Y P	Y
Visual observation of saturation	Y	Y[b]	Y P	Y
Watermarks	Y	Y	Y	
Drift lines	Y	Y	Y S	
Sediment deposits	Y	Y	Y S	
Drainage patterns (with caution)	Y	Y	N	
Observation of drainage, if any	N	Y	N	Y
Oxidized channels (rhizospheres) with living roots	N[c]	Y	Y[b] P	
Water-stained leaves	N	Y	N	
Scoured areas	N	Y	Y S	
Plant morphology adaptations	N[d]	Y[e]	Y[f] P S	
Hydric soil characteristics	N	Y	N	
Aerial photographs	N	Y	Y[g] P	
Sulfidic material	N[h]	N	Y[b] P	

[a]Minimum of 3 years of data collected during years of normal rainfall and correlated with long-term records.

[b]With caution.

[c]The use of oxidized rhizospheres is now accepted under the 1987 manual.

[d]Used as indicator of hydrophytic vegetation.

[e]See list of adaptations in text.

[f]Early spring or wet season, minimum of 5 years' data, evidence of inundation or saturation in most years.

[g]Some indicators are used as primary indicators others as secondary indicators, see text.

[h]Indicator of hydric soils.

based on soils alone. The 1991 proposed revisions require direct evidence of duration of flooding or saturation.

NFSAM uses the 1987 Corps manual's hydrology indicators. Additional indicators recognized by NFSAM include long-term stream gauge records, rainfall runoff and water budgets, long-range analysis of water tables by means of models, and analysis of drainage systems with scope-and-effect equations. Most NFSAM delineations are based on soil maps and photographs (Chapter 8). For field delineations, the form for entering hydrologic data in a routine wetland delineation form requires information about observed water, rainfall regime, water marks, drift lines, waterborne sediment, water-stained leaves, adaptations in plant morphology, the presence of oxidized rhizospheres, or other information similar to that provided by the indicators listed in the 1987 Corps manual.

Growing Season

Each manual uses growing season as the appropriate period for evaluating hydrology, but they define it differently.

The 1987 manual defines growing season as the portion of the year when soil temperatures at 19.7 in. (50 cm) below the soil surface are higher than biological zero (41°F; 5°C), but it allows approximation from frost-free days. Delineators who apply the 1987 manual most commonly use air temperatures derived from local weather records to determine the growing season. The 1989 interagency manual uses biological zero at 20 in. (50 cm) below the surface to determine growing season, but it also provides growing-season estimates by soil taxonomic temperature category and generalizes soil temperatures over large geographic areas on the basis of the growth of particular crops. Although the beginning and end of the actual growing season can vary by several weeks within a given temperature region or from site to site, the use of the temperature regions does allow the delineator to work with a fixed growing season and decreases the need for site-specific temperature information.

The 1991 proposed revisions do not use biological zero; they define the growing season as an interval extending from 3 weeks before to 3 weeks after the frost-free period as determined by use of local weather information. NFSAM defines growing season in the same way that the 1987 Corps manual does. Most frequently, the office delineations conducted by NRCS use aerial photographs taken well after the onset of the growing season.

Hydrophytic Vegetation

Under the definitions applied by all manuals, wetlands must have a prevalence of vegetation typically adapted for life in saturated soil. Interpretation of this characteristic requires identification of wetland species, establishment of thresholds for determining whether wetland species are prevalent, and a means of evaluating the contribution of species that occur in wetlands and in uplands. Table 4.5 compares the treatment of vegetation by the manuals.

Wetland Plant Species

The manuals differ somewhat in the wording of their definitions of wetland vegetation, but their meanings are quite similar. The 1987 Corps manual describes hydrophytic vegetation as follows:

the sum total of macrophytic plant life that occurs in areas where the frequency and duration of inundation or soil saturation produce permanently or periodically saturated soils of sufficient duration to exert a controlling influence on the plant species present.

TABLE 4.5 Comparison of Manuals: Vegetation

Characteristic	1987	1989	1991	NFSAM (field determinations)[a]
Use of Hydrophyte List[b] to determine indicator status (OBL, FACW, FAC, FACU, UPL) of plant species	Y	Y	Y	Y
Use of + and - to modify indicator	Y	N	N	Y
Hydrophytic vegetation; >50% of the dominant species OBL, FACW, or FAC[c]	Y	Y[d]	N	N
Hydrophytic vegetation; prevalence index[e] less than 3.0 using all species present[c]	N	Y[d]	Y[f]	Y
Other indicators of hydrophytic vegetation allowed (morphologic adaptations, documentation from technical literature, physiologic adaptations)	Y[e, g]	N[h]	N[h]	N
FAC-neutral option	Y	N[i]	N[j]	N

[a]Most NFSAM determinations are not made in the field. NFSAM incorporates the 1987 USACE Manual for field delineation matters that it does not address specifically.

[b]OBL, obligate; FACW, facultative-wet; FAC, facultative; FACU, facultative-upland; UPL, upland species.

[c]Where OBL, 1.0; FACW, 2.0; FAC, 3.0; FACU, 4.0; UPL, 5.0.

[d]If the hydric soil is present and wetland hydrology is verified, vegetation is assumed to be hydrophytic even if the vegetation criterion is not met. Such areas, however, are considered to be problem area wetlands and appropriate cautions are advised.

[e]Weighted average. A single number that summarizes quantitative data about a large number of species within a community and gives weight to each species' contribution to the final number in terms of an assigned value.

[f]Listed specific exceptions to this criterion.

[g]See text for list of adaptations.

[h]Some morphologic adaptations are used as indicators of hydrology.

[i]Although the FAC-neutral test is not explicitly listed as an option, one vegetation indicator (see footnote c) can be considered a type of FAC-neutral test.

[j]Sought comments of the use of this option and several variants of it.

The 1989 interagency manual uses the following wording:

macrophytic plant life growing in water, soil or on a substrate that is at least periodically deficient in oxygen as a result of excessive water content.

The 1991 proposed revisions define hydrophytic vegetation as

plants that live in conditions of excess wetness. For purposes of this manual, hydrophytes are defined as macrophytic plant life growing in water or on submerged substrates, or in soil or on a substrate that is at least periodically anaerobic (deficient in oxygen) as a result of excessive water content.

NFSAM uses the FSA definition (16 U.S.C. §3801(a)(9)), which states that hydrophytic vegetation is

> plants growing in water or in a substrate that is at least periodically deficient in oxygen during the growing season as a result of saturation or inundation by water.

Notwithstanding the differences among these definitions, all of the manuals rely on one FWS publication, the National List of Plant Species that Occur in Wetlands (P.B. Reed, 1988)—commonly called the Hydrophyte List—for identification of hydrophytic species and assignment of indicator status. The Hydrophyte List divides plants into five fidelity categories, by their wetland indicator status, that reflect "the range of estimated probabilities (expressed as a frequency of occurrence) of a species occurring in wetland versus non-wetland" (P.B. Reed, 1988, p. 8) (Chapter 5). The categories are as follows:

• OBL, obligate wetland plants, which almost always occur in wetlands (estimated probability >99%) but can occur rarely elsewhere (estimated probability <1%).
• FACW, facultative wetland plants usually occur in wetlands (estimated probability >67-99%) but also occur elsewhere (estimated probability 1-33%).
• FAC, facultative plants have a similar likelihood of occurring in wetlands and nonwetlands (estimated probability 33-67%).
• FACU, facultative upland plants sometimes occur in wetlands (estimated probability 1-33%) but more often in nonwetlands (estimated probability >67-99%).
• UPL, obligate upland plants occur rarely in wetlands (estimated probability <1%).

Determining Prevalence

The manuals differ in the indicators and specific criteria they set up for determining whether a site contains a predominance or prevalence of hydrophytic vegetation (Table 4.5). The 1987 Corps manual does not use the term "criterion" for vegetation but refers instead to "diagnostic environmental characteristics":

> The prevalent vegetation consists of macrophytes that are typically adapted to areas having hydrologic and soil conditions described in the following definition of wetlands: those areas that are inundated or saturated by surface or ground water at a frequency and duration sufficient to support, and that under normal circumstances to support, a prevalence of vegetation typically adapted for life in saturated soil conditions.

According to the 1987 Corps manual,

> any one of the following is indicative that hydrophytic vegetation is present:

a.   More than 50 percent of the dominant species are OBL, FACW, or FAC on lists of plant species that occur in wetlands.

b.   Other indicators, specifically: (1) visual observation of plant species growing in areas of prolonged inundation and/or soil saturation; (2) morphological adaptations; (3) technical literature, including taxonomic references, botanical journals, technical reports, technical workshops, conferences, and symposia, and the wetland plant data base of the National Wetland Inventory [currently the Hydrophyte List]; (4) physiological adaptations; and (5) reproductive adaptations.

In the case of the "other indicators" listed under (b) above, the 1987 Corps manual notes that "additional training and/or experience may be required to employ these indicators." Under the methods section, the 1987 Corps manual further specifies that for on-site inspections of areas of more than 5 acres (2 ha), if morphologic or physiologic adaptations are used to indicate hydrophytic vegetation, two or more of the dominant species must have these adaptations.

The 1989 interagency manual allows alternative criteria to show that wetland vegetation is present:

An area has hydrophytic vegetation when, under normal circumstances:

(1) more than 50 percent of the composition of the dominant species from all strata are obligate (OBL), facultative wetland (FACW), and/or facultative (FAC) species, or

(2) a frequency analysis of all species within the community yields a prevalence index value of less than 3.0 (where OBL = 1.0, FACW = 2.0, FAC = 3.0, FACU = 4.0, and UPL = 5.0).

CAUTION: When a plant community has less than or equal to 50% of the dominant species from all strata represented by OBL, FACW, and/or FAC species, or a frequency analysis of all species within the community yields a prevalence index value of greater than or equal to 3.0, *and* hydric soils and wetland hydrology are present, the area also has hydrophytic vegetation. (Note: these areas are considered problem area wetlands.)

The 1989 interagency manual states that wetland vegetation can be indicated by any of the following evidence:

1) OBL species comprise all dominants in the plant community; or

2) OBL species do not dominate each stratum, but more than 50 percent of the dominants of all strata are OBL, FACW, or FAC species (including FACW+, FACW-, FAC+, and FAC-); or

3) A plant community has a visually estimated percent coverage of OBL and FACW species that exceed the coverage of FACU and UPL species; or

4) A frequency analysis of all species within the community yields a prevalence index value of less than 3.0 (where OBL = 1.0, FACW = 2.0, FAC = 3.0, FACU = 4.0, and UPL = 5.0); or

5) A plant community has less than or equal to 50% of the dominant species from all strata represented by OBL, FACW, and/or FAC species, or a frequency analysis of all species within the community yields a prevalence index value of greater than or equal to 3.0, *and* hydric soils and wetland hydrology are present. (*Note:* In other words, if the hydric soil and wetland hydrology criteria are met, then the vegetation is considered hydrophytic. For purposes of this manual, these situations are treated as disturbed or problem area wetlands because these plant communities are usually nonwetlands.)

The 1991 proposed revisions set up a single prevalence index threshold as an indicator of hydrophytic vegetation:

An area meets the hydrophytic vegetation criterion if, under normal circumstances, a frequency analysis of all species within the community yields a prevalence index value of less than 3.0 (where OBL = 1.0, FACW = 2.0, FAC = 3.0, FACU = 4.0, and UPL = 5.0).

Specific wetland types that do not meet this requirement are listed as exceptions, including prairie potholes, playas, and vernal pools. Comments were sought on additional exceptions.

The 1991 proposed revisions do not give specific field indicators, although the methods section (Part III) refers to indicators of hydrophytic vegetation. As in the 1989 interagency manual, some adaptations of plant structure and morphology are used as indicators of hydrology but not of hydrophytic vegetation; physiologic and reproductive adaptations are not used as indicators.

For field delineations, NFSAM uses the numerical prevalence index in a manner similar to that of the 1991 proposed revisions. NFSAM also cross-references and incorporates by reference the hydrophytic indicators from the 1987 Corps manual.

Because both the 1987 Corps manual and the 1989 interagency manual refer to "50% of the dominant species" as a threshold for determining whether hydrophytic vegetation is prevalent, the term "dominant species" must be defined and methods must be established for measuring dominance and selecting dominant species. The 1987 Corps manual (pp. 16-17) defines "dominant species" in the section on characteristics and indicators as those that "contribute more to the character of a plant community than other species present, as estimated or measured in terms of some ecological parameter or parameters." In the methods section, dominant species are "those that have the largest relative basal area (overstory), height (woody understory), number of stems (woody vines), or greatest areal cover (herbaceous understory)." That is, a measure of dominance is established for each stratum, or layer, of the vegetation. For routine determinations, the measure of dominance is estimated visually and dominant species are determined subjectively. For comprehensive determinations, however, dominant species are selected by ranking the species in each stratum in descending order of dominance based on the appropriate measure for that stratum. The three species of highest rank from each stratum are selected as the dominant species if four strata are present. If only one or two strata are present, the five species of highest rank are selected. Thus, in the case of a plant community with four strata, 12 species (the three top-ranked in each layer of the vegetation) are selected as dominants. If 7 or more (more than 50%) of these dominant species are OBL, FACW, or FAC, then the community is predominantly hydrophytic according to the 1987 manual's "50% rule." In the case of a plant community with only two strata, 10 species are selected as dominants, and at least 6 must be OBL, FACW, or FAC if the community is to be classified as predominantly hydrophytic.

The 1989 interagency manual also ranks species in each stratum in descending order of the value of the dominance measure used for that stratum, but it selects dominant species differently:

> For each stratum (e.g., tree, shrub, and herb) in the plant community, dominant species are the most abundant plant species (when ranked in descending order of abundance and cumulatively totaled) that immediately exceed 50 percent of the total dominance measure (e.g., basal area or areal coverage) for the stratum, plus any additional species comprising 20 percent or more of the total dominance measure for the stratum.

For each stratum, all of the species are ranked in descending order of abundance. The abundances for all species in the stratum are totaled, and the cumulative abundance is then computed for each species on the list. Two thresholds are identified: 50% of the total, and 20% of the total. The dominants are species whose abundances fall above the 50% mark on the cumulative abundance list for the stratum, plus any other species that individually account for 20% or more of the total abundance. For example, if the herb layer contains one species with 90% cover, two species with 40% cover, one species with 20% cover, and one species with 10% cover, the total abundance (dominance measure) for this layer would be 200%, 50% of the total would be 100%, and 20% of the total would be 40%. Only the first three species would be considered dominants. This procedure is repeated for each stratum. The numbers of dominant species in all strata are totaled to obtain the total number of dominant species. If the herb layer had 3 dominant species, the shrub layer had 2 dominant species, and the tree layer had 3 dominant species, then the entire plant community would have 8 dominant species. If 5 or more (more than 50%) of these species are OBL, FACW, or FAC, then the community is predominantly hydrophytic according to the 1989 interagency manual's "50% rule." Like the 1987 Corps manual, the 1989 interagency manual uses visual estimates of dominance for routine determinations, and it establishes more detailed and quantitative methods for measuring dominance in comprehensive determinations. The method of selecting dominant species, however, is the same for all determinations. The 1989 interagency manual identifies five strata (tree, sapling, shrub, woody vine, herb) for which dominant species should be selected, plus a moss layer for some types of wetlands.

The 1989 interagency manual's method of selecting dominant species became acceptable for use under the 1987 Corps manual through the issuance of a regulatory guidance letter (RGL) by USACE in March 1992. The same RGL authorizes the use of five strata for determinations of dominant species, as did the 1989 interagency manual. Both the 1987 Corps and 1989 interagency manuals allow the same species to be considered dominant in more than one stratum.

The 1991 proposed revisions do not define dominant species, because all species are considered in calculating the prevalence index—the only indicator used for hydrophytic vegetation. NFSAM applies the methods of the 1987 Corps manual for routine determinations in the field. For comprehensive determinations, NFSAM uses the prevalence index, which does not require selection of dominant species.

Treatment of FAC Species and FACU-Dominated Wetlands

The manuals differ in their treatment of FAC and FACU species in determining whether the vegetation is hydrophytic. The differences affect wetland determinations most significantly where independent evidence of hydrology, vegetation, and soils is required. Areas that satisfy the criteria for hydrology and for soils can have plant communities dominated by FAC or FACU species. If FAC or FACU species are not treated as hydrophytic, regardless of evidence on hydrology and soils, such areas would not be classified as wetlands.

Discussion of this issue has focused on the "FAC-neutral test," which eliminates consideration of FAC species from determinations of prevalence. According to the 1987 manual, this option can be adopted by individual USACE districts if the district questions the indicator status of a facultative species and provides documentation to the USACE representative on the regional plant list panel (Chapter 5). Guidance issued by USACE in March 1992 on the use of the 1987 Corps manual provides that the FAC-neutral test may be used to help clarify a delineation where evidence of wetland hydrology or soils is weak, but it may not be used to exclude areas that otherwise qualify as wetlands.

The 1989 interagency manual does not use the term "FAC-neutral test." One field indicator of hydrophytic vegetation, however, could be interpreted as a FAC-neutral test. The primary way that the 1989 interagency manual handles FAC- and FACU-dominated wetlands, however, appears as number 5 in the list of field indicators of hydrophytic vegetation. This indicator specifies that where 50% or fewer of the dominant species are OBL, FACW, or FAC (where FAC or FACU species dominate), the vegetation is hydrophytic only if hydric soil and wetland hydrology criteria are met. Furthermore, the 1989 interagency manual treats these areas as disturbed or problem area wetlands and outlines special procedures for their evaluation.

The 1991 proposed revisions use only the prevalence index, which incorporates all species, for vegetation determinations. However, the authors of the revisions sought comments on six variants of the FAC-neutral test. FAC and FACU-dominated wetlands are treated as "exceptions to the three criteria"; they are wetlands that fail to satisfy all the criteria for hydrology, soils, and vegetation. The only named exceptions to the three criteria were pocosins, playas, prairie potholes, vernal pools, and three types of conifer swamps dominated by FACU species: white pine bogs of the Northeast and northern Midwest, eastern hemlock swamps and bogs in the Northeast, and tamarack bogs. The first four were included because they are "widely recognized wetlands that fail to meet the hydrology criterion." The possible exceptions on which comments were sought included pitch pine lowlands in the Northeast, jack pine and white spruce in evergreen-forested swamps in the northern Midwest, lodgepole pine bogs and muskegs in the Northwest and Alaska coasts, sugar maple and paper birch swamps and bogs in the upper Midwest, and longleaf pine wet savannahs of the Southeast. Other wetlands dominated by FAC and FACU species would be excluded under the 1991 proposed revisions.

NFSAM does not specifically address wetlands dominated by FACU species. When field delineations are done, the delineator uses all species, including FAC and FACU, in calculating the prevalence index. NFSAM incorporates by reference the 1987 Corps manual for vegetation, but the NRCS relies on a prevalence index that uses all species.

Hydric Soils

Each manual uses the definitions of hydric soils established by the National Technical Committee for Hydric Soils (NTCHS):

A hydric soil is a soil that in its undrained condition is saturated, flooded, or ponded long enough during the growing season to develop anaerobic conditions that favor the growth and regeneration of hydrophytic vegetation.

The third edition of "Hydric Soils of the United States," issued in 1991, modifies the definition by deleting the reference to hydrophytic vegetation. The manuals, however, continue to use the 1985 NTCHS definition. There are some differences between the manuals with regard to methods of identifying hydric soils (Table 4.6).

The field indicators of hydric soils are essentially the same in all of the manuals, and include: organic soils, histic epipedon, sulfidic material, aquic or peraquic moisture regime, reducing conditions, soil color, high level of organic matter at surface, streaking by organic matter, and organic pan. Correlation between the presence of wetland hydrology and the occurrence of hydric soil characteristics is well established, but the period of inundation or saturation required to produce them is less well understood (Chapter 5). According to all three manuals, hydric soils can be inferred if hydrologic observations indicate that threshold durations have been reached. In most cases, the 1987 Corps and

TABLE 4.6 Comparison of Manuals: Soils

Characteristic	1987	1989	1991	NFSAM
Soil definition	NTCHS	NTCHS	NTCHS	NTCHS
Field verification	Field evidence only	Field evidence, maps with field verification	Field evidence only	Field evidence, maps
Evidence for hydric soils	Assumes soil is hydric where OBL or OBL and FACW species with same abrupt boundary	Seven-day flooding demonstrates hydric soils[a]	15 days' inundation[a] 21 days' saturation only[a]	Seven-day flooding or 14 days' saturation at or near surface[b]

[a]Number of days saturated during the growing season.
[b]"Saturated to the surface" is when the water table is within 0.5 ft of the surface for coarse sand, sand, or fine sandy soils, or 1.0 ft of the surface for all other soils (NFSAM, 1994).

1989 interagency manuals require field identification of hydric soils for any delineation. Where there is strong evidence of wetland vegetation and hydrology, the 1987 Corps manual authorizes a wetland delineation without field verification of hydric soils. The 1989 interagency manual provides that soils need not be verified where all dominant plant species are OBL or where all dominant plant species are OBL and FACW and the wetland boundary is abrupt. For these two manuals, the characterization of the plant community comes ahead of soils or hydrology.

NFSAM gives criteria for hydric soils (Chapter 5) and also refers to "The Field Indicators of Hydric Soils in the United States", a field office technical guide, for evaluation of soils in the field. NFSAM relies heavily on soil maps (Chapters 5, 8). Soils are assessed first, and then hydrology is determined from aerial photographs.

Special Situations: Disturbed Areas, Problem Areas, Exceptions

Each manual takes a different approach to special cases (Table 4.7). The 1987 Corps manual separates "atypical situations" and "problem areas." Atypical situations involve alterations that obscure indicators of vegetation, soils, or hydrology. Alterations include discharge of dredged or fill material; fires, avalanches, volcanic activity, or changing river courses; and artificial wetlands. This manual also stresses the need to assess normal circumstances for an area. For example, if impounded water has become a normal circumstance, the area affected may be considered wetland. Methods to be used for site investigations in atypical situations also are given separately for vegetation, soil, and hydrology.

TABLE 4.7 Comparison of Manuals: Special Cases

Characteristic	1987	1989	1991
Disturbed areas	Areas subject to filling, removal of vegetation, levee or dam , construction wetlands newly created by human action or natural events	Areas that would have been classified as wetlands prior to disturbance	Same as 1989
Problem areas	Wetlands on drumlins, seasonal wetlands, prairie potholes, vegetated flats	FACU-dominated: evergreen-forested wetlands; wetlands on glacial till; variable seasonal wetlands; interdunal swale wetlands; river bars; vegetated flats; caprock limestone wetlands; newly created wetlands; wetlands on Entisols, red parent material, Spodosols, Mollisols	Newly created wetlands; wetlands on glacial till; mosaics; cyclical wetlands; vegetated flats; interdunal swale wetlands; springs and seeps; drought-affected wetlands
Exceptions	None listed	None listed	Pocosins, playas, prairie potholes, vernal pools, white pine bogs, eastern hemlocks, tamarack bogs, others as proposed

Problem areas, as described in the 1987 manual, are those for which application of the criteria is difficult, at least seasonally. Four categories are considered (Table 4.7). The 1987 manual requires them to be evaluated for wetland functions.

"Atypical situations" in the 1987 manual are "disturbed areas" in the 1989 interagency manual. These areas have been modified by human activities or natural events. The methods of site investigation of disturbed areas are the same as for atypical areas in the 1987 Corps manual, with two additional methods for characterizing hydrology. The 1989 interagency manual identifies a greater number of problem areas than does the 1987 Corps manual (Table 4.7). Both manuals provide detailed procedures for delineating problem wetlands.

The 1991 proposed revisions describe "disturbed wetlands" as those that would have met the criteria for hydrology, soils, and vegetation before their disturbance. The 1991 proposed revisions do not describe atypical wetlands, but they do describe atypical hydric soils (Table 4.7). The revisions use the same methods for site investigations of atypical wetlands that appear in the 1989 inter-agency manual, but they include more descriptive methods for ground water investigations. The 1991 proposed revisions list some types of wetlands as exceptions and problem areas (Table 4.7). Wetlands that are exceptions, as well as the problem area wetlands, are subject to more detailed procedures than are other wetlands.

For field delineations, NFSAM identifies "disturbed areas" as those in which the soils, vegetation, or hydrology have been altered so as to make standard wetland identification unreliable. NFSAM refers to and incorporates by reference the section of the 1987 Corps manual that addresses atypical situations for procedures to be followed when soils, vegetation, or hydrology have been disturbed.

Regulatory treatment of special situations illustrates very well the distinction between identification and boundary setting for wetlands on one hand and jurisdiction on the other. The reference definition of wetlands given in Chapter 3 makes no exclusions of wetlands on the basis of origin. The definition applies equally to ancient wetlands as well as wetlands of recent origin, to natural as well as artificial wetlands, and to wetlands created by intent as well as those created by accident. For reasons that are quite understandable in a sociopolitical context, the jurisdictional treatment of wetlands is much more complex.

Differences Resulting from Application of the Manuals

Comparisons among the manuals have produced many claims regarding the differences in results that can arise from their use. The manuals sometimes provide inconsistent guidance on the same subject. Also, each manual is organized differently, so comparisons among them can be misleading. It is difficult to ascertain whether the degree to which differences in delineation results occur because of misapplication of a manual or because of actual differences among manuals.

The office delineation method used by NFSAM does not lend itself to extensive comparison with other manuals. Wetland delineations conducted with office methods are susceptible to errors that do not affect field delineations (Chapter 8).

After field testing the 1991 proposed revisions and the 1987 and 1989 manuals, a four-agency team in the Pacific Northwest concluded that the 1991 proposed revisions would result in an overall reduction exceeding 50% of the acreage delineated as wetland under the 1989 and 1987 manuals. This was primarily because of the limited number of acceptable indicators of hydrology (personal communication, Oct. 29, 1991 to Larry Vinzant from Thomas Yocom, Robert A. Leidy, Nancy A. Dubbs, and Mary Butterwick). In the Mississippi Valley, scientists commenting on the 1991 proposed revisions indicated that 30% of the bottomland hardwood wetlands in Louisiana would cease to be delineated as wetlands if the 1991 proposed revisions were adopted. This estimate was based on field testing by USACE (Lower Mississippi Valley Division) and the Coalition to Restore Coastal Louisiana. Significant interannual variations in flooding and saturation were cited as reasons that much of the bottomland hardwood forest would fail to meet the hydrologic requirements (personal communication, Dec. 13, 1991 to Gregory Peck, EPA, from James G. Gosselink and G. Paul Kemp, Coalition to Restore Coastal Louisiana). A study by the Environmental Defense Fund and the World Wildlife Fund suggests that the hydrologic requirements of the 1991 proposed revisions would result in exclusion of approximately 50% of the remaining wetlands in the United States. Substantial areas of bottomland hardwood forest, northeastern and midwestern bog areas, 23% of the Everglades National Park, and 80% of the Great Dismal Swamp in Virginia and North Carolina would be dropped.

As a general matter, it seems certain that less area would be delineated as wetland under the 1991 proposed revisions than under the 1989 or 1987 manuals. The difference results primarily from the proposed requirement that hydrology, soils, and vegetation be documented separately, and from the limitations on indicators that can be used for each, especially hydrology. The 1987 and the 1989 manuals are the most similar of the group. Where there is a difference between the two, it generally results in less area delineated as wetland under the 1987 Corps manual than under the 1989 interagency manual. This is explained mainly by a broader and more flexible array of indicators in the 1989 interagency manual.

5

Wetland Characterization:
Water, Substrate, and Biota

INTRODUCTION

Much of the controversy over wetland delineation can be reduced to a single question: which characteristics can be used to identify wetland ecosystems and distinguish them from other ecosystems? Many wetland ecosystems and their boundaries can be identified unequivocally most of the time, some present difficulties at all times, and others do so under some circumstances. This chapter provides an analysis of the properties that characterize wetlands and distinguish them from other ecosystems. The major issues to be dealt with in this chapter are hydrology; soils; vegetation; other indicators of the substrate and biological criteria; and combinations of information on water, substrate, and biota.

HYDROLOGY

Wetlands are the interface for the major water reservoirs in the hydrologic cycle: surface water, ground water, atmospheric water, and, in some places, seawater. Standing water in wetlands is either the result of surface flooding or outcropping of the water table, which is the top of the saturated zone where pore pressure equals atmospheric pressure (Freeze and Cherry, 1979). Wetlands can exist where the surface is flooded for extended periods or where there is saturation because ground water moves or stands close to the land surface.

As explained in Chapter 3, recurrent, sustained saturation of the upper part of the substrate is the most basic requirement for wetlands. The importance of hydrology in the formation and maintenance of wetlands is well accepted, but the threshold conditions that satisfy the hydrologic criterion and the methods to be used for determining the presence or absence of wetland hydrology are still in need of study. Several important principles have been established as a framework for hydrologic assessment of wetlands.

Nature of Wetland Hydrology

The duration and frequency of saturation or inundation of a site vary according to the site's hydrogeologic setting, and they depend on regional differences in physiography and climate and on antecedent moisture conditions (Skaggs et al., 1991; Winter, 1992; Brinson, 1993a; Mausbach and Richardson, 1994). The duration of saturation or inundation can be depicted for a wetland's hydroperiod, on a graph that shows the position of the water table or standing water in the area over time. A wetland's hydroperiod integrates all aspects of its water budget (rainfall, evapotranspiration, runoff from adjacent areas, flooding, net seepage of ground water). A major technical challenge is to determine an average or characteristic hydroperiod for sites on which there are no hydrologic data, or for which hydrologic data cover only a short interval.

Figure 2.3 shows hydroperiods for selected wetlands. The elevation of the water surface is shown relative to the elevation of the land surface, which is arbitrarily set at zero. As shown by Figure 2.3, water levels in some wetlands (for example, a marsh maintained by ground water, or a tidal marsh) are always above or close to the surface. In contrast, water levels in bottomland hardwood forest might come close to the surface only during specific periods of the year. Water levels in a tidal salt marsh can fluctuate daily. The water levels in a fen, which is maintained mainly by continuous ground water discharge, fluctuate the least. In many wetlands that are wet only seasonally, direct evidence of wetland hydrology might not be obvious for relatively long periods.

The hydrologic boundary of a wetland is different from the hydrologic boundary of the watershed that contains it. The wetland is that locus of points in which the water balance produces enough saturation to maintain substrate and biota that are characteristic of wetlands. In contrast, the watershed that contains the wetland typically includes upland areas that share a common drainage pathway with the wetland. The wetland boundary might change over time as a complex function of factors that control the balance of terms in the water budget for the entire watershed. Climate change would be the most basic natural cause of change in the boundary of a wetland, but other factors—for example, sedimentation in channels, earthquakes, the activities of beavers, and land management practices—can alter hydrology and change the size of a wetland.

Need to Evaluate Wetland Hydrology

Because particular hydrologic conditions are essential requirements for wetlands, it is logical that hydrology be evaluated when wetlands are identified or delineated. This is now the case: All wetland delineation manuals require direct or indirect evidence of saturation or inundation at a frequency and duration reflective of wetland hydrology. Direct evidence is often difficult to obtain, however, because indicators of hydrology are much more variable on a short time scale than are the main indicators of substrate (hydric soils) or biota (hydrophytic vegetation). This is especially true for seasonal wetlands (like the bottomland hardwood forest, Figure 2.3), which can be without flooding or saturation for several months every year. The hydrologic status of such sites cannot be evaluated from one or even from several site inspections. A thorough hydrologic analysis, including the collection of field data over a period of several months (or, in some cases, over a year or more) could be required. Fortunately, hydric soils and hydrophytic vegetation are reliable indirect indicators of wetland hydrology and can be used to infer its presence when the hydrology has not been modified. When the hydrology of a site has been altered, soils and vegetation might not be reliable indicators, and the hydrologic status of the site must be evaluated independently. For all sites, hydrology must be evaluated at least to the extent of determining whether it has been changed. If it has, further direct hydrologic analysis is essential; if not, other indicators related to substrate (hydric soils) or biota (hydrophytic vegetation) can be used to infer hydrology, if the evidence from them is strong and consistent with such hydrologically relevant information as landscape position and surface indicators of hydrology. There are also many instances in which strong indirect indicators can be used to infer that wetland hydrology is not present, as in areas that contain extensive mammal burrows.

In some cases, a direct evaluation of hydrology is necessary. Drainage ditches, dams, or channel modifications can alter the hydrology of a site to the extent that the conditions that are necessary to sustain wetland vegetation or soils no longer exist, even though the soils are still classified as hydric and relict wetland vegetation is present. The opposite also can occur. For example, natural or anthropogenic modifications can create wetland hydrology on sites where the soils cannot be classified as hydric. In some cases, evidence from soils and vegetation is so unclear that a direct evaluation of hydrology is necessary. There are two questions to answer in a direct evaluation of hydrology: Is the site saturated or inundated for a sufficient duration and frequency to demonstrate that wetland hydrology is present? Where is the boundary of the zone that satisfies the hydrologic criterion?

Hydrologic Criterion

The thresholds (direct indicators) for the hydrologic criterion are normally defined in terms of the frequency or duration of continuous flooding or saturation within a given distance of the surface during the growing season. The long-term threshold for hydrology of a wetland is that which, at minimum, is necessary to maintain the vegetation or other organisms of wetlands as well as characteristic physical and chemical features of wetland substrate, such as hydric soils. Unfortunately, there is much uncertainty about the duration and frequency of saturation that define this threshold, especially because the threshold can be expected to vary from one region to another.

Chapter 4 discusses thresholds of saturation and the critical depth for saturation (the water table depth) as they are defined in federal delineation manuals. The depth and duration thresholds proposed for the water table vary from less than 1.5 ft (46 cm) for 7 days (1989 interagency manual) to 0 ft (saturation to the surface) for 21 days (1991 proposed revisions). The 1989 interagency manual's threshold refers only to mineral soils of low permeability (<6 in. [15 cm] per hour) that are poorly drained or very poorly drained.

The different thresholds specified in the federal manuals, when applied to the same sites, would correspond to widely different hydrologic regimes. Some thresholds would include sites that are well drained from an agricultural perspective (Skaggs et al., 1994); others would exclude recognized wetlands.

Discussions of the hydrologic thresholds for wetlands have generally emphasized the duration of flooding or saturation. Duration is important, but in fact wetland hydrology involves four related elements: saturation in relation to water table depth, duration of saturation and its relation to growing season, frequency of saturation or flooding, and critical depth of saturation.

Saturation in Relation to Water Table Depth

The water table is often assumed to be the boundary between saturated and unsaturated zones in soils. In some cases, however, allowances have been made for a zone of saturation that extends above the water table because saturation can occur in the capillary fringe (Bouwer, 1978; Freeze and Cherry, 1979). The capillary fringe, or tension-saturated zone, is the region immediately above the water table in which pores are fully saturated but the pressure head is negative, indicating that the water is held in place by surface tension.

The height of the capillary fringe above the water table can be determined theoretically from soil moisture retention curves. Large values for the height of the capillary fringe have been reported for soils with uniform pore size distributions. The surface layers of soils, however, usually have large pore spaces—caused by roots, burrows and other discontinuities—that empty under very little suction. For this reason, saturation caused by capillary action often extends only a small distance above the water table (a few inches). In the hydrologic assessment of wetlands, the water table depth need not be corrected for a capillary fringe unless field evidence shows that the capillary fringe is large. Wetlands sometimes can have finely grained soils that raise the zone of saturation significantly above the water table, in which case the water table is not a reliable guide to saturation. If not, the water table reasonably approximates the saturated zone for wetland soils and should be the main basis for direct assessment of the hydrology of wetlands.

Where the water table fluctuates, air is nearly always trapped as the water table rises (Bouwer, 1978). Even when relatively small samples of soil are inundated under laboratory conditions, air is trapped and the sample can be fully saturated only under suction. For example, Adam et al. (1969) report that 5-50% of the pore volume can contain air after initial stages of wetting. Because of the trapped air, which supplements the oxygen dissolved in the water, anaerobic conditions might not develop quickly even below the water table. With time, the air dissolves in the soil water and slowly diffuses to the atmosphere (McWhorter et al., 1973) or, in the case of oxygen, it is consumed by microbes and other organisms. The amount of air trapped as the water table rises depends on soil properties; antecedent soil water content; and whether saturation is caused by rainfall, seepage, or flooding.

Duration of Saturation and the Growing Season

Conventions for the direct evaluation of hydrology typically involve a numeric threshold for the number of days of continuous saturation necessary to maintain wetlands (Chapter 4). It is well recognized, that temperature affects the rate of oxygen depletion and redox depression in soils, as well as the sensitivity of plants to saturated conditions. Consequently, duration thresholds are attached specifically to the growing season, which is then referenced to soil or air temperatures; saturation at other times is discounted. The implied assumptions are that plants and soil organisms are uniformly active over the growing season and uniformly inactive and that the growing season can be defined by a standard convention for regions of widely differing climate. These assumptions are unrealistically simple, and they can lead to errors in evaluating hydrologic data.

Effects of Soil Temperature on Development of Anaerobic Conditions

Depletion of oxygen and subsequent suppression of redox potential by the conversion of oxidized substances to reduced substances is expected in any soil that is saturated for many days and that contains a significant amount of organic carbon. Recurrent depletion of oxygen and suppression of redox potential are characteristic of most wetlands and are responsible for creating and maintaining a number of the diagnostic features of wetland ecosystems. As explained in the section on soils, depletion of oxygen and suppression of redox potential are caused by the respiratory oxygen demand of roots and soil organisms. Among the soil organisms, microbes are most important. Microbes are the driving force behind extreme reduction of redox potential that is found in some wetlands.

Respiration rates of plants, animals, and microbes are strongly affected by temperature. As a rule of thumb, the rate of respiration doubles in response to an increase in temperature of 10°C (Peters, 1983). Thus the respiration rates of root tissues and of soil organisms, including microbes, is strongly affected by the temperature of soil. Because of the strong dependence of respiration rate on temperature, the degree of seasonal and regional variation in respiration rates is quite large. For example, the warming of a soil in the Midwest from 0°C in late winter to as much as 20°C in the last half of the summer would be expected to raise the oxygen demand of each microbial cell and each root hair in the soil by approximately fourfold. Similarly, a perennially warm soil, as might be found in Florida, shows a much higher respiratory demand on an annual basis than a perennially cold soil at very high latitude.

Because the demand for oxygen in a soil is strongly dependent on temperature, the speed with which anaerobic conditions develop in a soil varies from one month to another at a given site and also from one region to another. The definition of thresholds for the duration of saturation necessary to produce anaerobic conditions must take into account the effect of temperature on respiration. This explains why fixed saturation thresholds (e.g., 14 or 21 days) are only crude estimates of the actual time that is required for anaerobic conditions to develop at a given site. As explained below, the critical threshold for saturation of soils can be defined in a more sophisticated way by two possible approaches, which can be used separately or in combination: (1) definition of saturation thresholds specific to individual regions of the U.S. (see Chapter 7), or (2) use of a "degree-day" concept, which would allow time to be weighted by temperature, so that the critical duration is shorter when temperature is higher and longer when temperature is lower. These two possibilities could be developed independently, but ideally would be used together. For example, the first approximation of the duration threshold would be made independently for each region on the basis of information from that region. Within the region, the degree-day concept could be used to account for variation in the threshold that might occur as a result of seasonal variation or intraregional climate differences.

Soil temperatures change gradually over an annual cycle. For this reason, a much longer period of saturation might be required for anaerobic conditions to develop in the early spring than in summer, when soil temperatures are highest, even though both spring and summer are part of the growing season. The true critical duration would vary continuously with soil temperature if other factors, such as availability of organic matter, were constant. This is shown by Figure 5.1, where average monthly temperature for St. Louis, Missouri, is plotted and bars indicate the estimated time required (the duration threshold) for reducing conditions to develop after saturation of the soil profile with water. The duration threshold varies substantially, even within the growing season. Temperature also causes regional variation in the duration threshold of saturation. For example, the duration threshold would vary less for San Diego, California, than it would for Saint Paul, Minnesota.

In principle, the effects of temperature on the duration threshold for saturation could be estimated for any time of year in any climate if temperature were the only factor that affects critical duration. Because several other factors influ-

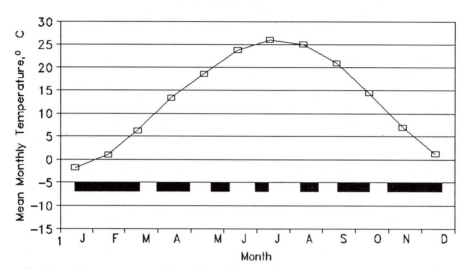

FIGURE 5.1 Mean monthly temperature of St. Louis, Missouri, and the length of continuous saturation required to develop anaerobic conditions in the root zone at various times
of year, as shown by the length of solid bars (W. Skaggs, unpublished data).

ence the rate at which anaerobic conditions or plant responses develop, however,
no simple estimate is likely to be realistic. Furthermore, current data are inadequate to define the duration threshold for saturation of wetlands over the wide
range of soils, climates, and wetland types in the United States. Information is
available for some regions, however, and duration thresholds can be approximated from information on the tolerance of a few sensitive upland plants to
flooding and saturation. More research is needed on relationships of the duration
of saturation to the development of wetland soils and vegetation, from which a
more flexible, temperature-based adjustment of the duration threshold can be
derived.

Definitions of Growing Season and Their Application to Wetlands

Cowardin et al. (1979) define the growing season as the frost-free portion of
the year, but they apply the concept only to saturation or inundation of nonsoil
substrates. The 1987 Corps manual applies the concept to inundation or saturation of soil, rather than of nonsoil substrates. The manual uses the growing
season through its adoption of the definition of hydric soils from the National
Technical Committee for Hydric Soils (Chapter 4). Growing season has thus

evolved from a minor constraint on the classification of nonsoil substrates to a major consideration in the identification of vegetated wetlands generally.

The most common use of the growing season concept is in agriculture. While information on growing season for crops may be useful in evaluating wetlands, the growing season concept as applied to wetlands relates specifically to wetland organisms (especially vascular plants), and not to crops.

Growing season has been defined as the period during which a given soil temperature at a specified depth is exceeded or as some function of the frost-free portion of the year. The 1987 Corps manual uses both definitions (Chapter 4). The 1988 Environmental Protection Agency (EPA) manual similarly defines growing season by its reference to biological zero (41°F, 5°C), but it does not mention frost-free days. Essentially the same approach appears in the 1989 interagency manual. A different definition appears in the 1991 proposed revisions, which define growing season as the interval from 3 weeks before to 3 weeks after killing frost, with exceptions for: "areas experiencing freezing temperatures throughout the year (e.g., montane, tundra, and boreal areas) that nevertheless support hydrophytic vegetation." The 1991 proposed revisions thus recognize errors in treatment of perennial cold regions as one of the flaws in earlier definitions of growing season (Bedford et al., 1992). In fact, the concept of biological zero, which is inherent in the use of growing season to define the metabolic activity of soils and plants, leads to numerous problems.

Biological Zero

The idea of biological zero is based on the notion that a limit of biological activity occurs at a specific temperature, below which, as stated in the 1987 Corps manual, "metabolic processes of soil microorganisms, plant roots, and animals are negligible." That manual places the temperature at 41°F (5°C), measured at a depth of about 20 in. (50 cm). This threshold fails for wetland communities in cold regions (Ping et al., 1992), and it might fail for some temperate communities as well (Dise, 1992). Furthermore, many wetland plants root at shallower depths (Tiner, 1991b; Bedford et al., 1992), which limits the relevance of soil temperature at this depth. Currently, the Hydric Soils List refers to the growing season as "the portion of the year when soil temperatures are above biologic zero in the upper part." This is more realistic than reference to 20 in. (50 cm), but "upper part" is not defined.

The use of biological zero is particularly inappropriate for defining growing season in permafrost wetlands. Pergelic Cryaquepts, which with histic Pergelic Cryaquepts (Appendix A, Soil Taxonomy) make up 65% of currently described permafrost soils in Alaska (Moore et al., 1993), have mean annual soil temperatures of ≤32°F (≤0°C) with active layers (seasonally thawed zones) averaging 20 in. (50 cm) and rarely exceeding about 3 ft (1 m) in thickness (Ping et al., 1992). Temperatures in the saturated zone often are only slightly greater than 0°C during the warmest weeks. For example, according to the 1989 interagency manual, Barrow, Alaska, would have a growing season of 0 days. The biological zero concept as developed for wetlands leads to the conclusion that shallow permafrost soils have no growing season, which runs counter to the reality that tundra and taiga ecosystems flourish on such soils.

Native plant species adapted to cool temperate, boreal, arctic, and alpine environments remain physiologically active at soil temperatures below biological zero (Tiner, 1991b; Bedford et al., 1992). Below-ground parts of arctic plants grow at biological zero (McCown, 1978, in Chapin et al., 1980; Chapin and Shaver, 1985) and absorb nutrients at low temperatures (Chapin and Shaver, 1985). Roots of deciduous taiga trees respire actively at 41°F (5°C) (Lawrence and Oechel, 1983), and their ability to absorb phosphate is relatively insensitive to temperature (Chapin, 1986).

Plant growth above ground also occurs at low soil temperatures, even under snow cover (subnivean). Arctic, alpine, and montane plant species grow (Billings and Bliss, 1959; Kimball et al., 1973; Kimball and Salisbury, 1974; Salisbury, 1984), flower (Bliss, 1971), or compete (Egerton and Wilson, 1993) in the subnivean environment at soil temperatures near freezing. Even in northern hardwood forest, spring-flowering herbs can develop leaves when soil temperatures are near 32°F (0°C) and there is partial snow cover (Vézina and Grandtner, 1965). Evergreen shrubs on exposed sites photosynthesize when the root zone is frozen (Webber et al., 1980), mosses and tundra graminoids photosynthesize when not covered by snow, and graminoids and the shrub *Dryas* initiate growth and photosynthesis within 1 day of snowmelt (Tieszen et al., 1980).

Tundra plants achieve high rates of production (Chapin et al., 1980) because their photosynthetic optima are from 18° to 54°F (10° to 30°C) below those of plants in temperate regions, and they often maintain significant rates of photosynthesis to 25°F (−4°C) (Chapin and Shaver, 1985). Some tundra and taiga mosses and lichens photosynthesize at >50% of maximum rates at 32°F (0°C) or 41°F (5°C) (Tieszen et al., 1980; Chapin and Shaver, 1985; Oechel and Lawrence, 1985). Other biological activity outside the frost-free period includes photosynthesis in alpine plants, subnivean growth of at least 20 plant species (including two winter annual cereals) at snowpack temperatures ≤32°F (0°C) (Salisbury, 1984), regreening of leaves and growth of roots in taiga plants (Kummerow et al., 1983; Tryon and Chapin, 1983), and growth of shoots in a temperate sedge (Bedford et al., 1988). Similarly, cyanobacteria associated with taiga lichens and bryophytes fix nitrogen at 38°F (3.5°C) (Alexander and Billington, 1986) and can be active for nearly 1 month after the average date of the first frost. Intact cyanobacterial crusts from subalpine habitats show no reduction in nitrogenase activity after repeated freeze-and-thaw cycles, and cyanobacterial nitrogenase activity of sedge meadow cores from a high arctic lowland are nearly 30% of maximum at 39°F (3.7°C) (Chapin et al., 1991).

Soil microbes also are active in tundra and taiga wetlands when the soil temperature is below biological zero. Bacteria from tundra soils respire to 20° or 19°F (–6.5° or –7°C) (Flanagan and Bunnell, 1980). Fungal biomass can increase within a temperature range of 32° to 26°F (0° to 2°C), but growth generally ceases below 27°F (–3°C) (Bunnell et al., 1980; Flanagan and Bunnell, 1980). Further evidence for microbial activity below nominal biological zero includes the presence of cold-adapted fungi in cold, acidic peat soils (Grishkan and Berman, 1993); in greater respiration rates and larger populations of some taiga microbes at 39°F (4°C) than at 68°F (20°C) (Sparrow et al., 1978); in overwinter increases in microbial biomass in near-freezing taiga soils (Zolotareva and Demkina, 1993); and in substantial early-winter carbon dioxide emissions from tundra and taiga soils (Zimov et al., 1993). The unfrozen isothermal zone (32°F [0°C]) that persists in the active layer of permafrost soils until heat loss is sufficient for phase change could provide a favorable environment for microbial activity (Zimov et al., 1993). Microbes oxidize >25% of estimated annual carbon fixation in a Wyoming subalpine meadow at winter soil temperatures of 33° to 35°F (0.5° to 1.5°C) (Sommerfeld et al., 1993). Wastewater treatment facilities, including natural and constructed wetlands subjected to wastewater discharge, also demonstrate significant microbial activity at low temperatures (S.E. Clark et al., 1970; Eckenfelder and Englande, 1970; Pick et al., 1970; Vennes and Olsson, 1970; Henry, 1974; Kent, 1987; Miller, 1989).

Hydric soils develop when soil microbial activity depletes oxygen and creates reducing conditions. Methane emission from saturated tundra and taiga soils demonstrates reducing conditions and suggests that these soils can become anoxic at temperatures below biological zero (Svensson, 1983, in Svensson and Rosswall, 1984; Whalen and Reeburgh, 1992). Winter methane fluxes from Minnesota peatlands (Dise, 1992) also provide evidence for reducing conditions in cold soils. Low redox potentials (in this case, <100 mV) were documented at groundwater temperatures below 39°F (4°C) at two tundra bioremediation sites (Jorgenson and Cater, 1992; Jorgenson et al., 1993). A great deal of evidence from field and laboratory studies shows that biological activity occurs below 41°F (5°C), especially in cold regions. This casts doubt on the validity of any universal value for biological zero.

Growing Season as Defined by the Frost-Free Period

The use of a "mean frost-free period" poorly represents the occurrence of soil and air temperatures at which biological activity can occur in arctic, subarctic, alpine, and some temperate regions. Wide interannual variability in the number of frost-free days at locations as diverse as Iowa (Bedford et al., 1992), coastal British Columbia (Banner et al., 1986), and interior Alaska (Bowling, 1984) suggests that in many years biological activity occurs over a period considerably longer than that defined by the average number of frost-free days. Growing season as defined by the frost-free period is particularly problematic in arctic

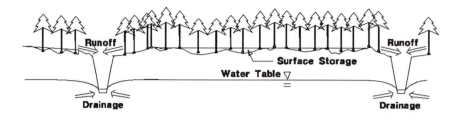

FIGURE 5.2 Drained wetland.

tundra, where subfreezing temperatures can occur at any time of year (Savile, 1972; Chapin and Shaver, 1985). Barrow, Alaska, for example, annually averages 16 frost-free days (Sharratt, 1992), but has 91 days with a mean daily air temperature above freezing (Brown et al., 1980). Similarly, a subarctic site has been shown to have a frost-free growing season of 97 days (Slaughter and Viereck, 1986) and a thaw season of about 176 days (Dingman, 1971). Subfreezing temperatures occur daily in equatorial alpine communities (Bliss, 1971; Beck, 1987, in Kalma et al., 1992), and they occasionally occur early in the growth period in midlatitude alpine plant communities (Billings and Bliss, 1959; Holway and Ward, 1965).

Interaction of Duration Threshold with Length of Growing Season

The appropriate duration threshold for the saturation of soils in wetlands depends on the definition of growing season. An analysis of growing season for a specific site will illustrate this point. The hydrology of a hypothetical drained wetland (Figure 5.2) was analyzed with the simulation model DRAINMOD, using the methods described by Skaggs et al. (1994). Analyses were conducted for a sandy loam hydric soil with a constant drainable porosity of 5%, parallel drainage ditches about 4 ft (1.2 m) deep and about 330 ft (100 m) apart, and average depressional storage of about 1 in. (25 mm). The drainage intensity was varied by changing the hydraulic conductivity of the soil profile which is about 8 ft (2.4 m). The hydrology was simulated over a 40-year period (1953-1992) by use of climatological data for Plymouth, North Carolina. The growing season, based on the average last date of 28°F (–2.2°C) in the spring and average first date of 28°F (–2.2°C) in the fall, is Mar. 30 to Nov. 7, or 222 days. Thus, the hydrologic requirement for a wetland, according to the 1987 Corps manual, is 11 days (5% of 222 days).

The number of years that exceed the 11-day duration threshold for saturation during the growing season is shown in Figure 5.3a as a function of hydraulic

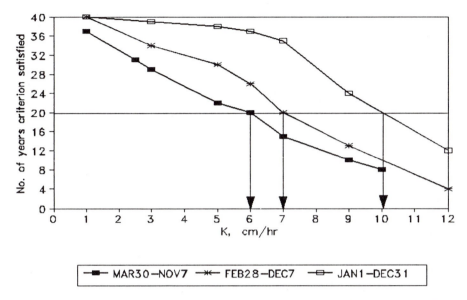

FIGURE 5.3(a) Results of a simulation for a wetland in Plymouth, North Carolina. The graph shows the effect of hydraulic conductivity and length of growing season on the number of years that the water table depth is less than 30 cm (11.7 in.) for at least 11 consecutive days during the growing season. The graph shows that critical permeabilities for the wetland threshold increase as the length of the growing season increases.

conductivity (K). Hydraulic conductivity of 2.34 in./hour (6 cm/hr) would cause the threshold to be exceeded in 20 of 40 years, which would just qualify the site as a wetland by the conventions of the 1987 Corps manual. Results differ if the 11-day threshold is evaluated over longer portions of the year. For example, if the whole year is considered, the 11-day threshold would be met or exceeded in 36 of 40 years for K = 2.34 in./hour (6 cm/hr). Increasing the length of the growing season without adjusting the duration threshold thus causes drier sites (with higher K) to meet a given duration threshold.

The result of holding the critical duration as a fixed percentage (5%) of the growing season, as is the convention of the 1987 USACE manual, is shown in Figure 5.3b. In this case, the critical durations for various hypothetical growing seasons were Mar. 30 to Nov. 7 growing season (duration, 11 days); Feb. 28 to Dec. 7 growing season (14 days); and the whole year (18 days). Thus, when duration is defined as a percentage of the growing season, the characterization of the site is to some extent normalized. If the entire year were treated as a growing season, however, some relatively dry sites would still tend to exceed the hydrologic threshold.

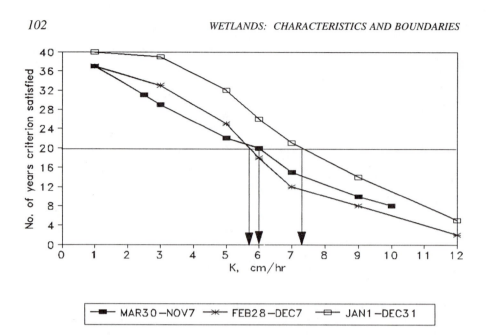

FIGURE 5.3(b)   Effect of hydraulic conductivity and growing season on the number of years that the water table depth was less than 30 cm (11.7 in.) for 5% of the growing season for the simulation of a wetland in Plymouth, North Carolina.

Resolving the Problem of Growing Season

Two general possibilities exist for resolving the problems caused by use of growing season in the identification of wetlands. The first is to abandon growing season as a constraint on the duration threshold for inundation and saturation and replace it with a system that links duration directly with temperature. The other is to redefine the growing season by region on the basis of careful scientific study of natural wetland communities and processes. The continuous change of plant and microbial activity with temperature provides a strong argument for the first approach (Tiner, 1991a; Bedford et al., 1992), but more thorough study of the physiologic activity of vegetation, soil microbes, and fauna in reference wetlands could permit the latter. Either approach would recognize more effectively the regional variation in duration thresholds.

Weaknesses in the growing-season concept, particularly for cold soils in which considerable metabolic activity can occur outside the present growing season, have already been summarized. In addition, estimates of the duration threshold are probably too short for places with long growing seasons. For example, Faulkner and Patrick (1992) analyze redox processes, water table depth, and wetland soil indicators on 24 bottomland hardwood forest sites over a range of elevations in Louisiana and Mississippi. For those sites, a change in the water table duration threshold for hydric soils from >7 days to >14 days would be justified, especially if saturation occurs early in the growing season when soil temperatures are low enough to slow microbial reduction. A similar study in South Carolina (Megonigal et al., 1993) reports that soils with hydric soil indicators within 1 ft (30 cm) of the surface were saturated at nearly 6 in. (15 cm) for at least 30 days. In this study, as well as the one by Faulkner and Patrick, the absence of sites saturated for shorter durations limits interpretation of events at the drier end of the moisture gradient.

More studies are needed in other regions and for other physiographic settings and wetland types, whether the use of the growing-season concept continues or is replaced by a more flexible time-and-temperature concept. In some cases, computer simulation models could be combined with field data to analyze the long-term hydrology of sites along the gradient from wetland to upland. In this way, soils and vegetation could be correlated with frequency and duration of saturation over the long term for specific regions or wetland types. This could expedite the refinement of duration thresholds.

Evaluation of duration thresholds for wetlands requires long-term data on water table depth and corresponding information on soil morphology and vegetation across a range of conditions. The lack of such data, except for a few locations, has limited development and refinement of thresholds in support of the hydrologic criterion. For some wetlands, simulation models can be used to predict water table fluctuations over long periods.

This approach was used by Skaggs et al. (1994) in evaluating seven proposed interpretations of the hydrologic criterion, including those of the federal manuals. The analysis showed that thresholds in the 1991 proposed revisions—flooding for 15 consecutive days or saturation to the surface for 21 consecutive days— characterize lands that are much wetter than those consistent with the 1987 or 1989 manuals. According to the simulation, the threshold given by the 1987 manual (water table <1 ft [30 cm], 14 consecutive days) would, for the North Carolina coastal plain, give corn yields that are approximately equal to observed average yields for standard agricultural drainage practice.

Frequency of Saturation

Delineation manuals for wetlands have not only specified thresholds for duration of saturation or flooding, but they also have incorporated the concept of "normal circumstances" or "average conditions." Average conditions are usually interpreted to mean those with a 2-year recurrence interval, or once in 2 years on average (10 out of 20 years). The threshold frequency for inundation probably varies, however, as a function of duration, especially in the western United States. For example, hydric soils form on sites that are saturated, flooded, or ponded long enough to develop anaerobic conditions. This might occur on sites that are anaerobic and reducing for brief periods nearly every year or on sites that are saturated and anaerobic for long periods, but not every year (such as the prairie pothole region). Similar reasoning applies to the interactions of duration and frequency essential for support of hydrophytic vegetation. In general, the duration threshold for saturation would increase as the frequency of saturation decreases. There is little scientific information on the relationship, however.

Critical Depth of Saturation

The rationale for determining the depth at which saturation should be evaluated is the response of plants to saturation of the substrate. Plants that are not adapted to frequent or extended periods of saturation within their rooting zones cannot survive in wetland environments. The depth of saturation, therefore, should be based on the depth of wetland plant roots. Only if saturation occurs within the plant rooting zone will it affect the establishment of wetland vegetation.

The few studies that have documented the depth distributions of roots in wetlands show that most roots are concentrated in the upper 1-2 ft (30-60 cm). Costello (1936) reports the rooting depths of several species growing in tussock meadows in Wisconsin. Arrowhead (*Sagittaria latifolia*) and *Carex riparia* (*C. lacustris*) rooted in the top 8 in. (20 cm) but that the tussock sedge (*C. stricta*) penetrated to 2 ft (60 cm). In a study of 15 annual and perennial species from freshwater tidal marshes, Whigham and Simpson (1978) found that all of the species except *Peltandra virginica* rooted in the upper 2 ft (60 cm) of substrate. Lieffers and Rothwell (1987) found that the roots of black spruce (*Picea mariana*) and tamarack (*Larix laricina*) were almost entirely restricted to the top 1 ft (30 cm) of substrate. Day and Montague (1980) found that in the Great Dismal Swamp most roots occur within the top 1 ft (30 cm) of the surface. In a study of several species common in fens (minerotrophic peatlands), Sjors (1991) found that, although some roots penetrate nearly 2 ft (60 cm), most roots and rhizomes concentrate in the upper 1 ft (30 cm). Although roots of some plants, and particularly trees, may extend more deeply than 1 ft (30 cm), the presence of an unsaturated zone above 1 ft (30 cm) may provide sufficient oxygen to meet the needs of most plants. Thus, evidence supports a depth of 1 ft (30 cm) as the critical zone for assessment of saturation, but further studies are clearly needed.

Interannual Variation

Variation in wetness from season to season and from year to year causes difficulties in identifying and delineating wetlands. This is especially true for sites that have been modified to such an extent that soils and vegetation are not reliable indicators of hydrologic status. Plant species can change from year to year in response to higher or lower water levels. For this reason, seed banks could provide valuable information on characteristic conditions. Temporal varia-

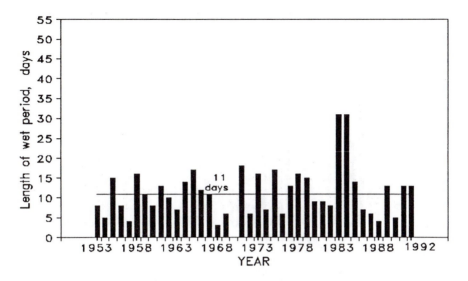

FIGURE 5.4 Length of longest continuous period that the water table depth would be less than 1 ft (30 cm) for a site that satisfies the duration threshold for saturation in 20 of 40 years, as simulated by DRAINMOD from climatological data from Plymouth, North Carolina.

tion of soil water is a typical result of variation in precipitation and evapotranspiration, but variation is more extreme in some regions than in others. On floodplains of large rivers, for example, the source of variation could be temporal variability of weather over a large region, whereas isolated wetlands could be affected by local variations. Variation also can be affected by structures such as dams or dikes.

An example of interannual variation in water table depth can be taken from a simulation for a site on sandy loam near Plymouth, North Carolina (Skaggs et al., 1991). The simulation was designed so that the duration threshold for wetlands as given by the 1987 Corps manual was just satisfied, which would require that the water table be within 1 ft (30 cm) of the surface for 5% of the growing season (5% of 222, 11 days) for half of the years. The longest span of days for any given year that the water table was within 1 ft (30 cm) of the surface during the growing season is shown in Figure 5.4 for each year of the 40-year simulation period (1951-1990). Although the site exceeded the hydrologic threshold for wetlands in 1 of 2 years, on average, there were several periods of 2 or 3 consecutive years when it did not exceed the threshold. In 2 years the water table was near the surface for more than 30 days; in several others it was in the top 1 ft (30 cm) of the profile for fewer than 5 days. These results demonstrate the limitations of short-term field data on borderline sites.

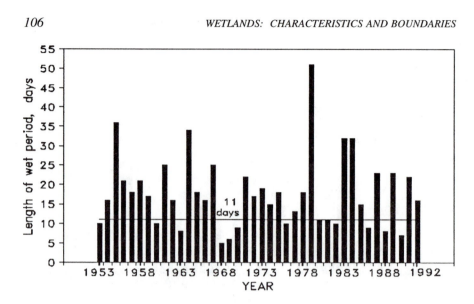

FIGURE 5.5. Length of longest continuous period that the water table depth is less than 1 ft (30 cm) for a site that satisfies the duration threshold for saturation in 30 of 40 years, as simulated by DRAINMOD from climatological data from Plymouth, North Carolina.

Year-to-year variability is a less serious problem for sites that are clearly wetland or upland. Simulation results for sites that exceed the hydrologic threshold in 75% (wetland) and 25% (nonwetland) of the years are given in Figures 5.5 and 5.6. For the wetter site (wetland), most years that do not show 11 consecutive days of saturation would have wet periods of within 2 or 3 days of that number. There is still one 3-year period (1968-1970), however, during which the threshold would not be exceeded. The drier site (nonwetland) would be below the threshold in most years but would occasionally exceed the threshold for 2 or 3 successive years (Figure 5.6). The simulations illustrate the influence of interannual variation on the hydrology of wetland sites. Analyses based on short-term water table data must consider antecedent and current precipitation and evapotranspiration as they relate to long-term patterns. Interannual variation increases as annual precipitation decreases.

Overview of Hydrologic Thresholds

There is not yet enough information about wetland hydrology and the response of soils, plants, and other wetland organisms to saturated soil to support a complete description of the conditions that demonstrate the presence of wetland hydrology for all soils, climates, and wetland types. Hydrologic thresholds can be estimated roughly, however, from the range of specific hydrologic conditions associated with wetland soils (Gilliam and Gambrell, 1978; Faulkner and Patrick,

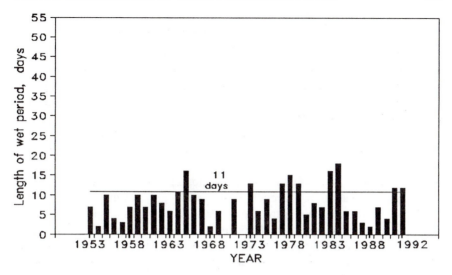

FIGURE 5.6. Length of longest continuous period that the water table depth is less than 1 ft (30 cm) for a site that satisfies the duration threshold for saturation in 10 of 40 years, as simulated by DRAINMOD from climatological data from Plymouth, North Carolina.

1992; Megonigal et al., 1993) and wetland organisms (Niering, 1985) and from moisture tolerances of upland plants (Joshi and Dastane, 1955; Luxmore et al., 1973; Howell et al., 1976; Carter, 1977; Evans et al., 1990, 1991). The data now available indicate that reasonable hydrologic thresholds would include a depth to water table of <1 ft (30 cm) for a continuous period of at least 14 days during the growing season, with a mean interannual frequency of 1 out of 2 years. This threshold is consistent with those defined for the formation of hydric soils (USDA, 1991) and would fall within the range of the convention used in the 1987 Corps manual of 5-12% of the growing season, except for those areas with growing seasons >280 days (such as southern California) or <112 days (such as Alaska). Overriding regional thresholds should be set for these areas.

The use of numeric thresholds for hydrology has been criticized because anaerobic conditions can develop within 1 or 2 days of flooding (Tiner, 1993). Although this can occur, the hydrologic threshold defines the limiting condition rather than the characteristic conditions. A natural system that quickly develops anaerobic conditions would likely satisfy the hydrologic requirements imposed by other indicators (by inference from hydrophytic vegetation). An extended period of saturation is required for anaerobic conditions to develop in soils that are infrequently saturated, especially if saturation occurs early in the growing season when soil temperatures are low. More scientific information is needed especially for areas where saturation itself, rather than anoxia, is responsible for the presence of hydrophytes.

Direct Methods for Evaluating Hydrology

Direct determination of the wetland boundary can be made by water table measurements along lines or transects of observation wells over 1 or more years, in combination with a hydrologic analysis that considers current and long-term average weather. Measuring the depth to the water table or the height of standing water is relatively easy. Pressure transducers and floats are routinely used to record water levels in wells (Freeze and Cherry, 1979). Although a water level record over a single year, which is sufficient to cover major seasonal hydrologic changes, might suffice, a longer record would be needed for cases that marginally satisfy the hydrologic requirements for duration of saturation and for sites with high interannual variation, especially in semiarid regions of the country.

A second direct method is the use of aerial photographs or spectral information, such as infrared images that document flooding. Spectral data or aerial photographs taken at the right time of year, coupled with measurements of precipitation and duration of flooding, are good indicators of wetland hydrology. Such information, however, documents inundation or saturation at the surface, and not saturation near the surface. Furthermore, it is necessary to have such information at a frequency sufficient to determine the length of the inundation.

One method of interpreting short-term (1-year) hydroperiod records would be to establish wetland reference sites that are subject to the same conditions and variations of climatology as are the sites being evaluated. Water table data could then be compared with data from the reference site; the comparison would show whether the test site is wetter or drier than the reference site. A disadvantage of this approach is that reference wetlands would be needed for many wetland types and for many locations.

Indirect Methods for Evaluating Hydrology

Indirect determinations of flooding or saturation can be made by observation or by calculation. As already explained, the strongest indirect evidence of wetland hydrology, if hydrology has not been altered, would be from hydric soils or hydrophytic vegetation. Other indirect hydrologic indicators include adaptations of vegetation to saturated conditions (multiple and buttressed tree trunks, adventitious roots, shallow root systems, polymorphic leaves, hypertrophied lenticels, inflated leaves and aerenchyma tissue). Unless relationships between the duration of saturation and the degree of plant tissue adaptation have been established for a particular region, however, such adaptations can be used as evidence for wetland hydrology only in support of more definitive indicators of hydrology, such as the presence of hydric soils or hydrophytes.

Other physical evidence of flooding includes silt marks, drift lines, surface scour, and channels. Extended surface flooding also causes fallen leaves to blacken. These phenomena, however, only indicate discrete hydrologic events and not long-term hydrologic conditions. They do not provide information on the duration and timing of inundation, which are the critical hydrologic factors that determine whether a landscape develops wetland characteristics.

Mathematical models also can be effective in evaluating the hydrologic features of a landscape. Models such as DRAINMOD (Skaggs, 1978; Skaggs et al., 1991) and SWATRE (Feddes et al., 1978) can be used to calculate the effects of hydrologic modifications (such as drainage ditches) on water table depth if they are used with long-term data on meteorology. Models also can be used to determine whether short-term measurements of water table and surface water elevations represent "normal" conditions.

Although models are powerful tools, their reliable application depends on specialized training and usually requires considerable data on soil properties and meteorology. Simulation models have been tested for some wetland types, but not for others. For this reason, modeling should not be viewed as a routine alternative to direct measurements. It might be possible, however, to use simulation models to prepare reference hydroperiods that include the effects of current and antecedent meteorological conditions. The recommendations from this section of the chapter are listed as recommendations 1 through 10 at the end of this chapter.

SOILS

Because the presence of hydric soil is the most common and useful general indicator to support the substrate criterion for wetlands, definitions and descriptions of hydric soils are of great practical importance to the identification and delineation of wetlands. Although soils are now used routinely in the diagnosis of wetland conditions, several scientific and technical issues require further study and refinement. Especially important are the conventions for identifying hydric soils under field conditions. It is also important that research continue to illuminate the conditions that lead to formation of hydric soils. Some wetlands may lack hydric soils (or lack soils altogether). Where hydric soils do occur, they are diagnostic of wetlands, unless hydrology has changed since they formed.

Concepts of Soil

Soil scientists define soil as (Soil Survey Staff, 1975)

the collection of natural bodies on the earth's surface . . . of earthy materials, containing living matter and supporting or capable of supporting plants out-of-doors. Its upper limit is air or shallow water. At its margins it grades to deep water or to barren areas of rock or ice.

The distinguishing features of this definition are that a soil is capable of supporting plants and that soil can be covered by "shallow water" but not by "deep water." This definition differs from the one used in geology, for which all unconsolidated materials above bedrock are considered soil (Bates and Jackson, 1987).

Soil scientists distinguish between rock-weathering processes that generate small particles of earthy material (beach sands, mud flats, river and lake bottom sediments, recently deposited alluvium, glacial rock flour), and soil-forming processes by which particles are altered over time through the interactions among climate, relief, parent material, and living organisms (Soil Survey Staff, 1992).

Until very recently, many wetlands were not considered to contain soil at all because of the sharp distinction made by soil scientists between rock weathering and soil formation. Soil-mapping conventions used between 1951 and 1993 (Soil Survey Staff, 1951), labeled many wetlands "miscellaneous land types"—lands that have little or no natural soil. Included in this category were alluvial land, beach, marsh, tidal marsh, fresh water marsh, salt water marsh, playa, swamp, tidal swamp, fresh water swamp, tidal swamp (mangrove), fresh water swamp (cypress), and tidal flat (Soil Survey Staff, 1951, pp. 306-311). Most of the nation's soil surveys were prepared by use of these conventions. Currently, beaches and playas are the only wetland-related features that remain in the miscellaneous land category (Soil Survey Staff, 1993, pp. 41-44). Also, areas that are permanently covered by water so deep that only floating plants are present are still not considered to have a substrate that is soil (Soil Survey Staff, 1993).

According to the Natural Resources Conservation Service (NRCS), "hydric soil" is a type of "technical soil grouping" that was developed "for the application of national legislation concerned with the environment and with agricultural commodity production" (Soil Survey Staff, 1993). Soils with "aquic conditions" experience continuous or periodic saturation and reduction (Soil Survey Staff, 1992). Soils with an "aquic moisture regime" are virtually free of dissolved oxygen due to saturation by ground water or by water of the capillary fringe (Soil Survey Staff, 1992). These and other terms used to describe and classify wet soils are discussed further in this chapter and in Appendix A.

Soil-Forming Processes in Wetlands

Accumulation of Organic Matter

Organic matter, which darkens the color of soil, tends to accumulate in wetlands because of the imbalance between primary production and decomposition (Mausbach and Richardson, 1994). Histosols are soils derived from organic matter, and they occur almost exclusively in wetlands (the exception being Folists, a very uncommon Histosol derived from decomposed leaves). Histic epipedons are surface layers of organic matter that reliably indicate hydric soils in the field, provided that they are correctly distinguished from other types of dark epipedons that are not reliable indicators. For example, soils with mollic epipedons (prairie soils) contain accumulated organic matter, but might or might not occur in wetlands. They are identified as problem soils in the 1989 manual.

Development of Anaerobic Conditions

Saturation of the pore space between soil particles decreases the movement of oxygen into the soil from the atmosphere, but biological activity that requires oxygen in the soil continues after saturation. As a result, soils that are saturated with water for many days typically become anaerobic—their free oxygen disappears and they show a decline in oxidation-reduction (redox) potential (Eh). Soils with an Eh ≤300 mV are generally considered to be anaerobic (reduced), but this threshold varies with soil pH. After soil oxygen becomes depleted, anaerobic microorganisms use other compounds in redox reactions, including manganese, iron, and sulfate. Factors that affect the development of anaerobic conditions include oxygen supply, abundant electron donors, and temperature.

Laboratory studies that are well-mixed soil-and-water slurries and supplemental organic carbon have shown depletion of soil oxygen in as little as 1 day (Turner and Patrick, 1968), but field studies indicate that oxygen depletion typically takes much longer than this in undisturbed wetland soil. Slow decline of oxygen is probably the rule where the organic content of soil is low. Vepraskas and Wilding (1983) show that a Texas coastal plain soil (Segno fine sandy loam: Typic Paleudalf) that was low in organic matter (<1%) was saturated from mid-February to early May before becoming sufficiently anoxic for reduction of iron to occur. Also, Faulkner and Patrick (1992) show that a Kobel soil (Vertic Haplaquept) supporting bottomland hardwood wetland vegetation was anaerobic (Eh ≤ 300 mV) for fewer than 7 days during the growing seasons of 1984 and 1985, even though it was saturated (water table depth ≤1 ft [30 cm] below the soil surface) for 77-78 days during the same 2 years. The water table for the Kobel soil was measured at these intervals and was generally exactly at 11.8 in. (30 cm) or just above. If a water table measurement exceeded the 12.2 in. (31 cm) threshold for two or more consecutive measurements, then the water table was considered to be ≤11.8 in. (30 cm) for all intervening days. It is likely that the water table at this site was below the 11.8 in. (30 cm) depth during the intervening days which allowed that depth to become aerobic. Therefore, the large discrepancy between anaerobic and saturated conditions for the Kobel and Norwood soils are likely artifacts of the methods. In the same study, Tensas (Aeric Ochraqualf) and Norwood soils (Typic Udifluvent) were saturated for 7-14 days without becoming anaerobic. This study (Faulkner and Patrick, 1992) was not, however, designed to determine the minimum time for development of anaerobic conditions. Because measurements were made only twice monthly in the spring, the large discrepancies between anaerobic and saturated conditions may be in part an artifact of the long interval between sampling dates. In the

Willamette River Valley of Oregon, long periods of soil saturation do not always result in anoxic conditions (Austin, 1993).

Daniels and Buol (1992) suggest that there are periods each year when low concentrations of dissolved organic carbon in soil water limit the rate of reduction reactions. Obenhuber and Lowrance (1991) found little evidence of microbial growth when dissolved organic carbon was below 4 mg/L. Daniels et al. (1973) found that some Ultisols are not reduced even when the temperature is above 41°F (5°C) and water is standing at the surface. Reducing conditions did not occur at a depth of about 3 ft (100 cm) in soils of the Willamette Valley, despite saturation for more than 50% of the wet season, because of low amounts of organic matter (Austin, 1993). The influence of organic carbon on soil redox conditions also has been shown in field studies by Ransom and Smeck (1986) and Meek et al. (1968) and in laboratory experiments by Bloomfield (1950; 1951), Ponnamperuma (1972), Gilliam and Gambrell (1978), Reddy et al. (1982), and Farooqi and deMooy (1983). Research on groundwater systems has shown that some microbes use hydrogen in lieu of carbon compounds as electron donors (Smith et al., 1994), but it is not known whether this occurs in wetlands.

Because most wetlands have an abundant supply of organic carbon from vegetation, prolonged saturation typically leads to anaerobiosis (McKeague, 1965; Vepraskas and Wilding, 1983; Ransom and Smeck, 1986; Josselyn et al., 1990; Faulkner and Patrick, 1992; Naiman et al., 1994). This issue requires more study, particularly for wetlands in arid climates where saturated soils commonly have only small amounts of organic carbon. Examples of such wetlands include playas, vernal pools, and parts of riparian zones in the western United States.

Anaerobic conditions develop more slowly in cold soils than they do in warm ones (Updegraff et al., 1995). For example, experiments on the surface layer of a hydric soil (Cape Fear, Typic Umbraquult) under controlled temperatures in the laboratory by Gilliam and Gambrell (1978) showed that 30 days' saturation was required to reach reducing conditions (Eh = 350 mV) at 77°F (25°C) as compared with 60 days at 59°F (15°C). The same soil at 41°F (5°C) did not reach reducing conditions in the 60-day experiment. Similar experiments on an upland soil resulted in reducing conditions after 5 days at 77°F (25°C), at 28 days at 59°F (15°C), and at 58 days at 41°F (5°C). It generally has been assumed that microbial activity and accompanying reduction reactions cease when soil temperatures are below 41°F (5°C) during the period of saturation (Soil Survey Staff, 1975; Pickering and Veneman, 1984), but several studies have demonstrated significant microbial activity at temperatures below 41°F (5°C). Furthermore, horizons with low chroma indicative of iron reduction occur in most mineral permafrost soils in the Canadian soil classification system (7 of 8 subgroups), and in several Alaskan permafrost soils. Therefore, it appears that the use of 41°F (5°C)—biological zero—as the threshold temperature below which anaerobiosis cannot develop is scientifically questionable.

Plants can sometimes affect the development of anaerobic conditions through evapotranspiration. In California, aerobic conditions can occur in the top layer of wetland soils despite high groundwater tables during the spring because soil moisture is removed by evapotranspiration (Josselyn et al., 1990). A similar effect can occur in moist climates (Appendix B, Kirkham Wetlands case study). Some soils retain oxygen when they are saturated because oxygenated water enters the soil continuously.

Redoximorphic Features

Redox reactions involving iron and manganese cause distinctive color variations in mineral soils that are subjected to continuous or recurrent anaerobiosis. Formerly called "gleying" and "mottling," these color variations are now called "redoximorphic features" (Appendix A). Ferric (oxidized) iron compounds generally exhibit high-chroma (bright) yellowish to reddish hues, whereas ferrous (reduced) compounds are green, blue, or have low chroma (they are grey). Periodic saturation of soils causes alternation of reduced and oxidized conditions. During saturation, iron is reduced to the ferrous form, which is soluble and can be translocated in the soil by water movement. During drainage, oxygen enters the soil and the ferrous iron is oxidized back to the ferric form, which precipitates in the soil because of its insolubility. Recurrence of this cycle over many decades concentrates these bright, insoluble ferric compounds. These "redox concentrations" (formerly called mottles) usually persist for decades, even if the conditions under which they formed have changed.

Distinctive color features also can form in similar ways near plant roots in anaerobic soils. If wetland plants are growing in soils where iron compounds have been reduced to the ferrous form, leakage of oxygen from the roots will cause the precipitation near the roots of yellowish-red ferric compounds, or oxidized rhizospheres, that can be distinguished from the surrounding reduced matrix (Appendix A). Oxidized rhizospheres, which mark the aerobic zones surrounding plant roots in saturated soils, are induced by the transport of oxygen through a system of air-filled cells connected by pores (aerenchyma) through which oxygen moves from leaves to roots (Luxmoore et al., 1970; Armstrong, 1971). For example, rice roots can cause marked increases in redox potential at a distance of 0.16 in. (4 mm) in a weakly reducing soil and 0.04 in. (1 mm) in a strongly reducing one (Flessa and Fischer, 1992). Vepraskas and Guertal (1992) showed that the development of oxidized rhizospheres is slow, and calculated that an iron-depletion zone (hypoalban) 0.08 in. (2 mm) wide would develop around an oxidized root channel within 16 years in a horizon saturated for 149 days each year if the surrounding soil originally had a free iron content of 3%.

Hydric Soils List

"Hydric Soils of the United States" (USDA, 1985)—also called the Hydric

Soils List—was first developed for the National Wetlands Inventory under the leadership of W. B. Parker, a soil scientist on assignment from the Soil Conservation Service (SCS, now NRCS) to the National Wetlands Inventory. Work on the list began in 1977. In 1981, NRCS formed an ad hoc committee, the National Technical Committee for Hydric Soils (NTCHS), charged with arriving at a definition for and list of hydric soils (Mausbach, 1992). NTCHS originally consisted of Parker, five other NRCS employees, and two academics. It was later expanded to include representatives from the U.S. Forest Service, the U.S. Fish and Wildlife Service (FWS), USACE, EPA, and the Bureau of Land Management. Members of the original NTCHS had experience predominantly with eastern soils, but the current members have experience with soils of the western states and Alaska as well. In April 1985, NTCHS was formalized by letter from then SCS Deputy Chief for Assessment and Planning Ralph McCracken, and was given a deadline of July 1, 1985, to complete the Hydric Soils List (Mausbach, 1992). The report of the NTCHS was published as a spiral-bound, unnumbered report (USDA, 1985) in October 1985, several months before adoption of the Food Security Act of 1985 and before the publication of any federal wetlands delineation manual. Use of the list was later adopted by reference in the 1987 rules implementing the Food Security Act.

The Hydric Soils List, which is now in its fourth edition (USDA, 1995), defines a hydric soil as "a soil that formed under conditions of saturation, flooding, or ponding long enough during the growing season to develop anaerobic conditions in the upper part," and states that "the following criteria reflect those soils that meet this definition":

1. All Histosols except Folists, or

2. Soils in Aquic suborder, Aquic subgroups, Albolls suborder, Salorthids great groups, Pell great groups of Vertisols, Pachic subgroups, or Cumulic subgroups that are:

   a. somewhat poorly drained and have a frequently occurring water table at less than 0.5 foot (ft) from the surface for a significant period (usually more than 2 weeks) during the growing season, or

   b. poorly drained or very poorly drained and have either:

      (1) a frequently occurring water table at less than 0.5 ft from the surface for a significant period (usually more than 2 weeks) during the growing season if textures are coarse sand, sand, or fine sand in all layers within 20 inches (in), or for other soils

      (2) a frequently occurring water table at less than 1.0 ft from the surface for a significant period (usually more than 2 weeks) during the growing season if permeability is equal to or greater than 6.0 in/h in all layers within 20 in, or

      (3) a frequently occurring water table water at less than 1.5 ft from the surface for a significant period (usually more than 2 weeks)

during the growing season if permeability is less than 6.0 in/h in any layer within 20 inches, or

3. Soils that are frequently ponded for long duration or very long duration during the growing season, or

4. Soils that are frequently flooded for long duration or very long duration during the growing season.

These "criteria" are referred to by number in the Hydric Soils List, which indicates by this means the rationale for including each soil: 1, 2A, 2B1, 2B2, 2B3, 3, or 4.

The hydric soils criteria are notable in several respects. First, all organic soils (Histosols) are defined as hydric (except for Folists, a very uncommon soil type derived from decomposed leaves), regardless of water table depth. Second, any soil that is frequently ponded or flooded during the growing season is defined as hydric, regardless of other soil characteristics or water table depth at other times of the year. Third, all other soils are defined as hydric on the basis of a combination of soil taxonomy and water table depth. Fourth, anaerobic conditions are not mentioned in the criteria, even though they are required by the definition. The criteria, therefore, combine both soil and hydrologic features. For some soils, only soil characteristics are used (e.g., Histosols); for other soils, only hydrologic characteristics are used (e.g., ponded and flooded soils); for still other soils, both are used.

The criteria for hydric soils are used to generate the Hydric Soils List from the NRCS Soil Interpretations Record (SIR) data base, also called the SOI-5 database, which is housed at the Iowa State University Statistical Laboratory. The SIR data base, which already existed when the Hydric Soils List was being developed, currently contains information on more than 25 soil properties for the approximately 18,000 soil series that are recognized in the United States (Lytle, 1993). Included among the soil properties are taxonomy, flooding (frequency, duration, months of year), drainage, water table (depth, kind, months of year), and ponding (depth, kind, months of year), all of which are used in identifying hydric soils. The water table data are categorical and entered in 0.5 ft (15 cm) increments. Thus, when the criteria state that water tables are at less than 0.5, 1.0, or 1.5 ft (15, 30, or 45 cm), the water tables are actually equal to or less than 0.0, 0.5, or 1.0 ft (0, 15, or 30 cm), respectively. That is, the soils on the hydric soils list for criteria 2A and 2B1 have water tables at 0.0 ft (0 cm), for criterion 2B2 at 0.5 ft (15 cm) or less, and for criterion 2B3 at 1.0 ft (30 cm) or less.

The existence of the SIR data base greatly facilitated development of the Hydric Soils List because computer programs could be used to select soils with the specific drainage classes (somewhat poorly drained, poorly drained, very poorly drained) and water table depths specified by criteria 2A, 2B1, 2B2, and 2B3. The primary purpose for developing the criteria, in fact, was to specify characteristics of hydric soils that could be drawn from the SIR data base. Unfortunately, the criteria developed for compatibility with the SIR data base were subsequently used in delineation manuals (1987, 1989, and NFSAM), for which they are less well suited. The most recent version of the Hydric Soils List specifies that "criteria 1, 3, and 4 serve as data base criteria and indicators for identification of hydric soils," whereas criterion 2 serves only to retrieve soils from the data base. Also, because the raw data that substantiate the SIR computer entries are located in the NRCS office of the state in which the soil was first described, the basis for specific computer entries can be difficult to verify.

Soils in the SIR data base that met the 1985 NTCHS requirements for hydric soils were listed in the first edition of the Hydric Soils List (USDA, 1985). In addition to listing hydric soils, this publication listed more than 200 soil series that are poorly or very poorly drained but not considered to be hydric because their water table is too far below the surface or because they flood at times other than the growing season.

The NTCHS definition of hydric soils has been changed three times since 1985. The first definition specified the capability of hydric soils, in an "undrained condition," to support hydrophytes. The definition in the second edition of the Hydric Soils List (USDA, 1987) struck the words "in its undrained condition" from the original definition. The definition in the third edition removed all reference to hydrophytic vegetation, added the phrase "in the upper part" with reference to development of anaerobic conditions, and added a sentence clarifying that the criteria reflect those soils that meet the definition. In the fourth edition, the idea that a soil must have formed under the conditions of saturation, flooding, or ponding was introduced.

The hydric soils criteria also have been changed with each new edition of the list. The 1987 changes in criteria specified minimum duration limits for saturation and ponding. The 1991 changes added soils in Pachic and Cumulic subgroups (Appendix A) and added new criteria for sandy soils in response to requests from the Florida office of NRCS to exclude "flatwood" soils from the list (Hurt and Puckett, 1992; Mausbach, 1992) (Appendix B). This was done by adding a new 2A1 criterion that requires the water table to be within 6 in. (15 cm) of the surface if soil textures are coarse sand, sand, or fine sand throughout the upper 20 in (50 cm). In 1994, criterion 2 was reworded to reflect changes in soil taxonomy (Soil Survey Staff, 1994) and to clarify the way in which water table data were used to select soils from the SIR data base.

Not only the criteria, but the list itself, can change as additional soil series are recognized and defined and as properties of existing soil series are revised on the basis of additional data. Requests for changes must follow specific procedures, as described in each edition (USDA, 1985; 1987; 1991; 1994). The procedures involve submission of data and rationale to NTCHS or the relevant state soil scientist. In a memo insert to the 1991 edition (USDA, 1991) dated Sep. 10, 1993, Soil Survey Division Director Richard W. Arnold states

These changes reflect refinements in knowledge of the soils of the United States. New soil series are recognized as soils are mapped in previously unmapped areas. These new series have always met hydric soil criteria, whether recognized as series or not, and thus represent an insignificant change in acreage of hydric soils. Soils that are removed from the list are mostly dry phases of existing hydric soils. These dry phases would not have met wetland hydrology criteria, thus represent an insignificant change in acreage of wetlands.

The Hydric Soils List gives the names of soil series, but does not include subdivisions of soil series (phases and types), nor does it include soil map units that might contain hydric soil series (a complex of hydric and nonhydric soils). NRCS has developed local lists, based on the Hydric Soils List, of map units that contain hydric soils for each county or parish in the United States. The local lists are available from NRCS state offices and are, according to the NRCS, "the preferred lists for use in making wetland determinations" (USDA, 1991).

Regional panels were not established for soils as they were for hydrophytes, but many NRCS state offices have commented on the Hydric Soils List. The state soil scientist apparently has some latitude for modifying the national criteria to develop a state hydric soils list and for recommending this to the NTCHS committee. For example, Hurt and Puckett (1992) report that Florida developed provisions requiring substantially longer duration of seasonal high water tables than that specified by the national criteria. Recommendations based on research were accepted by the NTCHS, thus reducing Florida's hydric soils list by 58 series (13% of the state) (Chapter 7).

Soil fidelity indicators—analogous to plant fidelity categories—could be used in classifying soils according to their hydrologic affinities. In 1991 NTCHS considered but did not adopt, the following classification (Mausbach, 1992):

Class 1. Obligate wet hydric soils
  - All Histosols
  - All Histic Subgroups
  - All Aquic Suborders that are very poorly drained
  - All Pell Great Groups that are very poorly drained
  - All Hydraquents
  - All Albolls that are very poorly drained
  - All Sulfa Great Groups
  - Sulfi subgroups of Aquic Suborders
Class 2. Facultative wet hydric soils.
  - All Aquic Suborders that are poorly drained
  - All Pell Great Groups that are poorly drained
  - All Salorthids
  - All Albolls that are poorly drained
Class 3. Facultative hydric soils
  - All Aquic Suborders that are somewhat poorly drained
  - All Pell Great Groups that are somewhat poorly drained
  - All Albolls that are somewhat poorly drained

Class 4. Facultative upland hydric soils
- All Aquic subgroups
- All other soils not listed in previous groups

A system of this type, if adopted by NTCHS, would greatly facilitate hydrologic inference from soils.

Use of Hydric Soils in Delineation

Soils that are recurrently or always anaerobic (hydric soils) are typical of wetlands, although some wetlands occur in the absence of anaerobic conditions. Of the wetland definitions discussed in Chapter 3, the only one that requires anaerobic conditions is that of the 1985 Food Security Act. Wetland delineation methods that require the presence of hydric soils as currently defined (USDA, 1991) would implicitly require anaerobic conditions because hydric soils by definition must be anaerobic in the upper part.

Anaerobic soils are a common and sufficient characteristic of wetlands, but not a necessary condition, of wetlands because some lack anaerobic soils. Springs, seeps, vernal pools, rocky beaches, sandy shores, upper intertidal zones, and some riparian systems are defined as wetlands by the National Wetlands Inventory (Cowardin et al., 1979) although they usually do not have hydric soils and they support characteristic wetland organisms. In arid regions or zones of irregular flooding, hydric soils might not develop in all wetlands, especially where water levels fluctuate widely from day to day, month to month, and year to year.

Some studies of soil-vegetation relationships have shown that hydrophytic communities can occur on soils that are not hydric (Veneman and Tiner, 1990; Light et al., 1993). These soils tend to be coarse-textured (loamy to sandy), and most occur on river floodplains subject to seasonal flooding. Hydrologic data collected in two of the studies confirm that these sites have wetland hydrology (Veneman and Tiner, 1990; Light et al., 1993). These examples demonstrate the importance of analyzing hydrology and biota where hydric soils are absent, and of confirming wetlands status hydrologically where hydric soils are absent.

Anaerobic conditions can alter soil properties in ways that reflect the frequency and duration of saturation with water. As early as 1964, Lyford showed that soil mottling could be used to estimate the seasonal maximum height of the water table, provided that there had been no artificial drainage. Since then, several studies have documented the relationships between soil morphology and depth to water table (McKeague, 1965; Latshaw and Thompson, 1968; Daniels et al., 1971; Boersma et al., 1972; Veneman et al., 1976; Vepraskas and Wilding, 1983; Conventry and Williams, 1984; Roman et al., 1985; Evans and Franzmeier, 1986; Watts and Hurt, 1991; Daniels and Buol, 1992; Faulkner and Patrick, 1992; Vepraskas and Guertal, 1992). When color, permeability, and internal drainage are considered together, they show a high correlation with water table regimes (Simonson and Boersma, 1972). Thus, soil characteristics are useful in separating wetlands from uplands.

Because most soil morphology characteristics take decades to develop, they reflect the average conditions of the past. In this respect, soils offer some advantages over plant communities as indicators of wetness. Plants are more subject to anthropogenic disturbance or to ephemeral changes in climate, and they can respond quickly to environmental extremes, especially if the vegetation is dominated by annuals rather than perennial species. If vegetation has been removed or does not give a clear indication of wetland or upland conditions, soils provide the only means for identification and delineation except for direct hydrologic study, which often is impractical. The greater temporal stability of soil morphology is a problem, however, in areas where hydrology has been altered or has changed naturally. An artificially drained muck farm, for instance, might have the same type of soil as an undisturbed fen, even though the muck farm is not a wetland. Likewise, floodplain soil that is no longer flooded because of the construction of river levees would retain its hydric features. This is particularly a problem in the alluvial plain of the lower Mississippi River where levee construction has modified the hydrology of vast areas of former wetland (Appendix B, Steele Bayou case study). In addition, hydrologic alterations might create wetlands where hydric soils have not yet formed. In such cases, hydrology or biota would better indicate wetland status.

Use of Soil Surveys

Soils in the United States have been surveyed and classified in a way that indicates relative wetness. The surveys are usually published for individual counties at scales of 1:15,840 or 1:20,000 and have a minimum map unit size of 2-3 acres (0.08-0.12 ha). Each soil map unit can have up to 25% inclusions of other soils; this percentage can be exceeded if the soils are similar to each other or if the soil-forming factors are very complex. Some soil-mapping units are complexes of intermingled soils. Wetland inclusions that are smaller than the minimum map unit size are sometimes indicated by special symbols.

Soil maps have scale limitations. Although scales of 1:15,840 and 1:20,000 are adequate for most agricultural uses, they do not permit detailed delineation of boundaries or landscape features. The minimum map unit size might be too large for some purposes, or boundary placement might not be sufficiently accurate. Because a line drawn with a standard pen (#1) represents about 25 ft (8 m) on the ground at a scale of 1:20,000, even a correctly placed boundary will not be very precise.

Soil surveys are not complete for the entire United States, and because the surveys for many parts of the country were published decades ago, they are outdated. Old surveys are not necessarily incorrect, but soil nomenclature has changed. Also, some soils have been altered by dredging, filling, impoundment, or drainage changes. Because natural areas are generally mapped in less detail than are agricultural areas, the accuracy of soil maps in areas that were formerly wetlands might be low.

Where they are available, county soil surveys are used in field wetland determinations. These surveys, when combined with the county lists of hydric soils designated by the NTCHS and state soil scientists, provide the delineator with an excellent starting point for a wetland determination. Although soil surveys provide excellent background information for wetland delineation, they are subject to error, and the presence of hydric soils should be verified at the site.

Field Indicators of Hydric Soils

Field observations are essential for accurate identification of hydric soils. Soil color is the field characteristic most commonly used to identify hydric soils because it usually indicates the oxidation state of iron compounds in the soil, which is related to soil wetness. Dark colors in soil also can indicate the presence of organic matter. However, soil colors must be interpreted on the basis of their location within a soil profile. For example, E horizons located just below the surface in many soils often have low chroma due to iron leaching, but they do not indicate the presence of hydric soils, unless accompanied by redoximorphic features. Soils derived from red parent material (weathered clays, Triassic sandstones, Triassic shales) are problematic because the red color can mask any redoximorphic features that might be present. Organic matter accumulation is only one cause of dark colors in soils; some minerals impart a dark color to the soils from which they are derived. The interpretation of soil color thus requires training and experience.

Because NTCHS has focused its attention largely on criteria for hydric soils and on the relationship between taxonomic categories and hydric soils, field indicators of hydric soils have not received as much attention as they probably deserve, given their practical importance. Numerous field indicators in common use by delineators were compiled by NRCS for field testing in February 1994. Synthesis of the field-testing results should be supported by a synthesis of scientific information explaining the basis and significance of various field indicators. In addition, and in context with the current testing of field indicators, NTCHS should consider the development of a classification system for assigning fidelity to hydric soils. A system of this type would facilitate the integration of soils into a tiered system for delineation (see sections on the Primary Indicators method and the Hierarchical Approach) by showing the degree of certainty that could be attached to a particular site-specific assessment of hydric soils. Recommendations for this section are at the end of this chapter numbered 11 through 22.

VEGETATION

The vegetation of wetlands is distinctive primarily because flooding and soil saturation create conditions that most plants cannot tolerate. Nearly 70% of the plant species that occur in the United States and its territories and possessions do not occur in wetlands (Reed, 1988). Saturation of soil with water effectively blocks the entry of oxygen from the atmosphere. Oxygen that enters the soil is readily depleted through plant roots and microbial populations. Lack of oxygen in the root zone is a source of stress for plants that lack special adaptations to bring oxygen to the roots from above or to function without oxygen in the root zone. The absence of oxygen in the root zone is only one of the stresses to which plants are subjected in hydric soils (Ponnamperuma, 1972; Gambrell and Patrick, 1978). After oxygen is consumed in the soil, some microorganisms can use other soil oxidants, such as nitrate and oxidized manganese and iron compounds, to carry on their metabolism. Under some conditions, this anaerobic microbial activity can produce toxic substances that add to the oxygen deficiency stress. Reduction of nitrate produces mainly nitrogen gas, which does not harm plants, but reduced manganese and iron can cause them stress. Also, if large amounts of organic matter are present, anaerobic bacteria can convert sulfate and organic sulfur compounds to hydrogen sulfide and other reduced-sulfur compounds that are especially toxic to plants. Organic acids and other reduced-organic compounds that are produced as a result of anaerobic microbial activity also can be toxic. Plants that grow in anaerobic soils must have special adaptations that allow absorption of nutrients and water without absorption of toxins (Crawford, 1983; Jackson and Drew, 1984).

The greater the reduction intensity of the soil, as measured by the redox potential, the more severe the stress on plants. Stress ranges from moderate, if created only by the absence of oxygen, to more severe, if created by the absence of oxygen and the presence of various toxic substances. Numerous plant species can grow if the only stress is the absence of oxygen; fewer species can tolerate multiple stresses.

Anoxia is not the only factor that can produce distinctive wetland vegetation. Plants that have exceptionally high requirements for water can be restricted to wetlands. For example, some plants require extended saturation for germination or vigorous growth (Sculthorpe, 1967). Plants on floodplains must be able to withstand the mechanical stress of moving water.

The scientific basis for using vegetation to identify and delineate wetlands is the strong relationship between continuous or frequently recurrent or sustained soil saturation and the development of communities dominated by plants specifically adapted for or requiring such conditions. These plants are called *hydrophytes*, and the plant communities are described as being dominated by *hydrophytic vegetation*. Communities composed of these plant species have been used for decades to identify wetlands (Hall and Penfound, 1939; Penfound, 1952; Martin et al., 1953; Dix and Smeins, 1967).

Hydrophyte List

All federal manuals use a national list of hydrophytes in their identification and delineation procedures. The U.S. Fish and Wildlife Service (FWS) began to develop the list in the mid-1970s as a basis for implementing its definition of wetlands (Chapter 3). Although the list was not published until the 1980s, its creation began a decade before the first delineation manual was devised. The "National List of Plant Species that Occur in Wetlands" (Reed, 1988, hereinafter the Hydrophyte List) serves as the basis for deciding which species should be designated as hydrophytes when vegetation is being classified for the identification or delineation of wetlands. To evaluate the Hydrophyte List and its current use in vegetation three elements must be considered: the definition of hydrophytes as used in the development of the list, procedures by which the Hydrophyte List and associated indicators of fidelity were developed, and the concept of ecotype as it applies to the list.

Definition of Hydrophyte

The current definition of hydrophyte derives from the early scientific literature in botany and plant ecology (Sculthorpe, 1967; Tiner, 1991a). Europeans used the term by the late 1800s and it was in common scientific usage by the early part of this century. Some early plant ecologists used the term only for plants that grow in water (Sculthorpe, 1967; Tiner, 1991a) or with their perennating organs submerged in water (Sculthorpe, 1967; Tiner, 1991a). Clements (1920; Weaver and Clements, 1938) and other American plant ecologists, however, proposed a broader definition that included plants growing either in water or in saturated soil (Sculthorpe, 1967). Weaver and Clements (1938, p. 424) explicitly included plants, of swamps, and wet meadows as hydrophytes. Hess and Hall (1945), followed by Penfound (1952), developed classification schemes in which they recognized terrestrial, aquatic, and wetland plants, and grouped the latter two types as hydrophytes (Sculthorpe, 1967). According to this convention, terrestrial species tolerate neither flooding nor soil saturation during the growing season, aquatic species tolerate flooding but not dewatering, wetland species tolerate both (Boulé, 1994). While acknowledging the difficulty of drawing sharp distinctions between some hydrophytes and plants of moist soils, Schulthorpe (1967) adopted the broader definition of hydrophyte used by American botanists.

All federal wetland manuals use the same general definition. According to Tiner (1991a), the manuals follow the usage of Daubenmire (1968) as given in his textbook on plant communities:

[H]ydrophytes are plants capable of growth in substrates that are at least period-ically deficient in oxygen as a result of high water content.

Hydrophytes can possess several adaptations that permit them to survive in saturated environments: physiologic adaptations, such as the capacity for anaero-bic respiration; anatomic and morphologic adaptations, including formation of aerenchyma (tissue with large spaces), adventitious roots (roots growing from unusual places), shallow root systems, hypertrophied lenticels (large internal pores), and pneumatophores (protruding roots); and life history adaptations, such as germination and seedling survival in saturated or flooded soil, dispersal in and by water, vegetative growth and regeneration from rhizomes or other organs that can survive submergence or soil saturation (Sculthorpe, 1967; Gambrell and Patrick, 1978; Keeley, 1979; van der Valk, 1981; Kozlowski, 1984; Crawford, 1987; Crawford, 1989; Ernst, 1990; Jackson, 1990). Many wetland plants pos-sess adaptations that allow them to survive in areas that are alternately wet and dry (Crawford, 1987). For example, the tussock sedge (*Carex stricta*) has a shallow root at the top of the tussock that functions when the base of the tussock is flooded as well as a deep root that passes through the tussock into the ground where water is present when there is none at the surface (Costello, 1936). The distributions of such plants are strongly correlated with continuous or recurrent sustained flooding or saturation of the soil surface.

Development of the Hydrophyte List

The Hydrophyte List was first drafted in 1976 by P.B. Reed of the National Wetlands Inventory, who remains its custodian (Reed, 1988). The definition of plant species that occur in wetlands as used in compiling the list is virtually synonymous with that of hydrophytes (from Reed, 1988):

[S]pecies that have demonstrated an ability (presumably because of morpholog-ical and/or physiological adaptations and/or reproductive strategies) to achieve maturity and reproduce in an environment where all or portions of the soil within the root zone become, periodically or continuously, saturated or inundat-ed during the growing season.

In 1982, after a search of almost 300 regional and state floras and regional wetland manuals and additions from the Fairchild Tropical Garden in Miami, the Hydrophyte List consisted of 5,244 species. It was divided into 13 regional lists (Chapter 7) corresponding to the geographic regions that were developed for the "National List of Scientific Plant Names" (USDA, 1982). This list of plant names, which was developed by the NRCS through a contract with the Smithsonian Institution, provided a standard nomenclature, a list of acronyms, and a range of distribution for each species.

Interagency review panels for the Hydrophyte List and regional lists (herein-after the national and regional panels) were established in 1983-1984. They consist of one representative each from the FWS, USACE, EPA, and NRCS. These representatives usually have been staff ecologists with a strong background in botany. The regional panels identified other potential reviewers, principally field botanists and ecologists associated with state and federal agencies and universities, who were sent the September 1982 version of the list and were asked to assign a wetland indicator status to as many species as possible. A total of 142 scientists (from 10 to 30 per region) responded.

FWS had created the wetland fidelity rating system on which indicator status is based in the 1970s during the development of its Annotated National Wetland Plant Species Data Base. In synthesizing information from hundreds of botanical sources on the habitats of the species, FWS staff observed that species could be separated into species that are excluded from wetlands (upland species, UPL), those that are restricted to wetlands (obligate species, OBL), and those that can occur in wetlands but that are not restricted to wetlands (facultative species). The facultative group was further subdivided into three categories corresponding to gradations of percentage occurrence in wetland (facultative wet, FACW; facultative, FAC; facultative upland, FACU) (Reed, 1988).

After examining the responses from the external reviewers, the regional panels assigned a regional indicator of habitat fidelity (OBL, FACW, FAC, FACU, UPL) to each species for which they had unanimous agreement. As a means of achieving interagency agreement, most of the regional panels adopted plus (+, more toward upland) and minus (−, more toward wetland) symbols for each of the three facultative categories. If a species does not occur in wetlands in any region, it is not on the Hydrophyte List. A species is given an NI (no indicator) if there is insufficient information to assign it to a category. Seven percent, or 483 species on the Hydrophyte List, are designated NI. An asterisk (*) after a designation indicates limited ecological information; 729 regional designations carry an asterisk. A question mark (?) denotes a tentative designation. NA (no agreement) was applied to the 28 species for which the regional panels could not reach consensus.

Each of the 6,728 plant species currently on the Hydrophyte List has a separate indicator for each region in which it occurs. The indicator assignment can vary from region to region because of ecotypic variation within species. Each species also has a national indicator status bracketing the range of regional indicators assigned to the species (such as FAC-FACW).

The lists are published in three formats: the Hydrophyte List, which contains the national indicator status and all regional indicator status assignments; regional lists; and state lists. The state and regional lists use the same indicator assignments. The Hydrophyte List and the regional lists are published in the FWS Biological Report series; publication of state lists is more informal. Although published versions of the Hydrophyte List and regional lists have not been revised since 1988, continuous feedback is solicited via the "Review Sheet for

Plant Species that Occur in Wetlands," which is used in revising the working versions of the lists. The national panel meets every 1-3 years to discuss changes.

The Hydrophyte List does not include mosses, although efforts are under way to include them (Reed, 1988). Mosses could dominate the herbaceous stratum in some areas and indicate either long-term or short-term hydrology, depending on the characteristics of the community. Their presence may indicate frequent saturation of the substrate. In fact, the ground layer of many wetlands with a peat substrate is dominated by mosses (Crum, 1988). *Sphagnum* mosses are almost entirely restricted to peatlands (bogs and fens) and many of the so-called brown mosses (such as *Cratoneuron filicinum, Calliergon giganteum, Campylium stellatum, Scorpidium scorpioides*) occur only in mineral-rich peatlands (fens) (personal communication, Aug. 1994, N. Slack, Russell Sage College).

The Hydrophyte List has often been used to assess vegetation in field studies that also include documentation of soils and hydrologic regime. The indications of the plant communities as derived from the Hydrophyte List have typically been consistent with information on soils and hydrology (Josselyn et al., 1990; Segelquist et al., 1990; Light et al., 1993). Many of the studies have led to questions about the regional assignment of particular species (Chapter 7). The species in question, however, have been few relative to the large number of species included in the studies.

Facultative Species and the Concept of Wetland Ecotypes

Species designated FAC and FACU pose particular problems in wetland identification and delineation because they are less restricted to wetland conditions than are OBL or FACW species. They are, therefore, less reliable indicators of a wetland. The wide distribution of FAC or FACU species is at least partly explained by the existence of ecotypes within the species. Ecotypes are distinct populations of plants within a species that have adapted genetically to specific conditions. They might be thought of as populations that are in the process of evolving to form separate species. For example, one ecotype of a particular plant species might be able to tolerate recurrent flooding or soil saturation, whereas another ecotype of the same species cannot. Numerous examples have been documented in the scientific literature, particularly for species that are widely distributed (Curtis, 1959; Ledig and Little, 1979; Huenneke, 1982; Crum, 1988; Abrams and Kubiske, 1990; Davy et al., 1990). Ecotypes of FACU species are particularly problematic. About 21% of the species on the Hydrophyte List are FACU species. As a category, FACU species are found most often in uplands, but wetland ecotypes of some FACU species might be essentially restricted to wetlands. The FACU species include a diverse collection of plants that range from weedy species adapted to exist in a number of environmentally stressful or disturbed sites (including wetlands) to species for which a portion of the gene pool (an ecotype) always occurs in wetlands. Both the weedy and ecotype representatives of the FACU category occur in seasonally and semipermanently flooded wetlands. The scientific literature is replete with examples of wetlands dominated by FAC and FACU species. These include red maple swamps (FAC) (Golet et al., 1993), hemlock swamps (FAC) (Niering, 1953; Huenneke, 1982), and southern swamps dominated by *Liquidambar styraciflua* (sweetgum) (FAC) and *Nyssa sylvatica* var biflora (black gum) (FAC) (Keeley, 1979). Tiner (1991a) lists 16 species of evergreen FACU species that have been documented in the literature as common or dominant plants in wetlands. An additional nine species of hardwood and herbaceous FACU species that are known to be common or dominant in wetlands of the Northeast are listed as well. Many of these species probably have ecotypes specifically adapted to wetlands. Although not well documented, ecotypes of FACW species might be well adapted to upland conditions and could even be restricted to upland habitats. Thus, species with FAC and FACU designations cannot be interpreted necessarily as indicating drier conditions than OBL or FACW species. For FAC and FACU species, the indicators of fidelity might not reflect the true strength of correlation with wetland conditions.

Some ecotypes of wetland species could be sufficiently distinct in their morphology or physiology to be given subspecific names and to be recognized in the field. Tiner (1991a) gives examples of seven species with recognized varieties that occur in different habitats and with different wetland indicator status. Because most wetland ecotypes cannot be distinguished easily from the overall population, however, FAC and FACU species will continue to pose problems in delineation.

Determining Predominance of Hydrophytic Vegetation

Many techniques have been used in characterizing plant communities (Mueller-Dombois and Ellenberg, 1974; Greig-Smith, 1983), and many of these have been evaluated for use in designating wetlands and defining their boundaries. A technique that works well for one wetland type or in one region might not work as well for another type or region. All techniques require knowledge of plant ecology, experience, good judgment, and knowledge of the vegetation of a region (Johnson et al., 1982a; Fletcher, 1983). Two approaches have been used in delineation manuals for assessing the predominance of hydrophytic vegetation: a measure of dominance, and a prevalence index. The two approaches, which are now used in field evaluations, are generally sound, although other techniques could also be used.

Measure of Dominance: The 50% Rule

Plant ecologists often describe vegetation in terms of its species composition (species list), and the relative abundances of species. Abundance can be quantified in terms of density (number of individuals in a given area), frequency (proportion of sampling units in which a species occurs), percentage cover (fraction of the sampling area covered by vertical projection of the plant onto the ground), or biomass (dry weight of all plants of a given species within the sampling unit). Typically, one or a few species will be quite abundant, several species will be moderately abundant, and most species will be rarer (Whittaker, 1978). The most abundant species are called the dominant species (Greig-Smith, 1983).

The 50% rule is one way of applying dominance measures to the classification of plant communities. Broadly speaking, the 50% rule requires that the most abundant species be used to determine whether the vegetation as a whole is predominantly (more than 50%) hydrophytic. Species of low abundance are ignored in the calculation of predominance. The underlying assumption is that the dominant species in a community reflect the hydrologic regime of a site over years or decades. In general, this assumption is sound. Over time, the environment favors species that are adapted to the physical characteristics of a site, including its hydrology. Species that cannot germinate, establish, grow, compete, and reproduce under the long-term hydrologic conditions will not attain dominance. Thus, the dominant taxa most reliably reflect the hydrologic regime, and can be used in distinguishing wetlands from uplands.

Application of the 50% rule requires knowledge of plant ecology and the exercise of sound judgment backed by experience. The choice of the measure of abundance (density, frequency, percentage cover, or biomass) will influence the results and should be appropriate to the growth habit of the plants (whether the plants are trees, bushes, or low groundcover) and the size of the sampling unit (Greig-Smith, 1983). In general, frequency data are not considered a good basis for estimating dominance because many small plants can influence the results excessively (Greig-Smith, 1983). All layers (strata) of the vegetation should be considered (V. Carter et al., 1988), but absolute abundance rather than rank abundance should be the basis for selection of dominant species. Species highly ranked in a given layer should not be included if their absolute abundances are significantly lower than the abundance of one or more species of lower rank in another layer. The purpose of considering all layers is to characterize the community as a whole. Under current methodologies, however, a species that is found in more than one layer can be dominant in each layer and will be counted as a dominant species more than once. If this species is maintained by some factor other than hydrology, the results can be misleading.

The effect of emphasizing dominant species and excluding rare species from vegetation analysis must be assessed in relation to the maintenance of biodiversity. For example, reliance on dominant species, which in some cases could be upland weeds temporarily invading a wetland, can lead to the misclassification of wetlands.

Another potential disadvantage of focusing on the dominant species is that other species in some cases will be better indicators of hydrologic regime. This problem is most likely to occur when the vegetation is marginally hydrophytic.

For example, it is possible under the 50% rule as formulated in the 1987 and 1989 manuals for a site to demonstrate that wetland vegetation is present if 51% of its dominant plant species are FAC. Strictly speaking, the remaining 49% of the vegetation, which could be UPL, need not be considered. Abundance of UPL species in association with FAC species, however, would indicate that the site is not wetland. Conversely, the vegetation of a FAC-dominated site where OBL or FACW species are distributed throughout the site, but constitute only 20% of the individuals, is strongly indicative of wetland.

Prevalence Index

In the early 1980s, FWS commissioned a study of procedures that could be used for designating wetlands based on the relative importance of hydrophytes (Wentworth and Johnson, 1986; Wentworth et al., 1988). The study led to development of a prevalence index for wetland delineation.

The prevalence index uses a single number, the index value, to summarize quantitative data on a large number of species in a community and weight the contribution of each species to the final number by use of an indicator value that reflects wetland affinity. In the plant ecology literature, this method, which was developed in the 1940s (Gauch, 1982), is called the method of weighted averages. It is a simple gradient analysis (Whittaker, 1978) that uses empirical data on the position of species along an environmental gradient, such as a moisture gradient (Gauch, 1982). Species are first assigned to categories. All species in a category then are given the same value of an index, which is based on the group's relative position on the environmental gradient, as determined by field observation (Wentworth et al., 1988). The final index for the community is the weighted average value—the sum of the products for all index values multiplied by some measure of abundance (frequency, percentage cover, biomass) for the species, divided by the sum of all abundance values for all species (Gauch, 1982; Wentworth et al., 1988).

Wentworth and Johnson (1986; Wentworth et al., 1988) developed the prevalence index for wetland delineation by applying the method of weighted averages with index values (OBL = 1, FACW = 2, FAC = 3, FACU = 4, UPL = 5) based on hydrophyte indicator status as defined by the Hydrophyte List (Reed, 1986). Dix and Smeins (1967) already had used the method to arrange plant communities along a moisture gradient from marsh to high prairie in Nelson County, South Dakota, and two other studies contracted by USACE in the early 1980s (Fletcher, 1983) evaluated methods closely related to the method of weighted averages. The USACE studies show that the method is limited primarily by the difficulty of assigning species to categories. Fletcher (1983) recommended a better basis for defining the groups. The development of the Hydrophyte List (Reed, 1986; 1988) later provided that basis.

Wentworth and Johnson (1986) also conducted statistical analyses of the method and evaluated several variants of weighted averaging. They found that weighted averaging by use of the Hydrophyte List is as accurate as any other method in separating upland from wetland species, and that removal of facultative species from calculations does not alter the results substantially. They demonstrated the strength of weighted averaging by comparing it with other methods of ranking, including use of personal experience, multivariate analysis, and the use of environmental data. Analysis of communities on the basis of presence and absence of species rather than relative abundance would not require the collection of quantitative data and thus would require less time to perform than computation of a prevalence index. Analysis on the basis of presence and absence would require inclusion of all species, however, whereas weighted averaging is relatively insensitive to the omission of rare species. Weighted averaging, as used in computation of the prevalence index, requires less skill for valid application than do other methods that are sensitive to the presence of rare species. When based on weighted averages, the prevalence index (PI) appears to be a sound method for separating wetland from nonwetland plant communities. Even without the inclusion of rare species, however, it does require considerably greater skill in plant identification and more time to use than estimation of dominance by the 50% rule. Its use should not be required except for controversial cases or where results based on dominant species alone are marginal. Studies that compare the use of the prevalence index and the 50% rule on the same sites are needed for a range of wetland types.

Evaluation of Thresholds

The thresholds used by the federal manuals for separating wetlands from other ecosystems on the basis of hydrophytic vegetation are 50% for the dominance measure and 3.0 for the prevalence index. These thresholds are not inherent in the methods themselves; they could be changed. In fact, several studies show that an index of 3.0 cannot be viewed as an unequivocal divide between hydrophytic and nonhydrophytic vegetation (Wentworth and Johnson, 1986; Carter et al., 1988; Wentworth et al., 1988; Scott et al., 1989; Josselyn et al., 1990; Segelquist et al., 1990). Exceptions occur on both sides of the threshold. For this reason, Wentworth and Johnson (1986) recommend that wetland designations not be made on the basis of vegetation alone for sites with indexes between 2.0 and 4.0 (Figure 5.7). For sites between 2.5 and 3.5, additional data on soils and hydrology should be mandatory; additional data on soils and hydrology are desirable for sites with 2.0-2.5 and 3.5-4.0.

Golet et al. (1993) have provided the only published data that allow direct evaluation of the 50% rule. Their data are primarily applicable to sites dominated by facultative species, as their sampling sites were. They found that the combined relative percentage cover of OBL, FACW, and FAC species exceeded 50% for both the shrub and herb layer across a moisture gradient between red maple

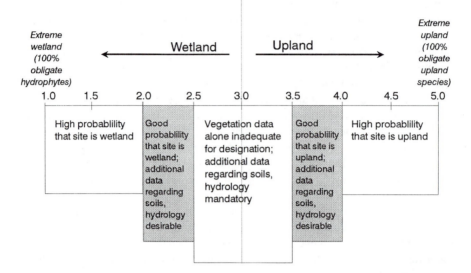

FIGURE 5.7 Recommended application of weighted and index averages for wetland identification. Varying degrees of confidence should be assigned to wetland or upland designation based on weighted or index average scores; scores that are farther from the theoretical wetland-upland boundary of 3.0 are considered to be better indicators of wetland or upland status (adapted from Wentworth and Johnson, 1986).

swamps and adjacent upland forests; the zone of 50% dominance of these three groups extended beyond the margin of hydric soils and beyond the likely hydrologic threshold for wetlands. Elimination of FAC species from the index, however, also caused errors of interpretation. Although the very poorly drained (hydric) soils had relative cover exceeding 50% for OBL plus FACW species, the communities of poorly drained soils failed to exceed the 50% threshold even though the soils, which were hydric, indicated wetland. This study shows that, for FAC-dominated sites, a vegetation index including OBL, FACW, and FAC species in the dominance measure will misidentify some upland sites as wetland but that exclusion of FAC species will misidentify some wetlands as uplands. Thus, multiple indicators are essential for such sites.

Further critical evaluation of the use of the 50% threshold is hampered by lack of other published data. Even so, it is clear that the limitations pertaining to the use of weighted averages also apply to dominance measures. That is, values near 50% for dominance or 3.0 for prevalence are subject to considerable uncertainty.

Visible Adaptations as Indicators of Hydrophytic Vegetation

The 50% rule and the prevalence index characterize the plant community as a whole through its species composition. As an alternative or supplement to the assessment of species composition, the visible adaptations of plants on a site have been used collectively as an indicator of wetland conditions. Although many adaptations to wetland conditions are not evident in the field, several adaptations in morphology and anatomy are easily observed, including pneumatophores, prop roots, hypertrophied lenticels, and buttressing. The development of these features has seldom been studied in relation to specific periods or frequencies of inundation or saturation, but they typically are seen where flooding or soil saturation is very frequent or of very long duration. Thus, if they are well developed and observed on many plants within an area, these adaptations provide strong evidence that the vegetation is hydrophytic.

Because many adaptations are internal, adaptations of wetland plants are not always observable in the field. Thus, whereas visible adaptations should be seen as indicative of wetland conditions where hydrology has not been modified, their absence does not necessarily indicate upland conditions. Guidance should be developed about the minimum abundance of plants with visible adaptations, as well as the degree of development of these adaptations, that would indicate wetland conditions. The use of these adaptations could speed the delineation process on some sites.

Treatment of Facultative Species

Three questions are relevant to the treatment of facultative species in identification and delineation of wetlands: Are some wetlands dominated by FAC or FACU species? If FAC and FACU species were excluded from a vegetation analysis, would the results be the same? How should the transition zones between wetlands and uplands, which typically contain species from a mixture of indicator categories, be treated?

Numerous wetlands are dominated by FAC or FACU species, either on a long-term basis or as part of natural changes associated with climatic cycles (Niering, 1953; Curtis, 1959; Weller and Spatcher, 1965; van der Valk and Davis, 1978; Ledig and Little, 1979; Huenneke, 1982; Sharitz and Gibbons, 1982; Schalles and Shure, 1989; Golet et al., 1993; Carter et al., 1994). Examples include wetlands that are inundated or saturated frequently or for extended periods of time: red maple (FAC) swamps (Golet et al., 1993), white pine (FACU) on deep peats (Curtis, 1959), and hemlock (FACU) on peat soils in New York (Huenneke, 1982).

Dominance by FAC or FACU species is sometimes caused by the presence of ecotypes of plant species that typically occur on uplands, as explained in the discussion of ecotypes. For example, Golet et al. (1993) found that one FAC species (red maple) was more abundant on the wettest sites (wetland ecotype) than on less wet sites, but the species also occurred in adjacent upland forests (upland ecotype). Dominance by FAC and FACU species also can be explained by climatic cycles, especially where the vegetation is not long lived. Some sites are dominated by OBL wetland species in wet years but not in dry years (Appendix B, prairie pothole case study). During dry years, the seed banks of these sites contain evidence of previous dominance by OBL and FACW species.

Computation of dominance or prevalence after removing FAC species (the "FAC-neutral test") is one way to deal with the ambiguities of facultative species. Few studies have been published, however, on the effect of the FAC-neutral test on vegetation assessments in FAC-dominated wetlands or uplands. As already mentioned, Golet et al. (1993) found that exclusion of FAC species did not clarify their analyses of red maple swamps and adjacent upland forests. Wentworth and Johnson (1986) found that exclusion of FAC species from their calculations had little effect on index averages based on abundance measures, and Carter et al. (1994) found that the FAC-neutral test based on species numbers erroneously showed all increments from wetland to upland to be wetland. It appears that a FAC-neutral test does not resolve the ambiguities in analyses of communities that contain FAC species. The FAC-neutral test should not be required for delineation until additional studies that compare vegetation analyses with and without FAC species have been conducted for a range of wetland types.

The wetland-upland transition zone, where facultative species might be expected to dominate, has been studied in several locations (Anderson et al., 1980; Johnson et al., 1982b; Fletcher, 1983; Roman et al., 1985; Carter et al., 1988; Allen et al., 1989; Carter et al., 1994). Of these reports, only two (Allen et al., 1989; Carter et al., 1994) give information on hydrology and soils as well as on vegetation. Johnson et al. (1982b) conclude that the vegetation of transition zones in the Upper Missouri River Basin and northern Florida generally had stronger affinities with wetland vegetation than with upland vegetation. Johnson et al. (1982b) attribute this to disturbance caused by wetland processes such as siltation during drawdown, ice scouring, and the variable hydrologic regime. The transition zones are typically rich in opportunistic species, many of which are herbaceous annuals classified as FAC or FACU.

Generally, studies of transition zones have shown that plant community composition shows no sharp discontinuities within the zone; that information on factors other than vegetation is needed to define a boundary within the zone; and that even with other information, the wetland boundary is, in ecological terms, more correctly represented as a band than as a line. These generalizations probably apply whether or not FAC species are considered. For example, Allen et al. (1989) found in red maple swamps that by use of the herb layer, which contained the largest proportion of non-FAC species, boundary zones were anywhere from 16 ft (5 m) to 150 ft (46 m) wide. Roman et al. (1985) separate upland from wetland and transitional zones, but they made no further separation on the basis of vegetation alone. Carter et al. (1988; 1994) could not locate a line, but they did locate a boundary zone.

Because facultative vegetation does not provide conclusive evidence, determinations regarding the hydrophytic nature of the vegetation must be based on information about substrate or hydrology. In the absence of hydrologic alteration and evidence to the contrary, it should be assumed that vegetation dominated by facultative species—or by species from a mix of indicator categories—and growing on field-verified soils that show strong evidence of being hydric (peat soils, or soils with strong redoximorphic features) is hydrophytic vegetation. Evidence from hydric soils is strong only if histosols or soils with non-relict redoximorphic features are strongly evident. If evidence from soils is not strong, hydrologic data should be required for determinations. Regional knowledge of FAC and FACU-dominated wetlands could provide the basis for setting criteria in specific regions (Chapter 7).

Vegetation and Hydrology

Scientific understanding of the relationship between vegetation and hydrologic regime is based on studies of the responses of individual plants to flooding and soil saturation (Meek and Stolzy, 1978; Jackson and Drew, 1984; Kozlowski, 1984; Crawford, 1987; Drew, 1988); and on the responses of plant communities to flooding and soil saturation (Hall and Penfound, 1939; Harris and Marshall, 1963; van der Valk and Bliss, 1971; Steward and Kantrud, 1972; Millar, 1973; Bedinger, 1979; Menges and Waller, 1983; Metzler and Damman, 1985; Paratley and Fahey, 1986; Damman and French, 1987; Golet et al., 1993; Carter et al., 1994). Several studies have shown that the absence of UPL plants corresponds to frequent or extended flooding or saturation (Jackson and Drew, 1984; Drew, 1988). However, because UPL species can become established during dry years or at any time on microsites that are elevated above the general wetland surface (Appendix B, Kirkham wetlands case study), some UPL species can be found in wetlands; the presence of some UPL species must be weighed against the abundance of OBL and FACW species. Dominance by UPL species provides conclusive evidence of infrequent flooding or saturation (upland); dominance by OBL or FACW species is strongly indicative of very frequent or extended periods of flooding or saturation (wetland). If the FACU and UPL species are dominant and OBL or FACW species are absent or of very low abundance, the vegetation strongly indicates that the area is not saturated frequently or for long durations. Conversely, dominance by OBL, FACW, or FAC species, if UPL species are absent or of very low abundance, is strong evidence that an area is saturated very frequently or for very long periods of time. The four studies used by Wentworth et al. (1988) to develop weighted averages for wetland designation support these conclusions, as do several of the studies reported in Scott et al. (1989) and Segelquist et al. (1990). An extensive analysis of regional studies would be required to refine further the relationships of species composition to specific hydrologic conditions (Chapter 7).

Vegetation and Soil Type

FWS commissioned several studies beginning in the mid-1980s that were intended to assemble data on the relationship between wetland plants and hydric soils; to test various delineation procedures based on plants against independent indicators of wetland character, including primarily hydric soils; and test the correlation of vegetation and soils with hydrology (Table 5.1). The results of the studies were published as FWS biological reports, and they are summarized by Scott et al. (1989).

The FWS studies and two studies based on similar methods (Carter et al., 1988; Josselyn et al., 1990) support several conclusions: Hydric soils and hydrophytic vegetation are closely related over a wide geographic range (Table 5.2). Correlations between hydrophytic vegetation and hydric soils are much stronger than are correlations between nonhydrophytic vegetation and nonhydric soils (Table 5.2), probably because the nonhydric soils studied were in wetland-upland transition zones rather than in more distinctly well-drained zones. Typically, transition zones show mixed indications for both vegetation and soils. Poor correspondence of soils and vegetation frequently can be related to misidentification of hydric soils, to disturbance leading to the presence of weedy or opportunistic species, or to the presence of species for which regional indicator status in the Hydrophyte List (Reed, 1988) is in error for the region of the study. There is a strong correlation between hydrophytic vegetation and hydric soils

TABLE 5.1 Soil-Vegetation Correlation Reports Commissioned by FWS

Wetland type	Reference
Rhode Island red maple swamps	Allen et al., 1989
Riparian zone of Butte Sink in the Sacramento Valley, California	Baad, 1988
Selected wetlands and uplands of northcentral Florida	Best et al., 1990
Pocosins of Croatan National Forest	Christensen et al., 1988
Riparian zones of the Gila and San Francisco Rivers, California	Dick-Peddie et al., 1987
San Francisco Bay Estuary, California	Eicher, 1988
Sandhills and Rainwater Basin wetlands of Nebraska	Erickson and Leslie, 1987
Coastal Mississippi wetlands	Erickson and Leslie, 1988
Prairie potholes of Beadle and Dauel Counties, South Dakota	Hubbard et al., 1988
Riparian and emergent wetlands, Lyons County, Nevada	Nachlinger, 1988
Connecticut River Floodplain, western Massachusetts	Veneman and Tiner, 1990
Arctic Foothills, Alaska	Walker et al., 1989

TABLE 5.2 Percentage Correspondence Between Hydric Soils and Hydrophytic Vegetation and Between Nonhydric Soils and Nonhydric Vegetation, by Vegetation Layer, for Soils Sampled Throughout the United States (From Segelquist et al., 1990)

| | Percentage Agreement | | | | |
Soil and Vegetation Associations	Herbaceous	Short Shrubs	Tall Shrubs	Trees	All Layers Combined
Hydric soils with hydrophytic vegetation	89	100	100	90	100
Nonhydric soils with nonhydric vegetation	85	50	53	50	58
Total	86	86	79	78	86

when the prevalence index is well below 3.0, or when OBL, FACW, and FAC species show 50% or more dominance; for index values near 3.0, the correlations are much weaker.

Use of Vegetation to Set Boundaries

Where vegetation is predominantly OBL, FACW, and FAC, and the topographic transition from wetland to upland is abrupt, boundaries will be obvious on the basis of vegetation alone. Where the topographic gradient is gradual, however, vegetation is likely to change gradually and boundaries will be obscure. Unfortunately, only a few studies provide data on vegetation, hydrology, and soils (Anderson et al., 1980; Allen et al., 1989; Veneman and Tiner, 1990; Golet et al., 1993; Light et al., 1993; Carter et al., 1994). Only the studies by Carter et al. (1988; 1994) include data across the wetland-upland transition; the others deal with relatively homogeneous stands of vegetation.

Three points seem to be well supported by the present information. First, within homogeneous stands, the data on vegetation, soils, and hydrology generally agree, but in transition zones between wetlands and uplands, information on vegetation might not correspond with information on hydrology and soils. Second, where information on vegetation, soils, and hydrology gives mixed indications, data on vegetation can indicate conditions either wetter or drier than shown by data on soils or hydrology. For example, Light et al. (1993) found in one instance that hydrologic data contradicted information on vegetation and soils. Carter et al. (1994) found that for one transect, vegetation data placed a boundary lower than that provided by use of data on either soils or hydrology; for another transect the reverse was true. Third, in FAC-dominated sites, information on soils is essential. For example, Golet et al. (1993) observed no distinct change in any of the vegetation layers over a transition from hydric to nonhydric soils on a FAC-dominated site.

Short-term variations in the composition of vegetation within the wetland transition zone can obscure the true boundary. Annuals respond most quickly and trees take the longest to respond to changes in prevailing hydrologic regime. Where several layers of vegetation are present, use of all layers can help to identify the boundary (Carter et al., 1994).

Knowledge of regional, interannual variation in vegetation within wetland transition zones is important (Chapter 7), but some general guidelines can be derived from existing studies. In the absence of hydrologic modification and where there is no evidence to the contrary, boundaries can be set on the basis of field-verified hydric soils and vegetation dominated by OBL and FACW combined with FAC and FACU species in the absence of UPL species. Dominance by UPL, FACU, and FAC species would provide strong evidence that the vegetation is not hydrophytic. In these cases, other evidence that the biological criterion is satisfied would be required, or long-term hydrologic evaluations would be necessary to establish wetland status. Recommendations from this section are listed as recommendations 23 through 27 at the end of the chapter.

OTHER INDICATORS OF THE SUBSTRATE AND BIOLOGICAL CRITERIA

Substrates occasionally meet the requirements of the wetland definition for continuous or recurrent saturation without coming under the classification of hydric soils. Some frequently saturated substrates do not develop hydric soil because they are frequently disturbed (mud flats, sand bars) or because they receive insufficient amounts of organic matter to support the development of hydric soil. Even when redoximorphic features are absent, however, saturation of the substrate with water over an extended interval is very likely to cause measurable chemical and physical change in the substrate. In substrates that fail to develop a permanent record of chemical change, the chemistry of the interstitial waters would need to be studied during the period of inundation to demonstrate that the substrate criterion is satisfied.

The biological criterion for wetlands is typically satisfied by vegetation analysis, although there are two general cases in which other organisms can be important. First, some wetlands lack vascular plants entirely, either because the plants have been removed or because the chemical or physical habitat is unsuited for their growth, as in the case of some playas or mud flats or areas where sulfide accumulation causes high vegetation mortality (Mitsch and Gosselink, 1993). The second possibility is that organisms other than vascular plants could be useful in evaluating the biological criterion even when vascular plants are present. For example, it might be technically simpler or more accurate in some cases to collect evidence on aquatic invertebrates (Garono and Kooser, 1994), algae, or mosses than it would be to collect evidence on vascular plants. These analyses also can prove valuable when vascular plant data are inconclusive. A draft list of hydrophytic mosses has been developed by FWS for this reason (personal communication, 1993, P.B. Reed, FWS).

The applicability of biological analyses other than the identification of vascular plants is largely a matter for regional evaluation (Chapter 7). Delineation manuals should, however, specify that indicators in support of the biological criterion can extend beyond the use of vascular plants. Several kinds of organisms should be acknowledged as potential biological indicators: aquatic invertebrates, algae or mosses that require inundation or saturation, and vertebrates that require inundation or saturation. Although not yet developed, lists of microbial and fungal indicators of saturation and inundation could be used as well. Biological indicators other than vegetation can serve either as an alternative or as a supplement to the use of vegetation. Recommendations that follow from this section of the chapter are listed as recommendations 28 and 29 at the end of Chapter 5.

COMBINING THE FACTORS

The practice of dividing the evidence required for wetland delineation into three categories—hydrology, soils, and vegetation—evolved in the 1980s (Huffman, 1981; Environmental Laboratory, 1987; EPA, 1988a). Before that time, wetland scientists and state agencies had used primarily vegetation to identify and delineate wetlands (Dix and Smeins, 1967; Stewart and Kantrud, 1971; Golet and Larson, 1974; Kusler and Bedford, 1975; Tiner, 1993). The use of multiple factors was adopted as a system of checks and balances intended to prevent misidentifications where soils or vegetation were relicts of former hydrologic conditions and in areas dominated by facultative plant species.

The use of three factors is now the basis for wetland identification and delineation by federal agencies (Chapters 3, 4). As conceived, the approach requires that evidence from all three categories be present at the time of delineation unless specific hydrologic data are available. Manuals differ, however, in the degree of independence they require for verification of hydrology, soils, and vegetation (Chapter 4).

From a scientific perspective, the issue encompasses two basic questions. The first is definitional: Do some wetlands inherently lack one or more of the three characteristics or fail to exhibit all three at some times? The second question is evidentiary: What evidence can be used to infer the existence of a characteristic that might not be obvious or present at the time of inspection? A third question can be asked as well: Are some properties or combinations of properties so distinctively characteristic of wetlands or uplands that no others are needed?

Necessity for Three Factors

The variables that characterize wetlands interact and are causally related. The primary causal agent, or master variable, is water, which creates wetlands through recurrent, sustained flooding or inundation at or near the surface of the substrate. The physical and chemical characteristics of the substrate, such as hydric soils, and the characteristic biota, such as hydrophytic vegetation, are effects caused by and dependent on a hydrologic regime; they are not independent variables. The studies cited in this chapter and numerous other studies of wetlands show this to be the case.

A logical extension of the causal relationships among the three factors is that effect (substrate, biota) can be used to infer cause (hydrology). For this reason, evidence supporting one criterion can be used to support another. The definition focuses on three factors, but the indicators of these need not come from three independent categories; the strength of causal relationships can be sufficient that indicators of one criterion can also be used for another. For example, if hydrologic conditions have not been altered, vegetation dominated by OBL and FACW species of plants provides evidence of wetland hydrology because of the strength of the relationship between development of this type of vegetation and frequent or prolonged flooding or saturation of the soil. Conversely, vegetation dominated by FACU and UPL species shows that the hydrologic criterion is not satisfied.

Although other indicators can be used to support the presence of wetland substrate and wetland biota, hydric soils and hydrophytic vegetation are the two most common indicators. The following discussion is framed, therefore, in terms of hydric soils and hydrophytic vegetation, but the logic applies to other indicators as well.

Coincidence of Characteristic Hydrology, Soils, and Vegetation

Wetlands sometimes do not show strong and direct evidence of wetland hydrology, soils, and vegetation. For example, fluctuating water levels are typical of wetlands (Wharton et al., 1982; Winter, 1989; Duever, 1990; Golet et al., 1993; Mitsch and Gosselink, 1993) (Chapter 2). As explained in the section on hydrology, the recurring presence of water in wetlands is more or less predictable over the long term, but it can be difficult to assess over short periods.

Vegetation is less variable over the short term than is hydrology, particularly for wetlands dominated by mosses or long-lived perennial herbaceous or woody plants, but variation can still present difficulties. Because perennial communities develop over several years to decades, their composition is an integrated expression of the hydrologic regime prevailing over the recent past. Although the relative abundance of individual species can change from year to year, the hydrophytic character of the overall community changes slowly in response to changes in the hydrologic regime. Annual or short-lived perennial species, however, can vary annually or even seasonally where water-level fluctuations are rapid or extreme.

Soils are least variable. Unless disturbed by cultivation or dredging, soil profiles consistently exhibit morphologic properties that reflect the long-term conditions under which they formed (Buol et al., 1980; Blume and Schlichting, 1985; Bouma et al., 1990; Mausbach and Richardson, 1994). The enduring nature of hydric soils, in fact, poses a problem for delineation because hydric soils persist long after they have been drained. Vepraskas and Guertal (1992) have proposed recently, however, that some relict features can be distinguished from some contemporary ones. Contemporary redox concentrations and depletions (Appendix A) along ped surfaces and root channels must not be overlain by other redder coatings that would indicate recent drainage. Contemporary manganese nodules with sharp boundaries are probably dissolving and therefore relict.

The coincidence of wetland hydrology, soils, and vegetation is likely to be irregular in the transition zone between wetland and upland (Anderson et al., 1980; Allen et al., 1989; Carter et al., 1994). In this zone, at the limit of the wetland, the water level fluctuations within the plant rooting zone can be the most extreme. Plant species composition at any given time will reflect a shifting competitive balance between species that are more and less tolerant of soil saturation or flooding. The balance will shift in response to changes in the frequency, duration, extent, and seasonality of surface flooding and soil saturation along the boundary. In drier years, facultative species will become more abundant and upland species can invade. In wetter years, the balance will shift toward obligate wetland plants. Because the soil changes very slowly, however, it will provide evidence of the composite hydrologic regime prevailing over years to decades.

Modified Approach to Evaluating Evidence

The studies cited in this chapter indicate that some modification is needed of the current approach to wetland identification and delineation. A strict requirement for independent evidence from hydrology, soils, and vegetation in identifying and delineating wetlands is often impractical, and it overlooks the strong causal relationships that unify the hydrologic regime with the other variables that characterize wetland ecosystems. It also makes delineations needlessly time-consuming when the weight of the evidence from two factors, rather than from three, is a sufficient indication of wetland status. Given the primacy of hydrology in maintaining wetlands, however, wetlands cannot be identified where evidence clearly shows the hydrologic conditions for wetlands to be absent.

Requirements for specific kinds of direct hydrologic data for delineations are not practical or necessary except when hydrology has been altered or other factors provide uncertain indications. Such requirements assume incorrectly that seasonal and interannual variability will be sufficiently small that the period of assessment will be an accurate reflection of the average condition or that long-term records will be available for most wetlands. Current information about wetland soils and vegetation, along with data from numerous field studies, shows that strong causal relationships can be established between hydrology, vegetation, and soils for the wetter end of the wetland continuum. Plant communities dominated by OBL, FACW, and FAC species and lacking an abundance of UPL and FACU species develop only where the prevailing hydrologic regime is one in which flooding or saturation of the soil is very frequent or extended. Histosols (except Folists), gleyed mineral soils, most mineral soils with low chroma matrixes and mottles, and mineral soils with well-developed depletion coatings develop only where sites are very frequently flooded or saturated for extended periods of time (Brinkman, 1970; Damman, 1979; Buol et al., 1980; Clymo, 1983; Vepraskas and Guertal, 1992; Mausbach and Richardson, 1994). These characteristics demonstrate the presence of wetland hydrology. The converse is true for vegetation dominated by UPL and FACU species and by soils that lack any sign of being hydric; these characteristics should be taken as strong evidence that the hydrologic criterion cannot be satisfied.

Many wetland scientists contend that some properties of hydric soils and some types of hydrophytic vegetation should be used as primary indicators of hydrology (Tiner, 1991a; 1993; Bedford et al., 1992; Golet et al., 1993; Carter et al., 1994). This is a valid principle where hydrology is unaltered. If the hydrology of a site has been altered, analysis of vegetation or soils can lead to erroneous conclusions. For such sites, the hydrologic criterion must be evaluated with field data, or modeling must be used to determine whether the site has been effectively drained.

A modification of the current approach to delineation would recognize the strength of causal relationships among factors rather than treating the factors as fixed and unrelated. Such an approach would not preclude assessment of all three factors for all wetlands, but it would broaden the evidence to be used in testing the indicators to see whether the criteria are satisfied, as follows, where hydrology has not been altered: It would allow inferences about wetland hydrology to be drawn from strong evidence in nonhydrologic categories—soils, vegetation, or other indicators of the substrate and biological criteria. It would allow the thresholds for indicators to vary as a function of the strength of evidence from other indicators and the presence or absence of conflicting information. For example, vegetation dominated by FAC species that occur on a nonhydric soil and lacking an abundance of OBL or FACW species would not exceed the threshold for the vegetation indicator, and vegetation dominated by FAC species on a strongly redoximorphic mineral soil and lacking an abundance of UPL or FACU species would exceed the threshold for vegetation. Variables other than hydric soils and hydrophytic vegetation could satisfy the substrate and biological criteria if strong causal relationships could be established between specific thresholds of these variables and recurrent, sustained flooding or saturation at or near the surface of the substrate.

The change reflected in this modified approach to delineation lies in the stringency of evidentiary requirements, which would vary as a function of the risk of error. As the risk increases, the evidence required to make a determination also would increase. Where the risk is low, direct information on all three criteria is redundant and would not be required. The modification would apply only in the absence of hydrologic alterations.

Two ways of implementing the modified approach to delineation have already been developed: primary indicators and hierarchical classification.

Primary Indicators

Tiner (1993) has proposed the Primary Indicators Method (PRIMET), which uses information on vegetation and soils unique to wetlands. It is intended only for use on sites where hydrology has not been significantly altered. The rationale for the method is as follows (Tiner, 1993, p. 53):

Wetlands are highly varied and complex habitats subject to different hydrologic regimes, climatic conditions, soil formation processes, and geomorphologic settings across the country. Within similar geographic areas, wetlands have developed characteristics different than adjacent uplands (nonwetlands) due to the presence of water in or on top of the soil for prolonged periods during the year. The visible expression of this wetness may be evident in the plant community and/or in the underlying soil properties. Consequently, every wetland in its natural undrained condition should possess at least one distinctive feature that distinguishes it from the adjacent upland. The "primary indicators method" (PRIMET) is founded on this premise.

The proposed list of primary indicators (Tiner, 1993) is short and, for the most part, conservative indicators (Table 5.3). For example, the vegetation indicators rely on OBL and FACW species or an exception morphological adaptations to frequent flooding. The soil indicators are field-verified properties known to result from prolonged seasonal high water tables such as a gleyed matrix or low chroma ped faces immediately below the surface layer. One indicator, surface encrustations of algae, has not been tested but seems reasonable; data on another, remains of aquatic invertebrates, are available only from a single set of studies (Euliss et al., 1993), the results of which suggest that it would be useful.

Tiner (1993) also provides a method for boundary determination: The boundary is located where no primary indicators are found. For wetlands subjected to cyclical drought (temporarily flooded red maple swamps or prairie potholes), Tiner recommends use of soil indicators. In drier wetlands, soils are more reliable than is vegetation because they provide evidence of seasonal saturation and long-term hydrologic conditions. In drought-prone areas, soils are more reliable because they respond less quickly than vegetation to short-term changes in hydrology. He also recommends using soil indicators for the boundaries of wet-

TABLE 5.3 Primary Indicators of Wetlands[a]

Vegetation Indicators of Wetlands

V1. OBL species comprise more than 50 percent of the abundant species of the plant
     community. (*An abundant species is a plant species with 20 percent or more areal
     cover in the plant community.*)
V2. OBL *and* FACW species comprise more than 50 percent of the abundant species of the
     plant community.
V3. OBL perennial species collectively represent at least 10 percent areal cover in the plant
     community and are evenly distributed throughout the community and not restricted to
     depressional areas.
V4. One abundant plant species in the community has one or more of the following
     morphological adaptations: pneumatophores (knees), prop roots, hypertrophied lenticels,
     buttressed stems or trunks, and floating leaves. (*Note:* Some of these features may be of
     limited value in tropical U.S., e.g., Hawaii.)
V5. Surface encrustations of algae, usually blue-green algae, are materially present. (*Note:*
     This is a particularly useful indicator of drier wetlands in arid and semiarid regions.)
V6. The presence of significant patches of peat mosses (*Sphagnum* spp.) along the Gulf and
     Atlantic Coastal Plain. (*Note:* This may be useful elsewhere in the temperate zone.)
V7. The presence of a dominant groundcover of peat mosses (*Sphagnum* spp.) in boreal and
     subarctic regions.

Soil Indicators of Wetlands

S1. Organic soils (except Folists) present.
S2. Histic epipedon (e.g., organic surface layer 8-16 inches thick) present.
S3. Sulfidic material (H_2S odor of "rotten eggs") present within 12 inches of the soil
     surface.
S4. Gleyed[b] (low chroma) horizon or dominant ped faces (chroma 2 or less with mottles *or*
     chroma 1 or less with or without mottles) present immediately (within 1 inch) below the
     surface layer (A- or E-horizon) *and* within 18 inches of the soil surface.
S5. Nonsandy soils with a low chroma matrix (chroma of 2 or less) within 18 inches of the
     soil surface *and* one of the following present within 12 inches of the surface:
     a. iron and manganese concretions or nodules, or
     b. distinct or prominent oxidized rhizospheres along several living roots, or
     c. low chroma mottles.
S6. Sandy soils with one of the following present:
     a. thin surface layer (1 inch or greater) of peat or muck where a leaf litter surface mat is
     present, or
     b. surface layer of peat or muck of any thickness where a leaf litter surface mat is
     absent, or
     c. a surface layer (A-horizon) having a low chroma matrix (chroma 1 or less and value
     of 3 or less) greater than 4 inches thick, or
     d. vertical organic streaking or blotchiness within 12 inches of the surface, or
     e. easily recognized (distinct or prominent) high chroma mottles occupy at least 2
     percent of the low chroma subsoil matrix within 12 inches of the surface, or
     f. organic concretions within 12 inches of the surface, or
     g. easily recognized (distinct or prominent) oxidized rhizospheres along living roots
     within 12 inches of the surface, or
     h. a cemented layer (orstein) within 18 inches of the soil surface.

TABLE 5.3 (Continued)

S7. Native prairie soils with a low chroma matrix (chroma of 2 or less) within 18 inches of the soil surface and one of the following present:

a. thin surface layer (at least one-quarter inch thick) of peat or muck, or

b. accumulation of iron (high chroma mottles, especially oxidized rhizospheres) within 12 inches of the surface, or

c. iron and manganese concretions within the surface layer (A-horizon, mollic epipedon), or

d. low chroma (gray-colored) matrix or mottles present immediately below the surface layer (A-horizon, mollic epipedon) and the crushed color is chroma 2 or less.

(Note: The native prairie region extends northward from Texas to the Dakotas and adjacent Canada.)

S8.Remains of aquatic invertebrates are present within 12 inches of the soil surface in nontidal pothole-like depressions.

S9.Other regionally applicable, field-verifiable soil properties associated with prolonged seasonal high water tables.

---

[a]The presence of any of these characteristics in an area that has not been drained typically indicates wetland. The upper limit of wetland is determined by the point at which none of these indicators is observed. Source: Tiner, 1993, Table 2, with permission from SWS.

[b]Gleyed colors are low chroma colors (chroma of 2 or less in aggregated soils and chroma 1 or less in soils not aggregated, plus hues bluer than 10Y) formed by excessive soil wetness; other nongleyed low chroma soils may occur due to (1) dark-colored materials (e.g., granite and phylites), (2) human introduction of organic materials (e.g., manure) to improve soil fertility, (3) podzolization (natural soil leaching process in acid woodlands where a light-colored, often grayish, E-horizon or alluvial-horizon develops below the A-horizon; these uniform light gray colors are not due to wetness.)

lands in gently sloping terrain, where the plant community often provides mixed indications. These principles are supported by the scientific literature.

PRIMET does not use hydrology as an indicator. Instead, vegetation and soils are used as indicators of hydrology. Tiner (1993) correctly points out that the visual signs of hydrology, including even direct observation of water, are indicators only of hydrologic events and not of their duration and frequency. Occasional flooding does not distinctively separate wetlands from uplands, many of which flood occasionally.

Hierarchical Approach

Another modified approach was outlined by the federal agencies that developed the 1989 manual. A tiered or hierarchical approach treats the evidence in accordance with the probability of reaching an erroneous conclusion. For example, a soil that shows only marginal signs of being hydric would not be accorded the same diagnostic value as a soil that is clearly hydric. Obvious wetland and upland would require less evidence than would problematic sites, such as those dominated by facultative species. Sites with soils and vegetation only weakly indicative of wetlands would require hydrologic evaluation. As with PRIMET, the approach would be applied only to sites without hydrologic modification.

The hierarchical approach is similar to PRIMET in seeking to use the strongest evidence, and only the evidence that is necessary and sufficient, for making determinations. It differs, however, in several ways. First, it relies on combinations of indicators rather than single indicators. Diagnostic combinations, which occupy the top tier of the hierarchy, are summarized in Table 5.4. Second, many of the indicators require the calculation of a prevalence index, which is much more time-consuming than is using a measure of dominance. Third, it allows the use of some off-site information, such as soil maps and aerial photographs, in combination with field verification. Fourth, it uses far fewer soil indicators than PRIMET does. Finally, it does not use plant morphology adaptations, algal crusts, *Sphagnum* moss, or aquatic invertebrates. In this sense, it is less comprehensive than PRIMET.

Future Delineation Manuals

Substantial knowledge of the nation's wetlands is embodied in the federal manuals that have been used to identify and delineate them. As a class of ecosystems, wetlands are remarkably diverse. Codifying this diversity into rules for recognizing the wetlands of the nation as a whole represents a significant challenge that the authors of the federal manuals generally have met well. Use of the manuals has helped to refine understanding of the essential characteristics of wetlands and to identify various problems with the manuals. A single federal manual whose core is drawn from existing manuals should be drafted. It should encompass the knowledge gained through the use of the manuals and recent refinements in scientific understanding of wetlands. This manual should be supported by the development of regional supplements that provide detailed criteria and indicators consistent with the federal manual (Chapter 7).

RECOMMENDATIONS

Improvements in the scientific understanding of wetlands since 1987 and refinement of regulatory practice through experience over almost a decade of intensive wetland regulation suggest that a new federal delineation manual should be prepared for common use by all federal agencies involved in the regulation of wetlands. This new manual should draw freely from the strengths of the existing manuals, and should not be identical to any of them. The recommendations that follow are intended to aid in its preparation.

1(a). In the absence of hydrologic alteration and evidence to the contrary,

TABLE 5.4   A List of Indicator Combinations That are Diagnostic of Wetlands According to the Federal Interagency Committee's Proposal for Use of Evidence in Wetland Determinations

1. A minimum of 5 years of direct observations of hydrology (e.g., ground water well data and tide or stream gauge records) during years of normal rainfall and correlated with long-term hydrologic records for the specific geographical area demonstrate that the area is inundated and/or saturated at a sufficient frequency and duration; or

2. Examination of aerial photographs [from] a minimum of 5 years (preferably from early spring or other wet parts of the year) and other off-site information, locally correlated with hydric soils and hydrophytic vegetation, reveals evidence of inundation and/or saturation in most years sufficient to support hydric soils and hydrophytic vegetation; or

3. Field verified plant communities, occurring on mapped hydric soils, with OBL species or OBL and FACW species representing more than 50 percent of the dominant species and no FACU and UPL species as dominants; or

4. Field verified plant communities, on mapped hydric soils, with a mean prevalence index ≤2.0; or

5. All field verified hydric organic soils (Histosols except Folists) dominated by facultative or wetter vegetation (P.I. <3.5); or

6. Field verified hydric mineral soils classified as a Histic subgroup of an Aquic Suborder, Sulfaquents, or Hydraquents, dominated by facultative or wetter vegetation (P.I. <3.5); or

7. Field verified organic surface layer 8-16 inches thick (or mineral histic epipedon) dominated by facultative or wetter vegetation (P.I. <3.5); or

8. Field verified gleyed subsoil immediately below the A, Ap, or E-horizon (gleyed according to the gley page of the Munsell Soil Color Book) dominated by FAC or wetter vegetation (P.I. <3.5); or

9. Field verified hydric mineral soils and one of the following plant communities where:
    (a) more than 50 percent of the dominant species are OBL and/or FACW species, or
    (b) more than 50 percent of the dominant species are FAC with OBL species present and UPL species absent, or
    (c) more than 50 percent of the dominant species are FAC, with OBL and/or FACW species present and FACU and/or UPL species absent, or
    (d) more than 50 percent of the dominant species are FAC, with OBL and FACW species more abundant (e.g., aerial coverage) than FACU and UPL species, or
    (e) the aerial coverage of OBL and FACW dominant species exceeds the aerial coverage of FACU and UPL dominant species, or
    (f) the mean prevalence index is less than 3.0; or

10. Hydric mineral soils are field verified using regional indicators of significant soil saturation, and other plant communities not listed above dominated by FAC species or having a mean prevalence index equal to 3.5, and indicators of wetland hydrology (refer to issue paper on wetland hydrology).

the presence of field-verified hydric soils can be used as strong evidence of wetland hydrology.

1(b). In the absence of hydrologic alteration and evidence to the contrary, vegetation dominated by OBL and FACW species, or by a combination of OBL, FACW, and FAC species can be used as strong evidence of wetland hydrology.

2. Procedures should be developed for evaluating hydrology at sites that have been hydrologically altered or from which soil, vegetation, or other important indicators of site hydrology have been removed.

3. Both the growing season and the hydrologic threshold for duration of saturation should be revised by region. Use of the growing-season concept in any form should be reevaluated for subarctic, arctic, and alpine regions as well as for the southwestern and tropical parts of the United States.

4. The growing-season concept should be replaced with a more flexible and defensible, temperature-based adjustment of the duration threshold and regionally-based criteria which would account for hydrology, biota, temperature, and substrate differences among regions.

5. If direct hydrologic evaluation is needed, as in the case of altered sites or when evidence from substrate and biota is not conclusive, the evaluation should be based on water table data or on evidence of anoxia. The relevant zone for evaluation is the upper plant-rooting zone—the upper 1 ft (30 cm)—and not the soil surface. Pending the development of more sophisticated approaches and of regional guidelines, and in the absence of evidence to the contrary, the duration threshold for saturation can be taken as 14 days over the growing season in most years (on average, at a frequency greater than one out of two years).

6. Indirect hydrologic indicators of flooding, such as water marks on trees, should not be used to determine the long-term hydrologic status of a site.

7. Mathematical modeling can be used in analyzing hydrologic alterations and in relating short-term hydrologic measurements to long-term hydrologic conditions.

8. Seasonal and interannual variation of weather must be considered in any direct evaluation of hydrology.

9. Research should be undertaken on the frequency, duration, recurrence interval, and seasonality of inundation or saturation required for the maintenance of specific regional wetland classes.

10. Guidelines should be developed for assessment of hydrologic alteration.

11. The Hydric Soils List is useful in the identification of wetlands; its continued development should be supported by NRCS.

12. Regional technical committees on hydric soils should be established for all U.S. states and territories. Each committee should report to NTCHS.

13. NTCHS should consider developing a system for assigning hydric soils to fidelity categories.

14. NTCHS should develop a list in which each soil is considered individually, rather than as a part of a taxonomic or soil drainage group. This would eliminate the need for the Hydric Soils List to reference water table depth.

15. Soil surveys and the Hydric Soils List serve as primary reference materials for delineations, but field delineations involving soils should be based on field indicators such as soil color and morphology.

16.   The Regional Field Indicators of Saturated Hydric Soils developed by NRCS should be evaluated for use in delineation.

17.   Field indicators of hydric soils should be evaluated for reliability; procedures are needed for revision of field indicators in response to field studies.

18.   NRCS should use its National Resources Inventory and other information (such as regional research projects) to determine the correlation of soil types, water table depth, redox potential, and vegetation.

19.   If the hydrology of a site has been altered, evidence from soils or vegetation must be used only with support from hydrologic analysis, including the characteristic frequency, duration, and depth of saturation.

20.   Assessment of problem soils (red or oxidized soils), or marginally hydric soils must be made by individuals experienced in identifying hydric soils.

21.   Lands on which hydrology has not been altered and on which hydric soils are present are wetlands and should be delineated as such, unless hydrologic and vegetation data do not support this conclusion.

22.   The absence of hydric soils, however, does not always indicate upland; analysis of hydrology and biota are needed for such lands.

23.   Scientific understanding of wetland soils and of correlations between plant distribution and wetland soils should be improved through research and monitoring.

24.   The Hydrophyte List is technically sound and should continue to serve as the basis for assigning species to wetland fidelity categories (obligate, facultative, etc.). Its continued improvement and revision should be supported by its sponsoring agency.

25.   The indexes for predominance of hydrophytic vegetation clearly separate hydrophytic from nonhydrophytic vegetation only when index values deviate substantially from the threshold; lands with hydrophyte dominance near 50% or a prevalence index near 3.0 cannot be assessed confidently without strong reliance on other indicators.

26.   An array of strong indicators that do not require use of formal indexes should be constructed and used in the field. Examples include the following, which should be applied only in the absence of significant hydrologic alteration:

•   Vegetation dominated by obligate and facultative-wet species will satisfy the biological criterion.

•   Vegetation dominated by obligate, facultative-wet, and facultative with no abundant upland or facultative-upland species will satisfy the biological criterion.

•   Vegetation dominated by facultative or facultative-upland species will satisfy the biologic criterion if it occurs on field-verified hydric soils with strong morphological indicators. If soils are not clearly hydric, hydrologic data will be essential.

27.   In the absence of hydrologic alteration or other evidence to the contrary, vegetation dominated by obligate and facultative-wet species, but with no abun-

dant upland or facultative-upland species, indicates that wetland hydrology is present, unless soils are non-hydric, in which case hydrologic information is needed. Conversely, vegetation dominated by upland, facultative-upland, and facultative species and with no abundant obligate or facultative-wet species should be considered nonhydrophytic and should indicate a nonwetland area, unless soils are hydric, in which case hydrologic information is needed.

28.   Boundary determinations involving vegetation analysis should be confirmed by analysis of substrate.

29.   Delineation manuals should specify that the list of indicators that support the biological criterion can include organisms other than vascular plants.

30.   Where biological indicators other than vegetation are used, quantitative thresholds should be developed if possible to allow standardization of the indicator for a particular region or for a particular type of wetland.

31.   The application of evidence to the assessment of wetlands should be modified. All three defining factors (water, substrate, biota) must be evaluated, even though in some cases evidence can be inferential. If hydrologic information is unavailable, and if hydrology has not been modified, the presence of wetland hydrology can be evaluated from information on substrate, if this information is definitive (for example, by the presence of hydric soils); from vegetation, when the hydrophytic nature of the vegetation is unequivocal; or from other indicators for which a strong relationship to recurrent, sustained saturation can be established. If neither substrate nor vegetation provides clear evidence, delineation will require hydrologic data. All evidence must be carefully weighed, however, when a delineation is made.

32.   Both the Primary Indicators Method (PRIMET) and the hierarchical approach are conceptually sound and should be studied for use in identifying and delineating wetlands.

33.   Federal agencies that regulate wetlands should hire regulatory staff that makes up a balanced mixture of expertise in plant ecology, hydrology, and soil science.

34.   Primary data on hydric soils, hydrophytic vegetation, and hydrology of wetlands should be assembled and analyzed statistically. The results should be published, and review panels for the Hydrophyte List and Hydric Soils List should use these analyses in revising the lists.

35.   Reference wetlands should be identified for long-term study of the relationships between water, substrate, and biota.

6

Especially Controversial Wetlands

INTRODUCTION

The wetlands and associated landscape features discussed in this chapter have been the subject of particular controversy because of their location, their unusual characteristics, or their regulatory status. They include permafrost wetlands, riparian ecosystems, isolated and headwater wetlands, especially shallow wetlands, agricultural wetlands, nonagricultural altered sites, and transitional zones. These areas are the source of many problems related to wetland regulation and delineation; their classification is particularly sensitive to changes in delineation procedures.

PERMAFROST WETLANDS

Permafrost is soil that has a temperature continuously below 32°F (0°C) for 2 years or more. This definition distinguishes permafrost from seasonal frost. The distribution of permafrost in the United States is restricted to Alaska and a few high alpine areas in the conterminous states. Except at latitudes and elevations so high that there is no summer thaw, permafrost is overlain by a zone of seasonal thaw called the active layer, which typically is 14-79 in. (25-200 cm) thick. Maximum depths of thaw are found where the climate is warmest and the soils are driest; minimum depths of thaw are found in the coldest and wettest environments.

North of the Brooks Range in Alaska, permafrost is generally continuous. In south-central and interior Alaska, permafrost is discontinuous, and it is generally found on north-facing slopes and poorly drained valley bottoms. The thickness of permafrost varies from almost 2,000 ft (600 m) in Northern Alaska to about 130 ft (40 m) or less in interior Alaska. The continuous permafrost areas of Alaska are mainly treeless tundra; discontinuous permafrost supports many plant communities, including forests.

At the southern limits of permafrost and in low regions, thickening of the active layer can occur readily if the thermal regime changes. Not only a warmer climate, but also fire and clearing of surface-insulating vegetation, can result in thawing of permafrost. Because permafrost is relatively impermeable to water, any change in its proximity to the soil surface can cause hydrologic changes.

Relevance of Permafrost to Wetland Formation

Permafrost contributes to wetland formation by retarding the downward movement of soil water (Dingman, 1975; Hobbie, 1984). Water retained near the ground surface can saturate the active layer and thus lead to the formation of hydric soils and the growth of hydrophytic vegetation. The presence of permafrost alone, however, is not always sufficient to create a wetland. Wetland formation is most likely where the active layer is shallow, hydraulic gradients are low, and mineral soils have low permeabilities. Under such conditions, saturation to the surface can occur for significant portions of the warm season. Conversely, thick active layers, steep slopes, and coarse-grained soils act against wetland formation in permafrost environments.

Permafrost wetlands are sometimes portrayed as uniform. Wetlands in permafrost environments vary, however, from brackish coastal marshes through shallow lakes and ponds to forests. Permafrost wetlands also occur on a variety of landforms ranging from flat coastal plains and river floodplains to steep north-facing slopes and alpine terrain. Soils in these areas can be mineral or organic, and the vegetation ranges from aquatic emergent to scrub-shrub and forest.

Dynamics of Permafrost Wetlands

Permafrost aggradation can create or restore wetland hydrology on forested sites. This process is especially important where permafrost is discontinuous. Aggradation can occur through primary succession on river floodplains as well as through postfire secondary succession on lowlands and on north-facing slopes of interior Alaska. Succession in these areas passes from hardwoods to spruce (Viereck, 1970; Foote, 1983). With succession, organic matter accumulates, especially in stands of white spruce (*Picea glauca*) and black spruce (*P. mariana*) with groundcover composed of feathermosses (Van Cleve et al., 1991). The accumulation of organic matter in turn affects the heat balance of the underlying soil. Dry peat reduces heat gain by the soil during summer, and frozen soil can accelerate winter heat loss because it has a high moisture content (Brown, 1963).

As a result, mean soil temperature declines when organic matter accumulates during succession. A lower soil temperature reduces the mean rate of decomposition (Fox and Van Cleve, 1983), which contributes to further accumulation of organic matter, particularly in old stands of black spruce (Van Cleve et al., 1983). This process can produce permafrost in primary successional stands on floodplains over periods of 200 years (Viereck, 1970), or on upland sites in only 25-50 years after a fire (Dingman and Koutz, 1974; Van Cleve and Viereck, 1983). Rising permafrost tables increase saturation of the active layer and create or restore wetland hydrology on sites where lateral drainage is weak. With increasing soil moisture, forested sites of interior Alaska tend toward hydrophytic communities characterized by black spruce, ericaceous shrubs, and *Sphagnum* mosses. Such sites remain wetlands until floodplain processes, fire, or anthropogenic disturbances reinitiate succession.

Treeless arctic wetlands share the dynamic nature of forested subarctic wetlands. On the Arctic Coastal Plain, for example, thermokarst lakes (thaw lakes) form, mature, drain, and reform (Carter et al., 1987). These cycles occur over several thousand years and cause lake basins to undergo vegetational succession after drainage (Billings and Peterson, 1980). Various phases of the thaw-lake cycle provide a variety of habitats for shorebirds and waterfowl (Bergman et al., 1977).

Other processes include the formation of low-centered frost polygons by ice wedges and thermal erosion of these wedges to form high-centered polygons on the tundra surface (Walker et al., 1980). Microrelief associated with these changing geomorphic features causes a fine-grained mosaic of soils and vegetation to develop on the tundra surface and contributes to the wide variety of tundra wetlands.

Disturbance of wetlands in the zone of discontinuous permafrost generally increases the thickness of the active layer. Increased thaw depth can temporarily eliminate wetland hydrology, as is the case after a fire (Van Cleve and Viereck, 1983) or after agricultural clearing (Ping, 1987), or it can increase the wetness of a site, as is common when melting of ground ice with consequent subsidence of the ground surface creates thaw ponds or lakes (Péwé, 1982). In contrast, wetlands in the continuous permafrost of the Arctic are less likely to lose wetland hydrologic characteristics after disturbance because the permafrost, which is both colder and more extensive in the Arctic, is less sensitive to changes in heat flux.

Tundra wetlands show a variety of geobotanical features influenced by permafrost processes and span a moisture gradient from lakes to shrub-tussock tundra (Walker et al., 1980; Chapin and Shaver, 1985). Perturbation of wetlands at the drier end of this spectrum generally increases their seasonal depths of thaw and causes ground surfaces to subside, thus forming depressions through consolidation of fine-grained soils with high ice content (Lawson et al., 1978; Lawson, 1986). Depressions of this type in level terrain usually retain moisture, and often become wetlands.

Regulation of Permafrost Wetlands

Many proposals have been made to regulate permafrost wetlands differently from nonpermafrost wetlands. For example, the Food Security Act wetland definition excludes some permafrost wetlands of Alaska (Chapter 3), which has 174.7 million acres (70.8 million ha) of wetland (Hall et al., 1994). Permafrost is in part responsible for this large amount of wetland, although pleistocene glaciation and associated fluvial and lacustrine deposits contribute to Alaska's wetlands (Péwé, 1975). Alaska accounts for one-sixth of the total land area of United States, and it has about 63% of the nation's remaining wetlands (Hall et al., 1994). The regulatory treatment of permafrost wetlands is significant regionally, because of the abundance of wetlands in Alaska, and nationally, because so much of the nation's wetlands are in Alaska.

Wetland formation by permafrost is influenced by latitude, topography, and climate, as are other mechanisms of wetland formation. Precipitation and evapotranspiration, for example, vary with latitude and climate in ways that affect many kinds of wetlands. Furthermore, studies of the National Wetlands Working Group (1988) in Canada show that permafrost wetlands have the same functions as other kinds of wetlands. To argue that saturated soils underlain by permafrost cannot be wetlands because they are a phenomenon of climate is akin to arguing that bottomland hardwood forests are not wetlands because they are a result of high river discharge. The sensitivity of permafrost wetlands to altered thermal regimes induced by anthropogenic disturbance or by fire also has been suggested as a reason for treating them as problem wetlands (Ping et al., 1992). Most wetlands are, however, similarly subject to loss or change by natural and anthropogenic forces. Because permafrost wetlands do not differ in their essential characteristics from other wetlands, separate regulatory treatment of them is not justifiable scientifically. Recommendations on permafrost wetlands can be found at the end of this chapter, numbers 1 to 3.

RIPARIAN ECOSYSTEMS

Land adjacent to a stream or river is often called a riparian zone or riparian ecosystem. The riparian zone is a characteristic association of substrate, flora, and fauna within the 100-year floodplain of a stream or, if a floodplain is absent, a zone hydrologically influenced by a stream or river (Hunt, 1988). Riparian ecosystems are maintained by high water tables and periodic flooding. Examples include bosques of the American Southwest, streamside communities along high-gradient streams of the Pacific Northwest and Rocky Mountains, gallery forests of prairie regions, cove forests of the eastern mountains, and wetlands and adjacent slopes that border streams of humid eastern states (Brinson et al., 1981). Riparian zones, which can be defined several ways, contain or adjoin riverine wetlands and share with them a multitude of functions including surface and subsurface water storage, sediment retention, nutrient and contaminant removal, and maintenance of habitat for plants and animals (Chapter 2).

Support of Biodiversity

Several studies document the importance of riparian ecosystems to regional biodiversity. Ohmart and Anderson (1986) conclude that the greatest densities of breeding birds in North America are found in riparian ecosystems, that more than 60% of the vertebrates in the arid Southwest are obligately associated with this ecosystem, and that another 10-20% of the vertebrates are facultative users of streamside vegetation. Mosconi and Hutto (1982) report that in western Montana, 59% of the species of land birds use riparian ecosystems for breeding, and 36% breed only there. Cottonwood and mesquite forests are very high in species richness of migratory birds (Stromberg, 1993). Thomas et al. (1979) found that 299 of the 363 species of land vertebrates in the Great Basin of southeast Oregon depend directly on riparian habitats or use them more than any other habitat type.

Current Regulation of Riparian Ecosystems

Riparian ecosystems are among the nation's highly valued and threatened natural resources (Johnson and McCormick, 1979). Alteration of riparian ecosystems has been of special concern in the West. Alteration has accompanied regulated activities such as gravel mining, bridge crossings, and the creation of new dams and diversions, and such unregulated activities as reduction of surface discharge or lowering of water tables due to ground water pumping or surface water withdrawal. Other activities that can alter riparian zones include clearing of land for agricultural development, logging, or recreation (Stromberg, 1993). Degradation of riparian habitat has also resulted from the spread of exotic species such as saltcedar and Russian olive. In some areas, native riparian plant and animal species are greatly suppressed or have become locally extinct (Stromberg et al., 1991).

Because of their proximity to flowing water, riparian ecosystems are closely associated with the maintenance of the physical, chemical, and biological processes of streams. Although widely recognized as important to the goals of the Clean Water Act, riparian zones are not fully protected by it. Some parts of riparian ecosystems are regulated because they are located at an elevation below ordinary high-water, which qualifies them as waters of the United States, or because they conform to regulatory definitions of wetlands. Other parts of riparian ecosystems are unregulated because they do not satisfy any of the broadly-used definitions of wetlands and they lie outside the ordinary high-water mark. Unregulated riparian areas in arid climatic regions such as the Southwest and the Great Basin include cottonwood-willow streamside forests as well as bosques on

the higher portions of floodplains. These riparian ecosystems often include jurisdictional wetlands (Appendix B, Verde River case study).

The overstory of arid zone riparian ecosystems is typically dominated by
phreatophytes, plant species that rely on water drawn from points below the water
table. Riparian phreatophytes of the West typically cannot live on uplands where
the water table is inaccessible. Thus, whereas upland species can tolerate drought,
riparian species avoid the effects of drought by use of shallow ground water near
streams or rivers. Although ground water is close enough to the surface to
support phreatophytes in arid zone riparian ecosystems, it is not close enough to
sustain a hydrophyte-dominated wetland. Furthermore, full inundation might
occur only during occasional floods at intervals of many years. Also, soils of arid
riparian ecosystems generally lack hydric properties because organic matter seldom accumulates in sufficient quantities to cause the development of
redoximorphic features and because saturation at or very near the surface is
infrequent.

Riparian ecosystems also can be found along headwater streams and annually inundated floodplains in humid regions such as the eastern United States and
the Pacific Northwest. Significant proportions of these riparian zones often
qualify as wetlands, but the uppermost portions typically do not. The upper
zones of floodplains do flood periodically, but not often enough to qualify as
wetlands. Even so, riparian zones outside wetland boundaries perform functions
that are similar or complementary to those of wetlands. Even where the riparian
zones of headwater streams are jurisdictional wetlands, however, protection is
weak because of Nationwide Permit 26, through which significant alteration of
headwater wetlands can occur (see following section on isolated and headwater
wetlands).

Since 1968, the National Flood Insurance Program has conditioned the availability of flood insurance on the adoption of local regulations designed to limit
construction in the 100-year floodplain. Areas that receive flood disaster relief
also must submit hazard mitigation plans for approval by the Federal Emergency
Management Agency. These statutory programs are supplemented by Executive
Order 11988, which directs federal agencies to avoid supporting development in
floodplains if there is a practical alternative. Although federal policies are not
oriented toward protection of the natural functions of floodplains, they have
slowed the alteration of floodplains. Many state and local governments have
supplemented the federal programs with even more restrictive regulations.
Complementary programs that acknowledge the importance of riparian zones in
hydrologic buffering and in the maintenance of water quality and biodiversity are
warranted but have not yet been developed.

Riparian zones may contain wetlands that meet the present regulatory definitions of wetland as well as the reference definition that is given in Chapter 3.
Examples include floodplain depressions that are inundated every year or in most
years, abandoned channel remnants that extend to contact with groundwater, or

that accumulate considerable precipitation that causes them to be wet for extended intervals. In addition, however, riparian zones often contain substantial amounts of land that cannot be classified as wetland according to present regulatory definitions or the reference definition given in Chapter 3. For example, a broad definition of the riparian zone would correspond to the high-water mark of the hundred-year flood near a river channel. The uppermost portion of this zone would be inundated only once every hundred years on average, and even when inundated, it might not retain water very long. Thus this upper margin of the floodplain would not meet the requirements for recurrent, sustained inundation or saturation at or near the surface. Vegetation in this part of the riparian zone would not be predominantly hydrophytic, although the zone might contain some phreatophyte species dependent on a water table several feet below the surface of the substrate. The substrate would not show any physical or chemical evidence of repeated, sustained inundation. Thus riparian zones are not wholly contained within the set of ecosystems defined as wetlands by existing regulatory definitions or by the reference definition of Chapter 3. This conclusion does not imply that riparian zones are unimportant to the goals of the Clean Water Act, or that riparian zones are not critically threatened in much the same way that wetlands are threatened, but rather that extension of the definition of wetland to cover all riparian zones would unreasonably broaden the definition of wetland and undermine the specificity of criteria and indicators that have developed around wetland delineation. A recommendation from this section can be found at the end of this chapter, recommendation number 4.

ISOLATED WETLANDS AND HEADWATERS

As explained in Chapter 4, Nationwide Permit 26 affects isolated wetlands and headwaters, by authorizing the filling of relatively small areas if the permitted activity is consistent with CWA regulations. Most of the nationwide general permits refer to categories of activities, such as construction of aids to navigation, rather than to categories of wetlands. Unlike the other nationwide permits, Nationwide Permit 26 authorizes discharge to wetlands on the basis of their position in the drainage network, rather than on the basis of the activity itself. It permits filling of up to 1 acre (0.4 ha) with no review and 10 acres (4 ha) with minimal review in headwaters and isolated waters. Isolated waters, which include vernal pools, playas, potholes, and alpine wet meadows, are defined as the nontidal waters of the United States that are not a part of a surface tributary system to interstate or navigable waters of the United States and that are not adjacent to such tributary bodies of water (33 CFR 330.2). Even though such wetlands qualify for protection under Section 404 jurisdiction, Nationwide Permit 26 excludes some types of wetlands from individual permit requirements, except when overridden by the USACE division engineer. Nationwide Permit 26 has been controversial because of the cumulative wetland losses that can result through its application, and it is the cause of more litigation than any other nationwide permit (Strand, 1993).

As indicated in Chapters 3 and 5, many functions of wetlands can be independent of isolation or adjacency. Even water quality functions might not be fully separate for isolated and other wetlands because of the ground water connections between isolated wetlands and surface waters. Special treatment of headwaters is also questionable, given that headwaters affect water quality downstream and perform many of the other functions of wetlands (Johnson and McCormick, 1979; Lowrance et al., 1984a, b; Peterjohn and Correll, 1984; Cooper and Gilliam, 1987; Cooper et al., 1987). The scientific basis for policies that attribute less importance to headwater areas and isolated wetlands than to other wetlands is weak.

Small, shallow wetlands that are isolated from rivers are frequently important to waterfowl. For example, pintail draw a substantial proportion of their diet from the shallowest potholes (personal communication, 1994, Carter Johnson, South Dakota State University). Although these wetlands make up only 4% of the surface water in the pothole region, they support a large percentage of the total populations of several of the most abundant species such as mallards, gadwall, bluewing teal, shoveler, and pintail (Kantrud et al., 1989b). Studies of the prairie potholes of the northern Plains states have shown why shallow potholes are especially important (Appendix B). Shallow potholes develop invertebrate populations earliest in the spring because they thaw earlier than do deeper potholes; invertebrates in turn provide critical early-season forage for the earliest waterfowl migrants of the Mississippi flyway. Similarly, for snowmelt-dependent depressional wetlands of the San Luis Valley of Colorado, in an area with 19,856 acres (8,039 ha) of wetlands, intermittently wet wetlands comprise the largest surface area (61%) and provide 81% of waterfowl food (personal communication, 1994, David Cooper, Colorado State University).

A recommendation from this section can be found at the end of this chapter, recommendation number 5.

ESPECIALLY SHALLOW OR
INTERMITTENTLY FLOODED WETLANDS

In some portions of the United States, including the arid West, annual rainfall is especially variable in total amount and in timing. Because wetlands in these areas may become completely dry for several years, the concept of average conditions can be difficult to apply. For example, Zedler (Bedford et al., 1992) showed that for San Diego, California, only 21 years out of 140 had total rainfall within 90-110% of the long-term average.

Because wetlands are important in meeting CWA goals, then the wettest of wetlands might seem to be the areas most in need of protection. Landscape position and other factors are also important, however. For example, wetlands in zones that flood only intermittently could be among the most important for storing flood waters; their capacity to reduce peak discharge would be negligible if they were always full.

It is sometimes difficult for the regulated public to understand how sites that are often dry can be classified as wetlands. Part of the reason, as explained in Chapters 2 and 5, is that intermittently flooded wetlands have a distinctive, water-dependent biota. Temporary wetlands support a variety of invertebrates, algae, or mosses that can persist over dry intervals as propagules (seeds, ephippia, spores). Propagules of these organisms are absent in uplands. Some upland plants and animals can colonize a wetland during prolonged dry periods, but the wetland biota will return with the water. For example, California's vernal pool fairy shrimp (*Branchinecta sandiegoensis*) can hatch within 48 hours and can complete its life cycle within 2 weeks (King et al., 1993; Simovich, 1993). Only about 15% of the eggs hatch at a time; if the first inundation period is short, a second wetting stimulates additional hatching. In this way, populations can be sustained even where inundation is brief and intermittent. During the long, dry summers, these same pools can be dry. They do not support extensive upland vegetation, however, because there is too much water for its establishment in the wet season and not enough in the dry season.

The dependence of fish species on temporarily wet habitats is discussed by Finger and Stewart (1987), who document a decline in spring-spawning sunfishes of southeastern Missouri after the reduction of spring flooding. Seasonally flooded bottomlands greatly increase the feeding areas for fish, as has been shown for the Atchafalaya Basin, in Louisiana. Lambou (1990) noted that 54% of the 95 finfish species use wooded areas of the basin for reproduction and 56% use them for feeding. The total harvest attributable to overflow areas was nearly 51,300 lbs/sq. mile (9,000 kg/km²) per year of finfish and nearly 400,000 lbs/sq. mile (70,000 kg/km²) per year of crawfish. Junk et al. (1989) report a strong relationship between the extent of accessible floodplain and fishery yields and production. During the rising floodwater period, fish take advantage of food and shelter in riparian wetlands.

Shallow wetlands could be especially valuable in maintenance of water quality because of their high ratio of sediment surface relative to water volume. For example, wetlands in Minnesota are more effective in removing suspended solids, total phosphorus, and ammonia during high flows when waters cover more of the higher-elevation areas of the wetland, while nitrate removal is more effective during low flow (Johnston et al., 1990).

Wetlands that are intermittently dry can retain wetland characteristics only if they are protected from physical alteration when dry. Delineation of intermittently dry wetlands can be justified by the same rationale as for other wetlands, and can follow the same methodology as delineation of other wetlands.

AGRICULTURAL WETLANDS

Agricultural wetlands are defined here as wetlands found on agricultural lands. Agricultural lands, in turn, are those that are intensively used and managed for food and fiber production and from which natural vegetation has been removed and cannot be used in making a wetland determination. Examples include cropland, hayland, and pasture composed of planted grasses and legumes; orchards; vineyards; and areas that support wetland crops such as cranberries, taro, watercress, and rice (NFSAM, 1994).

Agricultural and silvicultural activities and associated lands were originally exempted from the permitting requirements of CWA Section 404. This created a conflict within the federal government in that the USACE and EPA were encouraging wetland conservation through the act, whereas the U.S. Department of Agriculture was encouraging wetland drainage projects with federal subsidies. This changed when Congress passed the FSA "swampbuster" provisions (Chapter 4).

As a result of an executive decision by President Clinton in August 1993, the lead agency for delineating wetlands on all agricultural lands is now the Natural Resources Conservation Service (NRCS) of the U.S. Department of Agriculture (Chapter 4). NRCS is responsible for an estimated 20 million acres (8 million ha) of wetlands, or about 20% of the nation's remaining wetlands in the contiguous United States (Table 6.1). The cost to NRCS for carrying out these new responsibilities will be $15.6 million annually if intensively managed agricultural lands alone are delineated. If native grazing lands are included, the cost will be an additional $10.4 million per year (personal communication, 1994, Billy Teels, Wetlands Staff Leader, NRCS).

The current and historical use of agricultural land, and especially the date of conversion to cropland, are important in determining whether a tract can be

TABLE 6.1 Estimated Area of Wetlands for Which NRCS Is Responsible Under 1994 MOA

Category	Millions of Acres (ha)
Farmed wetlands	7 (2.8)
Wetlands farmed under natural conditions	3 (1.2)
Farmed wetland pasture-hay	9 (3.6)
Nonagricultural wetland inclusions within agricultural lands	1 (0.4)
Total	20 (8)

Source: Written response by Billy M. Teels, U.S. Natural Resources Conservation Service, June 22, 1994.

TABLE 6.2. Agricultural Wetlands and Wetlands in Agricultural Settings as Defined by the NRCS

Name	Definition
Wetland	Meets wetland criteria under natural conditions and has typically not been manipulated by alteration of hydrology or vegetation. Can be used only to produce agricultural commodity if natural conditions prevail.
Prior converted	Drained, filled, or manipulated before Dec. 23, 1985, sufficient to make production possible, and an agricultural commodity was planted or produced at least once before Dec. 23, 1985.
Farmed wetland	Manipulated and planted before Dec. 23, 1985 but still meets wetland criteria, i.e., not converted prior to that date; can produce agricultural commodities without loss of benefits and existing drainage systems can be maintained.
Farmed wetland pasture	Manipulated and used for pasture or hayland before Dec. 23, 1985; management similar to farmed wetland.
Converted wetland	Drained, dredged, filled, or otherwise manipulated to make production of an agricultural commodity possible.
Converted wetland for non-agricultural purpose	Converted for purposes other than producing agricultural commodities (trees, vineyards, fish farms, cranberries, roads, building, waste management structures, livestock ponds, parking lots).
Artificial wetland	Nonwetland converted to wetland through human activities.

considered for exemption under the swampbuster provisions. Table 6.2 lists some varieties of agricultural wetlands that are recognized by the National Food Security Act Manual, third edition. The switching point for history of these wetlands is Dec. 23, 1985, the date of FSA's enactment. Although implementation of the act is complicated, the basic concept is that wetlands that were drained or manipulated before that date can be maintained for agricultural production. Owners who drained or manipulated wetlands after that date are subject to federal penalties (Chapter 4).

All four federal agencies that deal extensively with wetlands (NRCS, EPA, USACE, and the Fish and Wildlife Service [FWS]) are participating in a new effort to improve and standardize wetland identification and delineation on agricultural lands. One potential concern, however, is that agricultural wetlands will begin to diverge as separate from those regulated by USACE and EPA. This divergence could be fostered by maintenance of separate delineation manuals for agricultural and nonagricultural wetlands. Several major differences based on policy rather than science are already apparent (Chapters 4 and 5).

Wetlands in the United States are often found in agricultural settings. In fact, a significant proportion of the 117 million acres (46.8 million ha) of wetland loss in the lower 48 states since the 1780s (Dahl, 1990) can be attributed to the conversion of wetlands to agricultural use. Much of this conversion has occurred in the upper Midwest and in the lower Mississippi River Valley. Shaw and Fredine (1956) attributed a loss of 45 million acres (18.2 million ha) primarily to the Swamp Land Acts of the mid-nineteenth century (Chapter 3). In addition, more than 57 million acres (22.8 million ha) of wet farmland, including some wetlands, was drained under the terms of the U.S. Department of Agriculture's Agricultural Conservation Program between 1940 and 1977 (OTA, 1984).

Between 1900 and 1990, except for the years of the Great Depression, there was a steady conversion of wet farmland to drained farmland (Gosselink and Maltby, 1990; Mitsch and Gosselink, 1993); an estimated 65% of this wet farmland was wetland (OTA, 1984). Between the 1950s and 1970s, most wetland conversions (87%) were caused by agricultural activity; from the 1970s to the 1980s, nearly 1.3 million acres (about 510,000 ha) or 54% of the conversion of palustrine wetland was caused by agricultural activity (Dahl and Johnson, 1991). As a result of wetlands protection legislation, especially FSA (Chapter 4), the loss rate has probably slowed, although few reliable data are available since the estimate by Dahl and Johnson. Although reduced in extent, wetlands that remain on farmed land are potentially subject to protection by CWA and FSA (Chapter 4).

Some wetlands are now being used agriculturally without being converted. For example, depressional wetlands are sometimes allowed to flood and develop naturally in wet years or wet seasons, but are used for crops in dry years or during the dry season (Chapters 4 and 5; Appendix B, prairie pothole case study). Some wetlands also are being created and restored on former agricultural land through federal incentive programs to promote the removal of drainage systems, filling of drainage ditches, or the breaking of drainage tiles (NRC, 1992). FWS estimates that, as result of the conservation reserve program within FSA, about 90,000 acres (36,450 ha) of wetlands was restored from 1987 to 1990, much of it farmland. About 43,000 acres (17,400 ha) of wetlands was restored in the upper Midwest alone between 1987 and 1992 (Mitsch and Gosselink, 1993). In 1990, NRCS began to administer a wetlands reserve program that has acquired easements on agricultural lands that were formerly wetlands (Chapter 4). In fiscal year 1994, $67 million was authorized for the program and approximately 590,000 acres (23,900 ha) of land was offered by landowners for restoration. This is far in excess of the goal of 75,000 acres (30,300 ha) for 1994. Another 25,000 acres (10,100 ha) will be restored to wetland status through the Emergency Wetland Reserve Program for the Midwest flood area (personal communication, 1994, Billy Teels, Wetlands Staff Leader, NRCS).

Agricultural wetlands are generally found in an extensively altered landscape where they can be particularly important for controlling water quality, preventing floods, and maintaining biodiversity. These wetlands are also of special interest because they are now being managed and protected under a different set of definitions and rules and by a different federal agency than are most other wetlands (Chapters 3 and 4).

Functions of Agricultural Wetlands

Wetlands in agricultural settings have the same range of natural functions as do wetlands elsewhere. In addition, they often receive sediment, nitrate, phosphate, organic matter, and pesticides associated with the agricultural practices on adjacent lands. There has been considerable research on the ability of wetlands in agricultural settings to serve as sinks for fertilizers such as phosphate and nitrate (Peterjohn and Correll, 1984; Jacobs and Gilliam, 1985; Cooper et al., 1986, 1987; Mitsch, 1992, 1994) and a limited number of studies show the potential for wetlands to adsorb agricultural pesticides (Rodgers and Dunn, 1992). The water quality improvement function is often well developed in these systems, although pollutants can cause stress. Because many former wetlands were drained for crop production, the hydroperiods of wetlands that remain on or near agricultural lands might have been altered and floodwater retention functions diminished. Thus, although the wetlands in agricultural settings are potentially valuable for maintenance of water quality, they can be significantly disturbed and can show reduced functional capacity. van der Valk and Jolly (1992) present the argument that natural wetlands in rural settings should not be used as sinks for processing of nonpoint source pollutants because natural wetlands have been greatly reduced in agricultural settings and should therefore be preserved for their habitat and recreational values. Also, these wetlands in many cases already receive significant amounts of agricultural runoff.

Differential Regulation of Agricultural Wetlands

There are several major differences in the regulation of agricultural and nonagricultural wetlands.

• Wetland delineations for agricultural lands routinely are based on aerial photography and soil maps; seldom on field data (Chapter 8).
• Wetlands have different definitions in the National Food Security Act Manual (NFSAM, 1994) and in the USACE manuals (Chapter 4).
• The burden is with the federal government, through the NRCS, to prove that an agricultural area is a wetland. With nonagricultural delineations, the applicant is typically required to submit a delineation showing that there are no wetlands on a site to be developed.
• There is no threshold date for exemption of wetland conversions of nonagricultural lands through the 1987 Corps manual, as there is for agricultural lands.
• There is no binding regulatory classification of nonagricultural wetlands.

  • Criteria for identifying agricultural and nonagricultural wetlands differ in some respects (Chapter 4) .

SITES ALTERED FOR NONAGRICULTURAL PURPOSES

Altered sites are those that have been changed recently by anthropogenic or natural events to the extent that one or more indicators of wetland character are absent, obscured, or provide information that is not representative of current conditions. Such sites can retain their original character, either as wetlands or as uplands, or their character might have changed or be indiscernible by a standard field assessment. Much of the North American landscape has been subject to some degree of perturbation, but many disturbances do not change the character of wetland ecosystems. Altered sites are those at which disturbance has been recent enough and extensive enough that normal conditions are not readily apparent by the indicators of hydrology, substrate, and biota. Special methods could be required for the assessment of such sites for wetland determination and delineation.

Types of Alterations

Anthropogenic activities other than agriculture that alter substantial areas of wetlands include logging and silviculture, peat and mineral mining, construction of roads, construction of reservoirs, building of commercial and residential structures, dredging and disposal for maintenance of navigation, introduction of exotic plant and animal species, and numerous other physical and biological disturbances. These activities involve alteration of wetlands by: draining, dredging, or filling; structural modification of the hydrologic regime; removal or alteration of vegetation and wetland substrate; and discharge of pollutants (Mitsch and Gosselink, 1993). Natural events that affect the formation and status of wetlands include floods, erosion, alluvial or sediment deposition, earthquakes, landslides, fires, stream channel changes, wildlife activity, and plant succession. The results of such events include: draining or filling; modification of hydrologic regime through the creation or destruction of landscape features; destruction or introduction of vegetation components; and release or sequestering of nutrients.

Although many changes can occur in altered wetlands, changes in vegetation, soils, and hydrology carry the greatest implications for the determination of jurisdiction or regulatory action. While the following alteration types are given primarily in terms of anthropogenic origins, some similar kinds of alterations can come about naturally as well:

  • Complete removal of vegetation, which typically includes the use of biological indicators. The removal of vegetation can decrease water retention time, thus decreasing the duration of saturation, or decrease the amount of evapotranspiration, thus increasing the duration of saturation.

• Partial removal of vegetation, which can alter the outcome of vegetation assessments. Selective removal of specific components (by overstory logging, burning of the herbaceous and shrub layers) also can cause hydrologic change.

• Herbicide treatment, which can remove specific vegetative components. Few herbicides are specific for hydrophytic species, but chemical specificity for herbaceous broadleaf plants, grasses, or woody vegetation can result in misleading results for plant surveys.

• Grazing or mowing, which can shift the composition of the plant community, often toward the xerophytic end of the spectrum.

• Planting or introduction of vegetation that can alter plant communities. Agricultural and silvicultural practices frequently result in total replacement of the natural plant community. Likewise, introduction or invasion by aggressive species can alter community composition. These actions also can influence the hydrology of a site.

Soil disturbances and associated ramifications include the following:

• Soil removal, which can change the results of soil analysis or alter the relative water retention capacity of the substrate, thus either increasing or decreasing the degree of saturation and vegetation of a site.

• Soil disturbance, which can complicate the assessment of soil character. It can destroy or mask some indicators and, through time, can reduce the hydric character of a soil. Where subsurface clay layers limit drainage, soil disturbance may also alter the hydrology of the site.

• Covering of the soil, which results in the burial of soils that are relevant to delineation. It also can alter the hydrology of the site, usually by decreasing the likelihood of saturation.

Hydrologic alterations and their associated ramifications include

• Increased drainage through ditching, dike removal, or tiling, which lowers water levels and shortens the duration of saturation.

• Water removal, which can reduce the likelihood of saturation.

• Water addition, which can result in higher water tables and greater amounts of saturation. Such changes can result in the formation of a wetland community through time; others can be ephemeral and of insufficient consequence to justify wetland status.

• Change in water retention, either through excavation or impediment to drainage, which can result in higher probability of saturation.

Hydrologic alterations can originate at some distance from a site and might not be directly related to its management. For example, municipal withdrawal of water from an aquifer can reduce the wetland character of sites that are connected to the aquifer. Such sites can retain indicators, such as hydrophytic vegetation or hydric soils, that developed before the hydrologic change. Conversely, impoundment of water can maintain a high water table near an impoundment.

Identification of Normal Conditions

In the assessment of altered sites it is important to have information about normal conditions before the alteration, normal conditions after the alteration, the timing of the alteration, and the origin of the alteration. Generally, the assessment of normal conditions subsequent to alteration is done through standard wetland delineation procedures. There are some exceptions to this, however, in that one or more important indicators can be absent or significantly altered. The timing and origin of the alteration usually can be ascertained either from a landowner or from other persons. When the determination of normal conditions must be made at altered sites, special methods must sometimes be used in assessing normal vegetation, soils, and hydrology.

Assessment of Altered Lands

Evidence of normal vegetation can be derived from

• Review of aerial photographs. Both the National Wetlands Inventory (NWI) and NRCS maintain aerial photographs of wetlands. These can be useful in assessment of normal conditions. Local runoff or meteorologic data should be used in identifying seasons and years when normal conditions would be most likely observed.
• Study of adjacent similar areas. Analysis of unaltered reference areas can provide information on the normal vegetation at an altered site.
• Interviews. Landowners and other persons can provide useful information on the previous vegetation of an altered site.
• Remnants. Remnants of a plant community can provide sufficient information to support a delineation. Trees can frequently be identified by their stumps as well as by leaf and mast remnants. Buried vegetation can sometimes be excavated and identified.
• Review of NWI or NRCS maps. NWI maps provide basic descriptive information on vegetation. NRCS maps also provide some information about vegetation.

Evidence of preexisting soils can be derived from

• Soil survey maps. Soil survey maps can provide useful information on soils, but care must be taken in interpreting them (Chapter 5).

• Soil samples. If the original soils have been buried, sampling pits will show the preexisting A horizon. Historic deposition, however, might have covered relict hydric soils that antedate CWA Section 404 enforcement. When the surface soils have been disturbed or removed, soil horizons immediately below the disturbed zone can be examined for indications of hydric character.

• Soils of adjacent areas. Soils tend to be of the same type in similar geomorphic positions on the landscape. When the preexisting soil has been removed or has otherwise been made unavailable for assessment, reference areas can be used to infer original soil types.

Evidence of preexisting hydrology can be derived from

• Hydrologic models. As discussed in Chapters 5 and 8, hydrologic models can provide evidence of hydrology prior to alteration.

• Topographic maps. Sites in close proximity on the landscape will tend to exhibit similar hydrology. In such cases, review of topographic maps based on preexisting conditions can be of assistance in evaluating hydrology. This evidence can be particularly useful for flood plains, where the primary factor of importance is elevation (Appendix B, Steele Bayou case study).

• Aerial photographs. Aerial photographs can provide evidence of standing water, but they do not indicate saturation. Aerial photographs only rarely provide indications of duration of inundation, but the use of gauging or meteorologic data can increase the utility of these photographs. Also, NRCS currently uses evidence of stunted vegetation as an indicator of wetland hydrology. Such evidence can be used to infer prealteration conditions in conjunction with corroborative information, such as position in landscape and presence of hydric soils. Vegetation can be stunted as a result of several factors, however, and should not be considered definitive without supporting evidence.

Limitations of Assessment Methods for Altered Sites

The assessment methods mentioned above are recommended by the 1989 interagency manual and the 1987 Corps manual. The results are subject to varying degrees of uncertainty, which can be reduced through the use of mutual kinds of evidence, which should be a priority for controversial cases. As is often true for standard delineations, the greatest uncertainty will likely be associated with the placement of the boundary line of a wetland. The establishment of the wetland boundary will involve professional judgment as well as technical analysis.

A recommendation concerning altered lands can be found at the end of this chapter as recommendation number 11.

TRANSITIONAL ZONES

On gentle gradients, or where microtopography causes wetlands to be interspersed with uplands on fine scales, the wetland boundary can be difficult to locate (Chapters 2 and 5). The same is true of marginal sites where wetland status is questionable because evidence is weak or inconsistent. These transitional and marginal areas have stirred debate and criticism of current and past identification and delineation of wetlands. In these difficult cases, the evidence must be carefully weighed against the minimum essential characteristics of wetlands, namely: hydrologic features associated with flooding or saturation and the presence of organisms and physical and chemical features that reflect continuous or frequently recurring saturation or flooding. Evidence should be calibrated regionally for specific wetland types to facilitate more consistent delineation; reference wetlands are useful for this purpose.

An approach that requires no conflicting evidence might have the effect of excluding some wetlands. In contrast, an approach that does not require strong evidence and that ignores conflicting evidence could include some uplands. For these reasons, the consequences of delineation procedures must be carefully considered on a regional basis. A recommendation concerning transitional zones is listed as recommendation number 11 at the end of this chapter.

RECOMMENDATIONS

1. Permafrost wetlands, which have structure and function similar to those of nonpermafrost wetlands, should be identified and delineated by the same principles as are other wetlands.

2. A better scientific understanding of permafrost wetlands should be developed.

3. The correlation of soils and hydrology as well as vegetation and hydrology should be studied for permafrost wetlands.

4. Riparian zones perform many of the same functions as do wetlands, including maintenance of water quality, storage of floodwaters, and enhancement of biodiversity, especially in the western United States. Although they typically contain wetlands, riparian zones cannot be defined wholly as wetlands by any broad definition. If national policy extends to protection of riparian zones pursuant to the goals of the Clean Water Act, regulation must be achieved through legislation that recognizes the special attributes of these landscape features, and not by attempting to define them as wetlands.

5. The scientific basis for special permitting of wetlands in headwaters or isolated wetlands is weak. Nationwide Permit 26 has been controversial because of the cumulative wetland losses that can result through its application. Conse-

quently, Nationwide Permit 26 should be reviewed for validity in the context of the Clean Water Act and for consistency with other permitting practices.

6. Especially shallow wetlands or wetlands that are only intermittently wet perform the same kinds of functions as other wetlands and can be delineated by the same procedures as those used for other wetlands.

7. Wetlands on agricultural lands should not be regulated differently from other wetlands. These wetlands may have many of the same attributes as do other wetlands, including maintenance of water quality, and there is no scientific basis for delineating them under definitions or federal manuals different from those applicable to other wetlands.

8. Wetlands in agricultural settings can enhance runoff water quality; the impairment of this function by agricultural practice should be considered when wetlands are proposed for agricultural use.

9. When wetlands are to be constructed or restored using agricultural lands, it is preferable to locate such projects near natural wetlands. Restoration on agricultural lands should be encouraged whenever these practices can reduce impairment of the remaining natural wetlands on or near agricultural lands.

10. Inference of wetland features that have been removed or changed by natural or anthropogenic means should be allowed as part of wetland delineation on altered lands. Federal manuals should instruct delineators on the valid use of inference for this purpose.

11. Application of delineation methods should be tested on transitional and marginal lands in all regions.

7

Regionalization

INTRODUCTION

Regional variation among wetlands affects the validity and usefulness of nationwide procedures for delineation. Not only wetlands, but also the upland ecosystems with which they interface, are regionally variable. This variation accounts for much of the difficulty in developing reliable procedures and indicators that can be used to establish wetland boundaries in all parts of the United States.

Gallant et al. (1989) define a region as an area that is to a certain extent homogeneous with respect to specific characteristics of interest for a particular purpose. Regionalization is "a method of reducing or eliminating details which do not, on the average, hold true over large areas" (Wiken, 1986). Regionalization for the purpose of wetland delineation, therefore, would require the identification of areas with some degree of homogeneity in wetland characteristics and the development of specific regional procedures or indicators.

A regionalized delineation approach involves several steps. First, regional boundaries must be circumscribed around an area with unifying properties. Second, the occurrence and fidelity of wetland indicators within that region must be determined. Finally, a regionally valid system must be adopted for applying indicators to wetland determinations. Regionalization thus extends beyond mere division of a national list of indicators into subsets (such as state lists) because true regionalization involves the regional adaptation of indicators and delineation methods.

Current wetland delineation methodologies already incorporate some regional elements. For example, regional hydrophyte and hydric soil lists supplement the broad national criteria and indicators for identification and delineation of wetlands. Regional offices for each of the four federal agencies that deal extensively with wetlands, i.e., U.S. Army Corps of Engineers (USACE), National Resources Conservation Service (NRCS), U.S. Fish and Wildlife Service (FWS), and U.S. Environmental Protection Agency (EPA) consider regional conditions as they identify and delineate wetlands. This chapter contains an evaluation of the ways in which wetland delineation is currently regionalized as well as the potential for increasing its regionalization.

HIERARCHY OF REGIONAL VARIATION

Wetlands, which occur at every latitude from the equator to the arctic, vary in precipitation, evapotranspiration, temperature, and insolation. Wetland hydrology, substrates, and biota reflect this climatic variation. Land forms also can be a cause of variation because of their relationship to regional geomorphology associated with such factors as glaciation and change in sea level. In addition, the composition and stratigraphy of underlying geologic deposits vary regionally and strongly influence wetland formation and characteristics. Wetland size, configuration, and hydrology are greatly influenced by climatic and geomorphic factors (Johnston, 1982; Winter, 1992; Brinson, 1993a).

Variation of wetlands occurs over a hierarchy of scale from continental to sites within a wetland (Table 7.1). The principal type of variation at the continental scale is physiographic regions as a result of climate, especially as it reflects temperature and precipitation. The balance between precipitation and evapotranspiration rates greatly influences the prevalence of wetlands in the landscape and the duration of inundation. Because variation in growing season occurs at this scale, many of the difficulties associated with the application of numeric

TABLE 7.1   Scales, Types, and Cause of Variation at Scales Arranged from Coarsest to Finest (Causes of Variation at Large Scales May Also Affect Smaller Scales)

Scale of Variation	Characteristic Type of Variation	Cause of Variation
Continental (U.S.)	Among physiographic regions	Climate
Physiographic region	Among wetland classes	Geomorphic setting, water sources, hydrodynamics
Wetland class	Size and connections to upland, aquatic, and other wetlands	Hydroperiod, soils, plant assemblages
Intra-wetland	Topographic position	Plant species composition, hydrologic status, redoximorphic features

thresholds (days of continuous saturation) could be minimized by regionalization at the continental scale. Appropriate regional boundaries for wetlands would divide some large states and cluster other small states. Many wetland delineators feel comfortable working within a region because it matches the geographic extent of their expertise in wetland flora and soils.

Variation occurs also within physiographic regions (Table 7.1). A given region may have all classes of wetlands which will differ substantially from one another in geomorphic setting, water sources, and hydrodynamics. For example, bogs, tidal marshes, and freshwater swamps can all be found within a single region. Classes often cluster, however, as mountainous areas tend to support riparian wetlands, whereas glaciated plains are rich in depressional wetlands.

Within a wetland class, variation is found in size and the connection of individual wetlands to other landscape units, including other wetlands that occur in vast wetland complexes. These connections influence functionally important processes such as the capacity for nutrient removal or the quality of habitat for estuarine dependent fish. Variation will be found in hydroperiod, soils, and plant assemblages.

The smallest scale relevant to characterization of wetlands is the intra-wetland scale. Topographic position within the wetland along the wetness gradient accounts for variation at this scale. Combinations of plant species, inundation and saturation, and redoximorphic soil features as they occur along the wetland to upland continuum, make this scale of variation the major focus of wetland delineation. Given the amount of variation at scales larger than that within a single wetland (Table 7.1), however, it is clear that excessive focus on individual sites could lead to the development of delineation systems that fail to account for variation at larger scales.

Regional Variation in Hydrology

Hydrologists have long recognized that the discharge characteristics of a stream are related to the size of its watershed. The hierarchical ordering of streams from the smallest rills in headwater reaches (first order) to rivers of continental scale (greater than sixth order) reflects the relationship of hydrology to scale (Leopold et al., 1964). Groundwater also can be divided into flow systems at local to regional scales (Toth, 1963; Freeze and Cherry, 1979). Groundwater flow systems of local scale have short subsurface flow paths recharged by infiltration on local uplands. These flow paths terminate in adjacent lowlands where the groundwater moves either to the water table or to surface waters. There is also some degree of water loss by evaporation and evapotranspiration.

Unlike local ground water flows, flow systems of intermediate scale (0.6 mi to tens of miles [1 km to tens of km]) have subsurface flow paths that bypass adjacent lowlands. Flow systems of regional scale have even longer flow paths

(6 mi to hundreds of miles [10 km to several hundred kilometers]) that discharge to major rivers and lakes.

Lakes, wetlands, and groundwater interact at a range of scales (Siegel, 1988; Winter, 1992). For example, Siegel and Glaser (1987) have shown that seasonal changes in the amount of groundwater reaching bogs in northern Minnesota is probably related to changes in the height of the water table on beach ridges located many miles away.

Regional contrasts in the groundwater hydrology of wetlands are very large. For example, in the humid northcentral and northeastern states, wetlands in surface depressions are usually located over groundwater discharge areas—where the direction of groundwater flow is upward (McNamara et al., 1992). In contrast, wetlands in the drier parts of the West often conduct water downward, thus causing local elevation of the underlying water table. Examples include prairie pothole wetlands in the northcentral states (Appendix B). Other wetlands, including some prairie pothole wetlands, recharge groundwater during wet weather but receive groundwater during dry weather (Winter, 1989).

In humid and dry regions alike, wetlands can be perched above and isolated from the regional water table wherever wetland soils do not drain efficiently. Isolation of wetlands from the regional groundwater table particularly occurs where hydrology has been altered by control structures and artificial drainage, as is the case on the Mississippi River Delta. The inundation and saturation of riparian wetlands and wetlands near the ocean or large lakes is mostly controlled by fluctuations in the water levels of the adjacent body of water.

Regional Variation of Soils

Climate, topography, and parent material (the geologic substratum from which a soil is derived) are three of the major soil-forming factors upon which classification of soils is based (Jenny, 1941). The proportion of hydric soils is highest for areas with relatively flat topography, glacial or coastal plain geomorphology, and high summer rainfall. In fact, climatic terms are used in the U.S. system of soil taxonomy to describe soil moisture (aquic, aridic, torric, udic, ustic, xeric) and temperature (pergelic, cryic, frigid, mesic, thermic, hyperthermic) (Soil Survey Staff, 1975). Because moisture and temperature are components of climate, soil nomenclature is inherently regional. Most wetland soils, however, fall within the aquic moisture regime, which reduces their climatic differentiation under soil taxonomy to temperature regimes only. Also, fewer regional distinctions are made in the mapping of wetland soils than in the mapping of upland soils because wetland soils are usually mapped in less detail. Many soil surveys use generic terms to classify wetlands (marsh, playa), or assign them to general soil series that occur in more than one state.

Regional Variation of Plants

A number of plant characteristics vary regionally. Plant life form is one of the most obvious of these. For example, forested wetlands dominate in the eastern U.S. (Shaw and Fredine, 1956), whereas nonwoody vegetation dominates wetlands in drier regions, such as the prairie pothole area. Growing seasons for plants differ substantially among regions, and plant phenology reflects the correlated regional variation in light and temperature (Chapter 5). Plants also are adapted to regional differences in soil chemistry related to geomorphology, physiography, and climate (high sediment loads in riverine wetlands or high salt content in wetlands of arid and semiarid zones).

Wetland vegetation consists of at least two groups of plants: those that require soil saturation to become established or to persist and those that tolerate it. Plants that are not found in wetlands are intolerant of the stresses associated with wetland edaphic conditions. As explained in Chapter 5, anaerobic conditions are the most common source of stress accounting for the absence of upland plants. Indicators that account only for the tolerance of wetland plants and the intolerance of upland plants are suitable for many regions and wetland types. For some wetland types in some regions, however, species composition reflects a requirement for wetness rather than a tolerance of anaerobic conditions. For example, in the upper salt marshes of California, plants such as *Salicornia subterminalis* (an obligate [OBL] wetland species), *Monanthochloe littoralis* (OBL), and *Atriplex watsonii* (a facultative wetland [FACW] species) become established because of their winter moisture requirements, even though inundation is rare (Nixon, 1982) and soils are oxygenated (Zedler, 1982; Callaway et al., 1990; Pennings and Callaway, 1992). Similarly, most wetland animals (aquatic invertebrates, fish) occur in wetlands because of their requirement for water rather than because of their tolerance of it.

A wetland plant species might require soil saturation for germination and establishment, yet be relatively intolerant of inundation as an adult. Such species are most likely to occur where water levels fluctuate widely, especially where rainfall, runoff, and standing water are episodic and unpredictable, as in the western United States. An example is *Salicornia virginica*, a salt marsh dominant species that is restricted to midintertidal areas because of its high moisture requirements for establishment, but that dies if the canopy is inundated (Zedler et al., 1992). Black cottonwood is considered a wetland species by current researchers, because it depends on the action of water to establish on unvegetated mineral soil. The seeds of this species germinate in sandy soils within two days after flood waters recede, and roots grow at a rate of 1 cm/day for about 40 days thereafter (personal communication, 1994, R. Stettler, University of Washington). Other cotton wood species have similar characteristics (Friedman, 1993). Cottonwood persists even when sedimentation rates are high because it can produce adventitious roots, thus adapting to burial of the root crown. In contrast,

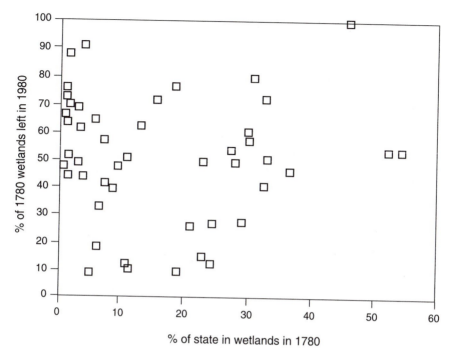

FIGURE 7.1 Comparison of wetlands in 1780 to wetlands in 1980 for all of the United States. Source: Dahl, 1990.

alder (*Alnus rubra*), a faculative (FAC) species often found in uplands, does not release seed coincident with spring flooding, nor do its seedlings produce adventitious roots.

Regional Variation in Abundance of Wetlands

Differences in geomorphology and climate were the cause of variation in wetland abundance among the states before to extensive European settlement. Use of the land resulted in a greater reduction of wetland area in some states than in others, however (Figure 7.1). In this way, anthropogenic influences have magnified natural variations in abundance of wetlands.

With scarcity, resources become more valuable, particularly if they perform a unique function, as does an oasis in a desert. With scarcity of wetland resources comes greater dependence of biota on wetlands for water and food, greater vulnerability of species when a wetland or unit of wetland area is lost, greater public concern over wetland loss, and greater need to protect the appropriate distribution of wetland patches that can sustain biodiversity.

REGIONALIZATION SCHEMES

Regional Classification Systems

The wetland classification system of Cowardin et al. (1979) acknowledges the importance of regionalization and incorporates Bailey's (1976) ecoregion map, which it modifies by the addition of 10 marine and estuarine provinces for North America (Figure 7.2). These regions, which do not appear on the National Wetland Inventory maps, are apparently unused at present.

Several classification systems are specific to particular regions. For example, Stewart and Kantrud (1971) devised a classification system specific to the glaciated prairie pothole region, an area of substantial interannual variability in wetness (Appendix B, prairie pothole case study). This classification system was introduced as a regional alternative to the FWS classification system in use at the time (Shaw and Fredine, 1956) (Chapter 3). In addition to seven types of prairie pothole wetlands, it contains six salinity classes and five hydrologic phases to account for long-term variation in hydrology, and it includes agriculture as a cause of variation. For the glaciated northeast, Golet and Larson (1974) classify freshwater wetland types on the basis of differences in plant life forms. Golet was later a coauthor of the work by Cowardin et al. (1979), which uses a life form approach to classifying wetlands (tree, shrub/scrub, emergent, moss/lichen). Among others, regional wetland classification systems have been developed for Alaska (Schempf, 1992), the southern U.S. (Penfound, 1952; Clark and Benforado, 1981), Ontario (Jeglum et al., 1974), and California (Ferren et al., 1994).

There have been some attempts to classify wetlands regionally according to geologic and hydrologic factors. Novitzki (1979) relates Wisconsin wetlands to water source and landform, Thompson et al. (1992) classifies Iowa fens according to their geologic setting, and Hollands (1987) classifies wetlands in glaciated regions by hydrology and vegetation.

Reports on regional wetland types have been commissioned by FWS, USACE, and EPA. Appendix A of the 1989 interagency manual lists several studies, including a series of "Community Profile" reports that synthesize the literature for a variety of wetland types. These studies provide information about basic wetland ecology that is essential to regionalization, but they generally focus on wetland interiors rather than boundaries. Other relevant regional report series include the FWS Soil-Vegetation Correlation reports (Chapter 5), Preliminary Guides prepared by the USACE (1978a,b,c,d,e; Huffman et al., 1982a,b; Huffman and Tucker, 1984) and transition zone studies commissioned by USACE (Johnson et al., 1982a; Fletcher, 1983).

Several climatic and physiographic schemes could serve as an ecological basis for regionalization. A modified version of Bailey's (1976) ecoregion map is proposed by Cowardin et al. (1979) for this purpose (Figure 7.2). A similar scheme is found in Omernik (1987), who divides the conterminous United States into 76 ecoregions based on land use, land surface form, potential natural vegetation, and soils (Figure 7.3). This scheme has been applied successfully in studies of water quality and fish distribution. Unfortunately, the Omernik system does not include Alaska, Hawaii, or U.S. possessions.

The U.S. Department of Agriculture has divided the country into 27 land resource regions based on physiography and crop potential. Statistically distinct intrastate map units are identified by sampling that was done for the Soil Conservation Service 1982 National Resource Inventory (Lytle, 1993). By acknowledging the influence of human activity, these subdivisions could more accurately portray current wetland status than do schemes based mainly on natural vegetation (Bailey, 1976; Omernik, 1987).

Several approaches could be used to regionalize wetlands on the basis of hydrology. The U.S. Geological Survey has divided the nation into hydrologic units consisting of watersheds for major rivers and coastal regions. This system has been used since 1977 for the National Stream Quality Accounting Network (Briggs and Ficke, 1977), and it is widely used for a variety of other surface water applications. EPA has developed a national "reach file," which divides rivers and streams into segments for which water quality data are collected and summarized. The U.S. Geological Survey and EPA systems would apply to wetlands that occur adjacent to rivers and streams, but would be less applicable to wetlands that receive primarily ground water or runoff.

Brinson (1993a) developed a hydrogeomorphic classification based on geomorphic setting, water source, and hydrodynamics (Table 7.2). A wetland's geomorphic setting is typically related to its capacity to store water and the pattern of water flow. Wetlands range regionally from bogs largely maintained by precipitation to tidal marshes inundated by seawater. In addition, the motion of water (hydrodynamics) can be used to distinguish among wetlands.

Winter (1992) identifies 8 basic physiographic settings in which wetlands form. By combining the physiographic settings with the climatic settings in which each occurs, he identifies 24 type settings for long-term wetlands research (Table 7.3). The wetland type settings are not "regional types" but are analogous to the species type concept. Winter recognizes that almost all wetlands are located where water becomes focused at breaks in the gradient of the water table, either because of depressions in the surface topography or because of changes in hydrogeologic conditions, such as permeability (Winter, 1992). He also recognizes that long-term hydrologic features are related to regional climate.

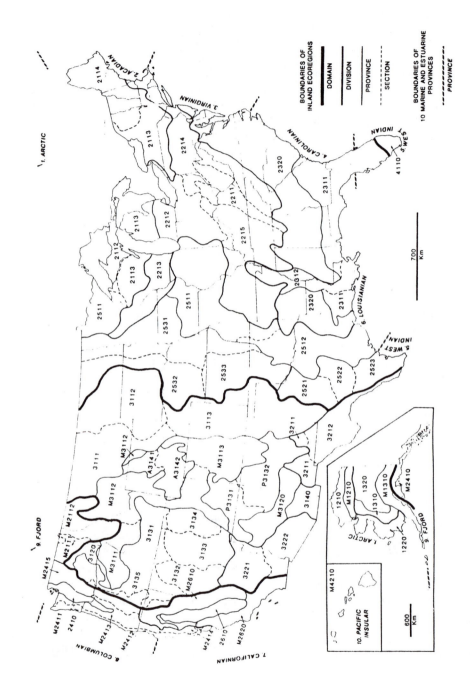

1000 Polar
1200 Tundra
  1210 Arctic Tundra
  1220 Bering Tundra
  M1210 Brooks Range
1300 Subarctic
  1320 Yukon Forest
  M1310 Alaska Range
2000 Humid Temperate
2100 Warm Continental
  2110 Laurentian Mixed Forest
  2111 Spruce-Fir Forest
  2112 Northern Hardwoods-Fir Forest
  2113 Northern Hardwoods Forest
  2114 Northern Hardwoods-Spruce Forest
M2110 Columbia Forest
  M2111 Douglas-fir Forest
  M2112 Cedar-Hemlock-Douglas-fir Forest
2200 Hot Continental
  2210 Eastern Deciduous Forest
  2211 Mixed Mesophytic Forest
  2212 Beech-Maple Forest
  2213 Maple-Basswood Forest + Oak Savanna
  2214 Appalachian Oak Forest
  2215 Oak-Hickory Forest
2300 Subtropical
  2310 Outer Coastal Plain Forest
  2311 Beech-Sweetgum-Magnolia-Pine-Oak
  2312 Southern Floodplain Forest
  2320 Southeastern Mixed Forest

2000 Humid Temperate
2400 Marine
  2410 Willamette-Puget Forest
  M2410 Pacific Forest (in conterminous U.S.)
  M2411 Sitka Spruce-Cedar-Hemlock Forest
  M2412 Redwood Forest
  M2413 Cedar-Hemlock-Douglas-fir Forest
  M2414 California Mixed Evergreen Forest
  M2415 Silver fir-Douglas-fir Forest
  M2410 Pacific Forest (in Alaska)
2500 Prairie
  2510 Prairie Parkland
  2511 Oak-Hickory-Bluestem Parkland
  2512 Oak + Bluestem Parkland
  2520 Prairie Brushland
  2521 Mesquite-Buffalo Grass
  2522 Juniper-Oak-Mesquite
  2523 Mesquite-Acacia
  2530 Tall-Grass Prairie
  2531 Bluestem Prairie
  2532 Wheatgrass-Bluestem-Needlegrass
  2533 Bluestem-Grama Prairie
2600 Mediterranean (Dry-summer Subtropical)
  2610 California Grassland
  M2610 Sierran Forest
  M2620 California Chaparral
3000 Dry
3100 Steppe
  3110 Great Plains-Shortgrass Prairie
  3111 Grama-Needlegrass-Wheatgrass
  3112 Wheatgrass-Needlegrass
  3113 Grama-Buffalo Grass

3000 Dry
3100 Steppe
  M3110 Rocky Mountain Forest
  M3111 Grand fir-Douglas-fir Forest
  M3112 Douglas-fir Forest
  M3113 Ponderosa Pine-Douglas-fir Forest
  3120 Palouse Grassland
  M3120 Upper Gila Mountains Forest
  3130 Intermountain Sagebrush
  3131 Sagebrush-Wheatgrass
  3132 Lahontan Saltbush-Greasewood
  3133 Great Basin Sagebrush
  3134 Bonneville Saltbush-Greasewood
  3135 Ponderosa Shrub Forest
  P3130 Colorado Plateau
  P3131 Juniper-Pinyon Woodland + Sagebrush Saltbush Mosaic
  P3132 Grama-Galleta Steppe + Juniper-Pinyon Woodland Mosaic
  3140 Mexican Highland Shrub Steppe
  A3140 Wyoming Basin
  A3141 Wheatgrass-Needlegrass-Sagebrush
  A3142 Sagebrush-Wheatgrass
3200 Desert
  3210 Chihuahuan Desert
  3211 Grama-Tobosa
  3212 Tarbush-Creosote Bush
  3220 American Desert
  3221 Creosote Bush
  3222 Creosote Bush-Bur Sage
4000 Humid Tropical
4100 Savanna
  4110 Everglades
4200 Rainforest
  M4210 Hawaiian Islands

FIGURE 7.2 Ecoregions of the United States after Bailey (1976) with the addition of 10 marine and estuarine provinces. Source: Cowardin et al., 1979.

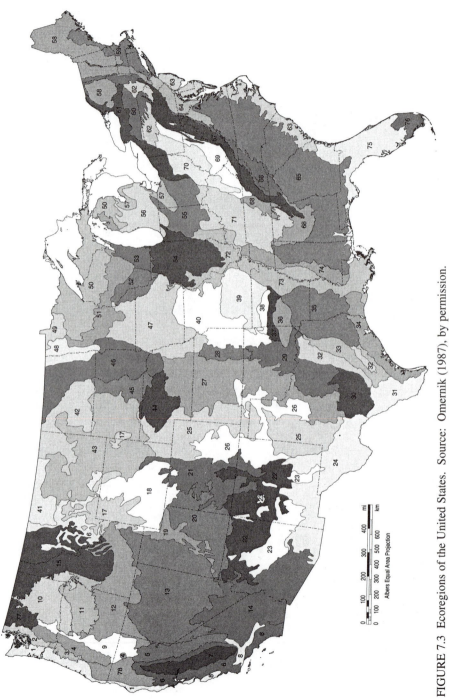

FIGURE 7.3 Ecoregions of the United States. Source: Omernik (1987), by permission.

TABLE 7.2 Hydrogeomorphic Classes of Wetlands Based on Geomorphic
Setting, Water Source, and Hydrodynamics (Brinson, 1993a)

Geomorphic setting	Principal Water Sources	Hydrodynamics	Example
Riverine, flood plain	Overbank, ground water discharge, overland flow	Unidirectional, horizontal	Bottomland hardwood forest
Depression	Precipitation, ground water discharge, overland flow	Vertical	Prairie pothole, Carolina bay
Slope	Ground water discharge	Unidirectional, horizontal	Minnesota fen
Peatland	Precipitation	Vertical	Bog, pocosin peatland
Flat	Precipitation	Vertical	Wet pine savanna, winter wet woods
Lacustrine fringe	Seiches[a]	Bidirectional, horizontal	Great Lakes marsh
Estuarine fringe	Lunar tides	Bidirectional, horizontal	Coastal salt marsh

[a]Harmonic water level fluctuations in large lakes resulting from wind relaxation after a period of setup.

CURRENT APPROACHES

Regionalization of Federal Agencies

The four federal agencies involved in wetland delineation are regionalized administratively, although their regional boundaries do not coincide (Figure 7.4). FWS has the fewest regions (seven), and NRCS has the most (virtually every county and parish in the United States is an NRCS district). Administration of the Clean Water Act Section 404 program by USACE is distributed among 36 districts plus 2 divisions that do not contain districts (Pacific Ocean Division, New England Division). USACE districts are generally bounded by major watershed divides, and are named for the city in which the district office is located. FWS and EPA regions are groups of states (Figure 7.4). NRCS regionalization is the most elaborate and hierarchical: At the county level are district offices, several counties are coordinated by an area office, the area offices are coordinated by a state office, and the state offices report to the national chief of NRCS.

The differences among agencies in regionalization complicate delineation of wetlands because a regional office might need to coordinate not only with other federal agencies, but also with the various regional offices of several agencies. This complexity will increase as NRCS, the most subdivided of the agencies, assumes its new lead role in classification of agricultural wetlands (Chapters 4 and 6).

TABLE 7.3 A Classification System for Wetland Hydrology Based on Climate and Physiography

Physiography	Climate	Region	States[a]
Terrace and scarp	Warm, dry	South Atlantic Coast	NC, SC, VA, MO
with coastal	Warm, wet	Gulf Coast	LA, MS, FL
lowland, including	Cold, dry	Northern Minnesota	MN
tidal			
Terrace within riverine	Cold, wet	Northern Appalachian valleys	New England
valley including	Warm, wet	Southern Appalachian valleys	TN, GA
adjacent upland	Cold	Northern Mississippi valley	MN, WI
and river	Warm	Southern Mississippi valley	AR, LA, MS
	Wet	Eastern tributary of Mississippi River (e.g., Ohio River valley)	KY, OH, IN
	Dry	Western tributary of Mississippi River (e.g., Missouri River valley)	ND, SD, NE, OK, TX
Steep slope adjacent	Cold, wet	North Appalachian uplands	NY, New England
to narrow lowland	Warm, wet	South Appalachia uplands	GA, TN
	Cold, dry	Rocky Mountains	CO, WY, MT, ID,
	Cold, wet	Sierras, Cascades	CA, OR, WA
Depression in large,	Cold, dry	North playas	NV
extensive lowland	Warm, dry	South playas	AZ, NM
Morainal depression	Cold, wet	East northcentral United States	WI, MI
	Cold, dry	West north central United States	ND, SD
	Cold, wet	Puget lowland	WA
Dune field	Cold, wet	East central United States	IN, MI
	Cold, dry	West central United States	NE, WY
	Cold, wet	West Coast	OR, WA
Sink hole	Warm, wet	Southwestern United States	FL
Other depression	Warm, dry	Southeastern United States	TX
Permafrost	Cold, dry	Northern Alaska	AK

[a]The geographic regions and states in table are not all inclusive of the physiographic type but only indicate where the type is well developed.

Source: Modified from Winter, 1992. Reprinted with the permission of the National Hydrological Research Institute, Environment Canada.

The USACE district office is usually the primary point of contact for Section 404 permits. Although all USACE districts use the same manual, there are minor differences among the districts in its implementation. Consultants who perform wetland delineations become accustomed to the standards of a district through their interactions with the staff in the district office, and can adjust their delineations accordingly. Organizational regionalization is not an ecological source of variation, but it is likely to cause some regional variation in wetland delineation.

Regional Lists of Hydrophytes and Soils

Regionalization is invoked in two ways through current delineation method-ologies: first, through the use of regional hydrophyte and state hydric soils lists and second, through the use of growing season, which varies regionally, in the application of soil saturation thresholds. The Hydrophyte List (Chapter 5) is divided into 13 regional lists (Figure 7.5). The 13 regions are assemblages of adjacent states or portions thereof. NRCS has developed from the national Hy-dric Soils List (Chapter 5) local lists of map units that contain hydric soils for each county or parish in the United States. These local lists contain details about soil categories within series ("phases" and "types" within a series) and map units that contain mixed soil series (a complex of hydric and nonhydric soils).

Regional panels were not established for soils as they were for hydrophytes, but the Hydric Soils List (USDA, 1991) was reviewed by NRCS state offices (Chapter 5). State soil scientists also have some latitude to modify the national criteria as necessary to develop state hydric soils lists, and they can petition NTCHS to modify criteria. In Florida, for example, NRCS developed special hydric soil indicators (Hurt and Puckett, 1992). These provisions require that seasonal high water tables persist for a period of 30 days or more, twice the time required nationally (usually more than two weeks) (USDA, 1991). Under these more restrictive thresholds, 13% of Florida that would have been classified as hydric soil under the national standard is classified as upland soil (Hurt and Puckett, 1992).

The decentralized nature of NRCS (Figure 7.4) makes it difficult to draw conclusions about regionalization of hydric soils. NRCS procedures tend to be described in internal memoranda rather than in published documents; the Florida example cited above was unusual in that it was published in a conference pro-ceedings. Also, it is not clear whether county and state lists differ, other than in geographic extent, from the national hydric soils list. This is an example of inconsistency that can occur when delineation is highly decentralized.

Hydrology and Growing Season

There is no hydrologic equivalent of the national lists of wetland plants or hydric soils. Descriptors of the complex wetland hydrologic system are usually limited to the relative height and seasonal variation in the water table or standing water or to indirect indicators of recent flooding. Although hydrologic indicators are used nationally in wetland delineation, the frequency and duration of satura-tion required for wetland formation and maintenance have not been summarized by region (Chapter 5). The lack of information about regional differences in the fundamental hydrologic requirements for wetlands is a serious weakness in the scientific foundation for wetland delineation.

The critical duration of continuous saturation for wetlands can be expressed

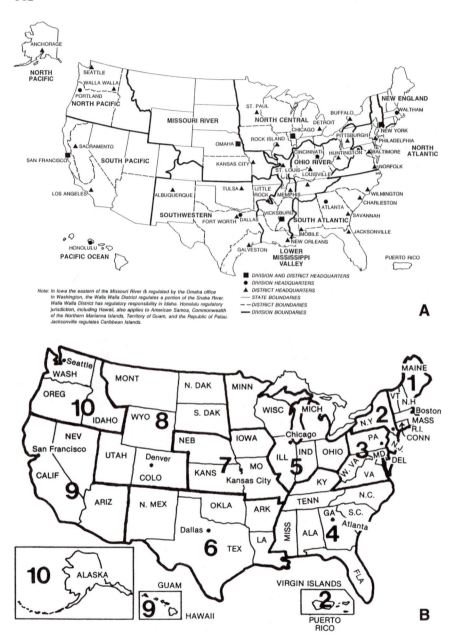

FIGURE 7.4 Regions of the four federal agencies with wetland delineation mandates. (A) U.S. Army Corps of Engineers, (B) U.S. Environmental Protection Agency, (C) U.S. Fish & Wildlife Service, (D) Natural Resources Conservation Service.

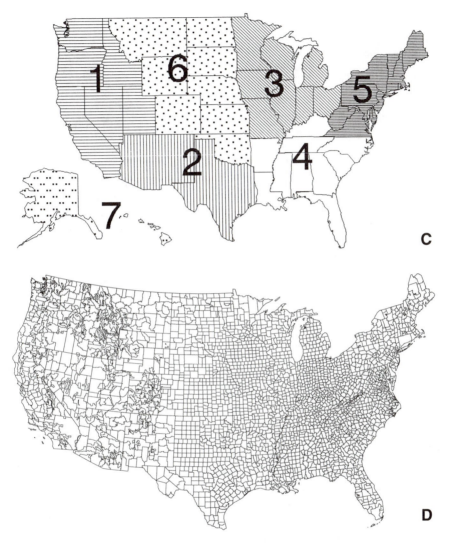

C

D

as a fixed number of days during the growing season or as a percentage of the growing season (Chapters 4 and 5). As explained in Chapter 5, substantial regional variation would be expected both for duration and for growing season, but information on duration and growing season is insufficient to allow clarification of this issue. Until a more sophisticated assessment is possible, reliance on duration should be questioned wherever duration data seem to conflict with information on plant associations and soil properties, and application of the growing-season concept should be reviewed and revised (Chapter 5).

FIGURE 7.5 Regions of distribution used for hydrophyte lists (Reed, 1988).

Regionalization is the best approach for establishing the relationship between growing season, duration of saturation, and the development of hydrophytes. If the plant lists that establish the relationship of hydric soils and their
attendant indicators are constrained to application within relatively homogeneous
climatic or physiographic regions, such as ecoregions (Omernik, 1987), then
growing season becomes a less critical variable, as does the saturation threshold.
Establishment of such a system would require more detailed information on the
relationship of vegetation, soils, and hydrology than is now available for most
regions.

The long-term goal for delineation systems should be to develop information
that establishes the relationship between wetland boundaries and hydrologic
thresholds for various wetland classes in relatively homogeneous climatic and
physiographic regions. Such data could then be applied to disturbed areas, including partially drained areas and areas where vegetation has been altered or
removed entirely. Because hydrologic thresholds for the maintenance of wetlands vary regionally in ways that may never be fully predictable from general
principles, the use of regional information that is specific to particular kinds of
wetlands will build a robust empirical foundation for regulatory practice. While
this approach is ultimately most desirable, it cannot be expected to evolve immediately. It presumes the availability of resources sufficient to document on the

basis of field studies the relationship between hydrology and wetland maintenance in every region for every major class of wetland. In the meantime, general
principles, such as those discussed in Chapter 5, will continue to play the dominant role in regions for which regionally specific information is not available.

Regional Applicability of Current Delineation Methods

Current delineation methods were developed predominantly in the eastern
United States, and as a result are most applicable there. For example, some of the
field indicators of wetland hydrology listed in the 1987 and 1989 manuals, such
as water marks, drift lines, waterborne sediment deposits, water-stained leaves,
buttressing, and multiple trunks are typically associated with floodplain forests of
the southeastern United States, and are less applicable where wetlands are maintained by ground water rather than by flooding. Also, the hydrologic zones for
nontidal areas listed in the 1987 Corps manual are based on information presented at a workshop on bottomland hardwood wetlands of the southeastern
United States (Clark and Benforado, 1981). Frequency of saturation as a potential hydrologic indicator was rejected in favor of duration by the authors of the
1987 Corps manual because of research on tolerances of species from southeastern bottomland forests (personal communication, 1993, R. Theriot, USACE
WES). Subsequent research in Florida has demonstrated, however, that wetlands
with hydric soils dominated by obligate hydrophytes can occur where flooding is
frequent (6-10 times each year) but of short duration (typically less than 1 week)
(Light et al., 1993). The scientists who prepared the 1987 Corps manual were
probably most familiar with the wetlands in the vicinity of the USACE Waterways Experiment Station in Vicksburg, Mississippi, where they worked, and
applied that knowledge in developing hydrologic indicators and thresholds. However, a truly generic wetland delineation system must incorporate information
from all parts of the country. Indicators that work well in a particular region can
cause errors of inclusion or omission when applied elsewhere.

ADVANTAGES AND DISADVANTAGES OF REGIONALIZATION

National lists of plants or soils, if not supplemented by regional lists, can be
unwieldy because they contain too much irrelevant information for a particular
site or region. Existing manuals do not, however, explicitly recognize the regional lists as part of a general effort toward regionalization. Instead, wetlands
that are not appropriately identified by use of a national manual often are identified as special cases or problems (Chapter 6). Although some of these cases are
associated with sites that have been hydrologically altered, cleared of vegetation,
or disturbed in other ways, it should not be necessary to assign undisturbed
wetland types to this category if regionalization is effective.

Delineation manuals need not be regionalized to the point of specifying a separate procedure for every wetland class. A single procedure cannot be sufficiently accurate, however, to accommodate all wetland delineations throughout the nation. Refinement of delineation would be easier if the nation were divided into 10-15 climatic regimes, each containing 3-4 physiographic regions. Regions defined in this way would show more internal homogeneity than regions defined solely by state boundaries. The regionalization schemes of Bailey (1976) (Figure 7.2) and Omernik (1987) (Figure 7.3) are examples of regionalization systems defined on the basis of climate and physiography.

The indicators and procedures for particular regions should be adapted to that region, but within boundaries prescribed by a central set of principles or conventions that apply to the entire nation. The advantage of this approach is that all regions, at least in principle, are treated alike. The equitable implementation of federal regulations and policies requires that there be some consistency in the application of wetland definitions. Regionalization of wetland delineation methods without central constraint could result in inconsistent treatment of wetlands from region to region. The aim of regionalization should be to improve the efficiency and accuracy of delineation without weakening regulatory principles.

Much of the interest in regionalization of wetland delineation derives from recognition that wetlands may differ substantially from one region to another. The identification of regionally valid indicators and the development of regional hydrologic thresholds will allow regulatory principles that are developed at the national level to be applied in a realistic and practical way throughout the nation. A parallel advantage, which is often overlooked, derives from the tendency of regional wetlands in a given class to be similar to each other. For example, prairie marshes or potholes of the upper midwest are more likely to be similar to each other than marshes in general. The greater uniformity among wetlands of a given class within a region will greatly facilitate the practicality and accuracy of wetland delineation following the development of regional indicators. Regional studies of indicators can demonstrate which indicators are highly reliable and easily diagnosed in the field, and these can be featured in the delineation process. While regionalization may be expensive to develop in the short run because of its greater demand for specific information, it may more than pay for itself in the long run through greater accuracy and efficiency of delineation.

RESEARCH TO SUPPORT REGIONALIZATION

The basis for regional identification of hydrophytes and hydric soils already exists, but it needs to be expanded and tested more thoroughly (Chapter 5). There is no regional framework for hydrology, despite the acknowledged regional differences in frequency and duration of saturation required for a wetland to develop hydric plant communities and hydric soils. Any national protocol defining hydrologic thresholds for wetlands should acknowledge regional variation.

Research especially relevant to regionalization can be accomplished by: the establishment of benchmark wetlands for long-term study, especially as related to hydrology; by validation of hydrologic modeling; and by field experiments on wetland indicators.

Benchmark Wetlands

Long-term benchmark studies have provided much of the scientific understanding of natural systems. For example, long-term biogeochemical and hydrologic studies of small watersheds such as at Hubbard Brook, New Hampshire (Likens et al., 1977), produced basic information on processes in forested uplands that has proven transferable to other forested watersheds in the same region. The U.S. Geological Survey long-term research programs on lake and ground water interaction, water budgets, and limnology provide other examples. Similarly, NRCS conducts its Natural Resources Inventory at the same sites every 5 years as a means of monitoring the status of the nation's soils, including those of wetlands. More specifically focused national benchmark wetland studies should be undertaken to provide a sound scientific basis for regional assessment of wetland hydrology and its relationship to hydrophytes and hydric soils. Winter (1992) describes a conceptual framework for such studies.

Validation of Modeling Experiments

Simulation modeling has come of age as a means of determining how natural and modified systems behave (Chapters 5 and 8). When it is supported with appropriate long-term meteorologic records and soils data, modeling can be used to estimate mean and variance for duration of saturation at specific sites in various regions. Modeling results should be tested against long-term monitoring of benchmark wetlands. Modeling should be used for systematically evaluating the sensitivity of wetlands to changes in the hydrologic features of different regions.

Field Experiments on the Reliability of Wetland Indicators

The reliability of most wetland indicators is not known for most regions. For example, how long and how often do particular types of environments need to be saturated to develop specific soil, vegetation, and other characteristics of wetlands? How long does it take for anoxia to develop in saturated soils under different conditions of flooding, temperature, and soil organic matter content? How does saturation at different times of the year influence the development of wetland characteristics? Future regional hydrologic studies should clarify how various vegetation and soil characteristics are related to hydrology, which in turn will show the reliability of specific indicators in specific regions.

IMPLEMENTATION OF REGIONALIZATION

Given the variety of wetland conditions that occur in the United States, regionalization of wetland delineation procedures must be expanded. The regional hydrophyte lists described in Chapter 5 are a good first step toward regionalization, but the boundaries of the 13 regions are not ecologically based. The Hydric Soils List is subdivided into state and county lists, but it does not represent an effective regionalization scheme because it is based on political boundaries. Regional indicators for wetland hydrology and hydric soils, both of which involve depth to water table, should be developed concurrently rather than separately.

Regional boundaries should be based on a combination of ecological, hydrologic, and physiographic characteristics, but in some cases can still follow the political boundaries that are currently used to distinguish organizational regions. Furthermore, a common set of regional boundaries should be used for all wetland indicators. Several ecology-based regionalization schemes already exist, such as that developed by Omernik (1987) (Figure 7.3), and they should be evaluated for broad use in wetland delineation.

Regionalization would be chaotic if each region developed its own methods and standards. Therefore, a national manual should be developed that contains criteria, methods, and procedures common to all wetlands. Regional supplements should then be developed. A uniform process should be required for development of regional standards. The process should involve all four agencies that participate in wetland delineation, and it should incorporate contributions and review by scientists outside the agencies and outside the regions. The review process that was used for regional hydrophyte lists is a reasonable prototype for regionalization of soils and hydrology.

RECOMMENDATIONS

1.   Wetland vary regionally to a great extent; regulatory systems must acknowledge this variation.

2.   Regions for wetland delineation should be redefined on the basis of physiography, climate, vegetation, and prevailing land use and should be used by all agencies for all wetland characteristics, including vegetation, soils, and hydrology.

3.   Regional protocols should conform with national standards that ensure consistency among regions.

4.   Regional delineation practices should be based on regional research and documentation.

5.   A uniform process should be used to develop regional standards; all federal agencies that assess wetlands (USACE, EPA, FWS, NRCS) should participate in the development of regional protocols.

6. Proposals for and review of regional practices should be solicited from scientific experts in the private and public sectors, both within and outside of the region.

7. The process that has been used to develop the regional hydrophyte lists is sound, as is the use of fidelity categories as a means of indicating regional differences.

8. Regionalization of hydric soils should be attempted by the use of regional fidelity categories analogous to those used for the Hydrophyte List.

9. Numeric thresholds for duration and frequency of saturation should be selected on the basis of their regional relationship to hydrophytic vegetation and hydric soils.

10. A central record should be maintained for the Hydrophyte List, as is currently done for the Hydric Soils List. Both records should be accessible via Internet, and both should contain information on the rationale for assignment of indicators.

8

Maps, Images, and Modeling in the Assessment of Wetlands

INTRODUCTION

Wetlands are sometimes delineated by use of aerial photography, satellite imaging, maps, or modeling, as an alternative to collecting field data. Offsite methods are recommended by the 1989 interagency manual for use in areas where "information on hydrology, hydric soils, and hydrophytic vegetation is known, or an inspection is not possible due to time constraints or other reasons." They are also the primary methods used by Natural Resources Conservation Service to delineate wetlands under the terms of the Food Security Act and by the Fish and Wildlife Service to map wetlands for the National Wetlands Inventory (NWI). Delineation of wetlands by offsite methods is subject to errors that do not affect delineation by use of data collected directly from the field. Offsite methods should be used only when their inherent limitations are recognized, as described here.

AERIAL PHOTOGRAPHY AND SATELLITE IMAGING

Aerial photography has been used to map wetlands for at least three decades (Olson, 1964; Anderson and Wobber, 1973; Seher and Tueller, 1973; Cowardin and Myers, 1974; Hardy and Johnston, 1975; Gammon and Carter, 1979; Johnston, 1984). Because the photographs provide a synoptic view of wetlands and their surrounding terrain, they facilitate rapid boundary determination. Interpretation of photographs is difficult, however, in areas where changes, vegetation, soils, or hydrology are indistinct or variable through time. Such areas are generally difficult to delineate by field methods as well.

Satellite remote sensing also holds promise for wetland delineation (FGDC, 1992), but it is not used routinely. When methods for the NWI were being evaluated in the late 1970s, it was determined that the images provided by satellites did not have sufficient spatial or spectral resolution to map wetlands reliably, and their use was rejected in favor of aerial photographs (Tiner, 1990). Recent research, however, suggests that satellite images could be superior for delineating wetland hydrology in some cases, particularly for agricultural areas. A review of the use of satellite data for mapping and monitoring wetlands, based on the experience of several private and public agencies, has been published by the Federal Geographic Data Committee (FGDC, 1992).

Detection of Standing Water

Aerial photographs are recommended by the 1987, 1989, and FSA manuals as suitable indicators of hydrology because they can provide direct evidence of inundation if they are taken when there is standing water on the soil surface and there is no obscuring vegetation. Interpretation of this type of photo requires little training; one merely looks for the dark areas associated with surface water. If photographs are available for several dates, they can provide a history of inundation. As with any hydrologic interpretation, soil moisture and antecedent precipitation must be considered, however.

Satellite images also can be used to detect standing water. The Landsat Thematic Mapper (TM) satellite detects energy returned from surface features in several wavelength bands. Band 5, which detects infrared wavelengths between 1.55 and 1.75 mm, is particularly useful for detecting soil moisture and standing water (Lillesand and Kiefer, 1979). The National Aeronautics and Space Administration (NASA) Space Remote Sensing Center in Huntsville, Alabama, used this band to map natural and farmed wetlands in the Yazoo River Basin in Mississippi and Arkansas as part of a pilot project for NRCS (R. Pearson, presentation to NRC Wetlands Characterization Committee, Nov. 23, 1993). A hydrologic model was used to determine the stage height corresponding to a 2-year flood, and TM images coinciding with those conditions were used to map fields that were inundated for 15 consecutive days, the FSA threshold for wetlands. Unlike aerial photography, which is done infrequently because of its high cost, TM images are acquired every 16 days as the satellite passes over the Earth. This allows NASA analysts to find a scene that coincides with flood conditions. This methodology also was tested for delineation of wetlands in the prairie pothole region of North Dakota (FGDC, 1992). Maps produced from TM images were adopted by NRCS for the Yazoo River Basin in Mississippi, but not for North Dakota, because their accuracy was considered too poor in the drier western half of the state (North Dakota State Conservationist, presentation at the National Interagency Memorandum of Agreement Meeting, St. Paul, Minnesota, May 18, 1994).

Other Factors

In the most sophisticated applications, the photo interpreter uses not only the tone or color in the photograph, but also landscape position, land slope, and the appearance of vegetation, to distinguish wetlands from uplands (Hardy and Johnston, 1975). Ancillary data, from soil surveys or topographic maps, also can be useful. The accuracy of interpretation is greatest where wetland boundaries coincide with changes in the density and structure of the dominant vegetation; wetlands that are easily discernible on the ground are generally also easiest to see in aerial photographs. Because an experienced interpreter uses a combination of clues to make a determination, keys and descriptions of methods are rare. Given the importance of aerial photography in the preparation of NWI and FSA surveys, however, there is a need for more explicit documentation on this delineation method.

Stereoscopic viewing of photographs greatly increases the accuracy of interpretation (Lillesand and Kiefer, 1979; Soil Survey Staff, 1993) because it shows topographic breaks, which help show wetland boundaries, and it reveals changes in vegetation height and shape that can indicate changes in soil moisture. Stereoscopic viewing also helps the interpreter locate wetlands because wetlands are more likely to occur in some topographic positions than in others. Stereoscopic interpretation is a standard procedure in preparation of the NWI (1990), but not in FSA inventories conducted by NRCS.

A boundary delineated on an aerial photograph corresponds to a zone on the ground with a width that equals the width of the line divided by the scale (the representative fraction) of the photograph. For example, a 0.0197-inch (0.05 cm) pen line on a 1:24,000 photo would represent 39 ft (11.85 m) on the ground. Although a boundary of this width could depict ecological reality, it would be insufficiently resolved for jurisdictional purposes.

People who work on the ground often have difficulty determining their location from a map or aerial photograph. The unfamiliarity of most nonspecialists with maps is a major disadvantage of delineating wetlands on aerial photographs: Even if an area is perfectly depicted, it can have little meaning if a bulldozer operator or tractor driver cannot relate the mapped boundary to a field location. The increasing accuracy and decreasing cost of global positioning systems are improving the georeferencing of ground locations, but this technology is not yet widely available at the fineness of resolution needed for wetland delineation.

WETLAND DELINEATION UNDER THE FOOD SECURITY ACT

In contrast to the field-intensive methods used to identify wetland boundaries for Clean Water Act Section 404 permits, wetland delineations required by FSA are done primarily by offsite methods. The 1990 FSA amendments direct NRCS to conduct a field wetland determination if possible whenever requested to do so by an owner or operator. In practice, field determinations are done only when an owner or operator questions the validity of the offsite determination.

Determinations Before 1994

After enactment of FSA, each state developed mapping conventions for indirect wetland determinations on agricultural lands, with technical guidance from the four NRCS National Technical Centers (Midwest, 1988; Northeast, 1989; South, 1989; West, 1988). Mapping conventions vary slightly by state because of regional differences in wetland characteristics and in the availability of data, but the general methodology is the same except where satellite remote sensing has been used. In all states, five land classes are differentiated: wetland (W), farmed wetland (FW), converted wetland (CW), prior converted cropland (PC), and artificial wetland (AW) (Chapter 6).

The primary source of data for FSA determinations is 35 mm aerial color slides that have been taken each year since the early 1980s by the Agricultural Stabilization and Conservation Service (ASCS). The slides, which are acquired primarily for confirmation of cropping claims under ASCS subsidy programs, are taken at a time of the year optimal for distinguishing crops, usually late June or July in the Midwest and West. Their use by NRCS for wetland determinations began later, and has not influenced the timing of their acquisition.

The mapping conventions from the four NRCS regions specify the following as photographic indicators of wetland: hydrophytic vegetation, water or drowned crop (mud), crop stressed by water (yellow leaves), lush crop in dry years, and differences in crop color caused by delay of planting. Steps in the delineation procedure described by the Midwest Center (1988), which are similar to those from the other three regions, are as follows:

1. Review NWI maps. All areas mapped by NWI are considered wetlands unless review of the ASCS slides indicates the contrary. Some wetlands shown by NWI might have been drained since the NWI photos were taken, or there can be errors on NWI maps.

2. Review the soil survey for evidence of wetlands (such as hydric soils).

3. Review ASCS color slides for the previous 5-7 years in conjunction with precipitation data collected 2 to 3 months before the date of the slide to determine prevailing climatological conditions at the time of photography. The slides are projected sequentially, and evidence of wetness over the 5 to 7 year interval is used to make decisions about the appropriate classification of the area.

The boundaries of areas determined to be wetlands are transferred to a 1:7,920 (8 in. = 1 mile) (20.32 cm = 1.61 km) ASCS enlarged black-and-white aerial photograph that is used as a base map.

The major disadvantage of the FSA approach is that, in many parts of the country, the slides are taken after surface waters have receded from wetlands. A further disadvantage is that air photo interpretation is monoscopic, rather than stereoscopic. The indicators of wetland are the color differences on the slides. There is no supplementary information about topography that stereoscopic interpretation or field inspection would provide. Thus, the appearance of stressed crops might be similar for an eroded hilltop and for a wetland depression.

The NRCS delineations are sent to the landowner for review. If the landowner contests the delineation, it is reviewed in the field by methods described in NFSAM, and corrected as necessary. There are four stages in the appeal process, corresponding to the four levels within NRCS: district, area, state, and national (Chapter 7). At the national level, there have been only about 200 appeals out of 2 million determinations (M. Fritz, U.S. EPA, presentation to NRC Wetlands Characterization Committee, Feb. 2, 1994); all other disputes either were resolved at a lower level or were not appealed to a higher level. FSA delineations are not subject to public review, and the wetland maps are not published. In addition to making wetland determinations, NRCS also prepares wetland inventory maps by use of ASCS 35 mm slides, aerial photographs, soil surveys, and NWI maps.

The Food, Agricultural, Conservation, and Trade Act of 1990 amended FSA to include a certification requirement for all wetland determinations. Determinations done before Nov. 28, 1990, become certified if the decision is appealed at least one level (to the district conservationist), or if the state conservationist determines that the inventories and mapping conventions are adequate and finds a sample of determinations in the field office to be accurate. Determinations done between Nov. 29, 1990, and Jan. 6, 1994, become certified if the decision is appealed at least one level (to the district conservationist), or if the decision is not appealed and the state conservationist determines that the inventories and mapping conventions are adequate, and if the affected persons are notified and given rights of appeal. Wetland determinations had been completed by these conventions for 60% of U.S. Department of Agriculture (USDA) program participants when, in 1991, NRCS offices were directed to discontinue mapping until a review of the FSA delineation manual could be completed (B. Teels, presentation to NRC Wetlands Characterization Committee, Sept. 15, 1993). From 1991 until the signing of the 1994 interagency Memorandum of Agreement (MOA), determinations were made by NRCS only as needed for evaluation of easements under the Wetlands Reserve Program (16 U.S.C. § 3837) or the Environmental Conservation Acreage Reserve Program (16 U.S.C. § 1230), and for cost-sharing under the Agricultural Water Quality Incentives Program (16 U.S.C. § 3838) (P.L. 101-624).

Determinations After 1994

On Jan. 6, 1994, the interagency MOA gave NRCS responsibility for making delineations for the swampbuster provisions of FSA and Section 404 of CWA (Chapter 4). Under the new MOA, representatives of U.S. Army Corps of Engineers (USACE), Environmental Protection Agency (EPA), FWS, and NRCS must concur in writing on the mapping conventions to be used in each state. Mapping conventions were discussed by representatives of all four agencies at an interagency meeting convened May 16-20, 1994, in St. Paul, Minnesota. Mapping conventions approved by the agencies for use at the state level will be reviewed by the headquarters of the signatory agencies to ensure national consistency. All wetland determinations done after Jan. 6, 1994, become certified on agricultural lands if approved mapping conventions were used. Determinations done on nonagricultural lands after Jan. 6, 1994, become certified if: USACE, under EPA review, makes the final wetland determination; if NRCS makes the determination on wetlands included within agricultural land; or if NRCS makes the determination by request on lands owned or operated by a USDA program participant (NFSAM Part 514.52).

The memorandum also establishes a monitoring and review process that is intended to improve wetland delineation. EPA will lead the signatory agencies in establishing interagency state oversight teams in periodic reviews of wetland delineations. Each team will attempt to reach agreement on wetland delineation issues that arise during these reviews, which will be conducted quarterly for the first year, semiannually for the second year, and annually thereafter. NRCS also will provide information to FWS about wetlands on NWI maps that are not verified as wetlands by NRCS mapping conventions or field investigation (NFSAM Part 513.31).

The third edition of NFSAM manual (Parts 513.30 and 527.4) contains general guidance for developing wetland mapping conventions that are consistent with mapping conventions previously used for FSA. In addition to the five wetland categories (W, FW, CW, PC, AW), Part 526.100 lists 19 new delineation categories related to various types and uses of agricultural wetlands.

NWI MAPPING

The purpose of the NWI is to map the wetlands of the United States for resource assessment rather than for regulation. NWI was begun by FWS in the mid-1970s and is still in progress. Maps are prepared by interpretation of photographic transparencies under stereoscopic magnification. Boundaries are drawn directly on the photos with a 0000 drafting pen, which on a 1:58,000 photo represents approximately 40 ft (12 m) on the ground. Photo interpretation and field checking are done by contractors from consulting firms, universities, and state and federal agencies, with quality control by NWI personnel. Interpreters are usually expected to spend 20 hours (2 1/2 work days) in the field for each 1:100,000 map (the equivalent of 32 1:24,000 topographic maps) (National Wetlands Inventory, 1990). Final map preparation is done by transfer of the wetland boundaries from the photographs to 1:24,000 maps (Figure 8.1).

Most of the aerial photographs used for NWI mapping were obtained by the U.S. Geological Survey (USGS) for general use and therefore are not always optimum for wetland mapping. Until the early 1980s, 1:80,000 (0.39 in. = 2,624 ft; 1 cm = 800 m) black and white panchromatic photos acquired by USGS were used. Each photo covers the equivalent of a 1:24,000 topographic quadrangle. After 1980, 1:58,000 (0.39 in. = 1,902.4 ft; 1 cm = 580 m) color infrared photos taken by the National High Altitude Photography program were used. This program was replaced in 1992 by the National Aerial Photography Program, which acquires 1:40,000 (0.39 in. = 1,312 ft; 1 cm = 400 m) color infrared aerial photography.

Because NWI maps depict wetlands that were present on the date of photography, wetland extent can be estimated incorrectly if atypical expansion or contraction of vegetation was occurring at the time of photography. Interannual variation causes fewer errors where ground water maintains wetland hydrology or where vegetation is resistant to interannual variation (such as in forested wetlands). Even though NWI is incomplete for much of the country (Figure 8.2), some of the earliest maps are 20 years old. The age of NWI maps is a particular problem in areas where agricultural and urban development have altered wetlands.

Wetland delineation on NWI maps is generally accurate areas where there is an abrupt change in hydrology, soil, or vegetation at the wetland boundary. In the prairie pothole region, for example, wetlands smaller than 1.24 acres (0.5 ha) are mapped routinely by NWI (Tiner, 1990). Mapping of wetlands in level landscapes, such as coastal or glaciolacustrine plains, is less precise because boundaries are not as evident. Forested wetlands are particularly difficult to map because foliage obscures the ground. Temporarily flooded, forested wetland is one of the most difficult types to map because, for most of the year, the water table usually lies below the surface.

NWI maps tend to be less inclusive of wetlands than are other wetland maps. Farmed wetlands usually are not included on NWI maps (NWI, 1990; NFSAM, 1994), and areas mapped as hydric soils on USDA soil surveys are generally much more extensive than are areas mapped as wetland on NWI maps (Street, 1993). In Washington and Tyrrell counties of coastal North Carolina, for example, only 19% of the hydric mineral soils were mapped as wetland by NWI, even though 82% of the hydric organic soils were mapped as wetlands (Moorhead and Cook, 1992). In the same area, Lukin and Mauger (1983) mapped as wetland nearly 35,000 acres (14,000 ha) that NWI showed as upland; the addition of these sites to the NWI maps would have increased the total wetland area by 16%. These three sites are clearly not a comprehensive sample, however, the NWI maps should be evaluated broadly in relation to field-delineated wetlands.

NWI was not designed to be used for regulatory delineation. It is a useful

FIGURE 8.1 NWI map (reduced) prepared from 1:58,000 color infrared aerial photographs.

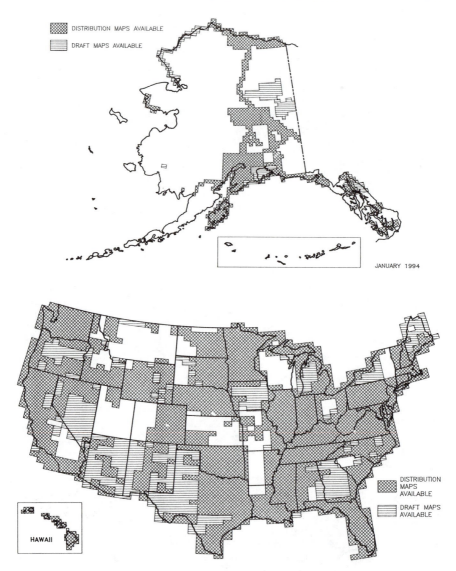

FIGURE 8.2 Status of NWI mapping as of January and February 1994.

source of background information for wetland delineations, and it is recommended as an ancillary data source by all federal delineation manuals (1987; 1989; NFSAM). Its utility as an ancillary data source varies regionally; it is least useful in areas where broad expanses of mineral soils with facultative vegetation and little topographic variation complicate wetland delineation. Given NWI's

utility for delineation in many parts of the country, however, as well as its importance in providing synoptic information about the nation's wetlands, it should be
completed.

GEOGRAPHIC INFORMATION SYSTEMS

Geographic information systems (GISs), computerized systems for the analysis and display of spatially distributed data, have great potential for use in management, regulation, and study of wetlands. A GIS can be used to store, retrieve,
and edit data; it can be used to create new data bases; and it can be used for
tabular, graphic, and digital presentation of information. A GIS offers numerous
advantages in extraction and analysis of data, and in the revision of data files
(Johnston et al., 1988a).

The primary disadvantages of GIS use are the time and expense required to
digitize maps, and the expensive equipment and trained personnel that are needed.
Also, a GIS data base is only as good as the source from which it was derived.

NWI maps are being digitized in a GIS-compatible format, which should
greatly increase their utility (Tiner and Pywell, 1983). This effort is progressing
even more slowly, however, than is map production. Digitizing is complete or
nearly complete for only 10 states: Delaware, Florida, Indiana, Illinois, Maryland, Minnesota, New Jersey, Rhode Island, Virginia, and Washington (Figure
8.3). Most of these states paid part of the cost of the work.

A GIS can be used as part of a spatial decision support system (SDSS) for
wetland delineation. An SDSS is a computerized system for data interpretation,
manipulation, and analysis that is used for support of complex decisions based on
spatially distributed information (Djokic, in press). It is designed to be interactive and easy to use. The solution procedure is developed interactively by the
user, who creates a series of alternative solutions and then selects the most viable.
This approach could be used with a wetland delineation decision tree and digital
information on soils, vegetation, and topography. An SDSS also could facilitate
management decisions about wetlands by putting them in a landscape or historical framework. For example, an SDSS could be used to evaluate the effect of
additional wetland loss relative to past wetland losses within a region.

Protection of wetland functions requires that wetlands be considered in context with the surrounding landscape. A GIS can be useful for this purpose. A GIS
can place individual wetlands in appropriate spatial context (such as in a watershed or in a waterfowl flyway) and can combine information about wetlands with
information about their surrounding environment. Empirical relationships between resource loss and measures of environmental degradation can be developed with a GIS (such as degradation of water quality, or loss of biodiversity).
Rates of change in number or extent of wetlands can be quantified with a GIS that
contains wetland maps for two periods. Transition probabilities derived from

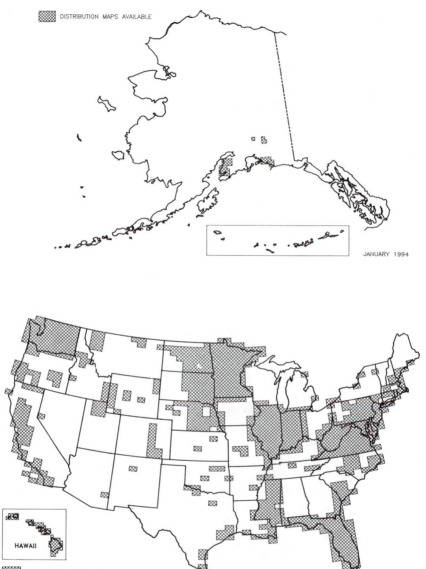

FIGURE 8.3 NWI digital data as of January and February 1994.

such analyses can then be used for predicting wetland trends (Pastor and Johnston, 1992).

A GIS can be used in assessments of cumulative environmental change (Johnston et al., 1988b; Johnston, 1994b). Disturbances that affect wetlands directly (such as the location of logged areas within wetlands) and indirectly (such as upstream sources of water pollution) also can be analyzed with a GIS.

A major barrier to the use of GISs has been the lack of suitable digital data on wetlands. Fortunately, this situation is changing. NWI maps are being digitized, and NRCS plans to digitize county soil survey maps under its Soil Survey Geographic Data Base program, which should facilitate identification of hydric soils (Reybold and TeSelle, 1989). EPA's North American Landscape Characterization program, which was developed in collaboration with the USGS EROS Data Center and the NASA Landsat Pathfinder program, will produce digital land cover maps from 1991 Landsat Multispectral Scanner images. It also will generate image-derived digital land cover change maps for the 1970s, 1980s, and 1990s (EPA, 1993). EPA has digitized all streams in the nation, coded by reach number, associated with its STORET water quality data base. USGS is producing digital elevation models (topographic data) for 7 1/2-minute areas corresponding to its 7 1/2-minute quadrangle series, and has digitized the watersheds it uses for its hydrologic units. These data bases could be useful for delineation, but their utility in a landscape context will rest on their accuracy and on the ability of wetland delineators to interpret them correctly.

HYDROLOGIC MODELING

Hydrologic models describe natural processes by representations that are either conceptual or mathematical (NRC, 1990). Conceptual models deal with interactions of hydrologic processes by the use of simplifying approximations and assumptions. For example, the accuracy of water budget estimates for most wetlands is limited by measurement difficulties, but this does not prevent the development of a conceptual model that shows how the budget components interact (Winter, 1988). A mathematical model can be developed from a conceptual model. The mathematical model makes specific quantitative estimates of the hydrologic characteristics of a watershed or wetland. The success of mathematical models is largely predicated on the validity of the underlying conceptual model. For example, the results of a mathematical model of water flow in a raised bog can be quite different if it is assumed that the bog is separated from or hydraulically connected to the water table. In general, it is difficult to describe with models both the flow system and the boundary conditions for natural systems. In such cases, models are best used to determine empirically what is possible or probable, even though they might not produce accurate predictions (Oreskes et al., 1994). The effects of modifications such as those caused by drainage ditches are generally easiest to describe because the boundary conditions and principal flow directions are better defined than they are for natural systems.

Mathematical Models to Assess Wetland Hydrology

There are two major applications of mathematical models in wetland hydrology. The first involves assessment of the hydrology of a site in relation to hydrologic thresholds for wetlands. Modifications by drainage or other activities can make it impossible to determine wetland status from soils and vegetation, both of which could be characteristic of the site's former hydrology but not of its altered condition. Models can be especially useful in assessing wetlands under such conditions. The second important application of models is in estimating or projecting the effects of cumulative wetland loss on regional hydrologic characteristics, particularly flood flows. Several of watershed-response simulation models, such as HEC2 (Bedient and Huber, 1988), have been developed to project flood flow in response to precipitation, soil moisture and depression storage, infiltration, ground water flux, evapotranspiration, and natural or constructed drainage systems.

Types of Mathematical Models

Mathematical models can be either analytical or numerical. Analytical models solve the fundamental equations for conservation of mass and fluid flow for steady-state processes and for transient events (Kirkham, 1957; van Schilfgaarde, 1974; Luthin, 1978). They are used to calculate water table response to drainage by open ditches and drainage pipes. Analytical models usually assume constant values for hydraulic properties of the soil (such as hydraulic conductivity and drainage porosity) and simple, well-defined boundary and initial conditions of the wetland. Although analytical models are mathematically exact solutions to the equations governing water flow, their application usually involves the use of approximations that can introduce errors.

Water in soil moves in three dimensions in the general case, but most analytical models treat it in one or two dimensions process. These approximations can be used in some situations to estimate the most probable location of the water table over a long period. Where the physical properties of soil and the sources of water vary widely in a wetland, however, analytical models are less likely to be successful. The wide range of models suitable for determining the steady-state and transient water table response to drainage is given by Kessler et al. (1973), van Schilfgaarde (1974), and Cohen and Miller (1983). Although analytical models can describe drainage processes and water table responses for steady rainfall and short-term drawdown, they are not generally applicable to describing water table fluctuations caused by the combined effects of rainfall, drainage, and evapotranspiration over long periods.

Numerical models can be functional (lumped parameter) or discritized (distributed parameter). Both solve the equations for fluid flow and conservation of mass. Functional models usually assume that the wetland behaves as a relatively uniform soil system with well-defined boundary conditions, although layers with different hydraulic properties can be considered. The water budget for the wetland is reduced to algebraic equations, and analytical algorithms are used to calculate flux as a function of water table position, depth, and spacing of natural or constructed drains, potential evapotranspiration, and the like. Unlike purely analytical models, which are usually used for steady-state conditions or short transient events, functional models can be used to project the rise and fall of water levels with time over a long period of record. Three well-known functional models that simulate wetland hydrology in drained areas are DRAINMOD (Skaggs, 1978; 1991), PHIM (Guertin and Brooks, 1986; Guertin et al., 1987), and SWATRE (Feddes et al., 1978). Functional models are effective tools for evaluating the hydrologic features of an entire wetland or certain specific points within a wetland. They are generally less useful for determining spatial differences in the water table regime for a wetland and adjacent upland.

Distributed-parameter numerical models are used for estimating detailed subsurface ground water flow and flood flows in watersheds. They are powerful, but they are difficult to construct and use (NRC, 1990). The study area (the flow domain) is partitioned into sections, each of which can be assigned values for the physical or hydraulic properties of the soil, rates of recharge and water loss, initial water levels, slope, storage capacity, and other variables that affect water movement and distribution. The numerical routines calculate water flow into and out of each section and for the domain as a whole. As with the analytical and functional models, distributed-parameter models originated primarily from two sources: they come from models that describe ground water processes and models that predict the performance of drainage systems. The most theoretically rigorous of these methods, the so-called exact approach, is difficult and expensive and can be applied only by an expert in ground water modeling. A basic limitation is the requirement of detailed descriptions of the properties of unsaturated soil and boundary conditions throughout the flow domain. These barriers will likely confine the use of distributed-parameter models to wetland research rather than to regulation.

Distributed-parameter ground water models have been used to determine the major controls over wetland ground water hydrology in many settings (Siegel, 1983; Winter, 1988; McNamara et al., 1992). A useful and easily applied distributed-parameter approach for modeling wetlands is based on numerical solutions to the Boussinesq equation. This approach is appropriate where subsurface water movement is primarily horizontal in the saturated zone. Models such as those developed by de Laat et al. (1981) and WATRCOM, developed by Parsons et al. (1991a,b), can be used to predict water table fluctuations continuously throughout a wetland on a continuous basis. By this means, the effect of a drainage ditch on the water table can be evaluated as a function of distance from the ditch. Boundaries that satisfy hydrologic conditions for wetlands can be determined from simulations of water table positions over long periods. Differences in soil properties and land uses from point to point in the wetland and adjacent upland also can be considered. These models can be applied to large, heterogeneous areas.

Model Selection and Application

The simplest model that will provide the required accuracy and resolution is the most desirable because the reliability of predictions often decreases with complexity. Hydrologic models require information on the physical attributes of the site, soils, vegetation, and climate. All data to be used in models are subject to uncertainty, so it is essential that the user consider the effects of uncertainty through the use of sensitivity analysis. Field data can increase the reliability of modeling. Often several months or even years of field hydrologic data on a wetland are insufficient for classification of a marginal site because of the inherent variability of hydrology (Chapter 5). In such cases, the field data can be used to test and calibrate a model, which can then be used for simulating water table conditions over a long period of record, providing a good basis for determining whether wetland hydrology exists on the site.

Advantages and Disadvantages of Hydrologic Modeling

Models offer several advantages. They can be used to analyze the effects of alterations, and thus provide a means of assessing wetland hydrologic conditions without reference to vegetation and soils, which might not be reliable indicators under these conditions. In addition, the assessment of the hydrology by use of models is not limited by short-term weather conditions. Models also can be used to predict the effects of agricultural drainage or other activities on the hydrology of adjacent wetlands, and the effects of wetland alterations on regional flood flows.

Models also have disadvantages. Because they are data intensive, they can be expensive and time-consuming. Their application also requires specialized training; if they are improperly applied, models can lead to erroneous conclusions. Overall, however, models should prove increasingly useful, particularly for quantifying hydrologic features of ecosystems for which direct hydrologic information is unavailable or inadequate.

QUANTITATIVE ANALYSIS OF BOUNDARIES

Boundary detection is one aspect of the analysis of spatial change. Although the position of an ecological boundary might be evident with little analysis, boundary detection can be difficult if the change is gradual (Hansen et al., 1988). The clarity of a boundary varies with the amount of change over distance, as well as with the overall magnitude of change. The most distinct boundaries are those for which there is a large change over a short distance.

Threshold values are often used to set ecological boundaries (Chapter 5). An example is the use of the prevalence index for vegetation to distinguish between wetland and upland. Although there can be statistically significant differences between the wetland and upland, it does not follow that the boundaries between them will be distinct.

Transect Data for Boundary Determination

The use of transects for determination of wetland boundaries is recommended by the 1987 and 1989 manuals. Biological, physical, or chemical data are collected along a perceived gradient and are analyzed for ecological discontinuities. Quantitative techniques can be used to locate and characterize ecological discontinuities along transects (Webster and Wong, 1969; Webster, 1973; Ludwig and Cornelius, 1987; Wierenga et al., 1987; Brunt and Conley, 1990), including transects across boundaries between wetland and upland. Extensive use of quantitative methods might be beneficial for application to gradients in redox potential, particularly in areas where vegetation and soils have been disturbed.

When suitably located and sampled, transects can provide a large amount of data with minimal effort. Because a transect locates only one or two points on a boundary, however, identification of an entire wetland perimeter requires multiple transects. Also, because transects are often placed perpendicularly to perceived boundaries, the data are biased toward visible gradients, and therefore could be unrepresentative of gradients that are not visible.

Detection of Boundaries with Image Analysis

Images provide information about the entire landscape, including boundaries. Information about boundaries can be extracted from an image by use of the moving-window technique, which involves a scan of the image with a two-dimensional window. The moving window technique can be applied to any 2-dimensional digital data, including aerial photography scanned with a video digitizer or scanning camera. For example, Johnston and Bonde (1989) have used "textural analysis," a moving-window technique that measures boundary contrast as the relative difference between the reflectance values of picture elements (Musick and Grover, 1991), to analyze boundaries within a Landsat satellite image of a portion of northern Minnesota. They applied this technique to a map of normalized difference vegetation index, which is a measure of the spectral properties of vegetation. Nellis and Briggs (1989) performed a similar analysis on the Konza prairie in Kansas.

Scientific vs. Legal Boundaries

Just as the interior of a wetland can be classified by soil type, vegetation, or other variables, its boundary can also be classified. A vector-based GIS, which depicts features as a series of connected points and lines, inherently classifies boundaries based on the features that are being separated and can be used to classify boundaries by other attributes. For example, a land cover map of Scotland produced by the Macaulay Land Use Research Institute uses different line widths to indicate the precision with which ecological boundaries are located (Aspinall et al., 1993). Similarly, boundaries could be classified by their strength (magnitude of change), width, or permanence. From a scientific perspective, wetland boundaries must be shown in some cases as broadly placed within a transition zone.

Land ownership and regulation in the United States are based upon discrete lines separating one piece of property from another. The mathematical analogue of this approach is classical set theory, in which space is discretely subdivided by use of threshold values rather than by probabilities. Herein lies a basic problem of wetland delineation: ecological properties often change gradually, rather than sharply, whereas legal boundaries are lines without width. The authors of the 1987 and 1989 manuals have done a credible job of establishing thresholds that compact a wetland boundary into widthless line, but legal boundaries will never be fully reconciled with ecological reality.

RECOMMENDATIONS

1. Aerial photography can be useful for wetland delineation and mapping if its timing, frequency, and scale are suited for making wetland determinations. Aerial photographs should be acquired specifically for wetland delineation in areas where these requirements are not met by existing photographs.

2. The interpretation of aerial photography should be done by personnel trained in this method of wetland determination and who have field knowledge of wetlands in the area being interpreted.

3. Monoscopic interpretation of aerial photography should be supplemented with information on topography and soils and should be validated by periodic field reconnaissance and regional assessments of accuracy.

4. The accuracy of offsite wetland determinations for agricultural lands should be evaluated comprehensively in the field before mapping conventions are adopted and wetland determinations are certified.

5. Remote sensing by satellite and high-altitude aircraft has promise for wetland delineation and should be evaluated further as a potential technique for wetland delineation where large areas of land are flooded seasonally.

6. Models, if verified in the field, should be accepted for analysis of the hydrology of some wetlands, including altered wetlands.

7. Documentation of wetland boundaries by use of global positioning systems should be encouraged as GPS technology is refined.

9

Regulation of Wetlands:
Administrative Issues

INTRODUCTION

The scientific study of wetlands rarely requires that the boundaries of wetlands be specifically defined. In contrast, both the regulators of wetlands and the regulated community must be able to establish, by application of scientific principles, the limits of individual wetlands that are subject to legal requirements administered through a regulatory system. In this sense, science, law, and policy are all relevant to the delineation of wetlands.

The complexity of the regulatory system produces administrative problems that can affect the scientific validity and consistency of wetland delineations, regardless of the underlying scientific basis for regulation. There are many agencies and private parties involved in wetland delineations and there is no system of uniform training or standard of knowledge and experience for delineators. This chapter considers these problems and their possible solutions.

CONSISTENCY AND RELIABILITY OF
WETLAND DELINEATIONS

The wetland delineation system should produce consistent, reliable results. If two qualified delineators apply the same standards, their delineations at a given site should be essentially the same. In other words, a landowner should be able to rely on the legal sufficiency of a wetland delineation, regardless of the agency that conducts or reviews it. If the delineation system yields highly variable or arbitrary results, there will follow a lack of confidence and respect among the regulated public. This is important because wetland delineations determine what private conduct is lawful; individuals can be fined or even imprisoned for filling a wetland (33 U.S.C. § 1319). Citizens lose faith in a legal system that is administered inconsistently even as it imposes penalties for noncompliance.

Consistency of wetland delineation is a widespread concern. Inconsistent delineation can arise from one or more of the following: confusion over delineation standards; inadequate training of delineators; improper application of delineation standards; use of excessive discretion in applying delineation standards; variations among wetland types or wetland disturbances; and regional differences, including different approaches to delineation by different offices of a given agency or different levels of government. Variability in delineation practices can result from inadequate training of delineators, misapplication of the delineation standards, or biased delineations by parties who desire a particular result. Regional bias can arise from regional variation in amount of wetland and in development pressures. There also are some problems among the field offices of various federal agencies over delineations performed by agencies other than their own. These systemic issues impede development of scientifically valid, consistently applied delineation standards.

Multiple Agencies

The involvement of so many federal agencies reduces the overall consistency of wetland delineations. Furthermore, the agencies that conduct wetland delineations allow significant regional or local autonomy (Chapter 7). The January 1994 Memorandum of Agreement (MOA) between the U.S. Army Corps of Engineers (USACE), Environmental Protection Agency (EPA), and Natural Resources Conservation Service (NRCS) for wetland delineations on agricultural lands is, however, intended to reduce the differences among agencies. The MOA guarantees the regulated party that delineation by one agency will be used by all three. In general, farm owners can rely on NRCS delineations for all federal regulatory purposes.

Although the MOA could reduce interagency differences administratively by establishing clearer lines of authority for agricultural lands, it will not improve the technical consistency of wetland delineations unless the delineations of NRCS achieve the same outcome as would delineations by EPA or USACE. It will be difficult for the public to accept that a particular set of landscape features is a legal wetland if delineated by USACE on nonfarm property, but not so if delineated by NRCS on a farm.

Joint training will improve consistency among the agencies. The agencies have different regulatory functions, however, which may result in differing attitudes toward protection of wetlands. As long as the agencies operate with different legal mandates, there can be inconsistency in wetland delineations across agency lines. Consolidation of all wetlands regulatory functions into a single federal agency, although difficult, would improve the consistency of wetland delineations. If several agencies must share wetland delineation responsibilities, then a common set of definitions and a common delineation manual should be used.

Standards for Expertise, Training, and Certification

The expertise necessary for delineation of wetlands should be clarified by the federal agencies that establish delineation protocols. Wetland delineators are expected to have some scientific background, but the type of training is not specified. This may contribute to the confusion of landowners, who can be unsure of the extent to which delineation is a technical or specialized task.

Wetland delineation requires scientific education at the college level, combined with specialized training in delineation methods and practices. Some knowledge of or familiarity with several scientific fields is needed for wetland delineation. Delineators should have some knowledge of plant taxonomy, botany, soil science, surface water hydrology, general ecology, wetland (or aquatic) ecology, sampling methodology, and plant morphology. Knowledge of ground water hydrology, geology, plant physiology, and perhaps other disciplines is also desirable. In addition, a wetland delineator must be familiar with regulatory requirements. There is, however, no established minimum of education or set course of training that will qualify a wetland delineator. Training programs, both private and government-sponsored, do not produce uniform results.

USACE has established a demonstration program for certification of wetland delineators (WDCP) (57 Fed. Reg. 62,312; 1992). The program operated between March 1993 and March 1994 in the states of Washington, Maryland, and Florida, but its full implementation had not occurred as of December 1994. WDCP involves a written test and a field practicum. A passing score for the written test in the demonstration program was 80%. Approximately 800 applicants took the written exam during the demonstration program, but fewer than 300 passed. Approximately 250 persons took the field practicum; more than 90% passed. USACE awarded provisional certification to those who passed both parts of the test. When USACE finalizes the program, provisionally certified delineators will be eligible for final certification.

Provisionally certified delineators are considered by USACE to have adequate knowledge and ability to perform wetland delineations. USACE expects that fully certified delineators will be able to train others in wetland delineation, and that proof of training with a certified delineator will be a prerequisite for delineators to become certified. Thus, WDCP anticipates that most of the training will be done by the private sector but that testing and certification will be done by USACE or in accordance with tests and standards set by USACE.

Other certification programs are offered by the private sector or by universities. The Society of Wetland Scientists (SWS) is a nonprofit scientific and educational organization that encourages the adoption of professional standards in all activities related to wetland science. SWS has developed a certification program designed to evaluate the education and experience of professional wetland scientists. The program is established to guide individuals, government agencies, the legal system, and the public in defining minimum standards of education and experience for professionals in the field of wetland science and to create and maintain public confidence in the advice and opinions of professionals by establishing a peer evaluation system involving education, experience, and ethical standards.

Applicants for SWS certification must have bachelors' degrees or the equivalent, with a specified range of science training. Certifications are awarded by the SWS Wetland Professional Certification Review Panel, composed of SWS members and appointed by the SWS Executive Board (SWS Bulletin, 1992). Certification constitutes recognition by SWS that, to the best of its knowledge, an applicant meets the minimum standards of education and experience adopted by the SWS, but it does not certify an individual's ability to perform delineations.

As shown by the USACE and SWS programs, certification of delineators raises several issues. For example, there are questions of national versus regional certification, and of familiarity with a delineation manual versus knowledge of basic scientific disciplines that underlie delineation. These choices and others involve a balance of time, expense, and possibly quality of delineation.

Certification of delineators will benefit the public as well as government agencies. The potential applicant, if informed, could contract with appropriately certified personnel, thereby obtaining some assurance that a delineation will be reliable. If a certification system is established, USACE might accept delineations from certified consultants only, after sufficient time passes to enable qualified consultants to become certified. On the other hand, a mandatory certification program involves expense.

Because delineation requires a substantial degree of expertise, the regulatory agencies must disseminate information about wetlands and their regulatory programs. Information such as wetland maps and sources of assistance should be made widely available. If the public is informed, compliance with the law will improve through cooperation with regulators and through physical protection of wetlands from inadvertent destruction. Public education can highlight the need for expertise in wetlands delineation.

Verification of Delineations

Wetland delineations vary in the degree to which they are subject to quality assurance and quality control. As a general matter, quality assurance is left to the discretion of regional or local agency offices. Federal agencies are now attempting to minimize interagency differences in wetland delineation, but they have not yet identified specific programs that assure quality.

Neither USACE nor EPA has a formal quality assurance process for wetland delineations. Supervisors regularly review wetland delineations, however, and EPA also uses interagency training and substantive guidance to improve the quality of wetland delineations. The USACE certification program, USACE regulatory guidance letters, and interagency memoranda of agreement concerning wetland delineations are also examples of attempts to ensure and standardize quality.

Most delineations for Clean Water Act Section 404 permit applications are done by private consultants. They are reviewed by USACE or EPA only if necessary for a Section 404 permit. Because review is not always necessary, and because a private delineation will not necessarily lead to a permit request, an inaccurate delineation is not always discovered, and, if it is not discovered, it cannot be corrected. In contrast, NRCS employees conduct all wetland delineations for the swampbuster program of the 1985 Food Security Act (FSA). Consequently, errors will affect directly the potential uses of agricultural lands. While there are limited ways the public can be protected for errors of delineation by private delineators, quality assurance of delineations within an agency such as NRCS is extremely important to maintain a fair regulatory system.

Standards of quality assurance for NRCS appear in its regulations and the third edition (1994) of the National Food Security Act Manual (NFSAM). These standards establish principles for quality control and prevention of fraud, waste, and abuse. The NRCS National Technical Center has quality assurance teams with nationwide responsibility for quality assurance, including training, technical assistance, and consistency. Each state must have a quality control program that is consistent with national guidance.

The January 1994 MOA also includes standards for interagency review of NRCS delineations. It requires interagency concurrence and training on methods (protocols) for office-based wetland delineations by use of aerial photographs and maps (Chapter 8), and it puts a high emphasis on consistency of wetland delineations across agency lines. EPA has an oversight role involving periodic review of determinations, and an appeal to agency headquarters is allowed when the agencies disagree. These provisions of the MOA have been incorporated into NFSAM. In addition, NRCS is leading interagency teams in field tests of regionalized hydric soil indicators (SCS, 1994).

Although interagency coordination is important, the agencies should not ignore internal quality assurance. Publication of substantive standards for wetland delineations is not the same as a system for quality assurance, which involves the enforcement of substantive standards. Also, a quality assurance system cannot compensate for unqualified delineators.

Properly implemented, a quality assurance system enables an agency to minimize and quantify errors. Such a system could also foster public confidence.

Uniformity and the Exercise of Professional Judgment

Predictable, uniform delineations are most easily achieved through strict standards. Strict delineation standards, however, allow minimal use of professional judgment, and this could be detrimental to the validity of delineation in complex or marginal cases. In addition, national delineation standards must be adaptable to regional differences in wetlands (Chapter 7). Some exercise of professional judgment is necessary in delineation of wetlands, but it must have limits. The standards for wetland delineation cannot be so subjective that government or private delineators have broad latitude in drawing jurisdictional lines.

Field testing and field verification of delineations should be used in establishing the balance between uniformity of standards and professional judgment. The agencies involved in delineation should maintain interagency and interdistrict communications on the use of professional judgment, and the results of field tests should be shared widely among the agencies. Establishment of regional indicators for wetland delineation also will reduce the necessity for broad exercise of professional judgment. Interaction between agency personnel and outside professionals could be encouraged by the development of regional advisory committees, participation of federal personnel in private and professional associations, and similar mechanisms.

Although wetland delineations are formally documented, they are not maintained in an accessible data base. This represents a great loss of potentially useful information. A usable record of wetland delineations would have many benefits: It would enable the government to ascertain the wetland acreage in the regulatory programs (such as acres permitted, not permitted, farmed); it would promote comparison among wetland delineations based on particular features (such as soils and vegetation); it would facilitate research on wetland delineations; it would provide access to records of prior delineations on specific parcels; and it could generate an overview for the entire federal regulatory program. Such a record also would be a means for determining whether professional judgment is being exercised arbitrarily in wetland delineation. A useful record of wetland delineations should be maintained in digital form and should be accessible electronically.

Resource Regulation and Private Rights

The government should be able to tell property owners, on relatively short notice, whether they risk breaking the law by conducting certain activities on private property. Fairness requires that if the law prohibits filling of wetlands, a landowner should be able to ascertain the wetland's location. This principle underlies the wetland delineation system's philosophy that federal delineations or federal reviews of private delineations should be done essentially at the time requested by the property owner. Field conditions, however, do not always allow accurate delineations to be conducted in all seasons. Seasonal variations, such as snow cover, or interannual variations, such as drought or unusual rainfall, can prevent reliable delineation or review of delineation. In general, wetland delineation should not be done when a short delay could greatly improve its validity. The need for accuracy must be weighed against the need for responsiveness to the landowner in administration of wetland delineations.

A variety of approaches could reconcile a property owner's need for timely delineation with the concern for the accuracy of delineation. Records of seasonal changes could be used by delineators. For example, difficulties caused by some types of seasonal change can be overcome by use of seasonally insensitive indicators or by regional knowledge of the nature of seasonal variations. This is part of the appropriate exercise of professional judgment with regard to field conditions. In other cases, seasonal difficulties might be insurmountable, and some delay should be allowed and expected: The applicant could be required to show evidence of the condition of the parcel during a more favorable season. Many government regulatory programs other than those involving wetlands require physical inspections that take time. Where wetland delineation cannot be undertaken on request, however, the factors that cause the delay must be explained and must be related to technical concerns for validity of delineation.

Use of Flow Diagrams and Charts

Decision trees and flow charts provide a method for structuring wetland delineations. With these tools, a delineator can minimize the collection and evaluation of redundant information. A decision tree is a diagram that portrays a sequence of alternative decisions as well as the probabilities associated with decision choices. A flow diagram provides a simple portrayal of the sequences involved in an analysis, but without attributing probabilities to particular steps.

The federal delineation manuals use flow diagrams as aids to delineation. These diagrams are graphic portrayals of the steps required, under each manual, to delineate a wetland. Such graphic alternatives to the text descriptions of delineation can be very helpful to the delineator.

Use of some of the most sophisticated flow charts could show, among other things, the probabilities of reaching particular conclusions. Given the degree to which wetland delineation involves the exercise of professional judgment, it would be useful to ascertain in probabilistic terms the likelihood of various kinds of outcomes for specific regions. This information could help to guide field delineation. For example, where particular decisions carry a substantial risk of error, the delineation manual could establish specific guidelines, such as a requirement for analysis by a technician with particular training.

CONCLUSIONS

A system of wetland delineation must be administered consistently. Wetland delineation standards must be understood by properly trained delineators, and delineations performed by different persons should have similar results on the same piece of ground. Public confidence in wetland delineations can be enhanced by a system that includes appropriate training and certification of delineators and dissemination of general information to the public about the nature of wetlands and the need for protection of this resource.

RECOMMENDATIONS

1. All federal agencies involved in wetland delineations should participate in jointly managed delineation training and should be part of a continuing-education program.

2. All federal agencies should use a single delineation manual that provides clear technical guidance and includes all rules and guidance.

3. Training for federal and private delineators must be rigorous. Agencies and professional associations should consider ways of disqualifying the results from unqualified wetland delineators.

4. The USACE program for certification of wetland delineators should continue, and should be available to federal and nonfederal personnel. Lists of certified delineators should be made available to the public.

5. Rigorous programs for quality control and quality assurance should be used by all agencies that conduct wetland delineations.

6. Records of wetland delineations should be maintained in a usable, accessible format that will enable the agencies to develop and release annually an inventory of wetlands subject to regulatory programs and to facilitate research and data analysis.

7. Central repositories should be developed for scientific substantiation of all indicators, including reference wetland sites.

8. Wetlands delineation should be postponed when a short delay might improve the accuracy of the delineation.

9. Consolidation of all wetland regulatory functions into a single federal agency would improve the consistency of wetland delineations but should not be implemented without appropriate oversight and quality assurance.

10

Functional Assessment of Wetlands

INTRODUCTION

Since wetlands were first subject to federal regulation in the 1970s, federal agencies have been attempting to develop techniques for assessing wetland functions. The motivations for assessing functions have been primarily the need to predict the effects of wetland alteration and to set appropriate requirements for mitigation. More recently, assessment of functions has been used to rank or categorize wetlands, which might ensure that wetlands with highly valued functions receive greater protection than wetlands in general. Assessing functions currently presents many challenges in methodology, but the problem is a subject of active research and conceptual development.

FUNCTIONS AND VALUES OF WETLANDS

Wetland functions are the physical, chemical, and biological processes that characterize wetland ecosystems, such as flooding, denitrification, provision of habitat for organisms, and support of aquatic life (see Chapter 2). Objective measurement of wetland functions falls within the realm of the natural sciences and, barring changes in the ecosystem being measured, is repeatable over time. Many wetland functions are considered useful or important by society. For example, inundation of wetlands can prevent flood damage elsewhere, denitrification can improve water quality, wetland habitat can help maintain waterfowl populations, and anaerobiosis can influence the development of unique plant communities that contribute to the conservation of biodiversity.

The value of a wetland is a measure of its importance to society. Wetland functions are valued to various degrees by society, but there is no precise, general relationship between wetland functions and the value of wetlands to society, and values can be difficult to determine objectively. Wetlands also have aesthetic values. A wetland's value can be weighed directly or relative to other uses that could be made of the site; thus, the location of a wetland affects its value to society. For example, wetlands in urban settings might have higher value for recreation and education or for alternative uses of the site than wetlands in undeveloped lands or far from population centers. Assessing the value of wetlands involves methods of social science, especially economics.

Decisions about whether to protect wetlands or how much to spend on wetland protection are policy decisions based in part on the value society places on wetlands. Part of that value depends on a sound scientific knowledge of what wetlands do, i.e., a knowledge of wetland functions. Indeed, some groups have suggested the creation of a national scheme that would designate wetlands of high, medium, and low value based on some general assessment of wetland functions that does not require field evaluation. Examples of categories that have been proposed as having low value include wetlands of under 10 acres (4 ha) or of some other specific size; fastlands, which are wetlands maintained behind dikes or levees; wetlands within industrial complexes or in intensely developed areas; wetlands affected by anthropogenic disturbance; artificial wetlands; frequently farmed wetlands; and regionally abundant types of wetland. As described above, however, it is usually not possible to relate such categories in a reliable way to objective measures of wetland functions, in part because the relationships between them are variable and in part because we do not have enough scientific knowledge. Wetlands of any of the categories can have a variety of wetland functions based on objective measurements (Bostwick, 1992). Examples include the prairie potholes of the upper midwest, which are isolated wetlands generally smaller than 10 acres (4 ha), but which provide vital wildlife habitat; and the wetlands of the Lake Calumet area in heavily industrialized southeast Chicago, which provide habitat for more than 170 bird species, of which 11 are listed by the state of Illinois as threatened or endangered (Kendall, 1990). The remainder of this chapter deals with the scientific assessment of wetland functions and its usefulness in planning.

GENERAL REQUIREMENTS FOR FUNCTIONAL ASSESSMENT

Important concepts in functional assessment of wetlands include functional capacity, predictors of function (indicators), and thresholds for functions. Functional capacity is the ability of an ecosystem to perform a function. An example would be kilograms of sediment removal per hectare per year. A predictor is an observable condition, the state of which is related to the capacity or ability of a wetland to perform a function. For example, morphometry of a wetland might serve as a predictor of sediment retention. A threshold is a functional discontinuity across which a wetland changes qualitatively. For example, a nutrient- or sediment-loading threshold is a condition above which a wetland's functional state would change. Thresholds apply to anthropogenic as well as natural conditions.

Use of functional assessment in conjunction with a Clean Water Act (CWA) Section 404 permit requires quick, simple, repeatable, and objective methods that are applicable or adaptable to a wide range of wetlands. Regulatory functional assessment should particularly facilitate analysis of wetland functions directly relevant to CWA's objectives.

METHODS OF FUNCTIONAL ASSESSMENT

Scientists and government agencies have been developing methods of functional assessment for wetlands over the last two decades. Measurement of wetland functions is fundamentally different from wetland identification or delineation. The system developed by Cowardin et al. (1979) for the National Wetlands Inventory, for example, was designed to describe classes of wetlands, arrange them in a system useful to resource managers, and provide a standard set of concepts and terms. The needs of federal agencies, however, often extend well beyond classification or delineation to planning and site selection, regulatory action, assessment of anthropogenic effects, management, mitigation, and acquisition of property. These have been the primary factors supporting the development of functional assessments (Lonard et al., 1981). Functional assessment allows comparison of a wetland to other wetlands or to other potential uses of a wetland site, and it shows the extent of compensatory mitigation that might be necessary if a wetland were altered.

The first attempt at evaluating wetland functions for regulatory purposes emerged in the USACE permit regulations of 1975, which were revised in 1977 and 1986. These regulations list wetlands that provide functions important to the public interest, including support of food chains and wildlife habitat, education and recreation, prevention of erosion, reduction of storm or flood damage, ground water discharge and recharge, water purification, and maintenance of biological diversity (33 CFR 320.4).

USACE (1979) developed a manual entitled "Wetland Values: Concepts and Methods for Wetlands Evaluation." Preparation of this manual was devised specifically to assist USACE field staff in making permit decisions. Technical guidelines in the manual that encompass physical, biological, and cultural factors permit at least qualitative approximation of functional efficiency (Reppert, 1981). The manual was developed from a large amount of information on the biological and ecological characteristics of wetlands. Information on some important wetland functions, including water quality improvement, shoreline protection, ground water recharge, and flood water storage, was sparse, however (Reppert, 1981).

In 1981 the U.S. Water Resources Council published an analysis of 20 functional assessment methods used by the USACE Waterways Experiment Station. USACE concluded that few methods could assess all functions of wetlands, and that some functions were assessed very subjectively by most methods. Habitat evaluation methods were the most common and the most elaborate. Hydrologic values were poorly integrated into evaluation methods, and there were few techniques for assessment of functions associated with recreation, heritage, or agricultural potential (Balco, 1981; Lonard et al., 1981). All of the methods that were reviewed included qualitative judgments by a resource manager or an interdisciplinary team.

In 1980, the U.S. Fish and Wildlife Service (FWS) published its own wetland evaluation method, the Habitat Evaluation Procedure (HEP), to replace its previous wetland valuation system, which was based on estimates of direct public use. HEP was designed primarily to evaluate the effects of proposed projects on fish and wildlife resources. The method is based on a numerical analysis of habitat quality and quantity, and measures functional capacity. The numerical analysis of HEP permits alternative plans to be compared. The procedure is done by a team of biologists who use file data, field observations, experience, statistical analysis, and simulation modeling to develop a habitat suitability model that expresses the quality of habitat through use of a habitat suitability index for individual species on a scale of 0-1. The scale is directly related to carrying capacity or abundance of a species per unit area. For instance, habitat units might be expressed as squirrels per acre, or coveys of quail or broods of ducks per acre (FWS, 1980). HEP is used extensively by FWS for impact assessment, but it is not used regularly in the wetlands regulatory programs of USACE or NRCS. Many regulators consider the method too time consuming, and regulators and wetland scientists consider it too narrowly focused on fish and wildlife to be used in routine regulatory assessments of wetlands.

A national assessment methodology was developed for the Federal Highway Administration (FHWA), as reported by Adamus and Stockwell (1983) and Adamus (1983). The Method for Wetland Functional Assessment—or the FHWA method, as it became known—uses an extensive literature review, including evaluation of a large volume of quantitative data, to build a series of evaluation algorithms that represent the functions of wetlands. The algorithms are sequential, dichotomous decision trees that use thresholds or binary responses to rank a wetland high, moderate, or low for a specific function or value. The FHWA method was designed specifically for use by state and federal highway departments, but was revised so that it could be used more broadly. The USACE concluded that the revised FHWA method might be useful for the CWA Section 404 permit program. A modified version, the Wetland Evaluation Technique (Adamus, 1987; Adamus et al., 1991) incorporates an interactive computer analysis program.

The FHWA method was intended to provide a means of using field observations to categorize the functions of wetlands relevant to the section 404 permit review process. The method has three separate procedures: threshold analysis of single wetlands, comparative analysis of two or more wetlands, and mitigation analysis for comparison of mitigation alternatives.

The FHWA algorithms incorporate the concepts of effectiveness, opportunity, and significance. A wetland could be potentially effective in performing a particular function, for example, but there might be no opportunity for it to do so, or the function might not be significant to society. These distinctions are particularly important for functions that have high value in modified or developed landscapes, such as flood water storage, sediment retention, or pollution abatement. Wetlands receive low ratings for such functions in undeveloped landscapes where the opportunity for the function does not exist. As a drainage is developed, its ranking for such functions increases, even though the wetland itself might become environmentally degraded. Similarly, the significance of the function—the degree to which a function is valued, used, or needed by society— is likely to increase as a landscape is developed.

Temporal changes in wetland contexts expose a failing of the FHWA and other methods that use the concepts of opportunity and significance. Regulatory or management decisions based on current contexts discount future wetland values. From an ecological perspective, such management is short-sighted for systems that could persist for hundreds or thousands of years.

The FHWA method recognizes that CWA objectives are not necessarily compatible with one another. As a wetland performs some functions to a higher percentage of its potential capacity, the capacity for other functions might decrease. For example, pollution abatement by a wetland could decrease its capacity to sustain wildlife. The original FHWA method ranks relative values of wetlands after consideration of the potential incompatibilities of functions. The second generation of the FHWA method (WET) uses a slightly different approach in that it ranks the probability that a wetland will perform a given function, and the significance of the function to society, rather than directly ranking the value of the wetland.

Another recent approach to wetland evaluation is the Hollands-Magee method (Hollands and Magee, 1986), which derives a numerical index for each function; it was developed for northeastern wetlands. Other examples include the Connecticut and New Hampshire methods (Amman et al., 1986; Amman and Stone, 1991), which use observable indexes of conditions and functions to derive rankings and can be used by nonspecialists; the Wisconsin method (Reed, 1986), which is a modification of the FHWA method; the New Jersey Department of Transportation modification of the FHWA method (McColligan, 1986); the Virginia Institute of Marine Science method for nontidal wetlands (Bradshaw, 1992); and the Evaluation of Planned Wetlands method (Bartoldus et al., 1994), which emphasizes mitigation design.

USACE published WET 2.0, a revised version of WET, in 1991. WET 2.0

uses a series of word models to evaluate a wetland relative to functions and values, such as ground water recharge, ground water discharge, flood flow alteration, shoreline and sediment stabilization, sediment and toxicant retention, nutrient removal and transformation, food chain support and export of production, wildlife diversity and abundance, diversity and abundance of aquatic life, uniqueness and heritage significance, and recreational uses. The results of the WET 2.0 evaluation are qualitative rankings of the probability that a wetland performs a given function (effectiveness), that its position in the landscape allows it to perform the function (opportunity), and that the function offers societal benefits (social significance) (Adamus et al., 1991).

WET 2.0 was the first widely used methodology to encompass all wetland functions, but it does not specifically account for regional variation of wetlands. The developers of WET 2.0 used an extensive literature review, including quantitative data, to build a series of independent evaluation models for the functions of wetlands.

The FHWA method, WET, and other methods that use rank present problems in the determination of compensation ratios for wetland mitigation because they do not give quantitative estimates of the functional capacities of altered wetlands and mitigated wetlands. In general, methods for wetland evaluation do not provide a means for direct comparison of wetlands on an areal basis, do not provide a basis for estimating mitigation ratios on an areal basis, are not readily adaptable to a variety of wetland types, and have data requirements that are too cumbersome for routine field application.

FUTURE METHODS OF FUNCTIONAL ASSESSMENT

Assessment Based on Hydrogeomorphic Classification and Reference Wetlands

A new procedure for assessment of wetland functions is being developed at the USACE Waterways Experiment Station (WES). The procedure differs from WET and some other assessment procedures in two important ways. First, it recognizes that wetlands exist under a wide range of climatic, geomorphic, and hydrologic conditions that can cause variation in functions among wetlands. Second, it uses functional indexes that can be quantified on a scale that is developed from reference wetlands. The functional indexes account for the need for functional assessment to strike a balance involving consistency, reliability, and scope of coverage under the constraints of time and resources that are available to regulatory programs.

The WES procedure uses the hydrogeomorphic wetland classification developed by Brinson (1993a). This system identifies five broad groups of wetlands on a national level. Wetlands within each group show similarities in function because of similarities in geomorphic setting, water source, and hydrodynamic features. Each of the groups is divided into regional subgroups. Subgroup divisions are based on landscape position and ecosystem type for wetlands of a given group. The functions that are most likely to be associated with a particular regional subgroup are assessed by the use of functional models that describe and define the relationship between wetland functions, the wetland ecosystem, and the landscape within which the wetland is located.

Reference wetlands in several regions are used in establishing relationships between hydrogeomorphic type, landscape, and functional capacity. These relationships form the basis for functional models that provide a scale for the functional capacity of individual wetlands across the range for a given hydrogeomorphic subgroup. The index values that result from the application of these models can be used in the evaluation of wetland alteration or to mitigation of wetland alteration.

The hydrogeomorphic approach is likely to improve the precision, consistency, reliability, and timeliness of functional assessment. Even so, it is subject to many of the same limitations that affect other procedures. Limitations involve quality and amount of background information, difficulty of incorporating a landscape perspective into the assessment, and difficulty in establishing relationships between functions and societal values.

The quality and amount of information relevant to functional assessment vary greatly among wetland types, wetland functions, and geographic regions. In general, physical functions are understood poorly by comparison with biological functions, and wetlands in the western United States have been studied less thoroughly than have been those in the eastern United States. Functional assessment models have of necessity drawn extensively on the technical literature and expert opinion. Primary research on functions within reference wetlands has been supported insufficiently in view of its relevance to quantification of functions through the use of functional indexes. The functional indexes represent only a qualitative approximation of the functional capacity of wetlands.

The hydrogeomorphic approach recognizes the reciprocal interactions of wetland ecosystems with the landscape. The functional analysis itself, however, is limited to functions that occur within the wetland. This reflects the difficulty in collecting data that will be relevant to an analysis of the relationship between the wetland and the entire landscape.

The hydrogeomorphic approach provides a measure of the ability of a wetland to perform a function, but it does not assign a measure of the importance or societal value to specific functions. Societal importance or value can be measured only through the analysis of a set of factors that are different from those that are considered in the assessment of wetland functions. Procedures for conversion of functions to societal value may become important, however, in establishing the relative importance of wetlands in the landscape.

Wetland Evaluation Under the National Food Security Act Manual

The Food Security Act of 1985 (P.L. 99-198), which establishes penalties for conversion of wetlands (Chapters 2 and 8), exempts some agricultural activities as having "minimal effect." The National Food Security Act Manual as revised in 1989 contains a procedure for determining minimal effects from a rudimentary wetland evaluation. Minimal effects include the conversion of less than 2% of a wetland smaller than 100 acres (40 ha), or 1 acre (0.4 ha) of a wetland larger than 100 acres. Actions that have a measurable effect on the hydrologic and biological functions of the remaining wetland are, however, not considered minimal, regardless of other considerations. Also, wetland conversions that exceed the size thresholds are not considered minimal, regardless of effects, unless accompanied by compensatory mitigation. The manual states that "[m]inimal effect determinations involving restoration must be supported by an assessment that indicates that wetland values lost as a result of the conversion have been fully replaced by restoration." These regulations (7 CFR § 12.5(b)(6)(F)) require the Natural Resources Conservation Service state conservationist, in consultation with FWS, to determine the mitigation acreage necessary to replace wetland functions or values.

The NFSAM procedure for a minimal-effect determination under the terms of FSA contains a checklist of 13 wetland functions that are to be designated as either present or absent. NRCS revised the determination procedure in March 1994 and incorporated a more elaborate wetland evaluation method. The new procedure, which appears in Section 527.6 of the third edition of NFSAM (NFSAM, 1994) includes a much broader range of wetland functions and requires that site evaluations include records of indicators of the presence or absence of specific functions. This procedure is modeled after the hydrogeomorphic classification system, and was it promulgated in anticipation of the adoption of a wetland evaluation procedure derived from this system by the federal regulatory agencies.

Relevance of Hydrologic Factors to Functional Assessment

The degree, frequency, and seasonality of inundation vary widely among wetland types (Chapters 2 and 7). Although hydrology is the most important factor explaining the development and maintenance of a wetland, other factors influence wetland functions. For example, the position of the wetland in the landscape, the uses of land in the surrounding watershed, the density of vegetation in the wetland, the soils and geologic features, the source of water, and the size of a wetland greatly influence function. The functional capacity of wetlands cannot be predicted from the frequency or duration of inundation alone, or from any other single characteristic.

RELEVANCE OF WETLAND ASSESSMENT TO
404 PERMIT APPLICATIONS

Assessment of wetland functions is required for a CWA Section 404 permit application, but not as part of the identification and delineation of a wetland. The first decision in the review of a permit application is whether a site that would be affected by the applicant contains wetlands or other waters of the United States subject to regulatory jurisdiction. If jurisdictional wetlands will be affected, the next step is to determine the location of the wetland boundary. Assessing wetland function is not necessary for either of these steps. Wetland evaluation is relevant to the issuance of a permit, however, because review of a permit application involves evaluation of probable effects and of reasonable ("practicable") alternatives for the proposed project. Corps regulations require that benefits of the proposed activity be balanced against its foreseeable detriments (33 CFR § 320.4(2)(i)). The U.S. Environmental Protection Agency's Section 404(b)(1) guidelines allow regulators to consider the relative functional capacity of a wetland when determining the environmental costs of a proposed project as compared with alternatives (R. Wayland and M. Davis).

Assessments of function also are used in determining mitigation requirements. The CWA Section 404 program requires that adverse effects be avoided, minimized, or compensated for through mitigation as a condition for issuance of a permit. Compensatory mitigation is determined in part by functional impairment of a wetland. According to USACE and EPA, the objective of compensatory mitigation is to provide, at a minimum, full replacement of wetland value (USACE and EPA, 1990). Replacement of value requires replacement of underlying wetland functions.

The degree to which a wetland performs a specific function of value to society does not influence regulatory jurisdiction. Conversely, many activities that can decrease the functional capacity of a jurisdictional wetland are not regulated. These activities include diversion of water from a wetland, flooding, diversion of sediment, shading, change of nutrient concentrations, indirect introduction of toxic substances, grazing, disruption of natural populations, and alteration of adjacent uplands.

USE OF FUNCTIONAL ASSESSMENT
IN WATERSHED PLANNING

Local or regional planning at the watershed level can provide a scientifically sound framework for consideration of variations in wetland functions. This would require evaluation of all wetlands within the boundaries of a particular watershed or planning area, accompanied by mapping of probable development patterns. Some wetlands could be identified as deserving stringent protection, while wetlands of lower significance could be identified as appropriate for general permits or other regulatory flexibility, although such a ranking system is not required under current law. Ranking or classification based on value is presently accomplished outside the regulatory framework by two processes: advanced identification programs (ADIDs) and special area management plans (SAMPs).

Advanced Identification (ADID)

Section 230.80 of EPA's 404(b)(1) guidelines (40 CFR § 230), allow EPA and the CWA Section 404 permitting authority to identify sites that are suitable or unsuitable to receive discharges of fill. The results of such an ADID wetland classification are advisory, not regulatory. Through ADID, developers and landowners benefit from predictability and consistency, and conservation interests can review and use information on wetland functions and values (EPA, 1988b).

ADID has been applied to areas ranging from 14 mi.^{2} (36.4 km^2) (Joliet, Illinois) to 4,200 mi.^{2} (10,920 km^2) (Rainwater Basin, south central Nebraska). As of December 1992, 35 ADID processes had been completed and 36 were in progress throughout the United States (EPA, 1992).

Special Area Management Plans

SAMPs were established under the Coastal Zone Management Act (CZMA) amendments of 1980 (16 U.S.C. § 1452). A SAMP is a plan for natural resource protection consistent with economic growth. It consists of policies, standards, and criteria for use of public and private lands and waters. Grants issued to states and communities for implementation of CZMA can be used for SAMPs in coastal zones.

USACE has adopted the SAMP concept for inland areas, as well as coastal areas. Its program is funded through a special studies segment of the USACE regulatory budget. The program is defined administratively, rather than legislatively, through a regulatory guidance letter originally issued in October 1986. According to the letter, SAMPs, which are labor intensive, can be justified only when an area is environmentally sensitive and under strong pressure for development, the plan is sponsored by a local agency, the public is fully involved, and all parties are willing to conclude the process with regulatory products. Ideal regulatory products include local or state approvals and a USACE general permit for specific activities and local, state, or EPA restrictions for undesirable activities (USACE, 1986). The identification of wetlands is a valuable component of many SAMPs. SAMPs generally go beyond ADIDs, however, in the numbers of interests and authorities involved and in the development of regulatory products.

Even within a given watershed, ranking systems and predetermined permit decisions are subject to a variety of criticisms. Prohibitive designations could raise legal questions about the confiscation of property without due process or just compensation, although policies such as transfer of development rights could reduce this concern. At the other end of the scale, the designation of some wetlands as having low value would seem to sanction their conversion to other uses. The role of a wetland in a region and the cumulative functioning of wetlands in a watershed or flyway also must be evaluated; this is the landscape perspective.

The National Wetlands Policy Forum of 1987 (Conservation Foundation, 1988) made several recommendations about wetland categorization (ranking). One was that agencies consider establishing regional general permits that would allow the conversion of a limited amount of wetland of low value in exchange for full compensatory mitigation. These permits would be issued only within the framework of an EPA-approved state wetland conservation plan. The compensation requirement would be consistent with the cost of acquiring, restoring, and managing wetlands in a location and of a type similar to those covered under the permit. The forum also recommended the establishment of wetland mitigation banks, consistent with state wetlands conservation plans, through which permit recipients could satisfy compensation requirements (Conservation Foundation, 1988). The regulated community has endorsed national policies that allow market mechanisms of this type to operate while protecting wetland functions and values (Hackman, 1993; Hahn, 1993; Marshall, 1993; Wennberg, 1993). The environmental community will expect programs that provide flexibility in the management of lower quality wetlands to also provide stringent protection for areas determined to be of high quality.

In addition to the flexibility provided in current policy to scale regulatory responses to the effects of specific projects and the functional capacity of specific wetlands, the regulatory program includes provisions for landscape-level planning processes that evaluate the relative value of wetlands. These processes, such as ADID programs and SAMPs, allow state and local agencies to work with federal regulatory agencies in surveying wetlands and ranking them according to their relative functional capacity or value. Through these landscape level planning processes, authorities and other interested parties can be integrated with the wetland regulatory program to achieve a mix of objectives within a specific geographic area.

CONCLUSION

Although it is possible to evaluate the functions of wetlands, the precision is low for some types of functions and in some regions. Progress is being made on the scientific basis for wetland evaluation. Functional assessment of wetlands is most useful in the context of watershed or landscape planning. This approach facilitates consideration of the interaction between the wetland and surrounding landscape features, as well as the location of the wetland in the watershed. Landscape-level planning provides a framework for incorporation of the interests of all affected parties. The creation of such a framework increases the likelihood that regulatory actions will be acceptable to all parties.

RECOMMENDATIONS

1. Analysis of wetland functions should be extended and refined, with emphasis on interactions between wetlands and their surroundings and on various hydrogeomorphic classes of wetlands in specific regions.

2. The procedures for identification and delineation of wetlands must be kept separate from the analysis of wetland functions.

References

Abrams, M. D., and M. E. Kubiske. 1990. Photosynthesis and water relations during drought in Acer rubrum L. genotypes from contrasting sites in central Pennsylvania. Functional Ecology 4:727-733.

Adam, K. M., G. L. Bloomsburg, and A. T. Corey. 1969. Diffusion of trapped gas from porous media. Water Resources Research 5:840:849.

Adamus, P. R., 1987. Wetland Evaluation Technique (WET): Volume II-Methodology. Vicksburg, MS: U.S. Army COrps of Engineers, Waterways Experiment Station.

Adamus, P. R., and L. T. Stockwell. 1983. A Method for Wetland Functional Assessment, Volume II. Washington, DC: Office of Research and Development, Federal Highway Administration, U.S. Department of Transportation.

Adamus, P. R., L. T. Stockwell, F. J. Clarain, Jr., M. E. Morrow, L. E. Rozas, and R. D. Smith. 1991. Wetland Evaluation Technique (WET), Volume I: Literature Review and Evaluation Rationale. Wetlands Research Program Technical Report WRP-DE-2. Vicksburg, MS: U.S. Army Corps of Engineers, Waterways Experiment Station.

Alexander, V., and M. M. Billington. 1986. Nitrogen fixation in the Alaskan taiga. Pp. 112-120 in Forest Ecosystems in the Alaskan Taiga, K. Van Cleve, F. S. Chapin, III, P. W. Flanagan, L. A. Viereck, and C. T. Dyrness, eds. New York: Springer-Verlag.

Allen, S. D., F. C. Golet, A. F. Davis, and T. E. Sokoloski. 1989. Soil-vegetation Correlations in Transition Zones of Rhode Island Red Maple Swamps. Biol. Rep. 89(8). Washington, DC: U.S. Fish and Wildlife Service.

Amman, A. P., and A. L. Stone. 1991. Method for the Comparative Evaluation of Non-tidal Wetlands in New Hampshire. Concord: Report NHDES-WRD-1991-3, New Hampshire Department of Environmental Services.

Amman, A. P., R. W. Franzen, and J. L. Johnson. 1986. Method for the Evaluation of Inland Wetlands in Connecticut. Hartford: Connecticut Department of Environmental Protection.

Anderson, K. L., M. W. Lefor, and W. C. Kennard. 1980. Forested wetlands in eastern Connecticut: Their transition zones and delineation. Water Resources Bulletin 16:248-255.

Anderson, R. R., and R. J. Wobber. 1973. Wetlands mapping in New Jersey. Photogrammetric Engineering 39:353-358.

Armstrong, W. 1971. Radial oxygen losses from intact rice roots as affected by distance from the apex, respiration and waterlogging. Physiol. Plant. 25:192-197.

Aspinall, R. J., D. R. Miller, and A. Richman. 1993. Data quality and error analysis in GIS: measurement and use of metadata describing uncertainty in spatial data. Pp. 279-290 in Proceedings ARC/INFO Users Conference, Vol.2. Redlands, CA: ESRI.

Austin, W. 1993. Duration of Saturation and Redox Potentials in Selected Willamette Valley soils. M.S. thesis. Oregon State University.

Baad, M.F. 1988. Soil-vegetation correlations within the riparian zone of Butte Sink in the Sacramento Valley of northern California. Fish and Wildlife Service, U.S. Department of the Interior, Washington, DC. Biol. Rep. 88(25).

Bailey, R. G. 1976. Ecoregions of the United States (map). Ogden, UT: U.S. Forest Service.

Balco, J. J. 1981. Assessing Wetlands Values—Evaluation Dilemmas. Pp. 421-429 in Selected Proceedings of the Midwest Conference on Wetland Values and Management, B. Richardson ed. Navarre, MN: Freshwater Society.

Banner, A., J. Pojar, and R. Trowbridge. 1986. Representative Wetland Types of the Northern Part of the Pacific Oceanic Wetland Region. British Columbia Minist. For. Res. Rep., Smithers, B.C. 45 pp.

Bartoldus, C. C., E. W. Garbisch, and M. L. Kraus. 1994. Evaluation for Planned Wetlands (EPW). St. Michaels, MD.: Environmental Concern.

Bates, R. L., and J. A. Jackson eds. 1987. Glossary of Geology. Alexandria, VA: American Geological Institute.

Beals. 1969. Vegetational change along altitudinal gradients. Science 165:981-985.

Bean, M. J. 1977. The Evolution of National Wildlife Law: Report to the Council on Environmental Quality. Washington, DC: Environmental Law Institute.

Bedford, B. L., N. R. Rapport, and J. M. Bernard. 1988. A life history of *Carex lasiocarpa* Ehrh. Ramets. Aquat. Bot. 30:63-80.

Bedford, B. L., M. B. Brinson, R. Sharitz, A. van der Valk, and J. Zedler. 1992. Evaluation of proposed revisions to the 1989 "Federal Manual for Identifying and Delineating Jurisdictional Wetlands." Report of the Ecological Society of America's Ad Hoc Committee on Wetlands Delineation. Bull. Ecol. Soc. Am. 73(1):14-23.

Bedient, P. B., and W. C. Huber. 1988. Hydrology of Floodplain Analysis. Reading, Mass: Addison-Wesley.

Bedinger, M. S. 1978. Wetland functions and values: The state of our understanding. Pp. 427-434 in Proceedings of the National Symposium on Wetlands, P. E. Greeson, J. R. Clark, and J. E. Clark eds. Lake Buena Vista, FL: American Water Resources Association.

Bedinger, M. S. 1978. Wetland functions and values: The state of our understanding. Pp. 427-434 in Proceedings of the National Symposium on Wetlands, P.E. Greeson, J. R. Clark, and J. E. Clark, eds. Lake Buena Vista, FL: American Water Resources Association.

Bergman, R. D., R. L. Howard, K. F. Abraham, and M. W. Weller. 1977. Water birds and their wetland resources in relation to oil development at Storkersen Point, Alaska. U.S. Fish Wildlife Service Resour. Publ. 129.

Bertness, M. D. 1991. Interspecific interactions among high marsh perennials in a New England salt marsh. Ecology 72:125-137.

Best, G. R., D. S. Segal, and C. Wolfe. 1990. Soil-vegetation Correlations in Selected Wetlands and Uplands of North-central Florida. Biol. Rep. 90(9). Washington, DC: U.S. Fish and Wildlife Service.

Billings, W. D., and K. M. Peterson. 1980. Vegetational change and ice-wedge polygons through the thaw-lake cycle in arctic Alaska. Arct. and Alpine Res. 12(4):413-432.

Billings, W. D., and L. C. Bliss. 1959. An alpine snowbank environment and its effect on vegetable plant development, and productivity. Ecology 40(3):388-397.

Blem, C. R., and L. B. Blem. 1975. Density, biomass, and energetics of the bird and mammal populations of an Illinois deciduous forest. Illinois Acad. Sci. Trans. 68:156-184.

Bliss, L. C. 1971. Artic and alpine plant life cycles. Ann. Rev. Ecol. Syst. 2:405-438.

Bloomfield, C. 1950. Some observations on gleying. J. Soil Sci. 1:205-211.

Bloomfield, C. 1951. Experiments on the mechanism of gley formation. J. Soil Sci. 2:196-211.

Blume, H. P., and E. Schlicting. 1985. Morphology of wetland soils. Pp. 161-176 in Wetland Soils: Characterization, classification, and utilization. Proceedings of a workshop held March 26 to April 5, 1984, anonymous ed. Los Baños, Philippines: Int. Rice Res. Inst.

Boersma, L., G. H. Simonson, and D. G. Watts. 1972. Soil morphology and water table relations, I. Annual water table fluctuations. Soil Sci. Am. Proc. 36:644-649.

Bostwick, P. 1992. Potential resource losses associated with nationwide regulatory wetland classification. Pp. 19-22 in Proceedings of a National Workshop: State Perspectives on Wetland Classification (Categorization) for Regulating Purposes, J. Kusler, ed. Berne, NY: Association of State Wetland Managers.

Boulé, M. 1994. An early history of wetland ecology. Pp. 57-74 in Global Wetlands-Old World and New, W. J. Mitsch, ed. Elsevier, Amsterdam.

Bouma, J., C. A. Fox, and R. Miedema. 1990. Micromorphology of hydromorphic soils: Applications for soil genesis and land evaluation. Pp. 257-278 in Soil Micromophology, L. A. Douglas, ed. New York: Elsevier Scientific.

Bouwer, H. 1978. Goundwater Hydrology. New York: McGraw-Hill.

Bowling, S. A. 1984. The variability of the present climate of interior Alaska. Pp. 67-75 in Proceedings of The Potential Effects of Carbon Dioxide-induced Climate Changes in Alaska, Conference, J. H. McBeath, ed. Univ. Alaska-Fairbanks, School of Agriculture and Land Resources. Manage. Misc. Publ. 83-1.

Briggs, J. C., and J. F. Ficke. 1977. Quality of the Rivers of the United States, 1975 Water Year—based on the National Stream Quality Accounting Network (NASQAN). Open-File Report 78-200. Reston, VA: U.S. Geological Survey.

Brinkman, R. 1970. Ferrolysis, a hydromorphic soil forming process. Geoderma 3:199-206.

Brinson, M. M. 1988. Strategies for assessing the cumulative effects of wetland alteration on water quality. Environ. Mgmt. 12:655-662.

Brinson, M. M. 1993a. A hydrogeomorphic classification for wetlands. Wetlands Research Program Technical Report WRP-DE-4. U.S. Army Corps of Engineers, Waterway Experiment Station. Vicksburg, MS: Bridgham and Richardson.

Brinson, M. M. 1993b. Changes in the functioning of wetlands along environmental gradients. Wetlands 13:65-74.

Brinson, M. M., B. L. Swift, R. C. Plantico, and J. S. Barclay. 1981. Riparian ecosystems: Their ecology and status. FWS/OBS-81/17. Washington, DC: U.S. Fish and Wildlife Service, Office of Biological Services.

Brown, R. J. E. 1963. Influence of vegetation on permafrost. Pp. 20-25 in Proceedings Int. Conference on Permafrost, Lafayette, Ind., 1963. Natl. Acad. Sci.-Natl. Res. Counc. Publ. No. 1287. Washington, D.C.

Brown, J., K. R. Everett, P. J. Webber, S. F. MacLean, Jr., and D. F. Murray. 1980. The coastal tundra at Barrow. Pp. 1-29 in An Arctic Ecosystem: The coastal tundra at Barrow, Alaska, J. Brown, P. C. Miller, L. L. Tieszen, and F. L. Bunnell, eds. US/IBP synthesis series: 12. Stroudsburg, PA: Dowden, Hutchinson & Ross.

Brunt, J. W., and W. Conley 1990. Behavior of a multivariate algorithm for ecological edge detection. Ecol. Mod. 49:179-203.

Bunnell, F. L., O. K. Miller, P. W. Flanagan, and R. E. Benoit. 1980. The microflora: composition, biomass, and environmental relations. Pp. 255-290 in An Arctic Ecosystem: The coastal tundra at Barrow, Alaska, J. Brown, P. C. Miller, L. L. Tieszen, and F. L. Bunnell, eds. US/IBP synthesis series: 12. Stroudsburg, PA: Dowden, Hutchinson & Ross.

Buol, S. W., F. D. Hole, and R. J. McCracken. 1980. Soil Genesis and Classification. Ames: Iowa State University Press.

Callaway, R. M., S. Jones, W. R. Ferren, Jr., and A. Parikh. 1990. Ecology of a mediterranean-climate estuarine wetland at Carpinteria, California: plant distributions and soil salinity in the upper marsh. Can. J. Bot. 68:1139-1146.

Carter, C. 1977. Drainage parameters for sugarcane in Louisiana. Pp. 135-143 in Proceedings of Third National Drainage Symposium, ASAE, St. Joseph, MI.

Carter, L. D., J. A. Heginbottom, and M. Woo. 1987. Arctic Lowlands. Pp. 583-628 in Geomorphic Systems of North America, W. L. Graf, ed. Geol. Soc. Am., Centennial Spec. Vol. 2, Boulder, CO.

Carter, V., M. K. Garrett, and P. T. Gammon. 1988. Wetland boundary determination in the Great Dismal Swamp using weighted averages. Water Resources Bulletin 297-306.

Carter, V., P. T. Gammon, and M. K. Garrett. 1994. Ecotone dynamics and boundary determination in the Great Dismal Swamp. Ecological Applications 4:189-203.

Chapin, D. M., L. C. Bliss, and L. J. Bledsoe. 1991. Environmental regulation of nitrogen fixation in a high arctic lowland ecosystem. Can. J. Bot. 69:2744-2755.

Chapin, F. S. 1986. Controls over growth and nutrient use by taiga forest trees. Pp. 96-111 in Forest Ecosystems in the Alaskan Taiga, K. Van Cleve, F. S. Chapin, III, P. W. Flanagan, L. A. Viereck, and C. T. Dyrness, eds. New York: Springer-Verlag.

Chapin, F. S., L. L. Tieszen, M. C. Lewis, P. C. Miller, and B. H. McCown. 1980. Control of tundra plant allocation patterns and growth. Pp. 140-185 in An Arctic Ecosystem: The coastal tundra at Barrow, Alaska, J. Brown, P. C. Miller, L. L. Tieszen, and F. L. Bunnell, eds. US/IBP synthesis series: 12. Stroudsburg, PA: Dowden, Hutchinson & Ross.

Chapin, F. S., III, and G. R. Shaver. 1985. Arctic. Pp. 16-40 in Physiological ecology of North American plant communities. B. F. Chabot and H. A. Mooned, eds. New York: Chapman and Hall.

Christensen, N. L., R. B. Wilbur, and J. S. McLean. 1988. Soil-vegetation correlations in the pocosins of Croatan National Forest, North Carolina. Fish and Wildlife Service, U.S. Department of the Interior, Washington, DC. Biol. Rep. 88(28).

Clark, E. H. II. 1993. Three little words: Understanding and implementing a "no-net-loss" goal. Prepared for the First National Wildlife Habitat Workshop, Winnipeg, Manitoba.

Clark, J. R., and J. Benforado, eds. 1981. Wetlands of bottomland hardwood forests, Proceedings of a workshop on bottomland hardwood forest wetlands of the southeastern United States. New York: Elsevier Scientific.

Clark, S. E., H. J. Coutts, and C. Christianson. 1970. Biological waste treatment in the Far North. Fed. Water Quality Adm. Alaska Water Lab, Fairbanks.

Clean Water Act, 33 U.S.C. §§1251-1387; 33 U.S.C. § 1319.

Clements, F. E. 1920. Plant indicators. Publ. 290. Washington, DC: Carnegie Inst.

Clymo, R. S. 1983. Peat, in Mires: Swamp, Bog, Fen, and Moor, Ecosystems of the World 4A, A. J. P. Gore, ed., Elsevier, Amsterdam, pp. 159-224.

Cohen, R. M., and J. Miller, III. 1983. Use of analytical models for evaluating corrective actions at hazardous waste sites. Pp. 85-97 in Proceedings of the Third National Symposium on Aquifer Restoration and Ground-water Monitoring, D. M. Nielson, ed. Worthington, OH: National Ground Water Association.

Conservation Foundation, The. 1988. Protecting America's Wetlands: An Action Agenda. The Final Report of the National Wetlands Policy Forum. Washington, DC: The Conservation Foundation.

Cooper, J. R., and J. W. Gilliam. 1987. Phosphorus redistribution from cultivated field into riparian areas. Soil Sci. Soc. Am. J. 51:1600-1604.

Cooper, J. R., J. W. Gilliam, and T. C. Jacobs. 1986. Riparian areas as a control of nonpoint pollutants. Pp. 166-192 in Watershed Research Perspectives, D. L. Correll, ed. Washington, DC: Smithsonian Institution.

Cooper, J. R., J. W. Gilliam, R. B. Daniels, and W. P. Robarge. 1987. Riparian areas as filters for agricultural sediment. Soil Sci. Soc. Am. J. 51:416-420.

Corps of Engineers Wetlands Delineation Manual. 1987. United States Army Corps of Engineers and U.S. Department of Defense. U.S. Tech. Rep. Y-87-1.

Corps Regulatory Guidance Letter 90-06, Expiration dates for wetlands jurisdictional delineations, reprinted in 57 Fed. Reg. 6591 (1992).

Costanza, R., S. C. Farber, and J. Maxwell. 1989. Valuation and Management of Wetland Ecosystems. Ecol. Econ. 1:335-361.

Costello, D. F. 1936. Tussock meadows in southeastern Wisconsin. Botanical Gazette 97:610-648.

Coventry, R. J., and J. Williams. 1984. Quantitative relationships between morphology and current soil hydrology in some Alfisols in semiarid tropical Australia. Geoderma 33:191-218.

Cowardin, L. M., and V. I. Myers. 1974. Remote sensing for identification and classification of wetland vegetation. J. Wildl. Mgmt. 38:308-314.

Cowardin, L. M. and V. Carter. 1975. Tentative classification for wetlands of the United States. Unpublished mimeographed report. U.S. Fish and Wildlife Service, Office of Biological Services.

Cowardin, L. M., V. Carter, F. C. Golet, and E. T. LaRoe. 1976. Interim classification of wetlands and aquatic habitats of the United States. U.S. Fish and Wildlife Service.

Cowardin, L. M., V. Carter, F. C. Golet, and E. T. LaRoe. 1979. Classification of wetlands and deepwater habitats of the United States. FWS/OBS-79/31. Washington, DC: U.S. Fish and Wildlife Service.

Cox, C. B., and P. D. Moore. 1993. Biogeography: An ecological and evolutionary approach. 5th edition. London: Blackwell Scientific.

Crawford, R. M. M. 1983. Root survival in flooded soils. Pp. 257-283 in Ecosystems of the World 4A, A. J. P. Gore. ed. New York: Elsevier Scientific.

Crawford, R. M. M. ed. 1987. Plant Life in Aquatic and Amphibious Habitats. British Ecological Society Special Publication No.5. Oxford: Blackwell Scientific.

Crawford, R. M. M. 1989. Studies in Plant Survival. Oxford: Blackwell Scientific.

Crawford, N. H., and R. K. Linsley. 1966. Digital simulation in hydrology: Stanford Watershed Model IV, Tech, Rept. 39, Stanford University, CA.

Crum, H. 1988. A Focus on Peatlands and Peat Mosses. Ann Arbor: University of Michigan.

Curtis, J. T. 1959. The Vegetation of Wisconsin: An Ordination of Plant Communities. Madison: University of Wisconsin Press.

Dahl, T. E. 1990. Wetlands losses in the United States 1780s to 1980s. Washington, DC: U.S. Department of the Interior, Fish and Wildlife Service.

Dahl, T. E., and C. E. Johnson. 1991. Wetland status and trends in the conterminous United States. Mid-1970s to mid-1980s. Washington, DC: U.S. Department of the Interior, Fish and Wildlife Service.

Damman, A. W. H. 1979. Geographic patterns in peatland development in eastern North America. Pp. 42-57 in Classification of Peat and Peatlands, Proceedings, Symposium International Peat Society, E. Kivinen, L. Heikurainen, and P. Pakarinen. eds.

Damman, A. W. H., and T. W. French. 1987. The ecology of peat bogs of the glaciated Northeastern United States: A community profile. U.S. Fish and Wildlife Service Biological Report 85(7.16):1-100.

Daniels, R. B., and S. W. Buol. 1992. Water table dynamics and significance to soil genesis. Pp. 66-74 in Proc. 8th Inter. Soil Correl. Mtg (VIII ISCOM): Characterization, Classification, and Utilization of Wet Soils, J. M. Kimble ed. USDA, Soil Conservation Service National Soil Survey Center, Lincoln, NE.

Daniels, R. B., E. E. Gamble, and S. W. Buol. 1973. Oxygen content in the ground water of some

North Carolina Aquults and Udults. Pp. 153-166 in Field Soil Water Regime, R. Bruce ed. Soil Sci. Soc. Am. Spec. Pub. 5.

Daniels, R. B., E. E. Gamble, and L. A. Nelson. 1971. Relations between soil morphology and watertable levels on a dissected North Carolina coastal plain surface. Soil Sci. Soc. Am. Proc. 35:781-784.

Daubenmire, R. 1968. Plant communities: A textbook of plant synecology. New York: Harper & Rowe.

Davis, S. M., and J. C. Ogden, eds. 1994. Everglades: The Ecosystem and its Restoration. Delray Beach, FL: St. Lucie Press.

Davy, A. J., S. M. Noble, and R. P. Oliver. 1990. Genetic variation and adaptation to flooding in plants. Aq. Bot. 38:91-108.

Day, J. W., Jr., T. J. Butler, and W. H. Conner. 1977. Productivity and nutrient export studies in a cypress swamp and lake system in Louisiana. In Estuarine Processes, M. Wiley ed. New York: Academic Press.

de Laat, P. J. M., R. H. C. M. Atwater, and P. J. T. van Bakel. 1981. GERGAM-A model for regional water management. In Water Resources Management on a Regional Scale, Proceedings of Technical Meeting 37, Vergl. Meded. Comm. Hydrol. Onderz. TNO 27:23-53, The Hague, The Netherlands.

Dennison, M. S., and J. F. Berry. 1993. Wetlands: Guide to Science, Law, and Technology. Park Ridge, NJ: Noyes.

Dick-Peddie, W. A., J. V. Hardesty, E. Muldavin, and B. Sallach. 1987. Soil-vegetation correlations in the Gila and San Francisco Rivers in New Mexico. Fish and Wildlife Service, U.S. Department of the Interior, Washington, DC. Biol. Rep. 87(9).

Dingman, S. L. 1971. Hydrology of the Glenn Creek watershed, Tanana River Basin, central Alaska. U.S. Army Cold Reg. Res. Eng. Lab. Res. Rep. 297.

Dingman, S. L. 1975. Hydrologic effects of frozen ground: Literature review and synthesis. U.S. Army Cold. Reg. Res. Eng. Lab. Spec. Rep. 218. 55 pp.

Dingman, S. L., and F. R. Koutz. 1974. Relations among vegetation, permafrost, and potential insolation in central Alaska. Arct. Alpine Res. 6(1):37-42.

Dise, N. B. 1992. Winter fluxes of methane from Minnesota peatlands. Biogeochem. 17:71-83.

Dix, R. L., and F. E. Smeins. 1967. The prairie, meadow, and marsh vegetation of Nelson County, North Dakota. Can. J. Bot. 45:21-58.

Djokic, D. In press. Towards general purpose spatial decision support system using existing technologies. Proc. 2nd Int. Conference/Workshop on Integrating GIS and Environmental Modeling. Sept. 26-30, 1993, Breckenridge, CO.

Drew, M. C. 1988. Nutrient uptake and acclimation to soil waterlogging and oxygen shortage in non-wetland plants. In The Ecology and Management of Wetlands, D. D. Hook. ed. Kent: Mackays of Chatham.

Duever, M. J. 1990. Hydrology. Pp. 61-69 in Wetlands and Shallow Continental Water Bodies, Vol. 1, B. C. Patten, ed. The Hague, The Netherlands: Academic Publishing.

Eckenfelder, W. W., Jr., and A. J. Englande. 1970. Temperature effects on biological waste treatment processes. Pp. 180-190 in R. S. Murphy and D. Nyquist, eds. International symposium on Water Pollution Control in Cold Climates, Univ. Alaska, Fairbanks, 1970. U.S. Government Printing Office.

Egerton, J. J. G., and S. C. Wilson. 1993. Plant competition over winter in alpine shrubland and grassland, Snowy Mountains, Australia. Arct. Alpine Res. 25(2):124-129.

Ehrenfeld, J. G., and J. P. Schneider. 1993. Responses of forested wetland vegetation to perturbations of water chemistry and hydrology. Wetlands 13:122-129.

Eicher, A. L. 1988. Soil-vegetation correlations in wetlands and adjacent uplands of the San Francisco Bay Estuary, California. Fish and Wildlife Service, U.S. Department of the Interior, Washington, DC. Biol. Rep. 88(21).

Elder, J. 1985. Nitrogen and phosphorus speciation and flux in a large Florida river wetland system. Water Res. Res. 21:724-732.

Energy and Water Development Appropriation Act of 1993, Pub. L. No. 102-377, 106 Stat. 1315 (1992).

Environmental Laboratory. 1987. U.S. Army Corps of Engineers wetlands delineation manual. U.S. Army Eng. Waterway Exp. Stn. Tech. Rep. Y-87-1.

EPA (U.S. Environmental Protection Agency). 1988a. EPA Wetland Identification and Delineation Manual (two volumes). W. S. Sipple, ed. Washington DC: EPA, Office of Wetlands Protection.

EPA (U.S. Environmental Protection Agency). 1988b. Use of advance identification authorities under section 404 of the Clean Water Act: Guidance to EPA regional offices. IM-89-2, March, 1988. Washington, DC: EPA, Office of Wetlands Protection.

EPA (U.S. Environmental Protection Agency). 1992. Summary of advanced identification projects under section 230.80 of the 404(b)(1) guidelines. December 21, 1992. 79 pp. Washington, DC: Office of Wetlands, Oceans, and Watershed Protection, Wetlands Division.

EPA (U.S. Environmental Protection Agency). 1993. North American Landscape Characterization (NALC), research brief. EPA/600/S-93/0005. Las Vegas, NV: U.S. EPA, Environmental Monitoring Systems Laboratory.

EPA (U.S. Environmental Protection Agency) and USACE (U.S. Army Corps of Engineers). 1993. Memorandum to the field: Appropriate level of analysis required for evaluating compliance with the section 404(b)(1) guidelines alternatives requirements. Washington, DC.

Erickson, N. E., and D. M. Leslie, Jr. 1987. Soil-vegetation correlations in the sandhills and rainwater basin wetlands of Nebraska. Fish and Wildlife Service, U.S. Department of the Interior, Washington, DC. Biol. Rep. 87(11).

Erickson, N. E., and D. M. Leslie, Jr. 1988. Soil-vegetation correlations in coastal Mississippi wetlands. U.S. Fish and Wildlife Service. Biol. Rep. 89(3).

Ernst, L. F. 1956. Calculation of steady groundwater in vertical cross-section. Netherlands J. of Agric. Sci. 4:125-131.

Ernst, W. H. O. 1990. Ecophysiology of plants in waterlogged and flooded environments. Aquat. Bot. 38:73-90.

Errington, P. L. 1963. Muskrat Populations. Ames: Iowa State University Press.

Euliss, N. H., D. M. Mushet, and D. H. Johnson. 1993. Use of macroinvertebrates to identify and delineate temporary and seasonal wetlands in the prairie pothole region. Wetland Symposium, Prairie Ecosystems: Wetland Ecology, Management and Restoration. Jamestown, ND: Northern Prairie Wildlife Research Center.

Evans, C. V., and D. P. Franzmeier. 1986. Saturation, aeration and color patterns in a toposequence of soils in north-central Indiana. Soil Sci. Soc. Am. J. 50:975-980.

Evans, R. O., R. W. Skaggs, and R. E. Sneed. 1990. Normalized crop susceptibility factors for corn and soybean to excess water stress. Trans. ASAE 33(6):1153-1161.

Evans, R. O., R. W. Skaggs, and R. E. Sneed. 1991. Stress day index models to predict corn and soybean relative yield under high water table conditions. Trans. ASAE 34(5):1997-2005.

Evans, R. O., and R. W. Skaggs. Stress day index models to predict corn and soybean yield response to water table management. Transactions, Workshop on Drainage Simulation Models, 15th Congress ICID, The Hague:219-234.

Ewel, K. C. 1990. Swamps. Pp. 281-323 in Ecosystems of Florida, R. L. Meyers and J. J. Ewel, eds. Orlando: University of Central Florida.

Ewel, K. C., and W. J. Mitsch. 1978. The effects of fire on species composition in cypress dome ecosystems. Florida Sci. 41:25-31.

Farber, S., and R. Costanza. 1987. The economic value of wetland systems. J. Environ. Mgmt. 24:41-51.

Farooqi, M. A. R., and C. J. deMooy. 1983. Effect of soil saturation on redox potential and microbial activity. Comm. Soil Sci. Plant Anal. 14:185-197.

Faulkner, S. P., and C. J. Richardson. 1989. Physical and chemical characteristics of freshwater wetland soil. Pp. 41-72 in Constructed Wetlands for Wastewater Treatment, D. A. Hammer, ed. Chelsea, MI: Lewis Publishers.

Faulkner, S. P., and W. H. Patrick, Jr. 1992. Redox processes and diagnostic wetland soil indicators in bottomland hardwood forests. Soil Sci. Soc. Am. J. 56:856-865.

FGDC (Federal Geographic Data Committee). 1992. Application of satellite data for mapping and monitoring wetlands. Technical Report 1, Wetlands Subcommittee, Federal Geographic Data Committee, Washington, DC.

Feddes, R. A., P. J. Kowalik, and H. Zaraday. 1978. Simulation of water use and crop yield. PUDOC, Center for Agricultural Publishing and Documentation, Wageningen, The Netherlands, 189 pp.

Federal Interagency Committee for Wetlands Delineation. 1989. Federal Manual for Identifying and Delineating Jurisdictional Wetlands. U.S. Army Corps of Engineers, U.S. Environmental Protection Agency, U.S. Fish and Wildlife Service, and U.S.D.A. Soil Conservation Service, Washington, DC. Cooperative technical publication. 76 pp. plus appendixes.

Ferren, W. R., P. L. Fiedler, and R. A. Leidy. 1994. Wetlands of the Central and Southern California coast and coastal watersheds: A methodology for their classification and description, draft report. U.S. Environmental Protection Agency, Region IX.

Finger, T. R., and E. M. Stewart. 1987. Response of fishes to flooding regime in lowland hardwood wetlands. P. 86-92 in W. J. Matthews and D.C. Heins, eds.

Fink, R. J. 1994. The National Wildlife Refuges: Theory, practice, and prospect. Harvard Environ. Law Rev. 18:1.

Fischer, D. H. 1989. Albion's Seed. New York: Oxford University Press.

Flanagan, P. W., and F. L. Bunnell. 1980. Microflora activities and decomposition. Pp. 291-334 in An Arctic Ecosystem: The coastal tundra at Barrow, Alaska, J. Brown, P. C. Miller, L. L. Tieszen, and F. L. Bunnell, eds. US/IBP synthesis series: 12. Stroudsburg, PA: Dowden, Hutchinson & Ross.

Flessa, H., and W. R. Fischer. 1992. Plant-induced changes in the redox potentials of rice rhizospheres. Plant and Soil 143:55-60.

Fletcher, S. W. 1983. Evaluation of methods for sampling vegetation and delineating wetlands transition zones in southern Louisiana, January 1979-May 1981. Technical Report Y-83-1. Vicksburg, MS: U.S. Army Corps of Engineers, Waterways Experiment Station.

Foote, M. J. 1983. Classification, description, and dynamics of plant communities after fire in the taiga of interior Alaska. U.S. Forest Service Northwest Research Station. Res. Pap. PNW-307.

Fox, J. F., and K. Van Cleve. 1983. Relationship between cellulose decomposition, Jenny's k, forest-floor nitrogen, and soil temperature in Alaskan taiga forests. Can. J. For. Res., 13(5):789-794.

Frayer, W. E., T. J. Monahan, D. C. Bowden, and F. A. Graybill, 1983. Status and Trends of Wetlands and Deepwater Habitat in the Conterminous United States, 1950s to 1970s. Department of Forest and Wood Science, Colorado State University, Fort Collins, CO.

Fredrickson, L. H., and F. A. Reid. 1990. Impacts of hydrologic alteration on management of freshwater wetlands. Pp. 71-90 in Management of Dynamic Ecosystems, J. M. Sweeney, ed. North Central Section, The Wildlife Society, West Lafayette, Indiana.

Freeze, R. A., and J. A. Cherry. 1979. Groundwater. Englewood Cliffs, N.J.: Prentice-Hall.

Friedman, J. M. 1993. Vegetation establishment and channel narrowing along a Great-Plains stream following a catastrophic flood. Ph.D. dissertation. University of Colorado, Boulder, CO.

FWS (U.S. Fish and Wildlife Service), Division of Ecological Services. 1980. Habitat as a Basis for Environmental Assessment. ESM 102, Release Number 4-80. Washington, DC: U.S. Department of the Interior.

Gallant, A. L., T. R. Whittier, D. P. Larsen, J. M. Omernik, and R. M. Hughes. 1989. Regionalization as a tool for managing environmental resources. EPA Research and Development Report EPA/ 600/3-89/060. Corvallis, OR: U.S. EPA Environmental Research Laboratory.

Gambrell, R. P., and W. H. Patrick, Jr. 1978. Chemical and microbiological properties of anaerobic soils and sediments. Pp. 375-423 in Plant Life in Anaerobic Environments, D. D. Hook and R. M. M. Crawford, eds. Ann Arbor, MI: Ann Arbor Science.

Gammon, P. T., and V. Carter. 1979. Vegetation mapping with seasonal color infrared photographs. Photogrammetric Engineering and Remote Sensing 45:87-97.

Garono, R. J., and J. G. Kooser. 1994. Ordination of wetland insect populations: Evaluation of a potential mitigation monitoring tool. Pp. 509-516 in Global Wetlands: Old world and new, W. J. Mitsch, ed. Amsterdam: Elsevier.

Gates, P. W. 1968. History of Public Land Law Development. For the Public Land Law Review Commission. Washington DC: U.S. Government Printing Office.

Gauch, H. G., Jr. 1982. Multivariate analysis in community ecology. New York: Cambridge Univ. Press.

Gelhar, L. W., and Wilson, J. L. 1974. Ground-water quality modeling. Ground Water 12:399-408.

Gilliam, J. W., and R. P. Gambrell. 1978. Temperature and pH as limiting factors in loss of nitrate from saturated Atlantic Coastal Plain soils. J. Environ. Qual. 7:526-532.

Glaser, P. H., G. A. Wheeler, E. Gorham, and H. E. Wright, Jr. 1981. The patterned mires of the Red Lake Peatland, northern Minnesota: Vegetation, water chemistry, and landforms. J. Ecol. 69:575-599.

Golet, F. C., and J. S. Larson. 1974. Classification of freshwater wetlands in the glaciated Northeast. U.S. Fish and Wildlife Service Resour. Publ. 116.

Golet, F. C., A. J. K. Calhoun, W. R. DeRagon, D. J. Lowry, and A. J. Gold. 1993. Ecology of red maple swamps in the Glaciated Northeast: A community profile. Biological Report 12. Washington, DC: U.S. Fish and Wildlife Service.

Gorham, E. 1991. Northern peatlands: role in the carbon cycle and probable responses to climatic warming. Ecol. Applications 1:182-195.

Gosselink, J. G., and L. C. Lee. 1989. Cumulative impact assessment in bottomland hardwood forests. Wetlands Vol. 9: Special Issue.

Gosselink, J. G., and E. Maltby. 1990. Wetland losses and gains. Pp. 231-322 in Wetlands: A Threatened Landscape, M. Williams, ed. Oxford: Blackwell Ltd.

Gosselink, J. G., L. C. Lee, and T. A. Muir, eds. 1990. Ecological processes and cumulative impacts: Illustrated by bottomland hardwood wetland ecosystems. Chelsea, MI.: Lewis Publishers.

Greenwalt, L. A. 1978. The National Wildlife Refuge System, in Wildlife and America, H. P. Brokaw, ed. Washington, DC: U.S. Government Printing Office.

Gren, I. M. 1995. Costs and benefits of restoring wetlands: two Swedish case studies. Ecological Engineering 4 (in press).

Greig-Smith, P. 1983. Quantitative Plant Ecology. Berkeley: University of California.

Grishkan, I. B., and D. I. Berman. 1993. Microflora of acid organogenic soils in the mountainous subarctic region of north-eastern Asia. Pp. 272-276 in Joint Russian-American Seminar on Cryopedology and Global Change, D. A. Gilichinsky, ed. Pushchino, Russia, 1992. Pushchino: Russian Academy of Science.

Guertin, P. D., P. K. Barten, and K. N. Brooks. 1987. The peatland hydrologic impact model: Development and testing. Nordic Hydrology 18:79-100.

Guertin, P. D. and K. N. Brooks, 1986. Modeling streamflow response of Minnesota peatlands. Pp. 123-131 in Watershed Management in the Eighties, E. B. Jones and T. J. Ward, ed. ASCE Symposium, Denver, CO.

Gunterspergen, G. R. and F. Stearns. 1985. Ecological perspectives on wetland ecosystems. Pp. 69-

95 in Ecological considerations in wetlands treatment of municipal wastewater, P. J. Godfrey, E. R. Kaynor, S. Pelczarski, J. Benforado, eds. New York: Van Nostrand Reinhold.

Hackman, F. H. 1993. Statement of the U.S. Chamber of Commerce on Reauthorization of the Clean Water Act of 1987. Testimony presented to the Subcommittee on Water Resources, House Public Works and Transportation Committee, May 12, 1993.

Hahn, R. W. 1993. Improving Water Resource Management in the United States: Suggestions for Reauthorizing the Clean Water Act (testimony before the Subcommittee on Public Works and the Environment, U.S. House of Representatives). American Enterprise Institute, Washington, DC.

Hall, J. V., W. E. Frayer, and B. O. Wilen. 1994. Status of Alaska wetlands. U.S. Fish and Wildlife Service, Alaska Reg., Anchorage. 32 pp.

Hall, T. F., and W. T. Penfound. 1939. A phytosociological study of a Nyssa biflora consocies in southeastern Louisiana. Am. Midland Nat. 22:369-375.

Hansen, A. J., F. di Castri, and R. J. Naiman. 1988. Ecotones: What and why? Bio. Intl. Spec. Iss. 17:9-45.

Hardy, E. E., and C. A. Johnston. 1975. New York State Wetlands Inventory: Technical report. Ithaca, NY: Cornell University.

Harris, L. D. 1988. The nature of cumulative impacts on biotic diversity of wetland vertebrates. Environ. Mgmt. 12:675-693.

Harris, S. W., and W. M. Marshall. 1963. Ecology of water-level manipulation on a northern marsh. Ecology 44:331-343.

Heinselman, M. L. 1970. Landscape evolution and peatland types, and the Lake Agassiz Peatlands Natural Area, Minnesota. Ecol. Mono. 40:235-261.

Henry, J. G. 1974. Psychrophiles in waste treatment. Pp. 305-331 in International symposium on wastewater treatment in cold climates, E. Davis, ed. Saskatoon, Sask., 1973. Inst. North. Stud. Environ. Can. Rep. No. EPS 3-WP-74-3.

Hess, A. D., and T. F. Hall. 1945. The relation of plants to malaria control on impounded waters with a suggested classification. J. National Malaria Soc. 4:20-46.

Hibbard, B. H. 1965. A History of the Public Land Policies. Madison: The Univerity of Wisconsin Press.

Hickman, S. 1994. Improvement of habitat quality for nesting and migrating birds at the Des Plaines River Wetlands Demonstration Project. Ecol. Eng. 3:485-494.

Hobbie, J. E. 1984. The ecology of tundra ponds of the Arctic Coastal Plain: A community profile. U.S. Fish and Wildlife Service FWS/OBS-83/25.

Hollands, G. G. 1987. Hydrogeologic classification of wetlands in glaciated regions. Pp. 26-30 in Wetland Hydrology, J. Kusler, ed. Berne, NY: Association of State Wetland Managers.

Hollands, G. G., and D. W. Magee. 1986. A method for assessing the functions of wetlands. In Proceedings of the National Wetland Assessment Symposium. Chester, VT: Association of State Wetland Managers.

Holway, J. G., and R. T. Ward. 1965. Phenology of alpine plants in northern Colorado. Ecology 46(1-2):73-83.

Howell, T. A., E. A. Hiler, O. Zolezzi, and C. J. Ravelo. 1976. Grain sorghum response to inundation at three growth stages. Trans. ASAE 19(5):876-880.

Hubbard, D. E., J. B. Millar, D. D. Malo, and K. F. Higgins. 1988. Soil-vegetation correlations in prairie potholes of Beadle and Deuel Counties, South Dakota. Fish and Wildlife Service, U.S. Department of the Interior, Washington, DC. Biol. Rep. 88(22).

Hudson, W. E., ed. 1991. Landscape Linkages and Biodiversity. Washington, DC: Island Press.

Huenneke, L. F. 1982. Wetland forests of Tompkins County, New York. Bull. Torrey Bot. Club 109(1):51-63.

Huffman, R. T. 1981. Multiple-parameter approach to the field identification and delineation of aquatic and wetland ecosystems. Technical Report EL-: Vicksburg, MS: U.S. Army Corps of Engineers, Waterways Experiment Station.

Huffman, R. T., and G. E. Tucker. 1984. Preliminary guide to the onsite identification and delineation of the wetlands of Alaska. Technical Report Y-78-9. Vicksburg, MS: U.S. Army Corps of Engineers, Waterways Experiment Station.

Huffman, R. T., G. E. Tucker, J. W. Wooten, C. V. Klimas, M. W. Freel, S. W. Forsythe, and J. S. Wilson. 1982b. Preliminary guide to the onsite identification and delineation of the wetlands of the South Atlantic United States. Technical Report Y-78-7. Vicksburg, MS: U.S. Army Corps of Engineers, Waterways Experiment Station.

Hunt, C. 1988. Down by the river. Washington, DC: Island Press.

Hurt, G. W., and W. E. Puckett. 1992. Proposed hydric soil criteria and their field identification. Pp. 148-151 in Proc. 8th Inter. Soil Correl. Mtg (VIII ISCOM): Characterization, Classification, and Utilization of Wet Soils, J. M. Kimble, ed. Lincoln, Neb.: USDA, Soil Conservation Service National Soil Survey Center.

Jacobs, T. C., and J. W. Gilliam. 1985. Riparian losses of nitrate from agricultural drainage waters. J. Environ. Qual. 14:472-478.

Jackson, M. B. 1990. Hormones and developmental change in plants subjected to submergence or soil waterlogging. Aquat. Bot. 38:49-72.

Jackson, M. B., and M. C. Drew. 1984. Effects of flooding on growth and metabolism of herbaceous plants. Pp. 47-128 in Flooding and Plant Growth, T. T. Kozlowski, ed. Orlando, FL: Academic Press.

Jefferies, R. L., A. Jensen, and K. F. Abraham. 1979. Vegetational development and the effect of geese on vegetation at La Perouse Bay, Manitoba. Can. J. Bot. 57:1439-1450.

Jeglum, J. K., A. N. Boissonneau, and V. F. Haavisto. 1974. Toward a wetland classification for Ontario. Information Report 0-X-215. Marie, Ontario: Canadian Forest Service, Sault Ste.

Jenny, H. 1941. Factors of Soil Formation. New York: McGraw-Hill.

Johnson, R. R., and J. F. McCormick. 1979. Strategies for protection and management of floodplain wetlands and other riparian ecosystems. USDA Forest Service GTR-WO-12. Washington, DC.

Johnson, W. C., R. A. Mayes, and T. L. Sharik. 1982a. Use of vegetation in delineating wetland borders in upper Missouri River Basin: North-Central United States. Technical Report Y-82-1. Vicksburg, MS: U.S. Army Corps of Engineers, Waterways Experiment Station.

Johnson, W. C., P. W. Reily, L. S. Andrews, J. F. McLellan, and J. A. Brophy. 1982b. Altered hydrology of the Missouri River and its effects on floodplain forest ecosystems. Blacksburg: Virginia Water Resources Center, Virginia Polytechnic and State University, Bulletin 139. 83 pp.

Johnston, C. A. 1982. Wetlands in the Wisconsin landscape. Wisconsin Academy Review 29:8-11.

Johnston, C. A. 1984. Mapping Wisconsin's wetlands. Wisconsin Natural Resources 8:4-6.

Johnston, C. A. 1991. Sediment and nutrient retention by freshwater wetlands: Effects of surface water quality. Critical Reviews in Environmental Control 21:491-565.

Johnston, C. A. 1994a. Ecological engineering of wetlands by beavers. Pp. 379-384 in Global Wetlands: Old and New, W. J. Mitsc,h ed. Amsterdam: Elsevier.

Johnston, C. A. 1994b. Cumulative impacts to wetlands. Wetlands 14:47-55.

Johnston, C. A., and J. P. Bonde. 1989. Quantitative analysis of ecotones using a geographic information system. Photogrammetric Engineering and Remote Sensing 55:1643-1647.

Johnston, C. A., B. Marlett, and M. Riggle. 1988a. Application of a computer-automated wetlands inventory to regulatory and management problems. Wetlands 8:43-52.

Johnston, C. A., N. E. Detenbeck, J. P. Bonde, and G.J. Niemi. 1988b. Geographic information systems for cumulative impact assessment. Photogrammetric Engineering and Remote Sensing 54:1609-1615.

Johnston, C. A., N. E. Detenbeck, and G. J. Niemi. 1990. The cumulative effect of wetlands on stream water quality and quantity: A landscape approach. Biogeochemistry 10:105-141.

Johnston, C. A., J. Pastor, and G. Pinay. 1992. Quantitative methods for studying landscape bound-aries. Pp. 107-125 in Landscape Boundaries: Consequences for Biotic Diversity and Ecological Flows, F. di Castri and A. Hansen, eds. New York: Springer-Verlag.

Jones, J. R., B. P. Borofka, and R. W. Bachmann. 1976. Factors affecting nutrient loads in some Iowa streams. Water Research 100:117-122.

Jorgenson, M. T., and T. C. Cater. 1992. Bioremediation and tundra restoration after a crude oil spill near Drill Site 2U, Kuparuk Oilfield, Alaska. 1992 Final Rep. prepared for ARCO Alaska, Inc. and Kuparuk River Unit by Alaska Biol. Res., Fairbanks, AK.

Jorgenson, M. T., T. C. Cater, and L. A. Nix. 1993. Cleanup, bioremediation, and tundra restoration after a crude-oil spill, S.E. Eileen exploratory well site, Prudhoe Bay, Alaska, 1992. Second Ann. Rep. prepared for ARCO Alaska, Inc. and Exxon Co., U.S.A. by Alaska Biol. Res., Fairbanks, AK. 45 pp.

Joshi, M. S., and N. G. Dastane. 1955. Studies in excess water tolerance of crop plants. II. Effect of different durations of flooding at different stages of growth, under different layouts on growth, yield and quality of maize. Indian J. Agron. 11(1):70-79.

Josselyn, M. N., S. P. Faulkner, and W. H. Patrick, Jr. 1990. Relationships between seasonally wet soils and occurrence of wetland plants in California. Wetlands 10:7-26.

Junk, W. J., P. B. Bayley, and R. E. Sparks. 1989. The flood pulse concept in river-floodplain systems, pp. 110-127 in D. P. Dodge, ed. Proceedings of the International Large River Symposium. Can. Spec. Publ. Ish. Aquat. Sci. 106.

Kalma, J. D., G. P. Laughlin, J. M. Caprio, and P. J. C. Hamer. 1992. The bioclimatology of frost: Its occurrence, impact and protection. Advances in bioclimatology-2. Berlin: Springer-Verlag.

Kantrud, H. A., J. B. Millar, and A. G. van der Valk. 1989a. Vegetation of wetlands of the prairie pothole region. Chapter 5 in A. van der Valk, ed. Northern Prairie Wetlands. Ames: Iowa State Univ. Press.

Kantrud, H. A., G. L. Krapu, and G. A. Swanson. 1989b. Prairie basin wetlands of the Dakotas: A community profile. U.S. Fish and Wildlife Service Bio. Rep. 85(7.28).

Keddy, P. A. 1990. Competitive hierarchies and centrifugal organization in plant communities. Pp. 265-290 in Perspective on Plant Competition, J. B. Grace and D. Tilman, eds. New York: Academic Press.

Keeley, J. E. 1979. Population differentiation along a flood frequency gradient: Physiological adaptations to flooding in Nyssa Sylvatica. Ecol. Mono. 49:89-108.

Kendall, P. 1990. Wetlands plan readied for third airport site. Chicago Tribune, March 27, 1990.

Kent, R. L. 1987. Wetlands wastewater treatment—Blue Quills School, St. Paul, Alberta. Pp. 233-240 in Proceedings of the Symposium: '87 Wetlands/Peatlands, C. D. A. Rubec and R. P. Overend, compilers. Edmonton, Alberta.

Kessler, J., N. A. de Ridder, M. G. Bos, and R. H. Messemaeckers, eds. 1973. Drainage principles and applications: Vol II. Theories of field drainage and watershed runoff. Bulletin 16. Wageningen, The Netherlands: International Institute for Land Reclamation and Improvement (ILRI).

Kimball, S. L., B. D. Bennett, and F. B. Salisbury. 1973. The growth and development of montane species at near-freezing temperatures. Ecology 54(1):168-173.

Kimball, S. L., and F. B. Salisbury. 1974. Plant development under snow. Bot. Gaz. 135(2):147-149.

King, J. L., R. C. Bruska, and M. Simovich. 1993. Crustacean communities of northern California vernal pools. Am. Zool. 33:79a.

Kirk, P. W., Jr. 1979. The Great Dismal Swamp. Charlottesville, VA: University Press of Virginia.

Kirkham, D. 1957. Theory of land drainage: The ponded water case. Pp. 139-181 in Drainage of Agricultural Lands, J. N. Luthin, ed. Madison, WI: American Society of Agronomy.

Konyha, K. D., R. W. Skaggs, and J. W. Gilliam. 1992. Effects of drainage and water management practices on hydrology. J. Irrig. Drain. Eng. 118(5):807-819.

Kozlowski, T. T. ed. 1984. Flooding and Plant Growth. Orlando, FL: Academic.

Kuenzler, E. J. 1989. Value of forested wetlands as filters for sediments and nutrients. Pp. 85-96 in Proceedings of the Symposium: Forested Wetlands of the Southern United States, D. D. Hook and R. Lea, eds. Gen. Tech. Rep. SE- 50. Southeastern Forest Experiment Station. Asheville, NC: U.S. Department of Agriculture, Forest Service.

Kummerow, J., B. A. Ellis, S. Kummerow, and F. S. Chapin, III. 1983. Spring growth of shoots and roots in shrubs of an Alaskan muskeg. Am. J. Bot. 70(10):1509-1515.

Kushlan, J. A. 1990. Freshwater marshes. Pp. 324-363 in Ecosystems of Florida, R. L. Myers and J. J. Ewel eds. Orlando, FL: University of Central Florida Press.

Kusler, J. A. 1985. Wetland Assessment: The Regulators Perspective. Pp. 2-8 in National Wetland Assessment Symposium, J. A. Kusler and P. Riexinger, eds. Chester, VT: Association of State Wetland Managers.

Kusler, J., and B. L. Bedford. 1975. Overview of state sponsored wetland programs. Pp. 142-147 in National wetland classification and inventory workshop proceedings, J. H. Sather, ed., University of Maryland, 1975. Washington DC: U.S. Fish and Wildlife Service.

Kusler, J. A., W. J. Mitsch, and J. S. Larson. 1994. Wetlands. Scientific American January:64B-70.

Lambou, V. W. 1990. Importance of bottomland hardwood forest zones to fishes and fisheries: the Atchafalaya Basin, a case history. Pp. 125-193 in J. G. Gosselink, L. C. Lee, and T. A. Muir, eds. Ecological processes and cumulative impacts: illustrated by bottomland hardwood wetland ecosystems. Chelsea, MI: Lewis Publ., Inc.

Latshaw, G. J., and R. F. Thompson. 1968. Water table study verifies soil interpretations. J. Soil Water Conserv. 23:65-67.

Lawrence, W. T., and W. C. Oechel. 1983. Effects of soil temperature on the carbon exchange of taiga seedlings. I. Root respiration. Can. J. For. Res. 13:840-849.

Lawson, D. E. 1986. Response of permafrost terraine to disturbance: A synthesis of observations from Northern Alaska, USA. Arct. Alpine Res. 18(1):1-17.

Lawson, D. E., J. Brown, K. R. Everett, A. W. Johnson, V. Komarkova, B. M. Murray, D. F. Murray, and P. J. Weber. 1978. Tundra disturbances and recovery following the 1949 exploratory drilling, Fish Creek, northern Alaska. U.S. Army Cold Reg. Res. Eng. Lab. Rep. 78-28.

Ledig, F. T., and S. Little. 1979. Pitch pine (Pinus rigida Mill.): Ecology, physiology, and genetics. Pp. 347-371 in Pine Barrens: Ecosystem and Landscape, T. T. Forman, ed. New York: Academic.

Leibowitz, S. C., B. Abbruzzese, P. R. Adamus, L. E. Hughes, and J. Irish. 1992. A synoptic approach to cumulative impact assessment: A proposed methodology. EPA/600/R-92/167.

Leopold, L. B., M. G. Wolman, and J. P. Miller. 1964. Fluvial processes in geomorphology. San Francisco: W.H. Freeman.

Lewis, W. M., Jr., F. H. Weibezahn, J. F. Saunders, III, and S. K. Hamilton. 1990. The Orinoco River as an ecological system. Interciencia 15:346-357.

Lieffers, V. J., and R. L. Rothwell. 1987. Effects of drainage on substrate temperature and phenology of some trees and shrubs in an Alberta peatland. Can. J. For. Res. 17:97-104.

Light, H. M., M. R. Darst et al. 1993. Hydrology, vegetation, and soils of four North Florida river flood plains with an evaluation of state and federal wetland determinations. U.S. Geological Survey, Water-Res. Invest. Rep. 93-4033:1-94.

Likens, G. E., F. H. Bormann, R. S. Pierce, J. S. Eaton, and N. M. Johnson. 1977. Biogeochemistry of a Forested Ecosystem. New York: Springer-Verlag.

Lillesand, T. M., and R. W. Kiefer. 1979. Remote Sensing and Image Interpretation. New York: John Wiley & Sons.

Lonard, R. I., E. T. Clarain, R. T. Huffman, J. W. Hardy, C. D. Brown, P. E. Ballard, and J. W. Watts. 1981. Analysis of methodologies used for the assessment of wetland values. Prepared by U.S. Army Corps of Engineers for the U.S. Water Resources Council, Washington DC.

Lowrance, R. R., R. L. Todd, and L. E. Asmussen. 1984a. Nutrient cycling in an agricultural watershed, I. Phreatic movement. J. Environ. Quality 13:22-27.

Lowrance, R. R., R. L. Todd, J. Fail, O. Hendrickson, R. Leonard, and L. E. Asmussen. 1984b. Riparian forests as nutrient filters in agricultural watersheds. BioScience 34:374-377.

Ludwig, J. A., and J. M. Cornelius. 1987. Locating discontinuities along ecological gradients. Ecology 68:448-450.

Lukin, C. G., and L. L. Mauger. 1983. Environmental geological atlas of the coastal zone of North Carolina: Dare, Hyde, Tyrrell, and Washington Counties. CEIP Report No. 32, North Carolina Coastal Energy Impact Program. Raleigh, NC: Department of Health, Environment and Natural Resources.

Luthin, J. N. 1978. Drainage Engineering. Huntington, NY: R.E. Krieger Publishing.

Luxmore, R. J., L. H. Stolzy, and J. Letey. 1970. Oxygen diffusion in the soil plant system. Agron. J. 62:322-332.

Luxmore, R. J., R. A. Fischer, and L. H. Stolzy. 1973. Flooding and soil temperature effects on wheat during grain filling. Agron. J. 65:351-364.

Lytle, D. J. 1993. Digital soils databases for the United States. Pp. 386-391 in Environmental Modeling with GIS, M. F. Goodchild, B. O. Parks, and L. T. Steyaert, eds. New York: Oxford University Press.

Marshall, D. 1993. Testimony of Duane Marshall, Union Camp Corporation, on behalf of the American Forest and Paper Association before the Water Resources and Environment Subcommittee, Committee on Public Works and Transportation, U.S. House of Representatives.

Martin, A. C., N. Hotchkiss, F. M. Uhler, and W. S. Bourn. 1953. Classification of wetlands of the United States. Spec. Sci. Rep.-Wild. 20. U.S. Fish and Wildlife Service.

Mausbach, M. J. 1992. History of the Development of Hydric Soil Criteria and Definition. Memo distributed to NRC committee April 20, 1994 in Fort Myers.

Mausbach, M. J., and J. L. Richardson. 1994. Biogeochemical processes in hydric soil formation. Pp. 68-127 in Current Topics in Wetland Biogeochemistry, Vol. 1. Louisiana State University: Wetland Biogeochemistry Institute.

McColligan, E. T., Jr. 1986. The New Jersey computer program for the wetland functional assessment method: An environmental management perspective. In Proceedings of the National Wetland Assessment Symposium, J. A. Kusler and P. Riexinger, eds. Chester,VT: Association of State Wetland Managers.

McKeague, J. A. 1965. Relationship of water table and Eh to properties of three clay soils in the Ottawa alley. Can. J. Soil Sci. 45:49-62.

McNamara, J. P., D. I. Siegel, P. H. Glaser, and R. M. Beck. 1992. Hydrogeologic controls on peatland development in the Malloryville Wetland, New York (USA). J. Hydrol. 140:279-296.

McWhorter, D. B., A. T. Corey, and F. M. Adam. 1973. The elimination of trapped gas from porous media by diffusion. Soil Sci. 116:18-25.

Meek, B. D., and L. H. Stolzy. 1978. Short Term Flooding. Pp. 351-373 in Plant Life in Anaerobic Environments, D. D. Hook and R. M. M. Crawford, eds. Ann Arbor, MI: Ann Arbor Science.

Meek, B. D., A. J. MacKenzie, and L. B. Grass. 1968. Effects of organic matter, flooding time, and temperature on the dissolution of iron and manganese from soil in situ. Soil Sci. Soc. Am. Proc. 32:634-638.

Megonigal, J. P., W. H. Patrick, Jr., and S. P. Faulkner. 1993. Wetland identification in seasonally flooded forest soils: Soil morphology and redox dynamics. Soil Sci. Soc. Am. J. 57:140-149.

Memorandum of Agreement. 1989. Between the Department of the Army and the Environmental Protection Agency. Concerning the determination of the geographic jurisdiction of the section 404 program and the application of the exceptions under section 404(f) of the Clean Water Act (Jan. 19, 1989).

Memorandum of Agreement. 1994. Among the Department of Agriculture, the Environmental Protection Agency, the Department of the Interior and the Department of the Army. Concerning the delineation of wetlands for purposes of section 404 of the Clean Water Act and subtitle B of the Food Security Act, Jan. 6, 1994, reprinted at, 59 Fed. Reg. 2920-2924.

Menges, E. S. and D. M. Waller. 1983. Plant strategies in relation to elevation and light in floodplain herbs. Am. Nat. 122(4):454-473.

Metzler, K. J., and A. W. H. Damman. 1985. Vegetation patterns in the Connecticut River floodplain in relation to frequency and duration of flooding. NatCan(Que) 112:535-549.

Millar, J. B. 1973. Vegetation changes in shallow marsh wetlands under improving moisture regimes. Can. J. Bot. 51:1443-1457.

Miller, G. 1989. Use of artificial cattail marshes to treat sewage in northern Ontario, Canada. Pp. 636-642 in Constructed Wetlands for Wastewater Treatment, D. A. Hammer, ed. Chelsea, MI: Lewis Publishers.

Minckley, W. L., and M. E. Douglas. 1991. Discovery and extinction of western fishes: A blink of the eye in geologic time. Pp. 7-17 in Battle Against Extinction: Native fish management in the American West, W. L. Minckley and J. E. Deacon, eds. Tucson: Univ. Arizona Press.

Mitsch, W. J. 1992. Landscape design an the role of created, restored, and natural riparian wetlands in controlling nonpoint source pollution. Ecol. Eng. 1:27-47.

Mitsch, W. J. 1994. A comparison of the nonpoint source pollution control function of natural and constructed riparian wetlands. Pp. 351-361 in Global Wetlands: Old world and new, W. J. Mitsch, ed. Amsterdam: Elsevier.

Mitsch, W. J., and J. G. Gosselink. 1986. Wetlands. New York: Van Nostrand Reinhold.

Mitsch, W. J., and J. G. Gosselink. 1993. Wetlands, Second Edition. New York: Van Nostrand Reinhold.

Mitsch, W. J., C. L. Dorge, and J. R. Wiemhoff. 1979. Ecosystem dynamics and a phosphorus budget of an alluvial cypress swamp in southern Illinois. Ecology 60:1116-1124.

Moore, J. P., D. K. Swanson, and C. L. Ping. 1993. Warm permafrost soils of interior Alaska. Pp. 104-111 in Joint Russian-American seminar on cryopedology and global change, D. A. Gilichinsky, ed. Pushchino, Russia, 1992. Pushchino: Russian Academy of Science.

Moorhead, K. K., and A. E. Cook. 1992. A comparison of hydric soils, wetlands, and land use in coastal North Carolina. Wetlands 12:99-105.

Morris, J., B. Kjerfve, and J. M. Dean. 1990. Dependence of estuarine productivity on anomalies in mean sea level. Limnol. Oceanog. 35:781-988.

Mosconi, S. L., and R. L. Hutto. 1982. The effect of grazing on the land birds of a western Montana riparian habitat: Range management impact. In Proceedings of the Wildlife-Livestock Relationships Symposium, J. M. Peek and P. D. Dalkeeds. Moscow, ID: Forest, Wildlife & Range Experiment Station, University of Idaho.

Moyle, P. B., and G. M. Sato. 1991. On the design of preserves to protect native fishes. Pp. 155-169 in Battle Against Extinction: Native fish management in the American West, W. L. Minckley and J. E. Deacon, eds. Tucson: Univ. of Arizona Press.

Moyle, P. B., and R. M. Yoshiyama. 1994. Protection of aquatic biodiversity in California. Fisheries 19:6-18.

Mueller-Dombois, D., and H. Ellenberg. 1974. Aims and Methods of Vegetation Ecology. New York: John Wiley and Sons.

Mulholland, P. J., and E. J. Kuenzler. 1979. Organic carbon export from upland and forested wetland watersheds. Limnol. Oceanog. 24:960-966.

Musick, H. B., and H. D. Grover. 1991. Image textural measures as indices of landscape pattern. Pp. 77-103 in Quantitative Methods in Landscape Ecology, M. G. Turner and R. H. Gardner eds. New York: Springer Verlag.

Nachlinger, J. L. 1988. Soil-vegetation correlations in riparian and emergent wetlands, Lyon County, Nevada. Fish and Wildlife Service, U.S. Department of the Interior, Washington, DC. Biol. Rep. 88(17).

Naiman, R. J., G. Pinay, C. A. Johnston, and J. Pastor. 1994. Beaver influences on the long term biogeochemical characteristics of boreal forest drainage networks. Ecology 75:905-921.

NRC (National Research Council). 1990. Groundwater Models, Scientific and Regulatory Applications. Washington, DC: National Academy Press.

NRC (National Research Council). 1992. Restoration of Aquatic Ecosystems: Science Technology and Public Policy. Washington, DC: National Academy Press.

NWI (National Wetlands Inventory). 1990. Photointerpretation conventions for the National Wetlands Inventory. St. Petersburg, FL: U.S. Fish and Wildlife Service.

National Wetlands Working Group. 1988. Wetlands of Canada. Ecol. Land Classification Ser., No. 24. Sustainable Dev. Branch, Environ. Canada. Montreal: Ottawa and Polyscience Publ.

Nellis, M. D., J. M. Briggs. 1989. The effect of spatial scale on Konza landscape classification using textural analysis. Landscape Ecol. 2:93-100.

NFSAM (National Food Security Act Manual). 1988. Title 180. 180-V-NFSAM, Second Ed. U.S. Department of Agriculture. Washington, DC: Soil Conservation Service.

NFSAM (National Food Security Act Manual). 1991. Amend. 6, Part 510.70, Subpart G. Soil Conservation Service August 1991.

NFSAM (National Food Security Act Manual). 1991. Amend. 7, 180-V-NFSAM. Second ed. Soil Conservation Service.

NFSAM (National Food Security Act Manual). 1994. Part 519, 180-V-NFSAM. Third ed. March 1994. Soil Conservation Service.

Niering, W. A. 1953. The past and present vegetation of High Point State Park, New Jersey. Ecol. Mono. 23:127-147.

Niering, W. A. 1985. Wetlands. New York: Alfred A. Knopf. 638 pp.

Nixon, S. W. 1982. The ecology of southern California coastal salt marshes: A community profile. FWS/OBS-81/55. Washington, DC: U.S. Fish and Wildlife Service, Office of Biological Services.

Novitzki, R. P. 1979. Hydrologic characteristics of Wisconsin's wetlands and their influence on floods, stream flow, and sediment. Pp. 377-388 in Wetland Functions and Values: The state of our understanding, P. E. Greeson, J. R. Clark, and J. E. Clark, eds. Minneapolis: American Water Resources Association.

Obenhuber, D. C., and R. Lowrance. 1991. Reduction of nitrate in aquifer microcosms by carbon additions. J. Environ. Qual. 20:255-258.

Oechel, E. C., and W. T. Lawrence. 1985. Taiga. Pp. 64-94 in Physiological Ecology of North American Plant Communities, B. F. Chabot and H. A. Mooney, eds. New York: Chapman and Hall.

Office of Technology Assessment (OTA). 1984. Wetlands: Their use and regulation. OTA-O-206. Washington, DC: U.S. Congress.

Ohmart, R. D., and B. W. Anderson. 1986. Riparian habitat. In Inventory and Monitoring of Wildlife Habitat. A. Y. Cooperrider, R. J. Boyd, and H. R. Stuart, eds. Denver: BLM.

Olson, D. P. 1964. The use of aerial photographs in studies of marsh vegetation. Maine Agricultural Experimental Station Tech. Serv. Bull. 13.

Omernik, J. M. 1987. Ecoregions of the conterminous United States. Annals Assoc. Am. Geog. 771:118-125.

Oreskes, N., K. Shrader-Frechette, and K. Belitz. 1994. Vertification, validation, and confirmation of numerical models in the Earth Sciences. Science 263:641-646.

Paratley, R. D., and T. J. Fahey. 1986. Vegetation-environment relations in a conifer swamp in central New York. Bull. Torr. Bot. Club 113:357-371.

Parsons, J. E., C. W. Coty, and R. W. Skaggs. 1991a. Development and testing of a water model (WATRCOM): Development. Trans. ASAE 34(4):120-128.

Parsons, J. E., Coty, C.W. and Skaggs, R.W. 1991b. Development and testing of a water model (WATRCOM): Field testing. Trans. ASAE 34(4):1674-1682.

Pastor, J., and C. A. Johnston. 1992. Using simulation models and geographic information systems to integrate ecosystem and landscape ecology. Pp. 324-346 in New Perspectives in Watershed Management, R. J. Naiman ed. New York: Springer-Verlag.

Penfound, W. T. 1952. Southern swamps and marshes. Bot. Rev. 18:413-436.

Pennings, S. C., and R. M. Callaway. 1992. Salt marsh plant zonation: The relative importance of competition and physical factors. Ecology 73:681-690.

Peterjohn, W. T., and D. L. Correll. 1984. Nutrient dynamics in an agricultural watershed: Observations on the role of a riparian forest. Ecology 65:1466-1475.

Peters, R. H. 1983. The Ecological Implications of Body Size. Cambridge, NY. 329 pp.

Péwé, T. L. 1975. Quaternary geology of Alaska. U.S. Geol. Surv. Prof. Pap. 835.

Péwé, T. L. 1982. Geologic hazards of the Fairbanks area, Alaska. Alaska Div. Geol. Geophys. Surv. Spec. Rep. 15.

Pick, A. R., G. E. Burns, D. W. Van Es, and R. M. Girling. 1970. Evaluation of aerated lagoons as a sewage treatment facility in the Canadian Prairie Provinces. Pp. 191-212 in Int. Symposium on Water Pollution Control in Cold Climates, R. S. Murphy and D. Nyquist, eds. Univ. Alaska, Fairbanks: U.S. Government Printing Office.

Pickering, E. W., and P. L. M. Veneman. 1984. Moisture regimes and morphological characteristics in a hydrosequence in central Massachusetts. Soil Sci. Soc. Am. J. 48:113-118.

Ping, C. L. 1987. Soil temperatures profiles of two Alaskan soils. Soil Sci. Soc. Am. J. 51(4):1010-1018.

Ping, C. L., J. P. Moore, and M. H. Clark. 1992. Wetland properties of permafrost soils in Alaska. Pp. 198-205 in Characterization, Classification, and Utilization of Wet Soils, J.M. Kimble, ed. Proc. Eighth Int. Soil Correlation Meeting (VII ISCOM) U.S. Soil Conservation Service, Natl. Soil Survey Center, Lincoln, NE.

Ponnamperuma, F. N. 1972. The chemistry of submerged soils. Adv. Agron. 24:29-96.

Preston, E., and B. L. Bedford. 1988. Evaluating cumulative effects on wetland functions: a conceptual overview and generic framework. Environ. Mgmt. 12:565-583.

Price, G. 1974. Wisconsin wetlands, 19th century (map). Water Resources Planning Section, Wis. Dept. of Nat. Resources, Madison, WI.

Ransom, M. D., and N. E. Smeck. 1986. Water table characteristics and water chemistry of seasonally wet soils of southwestern Ohio. Soil Sci. Soc. Am. J. 50:1281-1289.

Reddy, K. R., P. S. C. Rao, and R. E. Jessup. 1982. The effect of carbon mineralization on denitrification kinetics in mineral and organic soils. Soil Sci. Soc. Am. J. 46:62-68.

Reed, P. B. 1988. National List of Plant Species that Occur in Wetlands: National Summary. Biol. Report 88(24). Washington, DC: U.S. Fish and Wildlife Service.

Reed, R. T. 1986. Alternate Methodologies: The Wisconsin experience in modification of FHWA (Adamus) methodology. In Proceedings of the National Wetland Assessment Symposium. Chester, VT: Association of State Wetland Managers.

Reppert, R. T. 1981. Wetland Values, Concepts and Methods for Wetlands Evaluation. Pp. 385-393 in Selected Proceedings of the Midwest Conference on Wetland Values and Management, B. Richardson ed. Navarre, MN: Freshwater Society.

Reybold, W. U., and G. W. TeSelle. 1989. Soil geographic data bases. J. Soil Water Conserv. January-February:28-29.

Rodgers, J. H., and A. Dunn. 1992. Developing design guidelines for constructed wetlands to remove pesticides from agricultural runoff. Ecol. Eng. 1:83-95.

Roman, C. T., R. A. Zampella, and A. Z. Jaworski. 1985. Wetland boundaries in the New Jersey pinelands: Ecological relationships and delineation. Water Res. Bull. 21:1005-1012.

Salisbury, F. B. 1984. Light conditions and plant growth under snow. Pp. 39-50 in The Winter Ecology of Small Mammals, J. F. Merritt, ed. Pittsburgh: Spec. Publ. Carnegie Mus. Nat. Hist. No. 10.

Sather, J. H. ed. 1975. National Wetland Classification and Inventory Workshop Proceedings, University of Maryland. Washington, DC: U.S. Fish and Wildlife Service.

Savile, D. B. O. 1972. Arctic adaptations in plants. Can. Dep. Agric. Res. Branch Monogr. No. 6.

Schalles, J. F., and D. J. Shure. 1989. Hydrology, community structure, and productivity patterns of a dystrophic Carolina bay wetland. Ecol. Mono. 59(4):365-385.

Schell, D. M. 1983. Carbon-13 and carbon-14 abundances in Alaskan aquatic organisms: Delayed production from peat in arctic food webs. Science 219:1068-1071.

Schempf, J. H. 1992. Wetland classification, inventory, and assessment methods: An Alaskan guide to their fish and wildlife application. Habitat Division Technical Report 93-2. Juneau: Alaska Department of Fish and Game.

Sculthorpe, C. D. 1967. The Biology of Aquatic Vascular Plants. London: Edward Arnold.

Scott, M. L., W. L. Slauson, C. A. Segelquist, and G. T. Auble. 1989. Correspondence between vegetation and soils in wetlands and nearby uplands. Wetlands 9(1):41-60.

Segelquist, C. A., W. L. Slauson, M. L. Scott, and G. T. Auble. 1990. Synthesis of soil-plant correspondence data from twelve wetland studies throughout the United States. Biological Report 90(19). Washington, DC: U.S. Fish and Wildlife Service.

Seher, J. S., and P. T. Tueller. 1973. Color aerial photos for marshland. Photogrammetric Engineering 39:489-499.

Sharitz, R. R., and J. W. Gibbons. 1982. The ecology of southeastern shrub bogs (pocosins) and Carolina Bays: A community profile. U.S. Fish and Wildlife Service FWS/OBS-82/04: 1-93.

Sharratt, B. S. 1992. Growing season trends in the Alaskan climate record. Arctic 45(2):124-127.

Shaw, S. P., and C. G. Fredine. 1956. Wetlands of the United States: Their Extent, and Their Values for Waterfowl and Other Wildlife. Circular 39. Washington, DC: U.S. Fish and Wildlife Service.

Siegel, D. I. 1983. Ground water evolution of patterned mires, glacial Lake Agissiz peatlands, northern Minnesota. J. Ecol. 71:913-921.

Siegel, D. I. 1988. Evaluating cumulative effects of disturbance on the hydrologic function of bogs, fens and mires. Environ. Mgmt. 12:621-626.

Siegel, D. I., and P. H. Glaser. 1987. Groundwater flow in the bog/fen complex, Lost River Peatland, northern Minnesota, J. Ecol. 75:743-754.

Silverberg, S. M., and M. S. Dennison. 1993. Wetlands and Coastal Zone Regulation Compliance. New York: Wiley Law.

Simonson, G. H., and L. Boersma. 1972. Soil morphology and water table relations: II. Correlation between annual water table fluctuations and profile features. Soil Sci. Soc. Am. Proc. 36:649-653.

Simovich, M. 1993. Eubranchiopod community composition in California vernal pools. Am. Zool. 33:55a.

Sjors, H. 1991. Phyto-and necromass above and below ground in a fen. Holarctic Ecol. 14:208-218.

Skaggs, R. W. 1978. A water management model for shallow water table soils. Technical Report No. 134. Raleigh, NC: Water Resources Research Institute.

Skaggs, R. W. 1991. Drainage. Pp. 205-243 in Modeling Plant and Soil Systems, Agronomy Monograph No 31, ASA-CSSA-SSSA, J. Hanks and J. T. Richie, eds. Madison, WI.

Skaggs, R. W., J. W. Gilliam, and R. O. Evans. 1991. A computer simulation study of pocosin hydrology. Wetlands 11:399-416.

Skaggs, R. W., D. Amatya, R. O. Evans, and J. E. Parsons. 1994. Characterization and evaluation of proposed hydrologic criteria for Wetlands. J. Soil Water Conserv. 49(5):501-510.

Slaughter, C. W., and L. A. Viereck. 1986. Climatic characteristics of the taiga in interior Alaska. Pp. 9-21 in Forest Ecosystems in the Alaskan Taiga, K. Van Cleeve, F. S. Chapin, III, P. W. Flanagan, L. A. Viereck, and C. T. Dryners, eds. New York: Springer-Verlag.

Smith, R. L., M. L. Ceazan, and M. H. Brooks. 1994. Autotrophic, hydrogen-oxidizing, denitrifying bacteria in groundwater, potential agents for bioremediation of nitrate contamination. Appl. Environ. Microbiol. 60:1949-1955.

SCS (Soil Conservation Service). 1994. National Bulletin No. 450-4-1, TCH - Interagency Testing of the "Field Indicators of Hydric Soils of the United States." Feb. 15, 1994.

Soil Survey Staff. 1951. Soil Survey Manual. USDA Handbook 18. Washington, DC: U.S. GPO.

Soil Survey Staff. 1975. Soil Taxonomy. USDA Soil Conservation Service Agric. Handb. No. 436. Washington, D.C.: U.S. GPO.

Soil Survey Staff. 1992. Keys to Soil Taxonomy, fifth edition. SMSS Monogr. No. 19. Blacksburg, VA: Pocahontas Press.

Soil Survey Staff. 1993. Soil Survey Manual. USDA Handbook 18. Washington, DC: U.S. GPO.

Soil Survey Staff. 1994. Keys to Soil Taxonomy. 6th ed. USDA-SCS. Washington, DC: U.S. GPO.

Sommerfeld, R. A., A. R. Mosier, and R. C. Musselman. 1993. CO_2, CH_4, and N_2O flux through a Wyoming snowpack and implications for global budgets. Nature 361:140-142.

Sparrow, E. B., C. V. Davenport, and R. C. Gordon. 1978. Response of microorganisms to hot crude oil spills on a subarctic taiga soil. Arctic 31(3):324-338.

Stewart, R. E., and H. A. Kantrud. 1971. Classification of natural ponds and lakes in the glaciated prairie region. Resource Publication 92. Washington, DC: U.S. Fish and Wildlife Service.

Stewart, R. E., and H. A. Kantrud. 1972. Vegetation of prairie potholes, North Dakota, in relation to quality of water and other environmental factors. U.S. Bureau of Sport Fisheries and Wildlife, in collaboration with the U.S. Geological Survey. Washington, DC.

Strand, M. N. 1993a. Federal Wetlands Law. Environ. Law Rep. 23:10185-10215, 10354-10378.

Street, W. H. 1993. Field reconnaissance of National Wetland Inventory maps in the Carolina slate belt region of Durham County, North Carolina. M.S. thesis, Duke University, Durham, NC.

Stromberg, J. C. 1993. Riparian mesquite forests: A review of their ecology, threats, and recovery potential. J. Arizona-Nevada Acad. Sci. 27:111-124.

Stromberg, J. C., D. T. Patten, and B. D. Richter. 1991. Flood flows and dynamics of Sonoran riparian forests. Rivers 2:221-235.

Stromberg, J. C., B. D. Richter, D. T. Patten, and L. G. Wolden. 1993. Response of a Sonoran riparian forest to a 10-year return flood. Great Basin Naturalist 53(2):118-130.

Svensson, B. H., and T. Rosswall. 1984. In situ methane production from an acid peat in plant communities with different moisture regimes in a subarctic mire. Oikos 43:341-350.

SWS Bulletin. 1992. Certification of professional wetland scientists. March 9:1,18-22.

Szaro, R. C. 1990. Southwestern riparian plant communities: Site characteristics, tree species distributions, and size-class structures. For. Ecol. Mgmt. 33/34:315-334.

Tarlock, A. D. 1988. The law of water rights and resources. New York: Clark Boardman. Theriot, R. F. 1993. Flood Tolerance of Plant Species in Bottomland Forests of the Southeastern United States. Technical Report WRP-DE-6. Vicksburg, MS: U.S. Army Corps of Engineers.

Thomas, J. W., R. G. Anderson, C. Maser, E. L. Bull. 1979. Snags. Chapter 5 in Wildlife Habitats in Managed Forests of the Blue Mountains of Oregon and Washington, J.W. Thomas, tech. ed. Agr. Handbook 553. Forest Service, U.S. Department of Agriculture, Washington, D.C. 512 pp.

Thompson, C. A., E. A. Bettis, III, and R. G. Baker. 1992. Geology of Iowa fens. J. Iowa Acad. Sci. 99(2-3):53-59.

Tieszen, L. L., P. C. Miller, and W. C. Oechel. 1980. Photosynthesis. Pp. 102-139 in An Arctic Ecosystem: The coastal tundra at Barrow, Alaska, J. Brown, P. C. Miller, L. L. Tieszen, and F. L. Bunnell, eds. US/IBP synthesis series: 12. Stroudsburg, Pa.: Dowden, Hutchinson & Ross.

Tiner, R. W. 1984. Wetlands of the United States: Current Status and Recent Trends. National Wetlands Inventory, Fish and Wildlife Service, U.S. Department of the Interior, Washington, D.C. 19 p.

Tiner, R. W., Jr. 1990. Use of high-altitude aerial photography for inventorying forested wetlands in the United States. For. Ecol. Mgmt. 33/34:593-604.

Tiner, R. W. 1991a. The concept of hydrophyte for wetland identification. BioScience 41:236-247.

Tiner, R. W. 1991b. Wetland delineation 1991. Pp. 1-16 (plus tables) in Proceedings 1991 Stormwater Management/Wetlands/Floodplain Symposium, G. Aron and E. L. White, eds. University Park: Pennsylvania State Univ., Dept. Civil Eng.

Tiner, R. W. 1993. The primary indicators methods—a practical approach to wetland recognition and delineation in the United States. Wetlands 13(1): 50-64.

Tiner, R. W., Jr., and H. R. Pywell. 1983. Creating a national georeferenced wetland data base for managing wetlands in the United States. Pp. 103-115 in National Conference on Resource Management Applications: Energy and Environment, Vol. III - Issues in Forest, Habitat, and Wetland Management Using Remotely Sensed/Georeferenced Data.

Toth, J. 1963. A theoretical analysis of groundwater flow in small drainage basins. J. Geophys. Res. 68:4795-4812.

Tryon, P. R., and F. S. Chapin, III. 1983. Temperature control over root growth and root biomass in taiga forest trees. Can. J. For. Res. 13:827-833.

Turner, F. T., and W. H. Patrick, Jr. 1968. Chemical changes in waterlogged soils as a result of oxygen depletion. Trans. 9th Intern. Congress Soil Sci. 4:53-63.

U.S. Army Corps of Engineers (USACE). 1978a. Preliminary guide to wetlands of peninsular Florida. Technical Report Y-78-2. Vicksburg, MS: U.S. Army Corps of Engineers, Waterways Experiment Station.

U.S. Army Corps of Engineers (USACE). 1978b. Preliminary guide to wetlands of Puerto Rico. Technical Report Y-78-3. Vicksburg, MS: U.S. Army Corps of Engineers, Waterways Experiment Station.

U.S. Army Corps of Engineers (USACE). 1978c. Preliminary guide to wetlands of the West Coast states. Technical Report Y-78-4. Vicksburg, MS: U.S. Army Corps of Engineers, Waterways Experiment Station.

U.S. Army Corps of Engineers (USACE). 1978d. Preliminary guide to wetlands of the Gulf Coastal Plain. Technical Report Y-78-5. Vicksburg, MS: U.S. Army Corps of Engineers, Waterways Experiment Station.

U.S. Army Corps of Engineers (USACE). 1978e. Preliminary guide to wetlands of the interior United States. Technical Report Y-78-6. Vicksburg, MS: U.S. Army Corps of Engineers, Waterways Experiment Station.

U.S. Army Corps of Engineers (USACE). 1986. Regulatory Guidance Letter No. 86-10. Subject: Special Area Management Plans (SAMPs). Washington DC: Office of the Chief of Engineers.

U.S. Army Corps of Engineers (USACE) and EPA (United States Environmental Protection Agency). 1989. Memorandum of Agreement between the Environmental Protection Agency and the Department of the Army Concerning the Determination of Mitigation Under the Clean Water Act Section 404(b)(1) Guidelines.

U.S. Army Corps of Engineers (USACE) and EPA (United States Environmental Protection Agency). 1990. Section 404(b)(1) Guidelines Mitigation MOA "Questions and Answers."

U.S. Army Corps of Engineers (USACE). 1979. Wetlands Values: Concepts and Methods for Wetlands Identification.

U.S. Army Corps of Engineers (USACE). 1987. USACE Wetlands Delineation Manual. Environmental Laboratory, U.S. Army Eng. Waterway Exp. Stn. Tech. Rep. Y-87-1.

U.S. Department of Agriculture (USDA). 1982. National list of scientific plant names. Vol. I. List of plant names. Vol. II. Synonymy. SCS-TP-159. Washington, DC: Soil Conservation Service.

U.S. Department of Agriculture (USDA). 1985. Hydric Soils of the United States. Washington, DC: Soil Conservation Service.

U.S. Department of Agriculture (USDA). 1987. Hydric Soils of the United States, Second Edition. Washington, DC: Soil Conservation Service.

U.S. Department of Agriculture (USDA). 1991. Hydric Soils of the United States, Third Edition. Miscellaneous Publication Number 1491. Washington, DC: Soil Conservation Service.

Updegraff, K., J. Pastor, S. D. Bridgham, and C. A. Johnston. 1995. Environmental and substrate quality controls over carbon and nitrogen mineralization in a beaver meadow and a bog. Ecol. Appli. 5:151-163.

Van Cleve, K., and L. A. Viereck. 1983. A comparison of successional sequences following fire on permafrost-dominated and permafrost-free sites in interior Alaska. Pp. 1286-1291 in Proc. Int. Conference on Permafrost (Fourth), Fairbanks, AK, 1983. Washington DC: National Academy Press.

Van Cleve, K., L. Oliver, R. Schlentner, L. A. Viereck, and C.T. Dyrness. 1983. Productivity and nutrient cycling in taiga forest ecosystems. Can. J. For. Res. 13:747-766.

Van Cleve, K., F. S. Chapin, III, C. T. Dyrness, and L. A. Viereck. 1991. Element cycling in taiga forests: State-factor control. BioScience 41(2):78-88.

van der Valk, A. G. 1981. Succession in wetlands: A Gleasonian approach. Ecology 62(3):688-696.

van der Valk, A. G., and C. B. Davis. 1976. Changes in composition, structure, and production of plant communities along a perturbed wetland coenocline. Vegetation 32:87-96.

van der Valk, A. G., and C. B. Davis. 1978. The role of seed banks in the vegetation dynamics of prairie glacial marshes. Ecology 59:322-335.

van der Valk, A. G., and L. C. Bliss. 1971. Hydrarch succession and net primary production of oxbow lakes in central Alberta. Can. J. Bot. 49:1177-1199.

van der Valk, A. G., and R.W. Jolly. 1992. Recommendations for research to develop guidelines for the use of wetlands to control rural nonpoint source pollution. Ecological Engineering 1:115-134.

van Schilfgaarde, J. 1974. Nonsteady flow to drains. Pp. 245-270 in Drainage to Agriculture, J. van Schilfgaarde, ed. Madison: American Society of Agronomy.

Veneman, P. L. M., and R. W. Tiner. 1990. Soil-vegetation correlations in the Connecticut River floodplain of western Massachusetts. Biol. Rep. 90(6). Washington D.C.: U.S. Fish and Wildlife Service.

Veneman, P. L. M., M. J. Vepraskas, and J. Bouma. 1976. The physical significance of soil mottling in a Wisconsin toposequence. Geoderma 15:103-118.

Vennes, J. W., and O. O. Olsson. 1970. Microbiologic indicators of the efficiency of an aerated, continuous-discharge sewage lagoon in northern climates. Pp. 286-311 in Int. Symposium on Water Pollution Control in Cold Climates, R. S. Murphy and D. Nyquist, eds. Univ. Alaska, Fairbanks: U.S. Government Printing Office.

Vepraskas, M. J., and W. R. Guertal. 1992. Morphological indicators of soil wetness. Pp. 307-312 in Proc. 8th Inter. Soil Correl. Mtg (VIII ISCOM): Characterization, Classification, and Utilization of Wet Soils, J. M. Kimble, ed. Lincoln, Nebr.: USDA, Soil Conserv. Service National Soil Survey Center.

Vepraskas, M. J., and L. P. Wilding. 1983. Aquic moisture regimes in soils with and without low chroma colors. Soil Sci. Soc. Am. J. 47:280-285.

Vézina, P. E., and M. M. Grandtner. 1965. Phenological observations of spring geophytes in Quebec. Ecology 46(6):869-872.

Viereck, L. A. 1970. Forest succession and soil development adjacent to the Chena River in interior Alaska. Arct. Alpine Res. 2(1):1-26.

Walker, D. A., K. R. Everett, P. J. Webber, and J. Brown. 1980. Geobotanical atlas of the Prudhoe Bay Region, Alaska. U.S. Army Cold Reg. Res. Eng. Lab. Rep. 80-14.

Walker, M., D. Walker, and K. Everette. 1989. Wetlands and soil vegetation, Arctic Foothills, Alaska. Fish and Wildlife Service, U.S. Department of the Interior, Washington, DC. Biol. Rep. 89(7).

Want, W. L. 1989. Law of Wetland Regulation. New York: Clark Boardman.

Watts, F. C., and G. W. Hurt. 1991. Determining depths to the seasonal high water table and hydric soils in Florida. Soil Survey Hor. 32:117-121.

Weaver, J. E., and F. E. Clements. 1938. Plant Ecology. New York: McGraw-Hill.

Webber, P. J., P. C. Miller, F. S. Chapin, III, and B. H. McCown. 1980. The vegetation: pattern and succession. Pp. 186-218 in An Arctic Ecosystem: The coastal tundra at Barrow, Alaska, J. Brown, P. C. Miller, L. L. Tieszen, and F. L. Bunnell, eds. US/IBP synthesis series: 12. Stroudsburg, Pa.: Dowden, Hutchinson & Ross.

Webster, R. 1973. Automatic soil-boundary location from transect data. Mathematical Geology 5:27-37.

Webster, R., and I. F. T. Wong. 1969. A numerical procedure for testing soil boundaries interpreted from air photographs. Photogrammetria 24:59-72.

Weller, J. D. 1995. Restoration of a south Florida forested wetland. Ecological Engineering 4(in press).

Weller, M. W. 1981. Freshwater Marshes, Ecology and Wildlife Management. Minneapolis: Univ. of Minn. Press.

Weller, M. W. 1988. Issues and approaches in assessing cumulative impacts on waterbird habitat in wetlands. Environ. Mgmt. 12:695-701.

Weller, M. W., and C. E. Spatcher. 1965. Role of habitat in the distribution and abundance of marsh birds. Special Report No. 43. Ames: Iowa State University.

Wennberg, J. 1993. Statement of the Honorable Jeffrey Wennberg, Mayor of Rutland, Vermont, Vice Chair, the National League of Cities, Energy, Environment, and Natural Resources Committee before the Public Works and Transportation Committee, Subcommittee on Water Resources, U.S. House of Representatives. 11 pp.

Wentworth, T. R., and G. P. Johnson. 1986. Use of vegetation for the designation of wetlands. U.S. Fish and Wildlife Service 107.

Wentworth, T. R., G. P. Johnson, and R. L. Kologiski. 1988. Designation of wetlands by weighted averages of vegetation data: A preliminary evaluation. Water Resources Bulletin 24(2):389-396.

Whalen, S. C., and W. S. Reeburgh. 1992. Interannual variations in tundra methane emission: A 4-year time series at fixed sites. Global Biogeochem. Cycles 6(2):139-159.

Wharton, C. H., W. M. Kitchens, E. C. Pendelton, and T. W. Sipe. 1982. The ecology of bottomland hardwood swamps of the Southeast: A community profile. Fish and Wildlife Service, U.S. Department of the Interior, Washington, DC. FWS/OBS-81/37.

Whigham, D. F., and R. L. Simpson. 1978. The relationship between aboveground biomass of freshwater tidal wetland macrophytes. Aquatic Botany 5:355-364.

Whigham, D. F., C. Chitterling, and B. Palmer. 1988. Impacts of freshwater wetlands on water quality: A landscape perspective. Environ. Mgmt. 12:663-671.

Whittaker, R. H. 1967. Gradient analysis of vegetation. Biological Review 42:207-264.

Whittaker, R. H. 1975. Communities and Ecosystems, Second edition. New York: Macmillan Publishing.

Whittaker, R. H. 1978. Direct Gradient Analysis. Pp. 9-50 in Ordination of Plant Communities, R. H. Whittaker ed. The Hague, The Netherlands: W. Junk.

Wierenga, P. J., J. M. H. Hendrick, M. H. Nash, J. A. Ludwig, and L. A. Daugherty. 1987. Variation of soil and vegetation with distance along a transect in the Chihuahuan Desert. J. Arid Environments 13:53-63.

Wiken, E. 1986. Terrestrial ecozones of Canada. Ecological Land Classification Series No. 19. Ottawa: Environment Canada.

Winter, T. C. 1988. A conceptual framework for assessing cumulative impacts on hydrology of nontidal wetlands. Environ. Mgmt. 12:605-620.

Winter, T. C. 1989. Hydrologic studies of wetlands in the northern prairie. Pp. 16-54 in Northern Prairie Wetlands, A. Van der Valk, ed. Ames: Iowa State University Press.

Winter, T. C. 1992. A physiographic and climatic framework for hydrologic studies of wetlands. Pp. 127-148 in Aquatic Ecosystems in Semi-Arid Regions: Implications for Resource Management, R. D. Roberts and M. L. Bothwell, eds. N.H.R.I. Symposium Series 7. Saskatoon: Environment Canada.

Wright, J. O. 1907. Swamp and overflowed lands in the United States. U.S. Department of Agriculture, Circular 76. Washington, DC: U.S. Government Printing Office.

Zedler, J. B. 1982. The Ecology of Southern Californa Coasal Salt Marshes: A community profile. U.S. Fish and Wildlife Service, Biological Services Program, Washington, DC. FWS//OSB-81/54.

Zedler, P. H. 1987. The ecology of southern California vernal pools: A community profile. Biol. Report 85 (7.11). Washington, DC: U.S. Fish and Wildlife Service.

Zedler, J. B., C. S. Nordgy, and B. E. Kus. 1992. The ecology of Tijuana Estuary, California: A National Estuarine Research Reserve. Washington, DC: NOAA Office of Coastal Resource Management, Sanctuaries and Reserves Division.

Zimov, S. A., I. P. Semiletov, S. P. Daviodov, Yu. V. Voropaev, S. F. Prosyannikov, C. S. Wong, and Y.-H. Chan. 1993. Wintertime CO_2 emission from soils of northeastern Siberia. Arctic 46(3):197-204.

Zinn, J. A., and C. Copeland. 1982. Wetland Management, Congressional Research Service, The Library of Congress, Washington, DC.

Zolotareva, B., and T. Demkina. 1993. Soil biological activity and transformation of organic matter during winter. Pp. 321-325 in Joint Russian-American seminar on cryopedology and global change, D. A. Gilichinsky, ed. Pushchino, Russia, 1992. Pushchino: Russian Academy of Science.

APPENDIXES

APPENDIX
A

Soil Taxonomy

SOIL NOMENCLATURE 101

The U.S. system of soil taxonomy is hierarchical (Soil Survey Staff, 1975). The most general level in the hierarchy is soil "order": Alfisols, Andisols, Aridisols, Entisols, Histosols, Inceptisols, Mollisols, Oxisols, Spodosols, Ultisols, and Vertisols. Wetland soils occur in all 11 orders. Histosols are organic soils, formed almost exclusively in wetlands, whereas the other orders are mineral soils.

The second level in the taxonomic hierarchy is "suborder." Many wetland soils are in Aquic suborders, and they have an aquic moisture regime. Aquic suborders occur in all soil orders except Histosols, Oxisols, and Vertisols (wetland soils in these orders have other suborders). The names of Aquic suborders have two syllables, the first of which is "Aqu" and the second of which defines the soil order. For example, the suborder of Entisols that have an aquic moisture regime is "Aquents."

The third level in the taxonomic hierarchy is the "great group." The names of great groups are one word with three or more syllables, of which the last two denote the suborder. For example, an Aquent with very young sediments from frequent flooding is a "Fluvaquent."

The fourth level in the taxonomic hierarchy is "subgroup," used to modify the great group. For example, an "Aquic Xerofluvent" is an Entisol with very young sediments in a Mediterranean climate (Xerofluvent) that is saturated with water within 4.92 ft (1.5 m) of the surface during any period of most years. Aquic subgroups occur in all soil orders except Histosols.

253

The definition of "hydric soils" (Soil Conservation Service, 1991) distinguishes specific suborders, great groups, and subgroups so it is important to understand those terms.

SOIL MOISTURE REGIME

In soil taxonomy, "soil moisture regime" refers to the presence or absence either of ground water or of water held at a tension of less than 1500 kilopascals (kPa) (Soil Survey Staff, 1992, p. 34). Wetland soils generally have "aquic" or "peraquic" moisture regimes:

> Aquic moisture regime. The aquic moisture regime signifies a reducing regime in a soil that is virtually free of dissolved oxygen because it is saturated by ground water or by water of the capillary fringe. Some soils at times are saturated with water while dissolved oxygen is present, either because the water is moving or because the environment is unfavorable for microorganisms (e.g., if the temperature is less than 34°F [1°C]); such a regime is not considered aquic.

It is not known how long a soil must be saturated to have an aquic regime, but the duration must be at least a few days, because it is implicit in the concept that dissolved oxygen is virtually absent. Because dissolved oxygen is removed from ground water by respiration of micro-organisms, roots and soil fauna, it is also implicit in the concept that the soil temperature is above biologic zero (5°C) at some time while the soil or the horizon is saturated.

Very commonly, the level of ground water fluctuates with the seasons; it is highest in the rainy season, or in fall, winter, or spring if cold weather virtually stops evapotranspiration. There are soils, however, in which the ground water is always at or very close to the surface. A tidal marsh and a closed, landlocked depression fed by perennial streams are examples. The moisture regime in these soils is called "peraquic."

Although the terms *aquic* and *peraquic moisture regime* are not used either as criteria or as formative elements for taxa, they are used as an aid in understanding genesis.

These definitions are purely scientific, unrelated to any wetland regulation. Therefore, an "aquic soil" (Soil Survey Staff, 1994) might or might not be a "hydric soil" (SCS, 1991).

AQUIC CONDITIONS

The term *aquic conditions* was introduced in 1992 as a result of recommendations submitted to the Soil Conservation Service by the International Committee on Aquic Moisture Regime (ICOMAQ), which was established in 1982 (Soil Survey Staff, 1994). Soils with aquic conditions are those that currently experience continuous or periodic saturation and reduction. The presence of these conditions is indicated by *redoximorphic features* and can be verified, except in artificially drained soils, by measuring saturation and reduction. The following description of aquic conditions (saturation, reduction, and redoximorphic conditions) is from "Keys to Soil Taxonomy" (Soil Survey Staff, 1994, p. 25-29).

Elements of Aquic Conditions

1. **Saturation** is characterized by zero or positive pressure in the soil-water and can generally be determined by observing free water in an unlined auger hole. However, problems may arise in clayey soils with peds, where an unlined auger hole may fill with water flowing along faces of peds while the soil matrix is and remains unsaturated (bypass flow). Such free water may incorrectly suggest the presence of a water table, while the actual water table occurs at greater depth. Use of well-sealed piezometers or tensiometers is therefore recommended for measuring saturation.

The duration of saturation required for creating aquic conditions is variable, depending on the soil environment, and is not specified. Three types of saturation are defined:

a. Endosaturation - The soil is saturated with water in all layers from the upper boundary of saturation to a depth of 200 cm or more from the mineral soil surface.

b. Episaturation - The soil is saturated with water in one or more layers within 200 cm of the mineral soil surface and also has one or more unsaturated layers, with an upper boundary above 200 cm (78 in.) depth, below the saturated layer. The zone of saturation, i.e., the water table, is perched on top of a relatively impermeable layer.

c. Anthric saturation - This variant of episaturation is associated with controlled flooding (for such crops as wetland rice and cranberries), which causes reduction processes in the saturated, puddled surface soil and oxidation of reduced and mobilized iron and manganese in the unsaturated subsoil.

2. The degree of **reduction** in a soil can be characterized by the direct measurement of redox potentials. Direct measurements should take into account chemical equilibria as expressed by stability diagrams in standard soil textbooks. Reduction and oxidation processes are also a function of soil pH. Accurate measurements of the degree of reduction existing in a soil are difficult to obtain. In the context of Soil Taxonomy, however, only a degree of reduction that results in reduced Fe (iron) is considered, because it produces the visible redoximorphic features that are identified in the keys. A simple field test is available to determine if reduced iron ions are present when the soil is saturated. A freshly broken surface of a field-wet soil sample is treated with α, α'-dipyridyl in neutral, 1-normal ammonium-acetate solution. The appearance of a strong red color on the

freshly broken surface indicates the presence of reduced iron ions. Use of α, α'-dipyridyl in a 10-percent acetic-acid solution is not recommended because the acid is likely to change soil conditions, for example by dissolving $CaCO_3$.

The duration of reduction required for creating aquic conditions is not specified.

3. **Redoximorphic features** associated with wetness result from the reduction and oxidation of iron and manganese compounds in the soil after saturation with water and desaturation, respectively. The reduced iron and manganese ions are mobile and may be transported by water as it moved through the soil. Certain redox patterns occur as a function of the patterns in which the ion-carrying water moves through the soil, and of the location of aerated zones in the soil. Redox patterns are also affected by the fact that manganese is reduced more rapidly than iron, while iron oxidizes more rapidly upon aeration. Characteristic color patterns are created by these processes. The reduced iron and manganese ions may be removed from a soil if vertical or lateral fluxes of water occur, in which case there is no iron or manganese precipitation in that soil. Wherever the iron and manganese is oxidized and precipitated, it forms either soft masses or hard concretions or nodules. Movement of iron and manganese as a result of redox processes in a soil may result in redoximorphic features that are defined as follows:

a. Redox concentrations - These are zones of apparent accumulation of Fe-Mn (iron-manganese) oxides.

b. Redox depletions - These are zones of low chroma (2 or less) where either Fe-Mn oxides alone or both Fe-Mn oxides and clay have been stripped out.

c. Reduced matrix - This is a soil matrix which has a low chroma *in situ*, but undergoes a change in hue or chroma within 30 minutes after the soil material has been exposed to air.

d. In soils that have no visible redoximorphic features, a positive reaction to an α, α'-dipyridyl solution satisfies the requirement for redoximorphic features.

OTHER TERMS RELATED TO SOIL WETNESS

Natural Drainage Classes

Soils are assigned to natural drainage classes according to the frequency and duration of wet periods under conditions similar to those that existed when the soil developed (Soil Survey Staff, 1993). In the field, soil surveyors infer soil drainage by differences in soil color and in patterns of soil color. Soil slope, texture, structure, and other characteristics also are useful for evaluating soil drainage conditions. There are seven soil drainage classes, ranging from "very poorly drained" to "excessively drained." The three wettest categories, as defined in the Soil Survey Manual (Soil Survey Staff, 1993, pp. 99-100) are described below:

• *Very poorly drained.* Water is removed from the soil so slowly that free water remains at or very near the ground surface during much of the growing season. The occurrence of internal free water is very shallow and persistent or permanent.

• *Poorly drained.* Water is removed so slowly that the soil is wet at shallow depths periodically during the growing season or remains wet for long periods. The occurrence of internal free water is shallow or very shallow and common or persistent.

• *Somewhat poorly drained.* Water is removed slowly so that the soil is wet at a shallow depth for significant periods during the growing season. The occurrence of internal free water commonly is shallow to moderately deep and transitory to permanent.

Soil Inundation

Inundation is the condition of soil when an area is covered by liquid free water (Soil Survey Staff, 1993). Flooding is temporary inundation by flowing water. If the water is standing, as in a closed depression, the term "ponding" is used.

Older soil surveys used four classes of flooding frequency (Soil Survey Staff, 1951):

1. Floods frequent and irregular, so that any use of the soil for crops is too uncertain to be practicable.

2. Floods frequent but occurring regularly during certain months of the year, so that the soil may be used for crops at other times.

3. Floods may be expected, either during certain months or during any period of unusual meterological conditions, often enough to destroy crops or prevent use in a specified percentage of the years.

4. Floods rare, but probable during a very small percentage of the years.

REFERENCES

Soil Conservation Service. 1991. Hydric Soils of the United States, Third Edition. Soil Conservation Service, Miscellaneous Publication Number 1491. Washington, DC.

Soil Survey Staff. 1951. Soil Survey Manual. USDA Handbook 18. U.S. Government Printing Office, Washington, DC.

Soil Survey Staff. 1975. Soil Taxonomy. USDA Soil Conservation Service Agric. Handb. No. 436. U.S. Government Printing Office, Washington, DC.

Soil Survey Staff. 1992. Keys to Soil Taxonomy, fifth edition. SMSS Monogr. No. 19. Pocahontas Press, Blacksburg, VA.

Soil Survey Staff. 1993. Soil Survey Manual. USDA Handbook 18. U.S. Government Printing Office, Washington, DC.

Soil Survey Staff. 1994. Keys to Soil Taxonomy, 6th ed. USDA-SCS. U.S. Government Printing Office, Washington, DC.

APPENDIX

B

Case Histories

CASE HISTORY 1

Kirkham Wetlands, Talbot County, Maryland
Seasonal Hydrologic Change and Microtopography in Forested Wetlands

The Kirkham wetlands are typical of several hundred thousand acres of forested wetland in Maryland and adjoining states. These wetlands are located on flat topography and are supported hydrologically by the presence of ground water near the soil surface; the ground water is maintained by precipitation.

Figure B1.1 shows the location of the Kirkham wetlands, and the area can be used to illustrate many of the challenges for characterizing and delineating forested wetlands in Maryland and adjoining states. The U.S. Army Corps of Engineers (USACE) has obtained data on soils, vegetation, and surface hydrology, which would be typical support for delineations in this region. It also has gathered information on ground water, which typically is not available for delineations because it is expensive and time-consuming to collect and would delay the delineation process by at least a year if it were required.

The soils of the Kirkham site belong to the Elkton series (Elkton silt loam) and are classified as Typic Ochraquults. The soil profile consists of 4 to 10 in. (10.16-25.4 cm) of silt loam; the subsoil consists of about 30 in. (76.2 cm) of silty clay and silty clay loam. Below the subsoil is sand with much higher permeability. The soils have a dominant chroma of 2 or less below the A horizon. The soils show mottling caused by oxidized iron at depths where seasonal water saturation is characteristic.

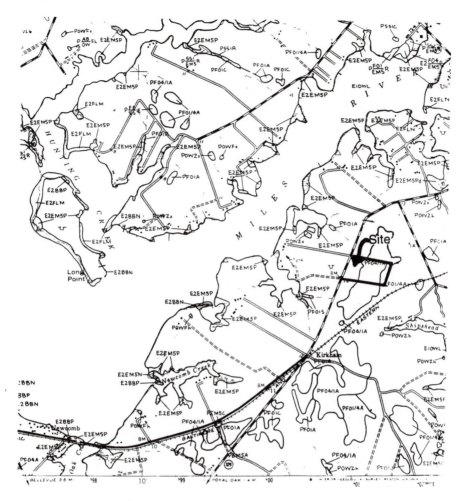

FIGURE B1.1 General location map for the Kirkham wetlands.

The dominant tree species throughout the site are loblolly pine (*Pinus taeda*) and red maple (*Acer rubrum*), as well as the shrub, and coast pepperbush (*Clethra alnifolia*) (Table B1.1). Red maple can appear in the understory, which is not rich in other species or in vines or herbaceous plants. Gaps could support other species, however. One large gap created by gypsy moth damage to trees showed an extensive growth of wool grass (*Scirpus cyperinus*), a facultative-wet (FACW+) species.

The indicator status of the plant community can change when the overstory is removed. For example, removal of trees could reduce depletion of ground

TABLE B1.1 Plant Community Composition for the Kirkham Site

Species	Common name	Status[a]	Location (station number) 1	2	3	4	5	6	7
Quercus alba	White oak	FACU-	-	-	-	-	-	-	-
Pinus taeda	Loblolly pine	FAC-	X	X	X	X	X	X	-
Acer rubrum	Red maple	FAC	X	X	X	X	X	-	X
Clethra alnifolia	Coast pepperbush	FAC+	X	X	X	X	X	X	X
Liquidambar styraciflua	Sweetgum	FAC	-	-	-	-	-	-	X
Parthenocissus quinquefolia	Virginia creeper	FACU	-	-	-	-	-	-	-
Toxicodendron radicans	Poison ivy	FAC	-	-	-	-	-	-	-
Fagus grandifolia	American beech	FACU	X	-	-	-	-	-	-
Vaccinium corymbosum	Highbush blueberry	FACW-	-	-	-	X	-	-	-
Carex intumescens	Bladder sedge	FACW+	-	-	-	X	-	-	-
Graminae	Grasses	—	-	-	-	-	X	-	X
Quercus falcata var. *pagodifolia*	Cherrybark oak	FACW	-	-	-	-	-	-	X

[a]FAC, facultative species; FACU, facultative-upland species; FACW, facultative-wet species.

water by evapotranspiration, thus converting sites from marginal or indeterminate to wetland. Soil compaction could have similar effects.

Some portions of the Kirkham site show surface hydrologic indicators of wetland status, including water marks on trees and blackened leaves. A site visit between January and May might show water standing at the surface over these portions of the site, but a visit at other times of the year would not. Because of microtopographic variation, which falls within a range of 29.25 in. (75 cm), large portions of the site show no evidence of surface hydrology. Figure B1.2, which gives surface contours, shows that the surface indicators of hydrology are distributed irregularly.

Water table data from wells show the hydrologic boundaries for wetlands at the Kirkham site. Figure B1.3 shows the records from a single well over a period of 3 years. Patterns from other wells at the site are similar, although the proximity of the water table to the surface depends on elevation at a particular location. As shown by Figure B1.3, there is a strong seasonal variation in the water table at the Kirkham site. The highest water tables are found in late winter or spring. It is clear from the well records that hydrologic classification based on well data

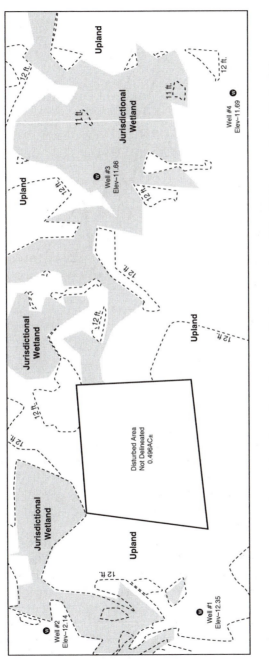

FIGURE B1.2 Microtopography and location of monitoring wells for a portion of the Kirkham wetlands (derived from a map prepared by USACE).

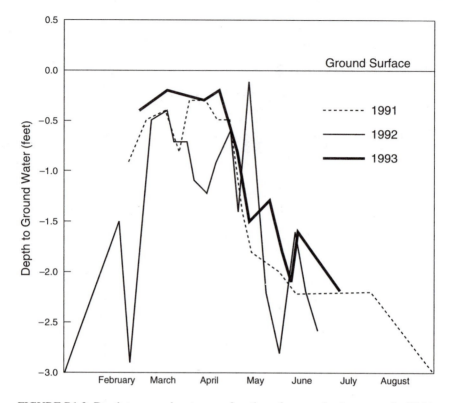

FIGURE B1.3 Depth to ground water as a function of season for 3 years at the Kirkham wetlands site.

would be erroneous if the well data did not include that portion of the year when the water table is highest. Furthermore, irregularities of timing in the rise of the water table from one year to the next suggest that a single datum taken at almost any time of the year could be in error.

USACE delineated the Kirkham site according to the guidelines in the 1987 manual (Figure B1.2). Hydric soils extended over the entire site and beyond the margin of wetland vegetation.

In this sense, the soils were important in contributing to the classification of the site as a wetland, but they were not useful in setting the boundary for the wetland according to the 1987 criteria. The boundary was drawn at the vegetative margin corresponding to 50% composition of species classified as FAC (facultative species) or wetter. This margin was then verified and refined by the use of surface indicators of hydrology, such as blackened leaves. Subsequent study of the data on ground water hydrology confirmed that the entire site would meet the hydrologic requirements for wetland classification. However, the study also showed that exclusive reliance on ground water data would have required 1 year or more of data collection because of the extreme seasonal variation in ground water levels.

Had the site been delineated by the 1989 manual rather than by the 1987 manual, delineation would have been simpler because it could have been based solely on the margins of hydric soils. This would have resulted in a slightly larger area for the delineation, given that the hydric soils extend further upslope than do the hydrophytic vegetation or the surface indicators of hydrology. Delineation according to 1991 proposed revisions probably would have resulted in exclusion of the site from classification as a wetland because of stricter requirements for classification of vegetation.

The future of the Kirkham wetlands could be beyond the influence of any delineation method. These wetlands are classified hydrologically as "isolated" because they are maintained by ground water rather than by a surface hydrologic connection to navigable waters. For this reason, the Kirkham wetlands are covered by Nationwide Permit 26, which allows conversion of wetland blocks of up to 1 acre (0.4 ha) without notification of USACE. It also allows conversion of 1-10 acre (0.4-4.0 ha) blocks with a pre-discharge notification but minimal review by USACE. Therefore, it is possible that all or part of the Kirkham wetlands could be incrementally altered under Nationwide Permit 26, regardless of the delineation boundaries.

CASE HISTORY 2

Yazoo National Wildlife Refuge
Lower Mississippi Valley
Relict Soils and Altered Hydrology

Wetlands occupied by bottomland hardwood forest account for many millions of acres in the southeastern United States (Clark and Benforado, 1981). The soils associated with these wetlands are frequently well suited for agriculture if they can be drained. Consequently, the total acreage of bottomland hardwood has declined substantially since the turn of the century (Gosselink and Maltby, 1990). This is well illustrated by Gosselink's study of the Tensas River bottomland of Louisiana (Gosselink et al., 1990) (Figure B2.1). Until the recent tightening of restrictions on drainage of wetlands for agricultural purposes (the "swampbuster" provisions of the Food Security Act of 1985), the rate of drainage and clearing often reflected fluctuations in the price of crops, principally soybeans, that could be grown on drained lands. In addition, use of lands subject to seasonal inundation has steadily become more practical with the introduction of new genetic strains that show rapid rates of maturation.

The lands of the Vicksburg District of the USACE illustrate several characteristics of extensive wetland supporting bottomland hardwood forest. The

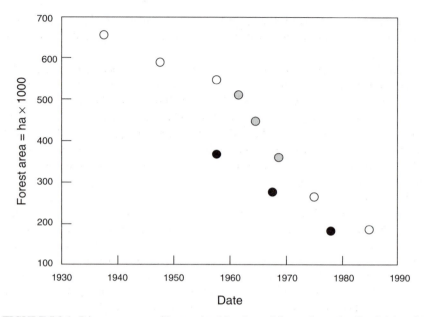

FIGURE B2.1 Disappearance of bottomland hardwood forest from the floodplain of the Tensas River, Louisiana. Different symbols indicate estimates from different sources. Source: Gosselink et al., 1990. Landscape conservation in a forest wetland watershed. BioScience 40:588-600. ©1990 American Institute of Biological Sciences.

Vicksburg District encompasses 45 million acres (18 million ha), including 18 million acres (7.2 million ha) of floodplain ("delta"). About 70% of the flood-plain is cleared. When identification and delineation of wetlands became an issue in the 1970s, the district identified 1.5 million acres (0.6 million ha) of wetland by the use of regional criteria for wetland delineation. In 1987, the first standard delineation manual was made available, but the district continued to use region-ally derived procedures that had been in use since the 1970s. When the 1989 manual was introduced, a quick assessment showed that literal interpretation of the 1989 criteria might increase the amount of jurisdictional wetland from 1.5 million acres (0.6 million ha) to 12 million acres (4.8 million). It became clear that this amount would be reduced substantially by exclusion of "prior con-verted" agricultural lands, but even so would result in a substantial increase in the area of jurisdictional wetland. Under current practice, the USACE Vicksburg District uses the 1987 manual for identification and delineation of wetlands. This approach defines approximately 4.5 million acres (1.8 million ha) of wetland in the district.

Studies of the Steele Bayou wetlands of the Yazoo National Wildlife Refuge have provided information on some of the issues that arise in the delineation of wetlands supporting bottomland hardwood forest. Steele Bayou is located just east of the Mississippi River north of Vicksburg (Figure B2.2). As is characteristic of the bottomland hardwood wetlands of this region, the Steele Bayou wetlands show a hydrologic regime that reflects seasonal flooding along the lower Mississippi River. Because the Steele Bayou is near the junction of the Yazoo River with the Mississippi, drainage is impeded as the Mississippi River reaches its seasonal peak discharge. Annual water level fluctuations in Steele Bayou can exceed 9 ft (3 m).

Bottomland hardwood forests and their adjacent aquatic and upland habitats of the southeastern United States are conventionally divided into six zones as defined by hydrologic characteristics (Larsen et al., 1981) (Figure B2.3). The zones can be loosely designated as aquatic (I), swamp (II), lower hardwood wetland (III), medium hardwood wetland (IV), upper hardwood wetland (V), and upland (VI). Delineation by the 1987 manual typically places the wetland boundary between zones IV and V.

Figure B2.4 shows the zonation of the Steele Bayou wetlands along a transect that has been used extensively for analysis of soils and hydrologic characteristics. The zones reflect elevation contours that extend from the water surface of the bayou up to a ridge that was formed as a natural levee when the Mississippi and its tributaries in this region probably followed somewhat different courses than they do today.

The soils of the Steele Bayou wetland range from Dundee series (Aeric Ochraquolt) on the ridge to Sharkey series (Vertic Haplaquept) at points nearer to the bayou. The Dundee soils are of medium to fine texture, generally poorly drained, and dark brown to gray-brown, often with mottling. Sharkey soils are poorly drained, with high clay content, and are typically dark gray to dark gray-brown. In a laboratory setting, all of the soils between the bayou and the ridge might be classified as hydric on the basis of chroma and under indicators. From the field setting, it is clear that the Dundee soil of the ridge is not inundated under the current hydrologic regime. The Steele Bayou site thus indicates the problem of relict soils: Hydric soils that formed under wetland conditions continue to show hydric characteristics after the hydrologic conditions change. Under these circumstances, the establishment of wetland boundaries by the use of soil can be unreliable unless soil phases that clearly reflect current conditions can be identified.

Detailed studies of oxygen content, redox potential, and water depth below the soil surface illustrate some of the critical differences for development of wetlands at the Steele Bayou site (Figure B2.5) (Faulkner et al., 1991). At location 1, along the ridge, the soil contains substantial oxygen and shows high redox potentials, consistent with the growth of plants that have poor tolerance for anaerobic conditions or for chemical conditions associated with low redox potentials. The water table remains 3 ft (0.9 m) or more below the surface at this site, regardless of season. In contrast, location 3 shows strong seasonal depletion of

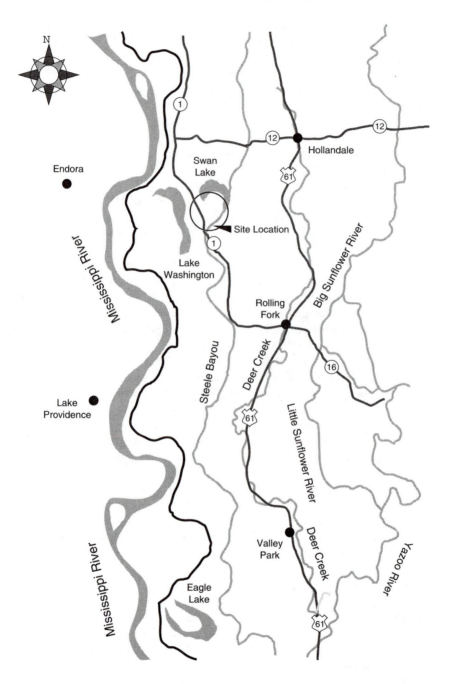

FIGURE B2.2 General location of the Steele Bayou site.

Zone	Aquatic ecosystem		Bottomland hardwood ecosystem				Bottomland upland transition
				Floodplain			
	I	**II**	**III**	**IV**	**V**	**VI**	
Name	Open water	Swamp	Lower hardwood wetlands	Medium hardwood wetlands	Higher hardwood wetlands	Transition to uplands	
Water modifier	Continuously flooded	Intermittently exposed	Semipermanently flooded	Seasonally flooded	Temporarily flooded	Intermittently flooded	
Flooding frequency, % of years	100	~100	51–100	51–100	11–50	1–10	
Flooding duration, % of growing season	100	~100	> 25	12.5–25	2–12.5	< 2	

FIGURE B2.3 Illustration of zonation for bottomland hardwood forests of the southeastern United States (from Theriot [1993] after Clark and Benforado [1981]).

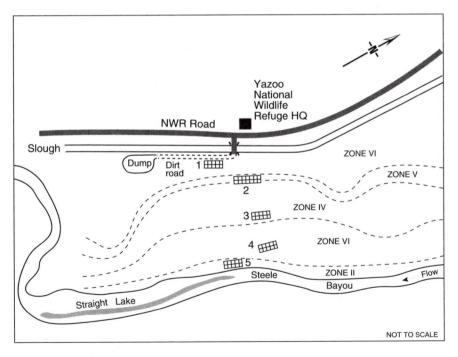

FIGURE B2.4 Map of the Steele Bayou site showing zonation.

Location 1 (Zone VI)

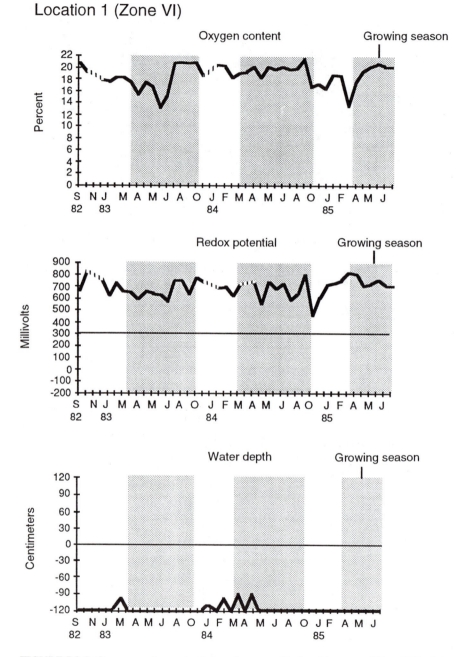

FIGURE B2.5 Oxygen, redox potential, and water table level in zones VI and IV of the Steele Bayou wetlands. Source: from Faulkner et al., 1991.

Location 3 (Zone IV)

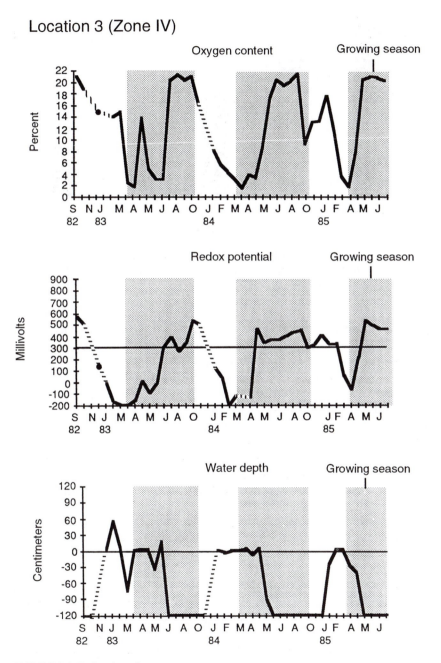

FIGURE B2.5 Continued

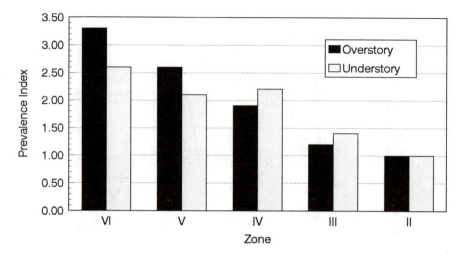

FIGURE B2.6 Change in abundance of wetland vegetation across zones in the Steele Bayou wetlands (data from USACE, Vicksburg District). A prevalence index below 3.0 indicates wetland vegetation.

oxygen and suppression of redox potentials. These seasonal events correspond to a rise in the water table to points reaching or exceeding the soil surface.

Woody vegetation in the Steele Bayou wetlands ranges from sassafras (*Sassafras albidum*), sweet gum (*Liquidambar styraciflua*), and oak (*Quercus nigra*) on the ridge to willow (*Salix nigra*) and cypress (*Taxodium distichum*) at the lowest elevations. The prevalence of other moisture-tolerant species increases steadily from the lowest to the highest elevations.

Theriot (1993) analyzed the association between vascular plant species and hydrologic regimes at 17 sites, including the Steele Bayou site, in the southeastern United States. Multivariate statistical analysis showed a strong association between community composition and hydrologic regime. Trees provided the best discrimination of sites, and herbaceous vegetation was least effective. The accuracy of classification based on tree species composition alone was 82%. This principle is illustrated for the Steele Bayou site by the graded change in community composition across hydrologic zones (Figure B2.6), which reflects the hydrologic gradient.

Hydrologic conditions at the Steele Bayou site have been affected by a drainage project that was completed in 1988. This USACE-sponsored project involved extensive wetlands mitigation in compliance with National Environmental Protection Act (NEPA) requirements. The project resulted in reduction of the level of the mean annual flood at Steele Bayou by about 23 in. (60 cm). Hydrologic change resulting from the project could be the basis for a change in the location of the wetland boundary and in a shift in the zonation of the Steele

Bayou area. Soils throughout the site will remain hydric, as they are now, even when hydrologic conditions change. Vegetation will probably change, but only gradually. Mature trees reflect hydrologic conditions over the past several decades and will not be affected quickly by a change in hydrologic conditions. However, recruitment of new individuals through the establishment of seedlings will be affected. In fact the first signs of this are already evident in the appearance of seedlings and young saplings of upland taxa at elevations lower than they have been found in the past. The Steele Bayou site thus provides a good example of the low sensitivity of woody vegetation to hydrologic change over the short term, even though community composition will change to reflect hydrology over the long term.

Until the hydrology changed, delineation of the wetland boundary at the Steele Bayou site was relatively straightforward on the basis of plant community composition and surface indicators of hydrology. At present, delineation would be more difficult, given that surface indicators of hydrology are beginning to disappear from the sites that still support a wetland plant community.

References

Clark, J.R. and J. Benforado (eds.). 1981. Wetlands of Bottomland Hardwood Forests. Elsevier, NY.

Faulkner, S.P., W.H. Patrick, Jr., W.B. Parker, R.P. Gambrell, and B.J. Good. 1991. Characterization of soil processes in bottomland hardwood wetland-nonwetland transition zones in the lower Mississippi River Valley. Contract Rep. WRP-91-1. Vicksburg, MS: U.S. Army Corps of Engineers, Waterways Experiment Station.

Gosselink, J.G., G.P. Shaffer, L.C. Lee, D.M. Burdick, D.L. Childers, N.C. Leibowitz, S.C. Hamilton, R. Boumans, D. Cushman, and S. Fields . 1990. Landscape conservation in a forest wetland watershed. BioScience 40:588-600.

Gosselink, J.G. and E. Maltby. 1990. Wetland losses and gains. Pp. 296-322 in M. Williams, ed. Wetlands: A Threatened Landscape. Blackwell, Oxford.

Larson, J.S., M.S. Beidinger, C.F. Bryan, S. Brown, R.T. Huffman, E.L. Miller, D.G. Rhodes, and B.A. Touche. 1981. Transition from wetlands to uplands in southeastern bottomland hardwood forests.

Theriot, R.F. 1993. Flood tolerance of plant species in bottomland forests of the southeastern United States. Vicksburg, MS: US Army Corps of Engineers Waterways Experiment Station Technical Report WRP-DE-6.

CASE HISTORY 3

Verde River Wetlands
Yavapai County, Arizona
Growing-Season Definitions and Western Riparian Lands

The Verde River, which joins the Salt River east of Phoenix, Arizona, drains an area of approximately 6,200 mi^2 (16,120 km^2), including 13 tributary watersheds (Figure B3.1) (Sullivan and Richardson, 1993). Over at least half of its

FIGURE B3.1 Location of the Verde River reach, containing Dead Horse Ranch State Park (Reach 2B).

length, the Verde River and the lower reaches of its tributaries support a well-developed riparian zone situated on lateral floodplain. In addition, the river channel and adjacent floodplain contain depressions that are moist at varying intervals, depending on their elevation above the river.

The riparian zone and river channel depressions of the Dead Horse Ranch State Park provide examples of several problems in delineation and identification of wetlands in the western United States. The Verde River channel in the vicinity of Dead Horse Ranch State Park contains depressions that were created by erosion at high flow. These depressions are typically a few feet to tens of feet in their longest dimension. They are most likely to be wet during the winter months, when river discharge can briefly occupy the entire channel. During the growing season, which extends from March through October in the lower reaches of the Verde River, these sites are likely to be dry. They lack extensive woody vegetation, although some support populations of the Goodding willow (*Salix gooddingii*). Herbaceous taxa include representatives of the obligate or facultative-wet categories such as bulrushes (*Scirpus americanus*), sedges (*Cyperis odoratus*), and rushes (*Juncus torreyi*). The presence of these plants, which require saturation or inundation for establishment and growth, suggests that the growing season is erroneously defined, at least with respect to wetland plants. The depressions also can lack soils, given that they are established through the movement of coarse sediment, and thus might not be easily defined by any criteria that require the presence of hydric soils. These wetlands are protected as waters of the Unites States because of their location within the normal high-water zone of the channel, but they are difficult to classify as wetlands because they lack soils and they fail to show the requisite hydrology during the formally defined growing season.

Above the river channel and separated from it by a steeply cut bank is a floodplain terrace that was established by floods of decadal or longer recurrence. This terrace contains depressions of varying size and depth that are comparable in dimensions to those found in the channel itself. The depressions show weak or negligible soil development and are inundated so seldom that they typically cannot meet the criteria for inundation or saturation, particularly during the growing season. Some of the depressions are deep enough to support wetland plants because of their proximity to ground water; others are not.

The entire riparian zone, which extends above the channel along the floodplain, presents severe problems in the identification and delineation of wetlands. This zone is not saturated annually. The underlying aquifer is relatively close to the surface (a few feet) but typically does not approach the surface closely enough to meet standard criteria for saturation at or "near" the surface. In fact, the entire system is established and maintained by floods that have recurrence intervals of many years, rather than annually, as would be the case in large portions of the southeastern bottomland hardwood forest (Zone II). Flooding redistributes the substrate, which is predominantly sand rather than hydric soil, and provides the essential conditions for establishment of key woody plants, such as cottonwood and willow (Stromberg et al., 1991). Once established, woody species can persist throughout their entire lifespan without additional flooding, because they are able to use the abundant water that is present in the phreatic zone. These woody species require inundation for establishment but, once established, can and typically do persist for very long periods of time without further inundation.

The riparian zone of the Verde River is dominated by Fremont cottonwood (*Populus fremontii*), Goodding willow (*Salix gooddingii*), salt cedar (*Tamarix chinensis*), alder (*Alnus oblongifolia*), and box elder (*Acer negundo*). Shrubs are not abundant, and herbaceous vegetation consists primarily of grasses, most of which lack wetland affinity because they grow in an environment that is seldom wet at the surface. The riparian zone lies above the normal high water mark and is therefore unprotected unless it can be classified as wetland.

The classification of western riparian zones such as those of the Verde River is problematic. Application of the 1987 USACE manual to these areas would probably show that they are not wetlands. The riparian zones of the west serve virtually all of the functions that are identified with bogs, swamps, and marshes of the wetter parts of the United States (Sullivan and Richardson, 1993). These zones are particularly important in stabilizing flood flows, which are especially destructive in arid zones such as the Verde River watershed. Vegetation stabilizes sediment, even under flood conditions. The riparian zones store and transport extensive alluvial water below the surface. Unique species associations of vegetation, vertebrates, and invertebrates are characteristic of the western riparian zones, which often are centers of biodiversity when compared with surrounding uplands. The recreational and aesthetic importance of these areas is also especially high. Surveys at the Dead Horse Ranch State Park site along the Verde River show 162 species of birds, including several listed as endangered and threatened species by the federal and state government; the avifauna includes shore birds, waterfowl, and tropical migrants. The channel and floodplain depressions of the Verde River can be classified as wetland only by liberal use of the guidelines now in use for identification of wetlands. It is also clear that the entire riparian zone performs the same functions that are performed by more easily identified wetlands in other parts of the country and that they are occupied by a distinctive flora that can be established only by inundation. The paradox is whether to include these areas by broadening the identification of wetlands, which might result in inadvertent inclusion of some eastern upland regions, to treat western riparian lands as wetlands by exception, or to regulate western riparian lands for their own sake, thus avoiding the problem of dealing with them through the wetlands classification system.

References

Stromberg, J.C., D.T. Patten, and B.D. Richter. 1991. Flood flows and dynamics of sonoran riparian forests. SEL and Associates.

Sullivan, M.E., and M.E. Richardson. 1993. Functions and values of the Verde River riparian ecosystem and an assessment of adverse impacts to these resources. USEPA Region IX, San Francisco, CA.

CASE HISTORY 4

Hydric Pine Flatwoods of Southwest Florida
Indistinct Margins and the Role of Fire

Flatwood wetlands of Florida consist of seasonally inundated lands that have sandy soils or sand substrates; a canopy that is often incomplete in coverage and consisting of slash pine; and a mixed understory of grasses, shrubs, and forbs that are tolerant of fire and inundation (Abrahamson and Harnett, 1990). In southwest Florida, this general wetland type takes the form of hydric pine flatwood, which occupies approximately 200,000 acres (80,000 ha). This wetland type has been reduced in extent by about 50% since 1970 (Birnhak and Crowder, 1974). Economic forces that have produced drainage of pine flatwood include commercial and residential development, citrus farming, and silviculture. Hydric pine flatwood is a distinctive regional wetland type that presents problems primarily associated with weak boundary definition and interaction between fire, water, and grazing.

The hydric pine flatwoods of southwestern Florida lie on a calcareous substrate derived from marine transgression and showing very little relief or slope (0.0016%). Because the terrain is flat, headwater streams are not well defined, and overland flow is the predominant means of water movement during the wet season. The hydric pine flatwoods are bordered by mesic and xeric pine flatwoods that are distinguished from them by vegetation, soils, and hydrologic characteristics. However, because of the gentle gradient, the margin between hydric zones, which are wetlands, and mesic or xeric zones, which are not, is indistinct. The gentle gradient in topography is reflected not only by gentle gradients in wetland indicators, but by a magnified importance of minor features of relief such as mounds that are only a few inches high and yet appear as mesic islands mixed with surrounding hydric terrain (Figure B4.1).

Southwestern Florida receives the bulk of its precipitation between May and September and shows a pronounced dry season between November and April. Toward the end of the dry season, the water table of hydric pine flatwoods can be as much as 3 ft (0.9 m) below the surface. In some cases, the water table is held by a hardpan that separates the surface aquifer from deeper aquifers. In spring, precipitation saturates the soil and raises the water table to the surface. Drainage is so weakly developed, and the amount of precipitation is so great, that the hydric pine flatwoods become fully inundated and remain so for at least 2 months. Water depths at the height of inundation reach as much as 3 ft, but they are characteristically in the vicinity of 1 ft. Adjacent mesic flatwoods also can be inundated, but to a shallower depth and over a shorter duration.

As precipitation declines, slow drainage of surface water occurs and the water table recedes below the soil surface and subsequently becomes very dry. Although the flatwoods show minimal relief, some mosaic elements, including

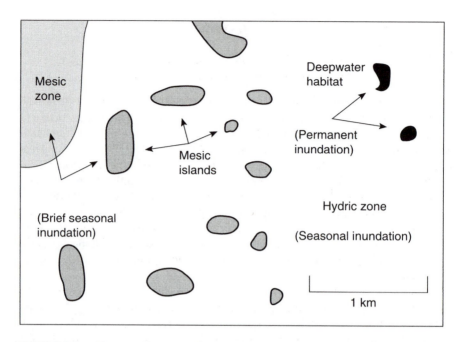

FIGURE B4.1 The margin of a hydric pine flatwood wetland in southwestern Florida. The appropriate wetland demarcation line would be between the hydric and mesic zones, but the transition is gradual and is marked by irregular inclusions of one zone within another.

sloughs and depressions, retain water throughout the dry season, and in this way introduce habitat diversity and refugia for organisms that require water continually.

The hydric pine flatwoods have distinctive vegetation. The canopy is dominated typically by slash pine *(Pinus elliottii* var. *densa)*. The understory is diverse and varied spatially in relation to such factors as frequency of fire, duration of drying, and depth of inundation. Some of the larger plants in the understory include cabbage palm *(Sabal palmetto),* wax myrtle *(Myrica cerifera),* and buttonbush *(Cephalanthus occidentalis)*. The canopy is discontinuous (10-20% coverage) (Beever and Dryden, 1992), and the number of species throughout the hydric pine flatwoods of southwest Florida is high: There are 992 plant species, including 98 that are federally listed (Beever and Beever, 1994). The flatwoods also support extensive seasonal growth of algae, aquatic invertebrates, and vertebrates associated with standing water.

The soils of the pine flatwoods are hydric. Even though sandy, they show weak polychromatic features that are associated with extended flooding. However, the transition from the hydric zone to the mesic zone is difficult to identify because the mesic zone itself can be inundated annually, but for a shorter interval, and because the lenses of nonhydric soils, reflecting minor variations in topography, can be intermixed with a background of hydric soils.

The hydric pine flatwoods have in the past been viewed as a successional transition to other ecosystem types (Duever et al., 1976). Now, however, they are believed to be highly stable under natural conditions (Beever and Beever, 1994). Natural stability is undermined by anthropogenic change in hydrology, fire, or grazing, all of which are important factors in maintaining the hydric pine flatwoods.

The seasonally dry condition of hydric pine flatwoods allows the vegetation to burn. In pre-Columbian times, burning probably occurred every 3-10 years (Beever and Beever, 1994) and was apparently patchy in its distribution so that the combustion chronologies, and therefore the plant community successional stages reflecting response to burning, made a mosaic on the landscape. Suppression of fire causes extensive vegetational change because the understory becomes predominated by the growth of plants that are eliminated or continually suppressed by frequent fire. In addition, accumulation of fuel in the understory over long periods ultimately could sustain a canopy fire that could damage or eliminate slash pine, which is tolerant of understory fires. Excessively frequent fire also can cause change in understory vegetation.

The delineation of boundaries for hydric pine flatwood is difficult. The interior of the hydric zone shows many diagnostic features of wetland status, including dried algal mats, remains of aquatic invertebrates, hydrophytic vegetation, and hydric soils. However, the margin of the hydric zone intergrades with the mesic area so subtly that it is difficult to find a line of demarcation (Figure B4.1). In some instances, the transition extends for miles, over which mesic islands interdigitate with hydric zones. Careful analysis of the soil could show the boundaries, but is impractical over large distances because of the extensive subsurface data collection that would be required. In practice, the most useful indicator is upland vegetation at the understory level, particularly the saw palmetto *(Serenoa repens),* which tends to come to the margin of the transition zone. However, heavy reliance on a single indicator could produce errors that could be avoided by more extensive analysis.

References

Abrahamson, W.G., and D.C. Hartnett. 1990. Pine flatwoods and dry prairies. Pp. 103-149 in R.L. Myers and I.I. Ewel, eds. Ecosystems of Florida. Univ. Central Florida Press.

Beever, J.W. III, and L.B. Beever. 1994. The effects of annual burning on the understory of a hydric slash pine flatwoods in southwest Florida (manuscript).

Beever, J.W. III, and K.A. Dryden. 1992. Red-cockaded woodpeckers and hydric slash pine flatwoods. Trans. 57th N.A. Wildl. and Nat. Res. Conf. 693-700.

Birnhak, B.I., and J.P. Crowder. 1974. An evaluation of the extent of vegetative habitat alteration in south Florida 1943-1970. South Florida Environ. Prot. Ecol. Rep. DI-SFEP-74-22. USDI. 22 pp.

Duever, M.J., J.E. Carlson, L.H. Gunderson, and L.C. Duever. 1976. Corkscrew Swamp, a virgin strand, ecosystems analysis at Corkscrew Swamp. Pp. 707-737 in H.T. Odum (ed.). Cypress Wetlands. 3rd Ann. Rept. on Research Projects. Nov. 1875-Dec. 1976. Center for Wetlands, Univ. Florida, Gainesville.

CASE STUDY 5

Prairie Pothole Region, North Dakota
Extreme Interannual Variation

The prairie pothole region, which extends from northwest Minnesota and Iowa across the Dakotas to Alberta (Figure B5.1), provides an excellent example of regionally distinctive wetlands that present special regulatory problems. The potholes, which are of glacial origin and lie on rolling till deposits, are a major landscape feature because of their abundance. Within the Dakotas alone, there are approximately 2.3 million that contain water at least temporarily (Kantrud et al., 1989). To the extent that they could be drained or filled, potholes could expand both the area of arable land and the convenience of farming, which is otherwise impeded by the necessity to circumnavigate these features in the culti-

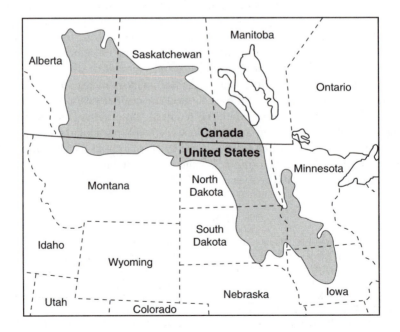

FIGURE B5.1. Distribution of prairie potholes.

vation of grains. Some potholes can be farmed in dry years without being drained, but most potholes cannot be farmed in wet years. Although drainage of potholes was practiced extensively in some parts of the Dakotas and Iowa before the enactment of wetland regulation, wetland regulatory determinations are now required. Some potholes are so shallow or small that they lack wetland features, but many are jurisdictional wetlands.

Although potholes are generally small, they have a wide range of physical characteristics. They have been divided into seven classes (Stewart and Kantrud, 1971). Class I potholes are designated ephemeral and are not wet with sufficient frequency to develop wetland soils or plants. Class II potholes are designated temporary. These often retain water for an extended period during the wet season, but can be dry or almost so in dry years. Seasonal potholes (Class III) retain water for a substantial period during the wet season in most years. Although semipermanent potholes (Class IV) almost always contain water, they can become dry in the driest season of the driest years, and the amount of water can vary substantially between years or between seasons. Permanent potholes (Class V) always contain water. Class VI includes alkaline basins that are wet only intermittently, and Class VII is for fens maintained by seepage. Classes III and IV are most common, Classes I and II are common, and the other classes are less abundant.

Precipitation comes to the North Dakota pothole region primarily in the spring and summer, and June is the wettest month (Kantrud et al., 1989), although potholes also can receive a substantial amount of water as a result of snowmelt after winters when snow accumulation is substantial. The seasonal sequence of events can differ for different classes of potholes. For example, the shallowest potholes thaw before the deepest ones and retain water readily over an ice seal in the soil below the wetland. Deeper potholes thaw later. Such variation in physical properties of potholes could be of considerable functional significance. For example, the potholes that thaw first are the only ones available to waterfowl that arrive early in the year.

Ground water plays an important role in sustaining the prairie potholes. The potholes can be divided roughly into three hydrologic categories: recharge, throughflow, and discharge. The recharge areas lie above ground water; they accumulate surface water (mostly from runoff fed by snowmelt) that subsequently recharges underlying ground water. The throughflow basins receive seepage from ground water, but also lose water back to the ground water pool on the lower end of the ground water gradient. The discharge basins receive upwelling ground water seepage and lost water mainly by evapotranspiration.

Hydrologic regimes affect the chemistry of potholes (LaBaugh et al., 1987; LaBaugh, 1989). Most potholes are at least moderately saline, but discharge potholes become highly saline. Saline conditions are often marked by a ring of salt deposits around the margin of the basin. The more saline potholes can have a distinctive vegetation and aquatic fauna (Kantrud et al. 1989). These basins often cannot be used for agricultural purposes, even if they are drained, because of the concentration of salts in the sediments above the tolerance of most crops.

The prairie potholes support a variety of herbaceous vegetation, but are usually without woody plants. The community composition of vascular plants is typically graded in concentric rings from the center or low-water mark of the pothole to a few feet above the mean high water-mark (Figure B5.2). The gradation reflects degrees of tolerance or competitive ability for individual plant species as a function of the duration and frequency of inundation.

Invertebrate fauna of the prairie potholes is diverse and abundant. It includes such taxa as the phantom midge (*Chaoborus*) and other dipteran larvae, odonates, cladocerans, ostracods, and many others. Large invertebrates tend to be especially abundant in the potholes because very few of the potholes contain fish. The fathead minnow (*Pimephales promelas*) is present in some of the Class V potholes, and some artificially deepened potholes have been stocked with game fish. However, the pothole waters are predominantly fishless and therefore support large populations of microinvertebrates that would otherwise be eliminated or reduced by fish.

The prairie potholes are famed for their support of waterfowl and wading birds; as much as half the waterfowl of North America originate from the pothole

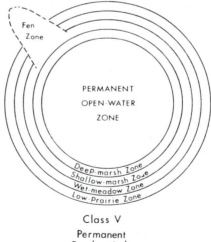

Class V
Permanent
Pond or Lake

FIGURE B5.2a The vegetation of a Class V (permanent) pothole, showing zonation. Source: Brinson, 1993.

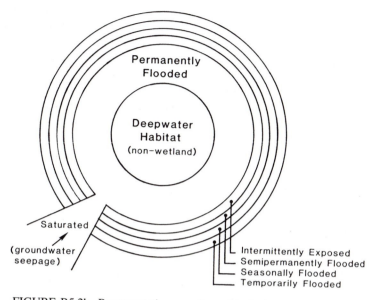

FIGURE B5.2b Representative zonation of hydrology in a prairie pot-hole. Source: Brinson, 1993.

region (Kantrud et al., 1989). Because of the high ratio of shoreline to surface area associated with these small bodies of water, the total area of shoreline available for waterfowl nesting is extremely large, and invertebrate populations provide abundant food. Less obvious but equally important is the role of potholes in ground water recharge and hydrologic buffering (Winter, 1989).

Prairie potholes that are farmed in dry years qualify as farmed wetlands under the Food Security Act of 1985. Farming often results in simplification of plant communities by cultivation, impairment of natural biodiversity by the use of herbicides, and physical disturbance (siltation, furrowing).

The soils of the entire prairie pothole region are characteristically dark. The pothole wetlands are underlain by hydric soils that are distinct, however, from the adjacent upland soils (Richardson et al., 1994). Careful examination of soils in the zone of frequent inundation shows the distinctive chroma and redoximorphic features that cannot be found on uplands.

Classification of the prairie potholes is a point of major practical concern, but delineation of pothole boundaries is far less so. Class I potholes (ephemeral potholes) are not considered jurisdictional wetlands and can be drained, filled, or cultivated without restriction by the Food Security Act of 1985. Other classes cannot be drained or filled. Therefore, the boundary between Class I and Class II and the validity of the typology are subject to scrutiny by agricultural landholders who could benefit economically from draining or filling, especially of shallow, nonsaline potholes. Because the intended use is agricultural rather than commercial or residential, the exact margin of a given pothole is of much less concern than is the legality of draining or filling for agricultural use.

The major complication in evaluating prairie potholes in relation to the regulatory guidance on wetland identification derives from the extreme hydrologic variability in the prairie pothole region. As shown in Figure B5.3, the amount of precipitation varies greatly, such that individual potholes can be deeply inundated for many weeks in the wettest years and barely moist at the surface in the driest years. To complicate matters further, both the vegetation and the invertebrate fauna of the potholes are adapted to widely varying hydrologic conditions. Thus, a pothole that appears to lack the biotic characteristics of a wetland in the driest years can in wet years have animal and plant communities that are clearly associated with wetlands.

Even a statistical analysis of the hydrologic irregularities in the pothole region is difficult because the interyear variability is neither random nor regular. There appears to be a certain amount of contagion in the hydrologic data base, suggestive of drought cycles running to a decade or more, but it is also possible to see some of the driest and some of the wettest conditions in two consecutive years (Figure B5.3). Thus, even with hydrologic records, it is difficult to compute reliably the recurrence, frequency, duration, and depth of inundation for individual potholes. Because of the high variability of vegetation, aquatic life, and hydrology over the short term, hydric soils are a particularly important indicator of wetland status in the prairie pothole region.

References

Brinson, M. M. 1993a. A hydrogeomorphic classification for wetlands. Wetlands Research Program Technical Report WRP-DE-4. U.S. Army Corps of Engineers, Waterway Experiment Station. Vicksburg, MS: Bridgham and Richardson.

Kantrud, H.A., G.L. Krapu, and G.A. Swanson. 1989. Prairie Basin Wetlands of the Dakotas: A Community Profile. U.S. Fish and Wildlife Service Biological Report 85 (7.28). 116 p.

LaBaugh, J.W. 1989. Chemical characteristics of water in wetlands and lakes in the Northern Prairie of North America. Pp. 56-90 in A.G. van der Valk (ed.). Northern Prairie Wetlands. Iowa State University Press, Ames, IA.

LaBaugh, J.W., T.C. Winter, V.A. Adomaitis, and G.A. Swanson. 1987. Hydrology and chemistry of selected prairie wetlands in the Cottonwood Lake area, Stutsman County, North Dakota, 1979-82. U.S. Geol. Surv. Prof. Pap. 1431. 26 p.

Richardson, J.L., J.L. Arndt, and J. Freeland. 1994. Wetland soils of the prairie potholes. Advances in Agronomy 52:121-171.

Stewart, R.E., and H.A. Kantrud. 1971. Classification of natural ponds and lakes in the glaciated prairie region. Bureau of Sport Fisheries and Wildlife Resource Publication 92. 56 pp.

Winter, T.C. 1989. Hydrologic studies of wetlands in the northern prairie. Pp. 16-54 in A.G. Van der Valk, ed. Northern Prairie Wetlands. Iowa State University Press, Ames, IA.

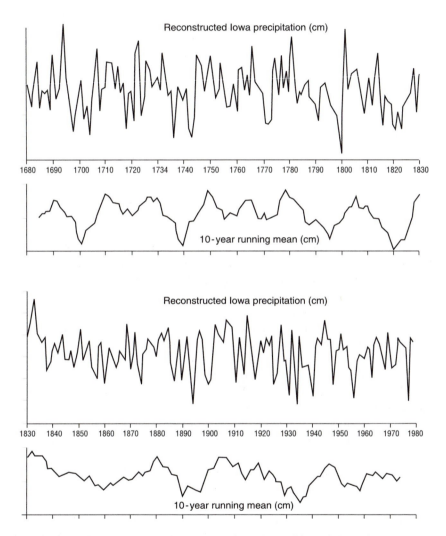

FIGURE B5.3 Long-term hydrologic record from the prairie pothole region reconstructed from historical records and tree ring data.

APPENDIX
C

Glossary

abiotic—nonliving (usually refers to substances or environmental factors).

adventitious root—root that grows from plant parts other than the primary root. Often develop in flood-tolerant and flood-intolerant plants just above the anaerobic zone when the plants are flooded; can develop when plants are engulfed by sediment or moss.

aerenchyma—tissue with numerous large intercellular spaces; common in the roots and stems of many aquatic and wetland plants. Facilitates oxygenation of the roots and allows plants to survive in saturated and inundated soils.

aerobic—growing or proceeding only in the presence of free oxygen, as in aerobic respiration. Living, active, or occurring only in the presence of oxygen.

aggradation—deposition of alluvial materials resulting in increased elevations. In permafrost, it is a rise in the permafrost table.

alluvium—sediment deposited by flowing water, as in a river bed, flood plain, or delta.

altered wetland—area affected by anthropogenic or natural events, such that one or more indicators of relative wetland character is absent, obscured, or provides information no longer representative of original condition.

anaerobic—growing in the absence of molecular oxygen, as in aerobic bacteria. Occurring in the absence of molecular of oxygen, as in biochemical processes.

anoxic—absence of molecular oxygen.

aquic soil—soil that currently experiences continuous or periodic saturation and reduction. Presence indicated by redoximorphic features and verified by measuring saturation and reduction, except in artificially drained soils.

artificial drainage—removal of free water from soil by surface mounding, ditches, or subsurface tiles to the extent that water table levels are changed significantly in connection with specific land uses.

artificial wetland—wetland constructed where one did not exist before.

bajada—broad alluvial slope extending from the base of a mountain range out into a basin, formed by coalescence of separate alluvial fans.

biogeographic region—any region delineated by its biological and geographic characteristics.

bog—a nutrient-poor, acidic-peat-accumulating wetland. Used in the restrictive sense to refer to those peatlands that receive all of their water from rain and snow—ombrotrophic bogs. Also used for any nutrient-poor, acidic peatland with a distinctive plant community of peat mosses (*Sphagnum* spp.), ericaceous shrubs, and sedges or coniferous trees. This broader use of the term thus includes weakly minerotrophic peatlands—poor fens.

bosque—dense growth of trees and underbrush, normally applied to arid riparian zone.

bryophyte—nonvascular plant, composed of moss and liverwort or hornwort (or hepatics). Inhabits a range of habitats from dry, barren rocks to submerged objects, but most frequent where an abundance of moisture is assured. Some bryophyte species are the dominant vegetation in bogs and poor fens.

categorize—to put into any of several fundamental and distinct classes to which entities or concepts belong. A category is a division within a system of classification.

chroma—the relative purity of saturation of a color. The intensity of distinctive hue as related to greyness. One of the three variables of color.

cienega— swamp or marsh in the southwestern U.S., especially one formed and fed by streams or ground water discharge.

classify—to assign to a category.

converted wetland—see *prior converted wetland*.

criterion—a standard on which a judgment or decision may be based.

depressional wetland—wetland occurring in a depression in the landscape so that the catchment area for surface runoff is generally small.

disturbed area—area where vegetation, soil, or hydrology have been significantly altered, making a wetland determination difficult.

ecoregion—ecological region that has broad similarities to other regions with respect to soil, relief, and dominant vegetation.

ecotype—genetically distinct populations within a species that are adapted to the local conditions.

edaphic—related to chemical and physical soil conditions, not including climate.

eluvial—the removal of soil material in suspension from a layer or layers of soil.

Entisol—mineral soil of slight or recent development. An order of the USDA soil taxonomy.

epipedon—diagnostic horizon formed at the soil surface, used in the classification of soils. Properties should be determined after mixing the surface soil to a depth of 7.02 in (18 cm), or the whole soil if its depth to bedrock is less than 7.02 in (18 cm).

ericaceous—of, relating to, or being a heath (shrubby evergreen) or of the heath family Ericacea.

eutrophication—process by which a body of water becomes highly productive either naturally or by pollution rich in dissolved nutrients (such as phosphates). Eutrophic lakes are often shallow, with a seasonal deficiency in dissolved oxygen.

evapotranspiration—loss of water from the soil both by evaporation and by transpiration of the water from the plants growing thereon.

facultative species—plant species that do not always occur in wetlands. One of five indicator categories used in determining whether the vegetation of a site is or is not hydrophytic. Facultative (FAC) species have a similar probability of occurring in wetlands and nonwetland sites. Facultative-wet (FACW) species have a higher probability of occurring in wetlands than in nonwetland sites. Facultative-upland (FACU) species have a higher probability of occurring in nonwetland sites than in wetlands.

farmed wetland—area in which farming is compatible with wetland status.

fen—minerotrophic, peat-accumulating wetland. Includes all peatlands that receive water that has been in contact with mineral soils, in contrast to ombrotrophic bogs, which receive only rainwater and snow. Includes both weakly minerotrophic peatlands (poor fens) that are acidic and strongly minerotrophic peatlands (rich fens) that are alkaline. Fens support a range of vegetation types, including sedge and moss-dominated communities and coniferous forest.

Folist—Histosol derived from leaf litter.

fringe wetland—wetland near a large body of water, most typically the ocean, that receives frequent and regular two-way flow from astronomic tides or wind-driven fluctuations in water-level.

geomorphology—study of characteristics, origin, and development of land forms.

gleyed—soil developed under conditions of poor drainage, resulting in reduction of iron and other elements, manifested by the presence of neutral grey, bluish, or greenish colors as reduced matrix or redox depletions (see Appendix A).

Histosol—soil that has organic materials in more than half of the upper 32 in (80 cm) or of any thickness if overlying bedrock. Formed almost exclusively in wetlands. An order of the USDA soil taxonomy.

hydric soil—soil that is saturated, flooded, or ponded long enough during the growing season to develop anaerobic conditions in the upper part (1991 National Technical Committee on Hydric Soils definition).

hydrogeomorphic—of or pertaining to a synthesis of the geomorphic setting, the water source and its transport, and hydrodynamics.

hydromorphic—used to describe a wetland classification method based on position in the landscape, water sources, and factors that control the velocity of the water as it passes through the wetland.

hydroperiod—depth, duration, seasonality, and frequency of flooding.

hydrophyte—any plant growing in water or on a substrate that is at least periodically deficient in oxygen as a result of excessive water. Plants typically found in wetland habitats.

illuvial horizon—soil layer or horizon in which material carried from an overlaying layer has been precipitated from solution or deposited from suspension.

indicator—organism, ecological community, or structural feature so strictly associated with a particular environmental condition that its presence indicates the existence of the condition.

isolated wetland—wetland not adjacent to another body of water.

landscape ecology—specialty that deals with the patterns and processes of biological systems in spatially and temporally heterogeneous environments at the scale of landscapes, i.e., generally hundreds to tens of thousands of acres.

landscape perspective—method of viewing the interactive parts of a geographic area that are not necessarily all within a single watershed.

lenticel—pore in the stem of a woody plant through which gases are exchanged between the atmosphere and stem tissues.

lotic—pertaining to or living in flowing water.

lysimeter—device for measuring the percolation of water through soils and for determining the soluble constituents removed in the percolate.

marsh—wetland characterized by frequent or continual inundation, emergent herbaceous vegetation such as cattails and rushes, and mineral soils.

mesocosm—in aquatic biology, an artificial system used for study that is larger than typical aquaria and smaller than lakes.

mire—peat-accumulating wetland (European definition).

Mollisol—soil common to the world's grasslands, characterized by a dark surface layer rich in organic matter. An order of the USDA soil taxonomy.

monotypic—being the only representative of its group, or more commonly, having only one type, e.g., a genus or plant community consisting of a single species.

morphology—branch of biology that deals with form and structure; also form and structure of an organism or any of its parts, or of soil.

obligate wetland species—plant species that almost always occur in wetlands. One of five indicator categories used in determining whether the vegetation of a site is hydrophytic.

offsite determination method—a technique for making a wetland determination in the office.

ombrotrophic bog—peatland that receives precipitation as the sole source of water. Generally peat has accumulated enough to isolate the plants from acquiring nutrients from the underlying mineral strata. The elevated surface is indicative of tertiary mines.

onsite determination method—a technique for making a wetland determination in the field.

opportunity cost—in economics, the cost in lost opportunity or flexibility of investing a resource (usually money or time) in a particular instrument or project, thus making the resource unavailable for other investments.

oxic—oxygenated.

oxidized rhizosphere—precipitation of yellowish-red ferric compounds around the roots and rhizomes of plants growing in frequently saturated soils that otherwise exhibit a reduced matrix. Caused by the transport of oxygen from leaves to roots and rhizomes through a system of air-filled pore space in plant tissue (aerenchyma).

Oxisol—thick, weathered soil of the humid tropics, largely depleted in the minerals that promote fertility. An order of the USDA soil taxonomy.

paludification—landscape phenomenon of the accumulation of organic matter on a mineral soil thus forming a Histosol. One process by which a peatland forms through the waterlogging of formerly terrestrial or upland habitats.

panchromatic—sensitive to light of all colors in the visible spectrum.

parameter—originally mathematics, often used more broadly. In this report, either a quantity or a constant whose value varies with the circumstances of its application (e.g., the radius of a circle), or a set of properties (usually physical) whose values determine the characteristics or behavior of something (e.g., atmospheric parameters, wetland parameters).

peat—deposit of partially decomposed or undecomposed plant material, or both. Can contain the remains of mosses, sedges, and other herbaceous plants or of trees and shrubs. Accumulates only in places that are sufficiently wet to prevent decomposition from keeping pace with the production of organic matter.

peatlands—generic term used to refer to all peat-accumulating wetlands—bogs and fens.

phreatophyte—plant that has a well-developed, deep root system that allows it to extract water from the permanent water-table (phreatic zone).

playa lake—shallow depression similar to a prairie pothole, abundant on the Southern High Plains on a tableland south of the Canadian River in Texas and New Mexico, characterized by annual or multiyear cycles of drydown and filling.

pneumatophore—specialized root formed on several species of plants occurring in frequently inundated habitats. The root is erect and protrudes above the soil surface. In some species promote root aeration in water-logged habitats.

pocosin—upland swamp of the coastal plain of the southeastern U.S.

prairie pothole—shallow, marshlike pond, particularly as found in the Dakotas and central Canadian provinces.

prevalence index—weighted average. A single number that summarizes quantitative data about a large number of species within a community and gives weight to each species' contribution to the final number in terms of an assigned value.

prior converted wetland—wetland converted to farmable land before Dec. 23, 1985.

propagule—structure of an organism involved in dispersal and reproduction, as in the seeds or spores of plants.

pulse-subsidy concept—the addition of nutrients in short intervals along with flooding.

redox potential—oxygen-reduction potential. A measure of the electron pressure (or availability) in a solution. Often used to quantify the degree of electrochemical reduction of wetland soils under anoxic conditions.

regionalize—to divide into regions or administrative districts.

restoration—return of an ecosystem to a close approximation of its condition prior to disturbance.

riparian ecosystem—ecosystem that has a high water table because of its proximity to an aquatic ecosystem or to subsurface water. Usually occurs as an ecotone between aquatic and upland ecosystems, but with distinctive vegetation and soils. Aridity, topographic relief, and presence of depositional soils most strongly influence the extent of high water tables and associated riparian ecosystems. Most commonly recognized as bottomland hardwood and floodplain forests in the eastern and central United States and as bosque or streambank vegetation in the West. Characterized by the combination of high species diversity, density, and productivity. Continuous interactions occur between riparian, aquatic, and upland terrestrial ecosystems through exchanges of energy, nutrients, and species.

riparian vegetation—vegetation growing close enough to a lake or river that its annual evapotranspiration is a factor in the lake or river regimen.

riverine wetland—wetland system of less than 0.5 ppt ocean salts, exposed to channelized flow regimes. Categorized according to flow regimes such as tidal waters, slow-moving waters with well-developed floodplains, fast-moving waters with little floodplain, and intermittent systems.

saturation—condition in which all pore spaces are filled with water to the exclusion of a gaseous phase.

soil matrix—the portion of a given soil that has the dominant color. In most cases, the portion of the soil that has more than 50% of the same color.

spodic horizon—mineral soil horizon characterized by the illuvial accumulation of aluminum and organic carbon with or without iron.

Spodosol—mineral soil that has a spodic horizon. An order of the USDA soil taxonomy.

swamp—emergent wetland in which the uppermost stratum of vegetation is composed primarily of trees.

thermokarst—topography created by the thawing of ice-rich permafrost and characterized by a complex, uneven ground surface that includes mounds, sink holes, tunnels, caverns, short ravines, lake basins, and circular lowlands. Occurs in unconsolidated materials, often loess.

tidal marsh—saltwater or brackish wetland dominated by herbaceous vegetation and subject to tidal flow. Can be flooded regularly (elevations low enough to be inundated by nearly all tides) or irregularly (too isolated to be inundated by all tides).

tidal subsidy—augmentation or support of water tables by tidal fluctuations; the way in which nutrients are added and toxic materials removed from areas of greater tidal energy.

vernal pool—shallow, intermittently flooded wet meadow, generally covered by water for extended periods during the cool season but dry for most of the summer. Used most frequently to refer to such habitats in the Mediterranean climate region of the Pacific coast.

Vertisol—clay-rich soil in which deep cracks form in the dry season. An order of the USDA soil taxonomy.

water budget—balance between the inflows and outflows of water.

watershed—surface drainage area that contributes water to a lake or river.

wet meadow—any type of wetland dominated by herbaceous vegetation (frequently sedges of the genus *Carex*) and with waterlogged soil near the surface but without standing water for most of the year.

wetland mitigation—the practice of allowing unavoidable losses of wetland in exchange for their replacement elsewhere through restoration or through creation of new wetlands.

wet prairie—herbaceous wetland dominated by grasses rather than sedges and with waterlogged soil near the surface but without standing water for most of the year.

zonation—state or condition of being marked with bands, as of color or texture. Wetland vegetation often exhibits distinct zones characterized by plant communities composed of different species.

APPENDIX

D
Committee on Wetlands Characterization
Biographical Sketches

WILLIAM M. LEWIS, JR., *Chair* is Professor, Department of Environmental, Population, and Organismic Biology at the University of Colorado, Boulder, and also serves as Director of the Center for Limnology at CU-Boulder. Professor Lewis received his Ph.D. degree in 1974 at Indiana University with emphasis on limnology, the study of inland waters. His research interests, as reflected by over 120 journal articles and books, include productivity and other metabolic aspects of aquatic ecosystems, aquatic food webs, composition of biotic communities, nutrient cycling, and the quality of inland waters. The geographic extent of Professor Lewis's work encompasses not only the montane and plains areas of Colorado, but also Latin America and southeast Asia, where he has conducted extensive studies of tropical aquatic systems. Professor Lewis has served on the National Research Council Committee on Irrigation-Induced Water Quality Problems and is currently Chair of the NRC's Glen Canyon Environmental Studies Committee. He is also a member of the NRC's Water Science and Technology Board. Professor Lewis is currently a member of the Natural Resources Law Center Advisory Board.

BARBARA LYNN BEDFORD received her B.A. from Marquette University in theology, her M.S. and Ph.D. in land resources from the University of Wisconsin-Madison. She is presently an assistant professor in the Department of Natural Resources at Cornell University. For ten years (1980-1990) she was Associate Director, and for a year (1991) the Director, of the Ecosystems Research Center of Excellence at Cornell University. She is a wetlands consultant to EPA's Science Advisory Board and recently served as a member of the Management Advisory Group to the Assistant Administrator for Water at EPA. Prior to assuming her academic positions, she worked with local and state government agencies, in wetlands mapping inventory, classification and development of wetlands regulations. Her research includes plant ecology of freshwater ecosystems; application of ecological knowledge to environmental assessment, regulation and management; response of wetland plants and communities to changes in hydrology and nutrient loading; and influence of plant species on wetland ecosystem processes.

FRED P. BOSSELMAN is currently professor of Law, Chicago-Kent College of Law. His areas of research include land use planning. He received his B.A .from the University of Colorado, Boulder, and his J.D. from Harvard Law School. He is a member of the Board of Advisors of the American Law Institute's Restatement of Property and the Board of Directors of the Sonoran Institute, on the editorial boards of the *Land Use* and *Environmental Law Reporters,* the *Practical Real Estate Lawyer*, and the *Land Use Law and Zoning Digest*. He is co-chair of the annual Land Use Institute sponsored by the ALI-ABA Committee on Continuing Legal Education. He is past president of the American Planning Association, past assistant chair of the National Policy Council of the Urban Land Institute, and was a member of the Board of Directors of the National Audubon Society and the American Society of Planning Officials.

MARK M. BRINSON received his B.S. from Heidelberg College, his M.S. from University of Michigan, Ann Arbor, and his Ph.D. (botany) from the University of Florida. He is currently Professor of biology at East Carolina University. He spent 1 year as an ecologist with the Office of Biological Services at the U.S. Fish and Wildlife Service. He provided testimony before the congressional committees on the functioning of wetlands and delineation issues. He has worked on the cycling of nitrogen, phosphorus and carbon in swamp forests, estuaries and marshes. Current research deals with the response of coastal wetlands to rising sea level. He is working on functional assessment of wetlands based on reference wetlands as scalars.

PAUL ALLEN GARRETT is an Ecologist with the Federal Highway Administration (FHWA). He received his B.S. in biology from Memphis State University and his M.S. in zoology and Ph.D. in botany from Montana State University. He has participated as senior biologist with several projects involving wetlands identification, classification, and functional analysis. He presently is involved in developing and administering wetland research programs for FHWA, as well as serving on the interagency group on Federal Wetlands Policy.

CONSTANCE HUNT received her B.S. in wildlife biology from Arizona State University, and her M.A. in public policy from the University of Chicago. She is a senior program officer with the World Wildlife Fund, where she is responsible for the management of programs to promote wetland restoration and conservation of biodiversity on private lands (1993-). From 1990-1993, she was program manager and coordinator for Lakewide Management Plans of the U.S. Environmental Protection Agency, where she developed lakewide management programs for reducing pollution in the Great Lakes. From 1987-1990 she was a biologist with the U.S. Army Corps of Engineers, where she created, coordinated, and implemented intergovernmental conservation plans for stream basins and wetland complexes in accordance with section 404 of the Clean Water Act. She also performed wetland evaluations and delineations, permit processing, and environmental impact analysis.

CAROL A. JOHNSTON received her B.S. in natural resources from Cornell University, her M.S. in land resources and soil science from the University of Wisconsin, and her Ph.D. in soil science from the University of Wisconsin. Currently she is a Senior Research Associate with the Natural Resources Research Institute at the University of Minnesota. From 1978-1983 she directed the Wisconsin Wetlands Inventory for the Wisconsin Department of Natural Resources, and in 1989-1990 was a Research Ecologist with the Environmental Protection Agency. Dr. Johnston is currently a member of the NRC Water Science and Technology Board. Her research interests include wetland soils, biogeochemistry, and mapping; effects of land/water interactions on surface water quantity and quality, spatial and temporal variability of wetland processes; and geographic information systems.

DOUGLAS L. KANE received his B.S. in civil engineering and M.S. in civil engineering and water management from the University of Wisconsin, and his PhD in civil engineering from the University of Minnesota. Currently, he is director of the Water Research Center and a professor of water resources and civil engineering at the University of Alaska, Fairbanks. His research focuses on ground water hydrology, snow hydrology, hydraulics, water resources engineering, and cold regions hydrology.

A. MICHAEL MACRANDER received his B.A. from Tarkio College, spent two years of graduate work at Northern Arizona University, and received his Ph.D. from the University of Alabama. He is presently Senior Environmental Specialist at Corporate Environmental Affairs at Shell Oil Company. He is responsible for providing technical support and guidance on issues related to the identification and protection of sensitive ecological resources. He has specific responsibility for wetlands, threatened and endangered species, ecological risk assessment, and oil spill response. From 1983-1991 he was an Associate Researcher at the University of Alabama where he worked in the design and use of biological information systems including the Southwest Regional Floral Information System.

JAMES C. McCULLEY IV received his B.A. and M.S. in biology from Rutgers University. He is President of Environmental Consultants, Inc., a firm specializing in wetland delineations, wetland permitting, wetland mitigation, wetland assessment, water quality studies, ground water monitoring, violation resolution, expert witness testimony, and natural resource studies, as well as other services. He has represented the Homebuilders Association of Delaware on several panels, including the Governor's Wetlands Steering Committee, the Governor's Freshwater Wetlands Roundtable, the New Castle County Executive's committee to formulate a wetlands policy. He advises the Homebuilders Association of Delaware on wetland and other environmental issues.

WILLIAM JOSEPH MITSCH received his B.S. from University of Notre Dame, his M.E. and his Ph.D. in environmental engineering science from University of Florida. Since 1986 he has been professor of natural resources and environmental science at Ohio State University. He previously taught at Illinois Institute of Technology and the University of Louisville. His research interests include wetland ecology and management; biogeochemical cycling; ecological engineering; ecological modelling; water quality role of wetlands; and energy flow in ecological and human systems. He has coauthored the textbook *Wetlands*, chaired the 1992 INTECOL conference on wetlands, serves on the editorial board of several journals and is editor-in-chief of *Ecological Engineering*.

WILLIAM H. PATRICK, JR. received his B.S., M.S. and his Ph.D. in soils science from Louisiana State University at Baton Rouge. He joined the faculty of Louisiana State University in 1953 where he has served as Boyd Professor of Marine Science since 1978. He received an honorary doctorate degree from Ghent University, Belgium,. His research interests include physicochemical properties of and reactions in soils, particularly wetland soils.

ROGER A. POST received his B.S. in wildlife management from the University of Alaska-Fairbanks, and his M.S. in forest zoology from the SUNY College of Environmental Science and Forestry. He has worked in environmental consulting and governmental focusing on mitigation of impacts of large construction projects and currently is a habitat biologist with the Alaska Department of Fish and Game. As habitat biologist he published a report reviewing the functions, species-habitat relationships, and management of arctic wetlands, and is preparing a functional profile of black spruce wetlands in Alaska. He has prepared reports on restoration of Arctic-tundra wetlands, management of nonpoint-source pollution related to placer mining, and a restoration plan for a mined stream system.

DONALD I. SIEGEL is a Professor of Geology at Syracuse University where he teaches graduate courses in hydrogeology and aqueous geochemistry. He holds B.S. and M.S. degrees in geology from the University of Rhode Island and Penn State University, respectively, and a Ph.D. in Hydrogeology from the University of Minnesota. His research interests are in solute transport at both local and regional scales, wetland-ground water interaction, and paleohydrogeology. He was a member of the NRC's Committee on Techniques for Assessing Ground Water Vulnerability.

RICHARD WAYNE SKAGGS received his B.S. and his M.S. in agricultural engineering from the University of Kentucky and his Ph.D. in agricultural engineering from Purdue University. He has served on the faculty in the Biological and Agricultural Engineering Department of North Carolina State University since 1984. Currently, he is the William Neal Reynolds Professor at NC State. His expertise is in agricultural drainage and related water management for poorly drained soils; hydrology of low relief and high water table watersheds. He has made scientific contributions in the development of computer simulation and mathematical models to quantify the performance of drainage and water table control systems. His current interests are in determining and developing methods to describe the effects of water management and farming practices on drainage water quality and hydrology; applying models to describe the hydrology of certain types of wetlands. He is a member of the National Academy of Engineering.

MARGARET (PEGGY) STRAND received her B.A. in history from the University of Rochester, her M.A. in history from the University of Rhode Island, and her J.D. from Marshall Wythe School of Law at the College of William and Mary. She is a partner with Bayh, Connaughton & Malone, P.C., Washington, DC, where she provides counsel on environmental compliance and conducts environmental litigation, focusing on EPA-administered regulatory programs. Prior to that, she was chief of the Environmental Defense Section of the US Department of Justice, where she was involved in environmental policy issues including wetlands regulation and enforcement. She serves on the editorial board of the Environmental Law Reporter and the Federal Facilities Environmental Compliance Journal. She is the author of *Federal Wetlands Law*, a primer published by the Environmental Law Institute in 1993. Ms. Strand is a member of the NRC Board on Environmental Studies and Toxicology.

JOY B. ZEDLER holds a Ph.D. in botany (plant ecology) from the University of Wisconsin. Since 1969, she has been at San Diego State University (SDSU) and is currently a professor of biology at SDSU and director of the Pacific Estuarine Research Laboratory. Her research interests include salt marsh ecology; structure and functioning of coastal wetlands; restoration and construction of wetland ecosystems, effects of rare, extreme events on estuarine ecosystems; dynamics of nutrients and algae in coastal wetlands; and use of scientific information in the management of coastal habitats. She helped develop the wetland research plan for the EPA and participated in the literature review on the status of wetland restoration. She was a member of the NRC's Committee on Restoration of Aquatic Ecosystems, and is a former member of the NRC's Water Science and Technology Board.

Index